FIQH AL ZAKAH
(VOLUME I)

A COMPARATIVE STUDY OF *ZAKAH*, REGULATIONS AND PHILOSOPHY IN THE LIGHT OF QUR'AN AND *SUNNAH*

DR. YUSUF AL QARADAWI

Dar Ul Thaqafah

Dar Ul Thaqafah

2023 CE – 1444 H

Translation of the Qur'ān

It should be perfectly clear that the Qur'ān is only authentic in its original language, Arabic. Since perfect translation of the Qur'ān is impossible, we have used the translation of the meaning of the Qur'ān throughout the book, as the result is only a crude meaning of the Arabic text.

Qur'ānic verses appear in speech marks proceeded by a reference to the Surah and verse number. Sayings (*Hadith*) of Prophet Muhammad ﷺ appear in inverted commas along with reference to the Hadith Book and its Reporter.

(Peace be upon him) ﷺ – صلى الله عليه وسلم

(Glory to Him, the Exalted) ﷻ – سبحانه وتعالى

*IN THE NAME OF ALLAH
THE MERCIFUL,
THE MERCY - GIVING*

FIQH AL ZAKAH
(VOLUME I)

A COMPARATIVE STUDY OF *ZAKAH*, REGULATIONS AND PHILOSOPHY IN THE LIGHT OF QUR'AN AND *SUNNAH*

BY
DR. YUSUF AL QARADAWI

TRANSLATED BY:
DR. MONZER KAHF

CONTENTS

Page

Advisory Committee for Approving Publications at Centre for Research in Islamic Economics

Sheikh Dr. Salih Ebin Humade

Prof. Dr. Mohammad Umer Zubair

Dr. Mohamed Ali Elgari

Dr. Mohammad Ebin Muslim Al-Raddady

FOREWORD

In the hierarchy of Islamic faith and religious duties *zakat* is next only to the acclamation of Allah's unity and prophecy of Muhamnad (peace be unto him) and the five daily prayers. It is rather significant that a measure of far reaching economic consequences should find such a high place in that hierarchy and be counted as one of the five pillars o Islam. *Zakat* is doubly important in the way of life that is Islam. On the one hand it is a means of spiritual purification and on the other a way to regain balance and equilibrium in social and economic life. One would expect religious scholars as well as economists not to miss these points and pay due attention to this unique institution. However, the subject of *zakat* did not attract the attention of contemporary scholars to an extent commensurate with its importance. There is a need for economists, legal experts and shariah scholars who would elaborate and analyze the law of *zakat* in a contemporary manner.

Sheikh Yusuf al Qardawi's book is one of those exceptions to the above which give one the needed hope and reassurance to carry on. First published more than twenty five years ago, Fiqh al *Zakat* still remains unparalleled in its comprehensiveness exposition and depth. It is, therefore, with great pleasure that we present it to the English reading public.

Zakat has always been a priority subject with us at the Centre for Research in Islamic Economics, King Abdulaziz University, Jeddah. Besides the papers on *zakat* included in the proceedings of the First International .Conference on Islamic Economics, published under the titles Studies in Islamic Economics (1980) and al Iqtisad al Islami (1980) the Centre has also published *Fatawa al Zakat* (1985) by Sheikh Abul A'al al Mawdudi and Prof. M. Raquibuzzaman's *Some Administrative Aspects of the Collection and Distribution of Zakat....*" (1987). Of special significance is our Arabic translation of the *Zakat Manual* prepared by the Central *Zakat* Administration in Pakistan. Translated by Rafic al Misri and comprising 526 pages, *Kitab al Zakat: Qanunuha, Idaratuha, Muhasabatuha, Muraja'atuha* (1984), is a compendium of operational details without any parallel in modern times.

We hope these modest efforts for promoting *zakat* studies will help in attracting greater attention to the subject. The Centre will be glad to support further studies on the subject and welcomes any proposal for studying its legal, historical, and contemporary economic aspects.

Our author hardly needs an introduction. Dean of Shariah College at University of Qatar, and member of several Academies of Islamic Jurisprudence and Shariah Advisory Bodies to Islamic financial institutions, Egypt born Sheikh al Qardawi is also a popular writer and frequent speaker on the subjects of Islam, contemporary Islamic movements and the economic system of Islam. We feel honored in presenting his magnum opus on *zakat* to the English readers. However, no scholarly work can be the last word on any subject. The same applies to this work, especially now that recent attempts to implement *zakat* in several countries - most were made after the book was written - have thrown up new problems. We hope the publication of an English version of Qardawi's book will bring unattended issues into sharper focus while improving our understanding of the many issues already discussed.

We are very grateful to Sheikh al Qardawi for his generous permission to translate and publish his book. Thanks are also due to Monzer Kahf in whom we found an excellent translator befitting the text. Abdul Azim Islahi's meticulous review of the translation has also helped in bringing out an error-free translation to the best of our capacity: For, Allah alone is free of error, and to Him we turn for help and forgiveness.

Mohamad Ali Elgari
Director
Centre for Research in Islamic Economics
King Abdulaziz University
Jeddah.

TRANSLATOR INTRODUCTION

Dr. Yusuf al Qardawi has his own style in Arabic writing. Being not only an academic scholar (currently he is the dean of college of *Shari'ah* at the university of Oatar, in Doha, Qatar) but also an enthusiastic preacher by his nature, his style can be described as detail and long breathed. The book *Fiqh al Zakah*, itself is highly scholarly but it does not miss the spirit of an activist or the zeal of a religious writer.

The general approach adopted in this translation is to elucidate the meaning of the Arabic sentence in English instead of going word by word, yet in so doing I attempted not to miss his original ideas , words and sequence as much as possible. Some details are omitted in a few cases, e.g. the comparison of nisab in Egyptian golden currency of the beginning of the 20th century. A few paragraphs are abridged and other summarized when the translator felt that they contain details of no interest to the English reader. Sometimes a few words are added when translation did not convey the intended meaning completely. Additions are usually put within brackets.

Except when the meaning of the Arabic origin was not lent to English expression transliterated Arabic words were not used. Thus the use of Arabic words in the English text is minimized to idioms and Arabic words given religious contents that have no equivalent in English. The letters (J) and (P) are put to mean "Jalla Jalaluh", and "Peace and Prayer be on him" after the words God and the Prophet respectively. The more common expression after the word God is Subhanahu wa Ta'ala, but it was avoided in order to escape symbolizing it by the letter(s) which is used often for plural.

Monzer Kahf

GLOSSARY*

A.

Abandoned
:   [matruk al Hadith متروك الحديث], for a narrator of sayings, when his narrations are not admitted by the standard rules of sayings scrutinization.

Absurd
:   [Hadith munkar حديث منكر], for a saying, rejected as denied approval by standard rules.

Agreed upon
:   [muttafaq 'alaih متفق عليه], for a saying, reported by both al Bukhari and Muslim.

Ahkam
:   [أحكام] p. of hukm, rulings of *Shari'ah* and its conjunctions.

Ahl al Bait
:   [أهل البيت], family of the Prophet (P), i.e. descendents of his great grand father, Hashim and the latter's brother al Muttalib.

Ahl al Hadith
:   [أهل الحديث], specialists in the studies of the Prophet's sayings. It refers sometimes to a quasi school of fiqh characterized by emphasizing sayings at the expenses of analogy.

Ahl al Ra'i
:   [أهل الرأي], or people of opinion: those scholars who believe in rationale based on logical analysis, especially analogy, as one of the sources of deriving *Shari'ah* rulings and *ahkam*. They usually include, among others, the Hanafites and the Malikites.

---

* This glossary includes only important words terms; sentences and expressions which appear in the text - not defined - and have special specific meaning in *Shari'ah*.

Ahl al Ra'i   :   [اهل الرأي], People of opinion methodology of jurisprudence which depends heavily on logical derivation of rulings.

Ahl al Kitab   :   [اهل الكتاب] People of the book, Christians and Jews.

Ahl al Harb   :   [اهل الحرب],People of War, non-Muslims with whom Muslims are in a state of war.

Ahl al 'Ahd   :   [اهل الذمة , اهل العهد], non-Muslims permitted in Muslim State
or Ahl al Dhimmah   temporarily or permanently.

al Salaf   :   [السلف], Predecessors, ancestors, it refers to the early few generations of Islam.

al Tajir al Mudir   :   [التاجر غير المحتكرالتاجر المدير] Non- Monopolistic trade merchant who has no storage facilities, thus he works on a negligible amount of inventory, buying or selling.

Amwal   :   [أموال] (p. of maL), generally, all kinds of assets and incomes. For detail definition see p......... of vol. 1.

Analogy   :   [Qias قياس], logical approach of deriving a *hukm* from known *ahkam* on the basis of similarity in the recognized reason of the known hukm.

Annul   :   (n: annulment, nasakha ونَسَخَ, Naskh نسخ]: to eliminate, used with reference to Qura'nic verses, as to eliminate either a text of a verse, its meaning and implication, or both.

Ansar   :   (plural, its sing. is Ansari),[انصار ، أنصاري]   (supporters): people of al Madinah who accepted the religion of Islam and became companions of the Prophet (P) after he migrated to them.

Ardab   :   [اردب], a volume measure used especially for grain.

Authentic	:	[correct صحيح] with respect to sayings, a saying whose chain of narrators is (1) linked continuously without interruption, and (2) consists of trustworthy persons both in morality and faith and in memory provided that its text is not odd شاذ or there is a good reason to reject it معلول.

B.

Books	:	See, two correct Books under letter T.

C.

Commentary; Explanatory	:	[Tafsir, تفسير], With respect to Qur'an, explanation of the Qur'an, usually composed of several volumes.
Commentator	:	[Mufassir مفسر], Writer of a commentary.
Companion	:	[Sahabi صحابي], a person who saw the Prophet Muhammad (PBUH), while he was a believer and died as a Muslim.
Correct	:	[sahih صحيح], with respect to sayings, see authentic.

D.

ضعيف	:	[Weak], with respect to a saying, when it is below the level of acceptability in regard to its chain or text.
Dinar	:	[دينار], a golden coin, used as currency, Equals one Mithqal of weight.
Dirham	:	[درهم], a silver coin, used as a currency, one dinar equals 10 dirhams.
Disregarded; Discarded	:	[Matruk متروك], with respect to a saying, when the saying is not accepted from the point of view of one of its narrators being abandoned.

<u>F.</u>

Fair   :   [Salih al Hadith صالح الحديث], for sayings' narrators, a narrator whose reports are just accepted with minimum trustworthiness, but not ranked highly in trustworthiness.

Fiqh   :   [فقه], the science of knowing details of the Ahkam of *Shari'ah.*

Followers   :   the generation of Muslims who met the Companions or any of them but not the Prophet (P).

Furq   :   [فرق], a volume measure.

<u>G.</u>

Ghanam   :   [غنم] sheep and goats.

Ghanimah   :   [غنيمة , pl. Ghana'im غنائم], property of the enemy acquired in war.

Ghusl   :   [غسل], flowing water all over the body. It could be required or only desired.

Good   :   [حسن Hassan], for a saying, a degree of acceptability of a saying putting it below the correct one, but still in the range of acceptability.

Gift of thanks   :   [هدي Hadiy], sacrificial animal (camel, cow,sheep or goat) taken to be slaughtered on the occasion of performing pilgrimage to Makkah's holy places.

<u>H.</u>

Hadith   :   [حديث], saying attributed to Prophet (P) Categorically it includes what he said, did, or approved.

Hadiy   :   [هدي], see Gift of thanks.

Hanafi (or Hanafite) : [حنفي], a follower of jurisprudence initiated by Abu Hanifah (d.150 H.) also adjective of that school.

Hanbali Hanbal (or Hanbalite) : [حنبلي], a follower of jurisprudence initiated by Ahmad bin Hanbal (d. 241 H.). also adjective of that school.

Hijaz : [حجاز], the central western part of Arabian peninsula, it includes Makkah and Madinah.

Hukm : [حكم], singular of Ahkam, see Ahkam.

I.

Ihram : [احرام], a special state required for entering Makkah on pilgrimage or 'Umrah (a special visit to Makkah holy places outside the pilgrimage season), it entails intention, non-sewed garment (for men) and observation of certain conduct.

Ijma' : [إجماع], unanimity, agreement among all scholars on certain ruling.

Ijtihad : [اجتهاد], excertion of effort in finding a ruling on something not mentioned clearly, according to certain known methodology.

Imam : [إمام] leader in his field.

Imami : [إمامي], a follower or adjective of the Shi'ite school of jurisprudence led by the 12 Imams descending from the family of the Prophet (P).

J.

Jihad : [جهاد], use of military force to defend Islam, its people and land, or religious freedom of any people.

Jizyah : [جزية], a poll tax imposed on non Muslims who are defeated in jihad and stay under the Islamic state's authority in exchange for their protection and security.

K.

Kaffarah : (Pl. Kaffarat) [كفارة], givings to poor and needy in recompense or a loss of certain kind of worship, eg. feeding three poor persons one meal for unfulfilled sweare.

Khaybar : [خيبر], a small town located north west of Arabian peninsula, 170 km. north of Madinah.

Khalifah : [خليفة], pl. Khulafa', the head of the Islamic state in the Islamic political system.

al Khulafa' al Rashidin : [الخلفاء الراشدين], the four successors of the Prophet (p) in heading the first Islamic state in Madinah, Abu Bakr, 'Umar, 'Uthman and 'Ali. They ruled during the period of 11-4O H., called the Wise Successors.

Khilafah : [خلافة], name of the position of the head of state in Islamic political system.

Kiyas : [القياس المرسل] Loose Analogy

L.

Linked : [Muttasil متصل], for a saying, when its chain is complete to the Prophet (p).

M.

Munqati' : [منقطع], for a saying, when its chain is not complete by missing two Interrupted consecutive links.

Ma'dan : [معدن] Metal.

Mahr : [مهر], an amount granted to the bride as part of the marriage contract.

Mal : (Plural Amwal), see Amwal.

Maliki : [مالكي] or Malikite, a follower of the school of jurisprudence led by Malik bin Anas (d. 170 H.) also adjective of that school.

Muhajir (s) : [Muhajir ' مهاجر], Immigrants from Makkah who accepted Islam at the time of the Prophet (P) and migrated to Madinah because of persecution.

Mulk : [ملك], ownership.

Minbar : [منبر], a stand in the Mosque for the speech given on Fridays.

Mithqal : [مثقال], a weight measure, equals on dinar of Gold, used sometimes to mean one dinar of gold.

Monopolistic : [al tajir al muhtakir التاجر المحتكر], has storage trader who
trader or Merchant facilities and keeps merchandize until prices improve.

Mudallis : [مدلس], in saying narrators, a person who does not state the person from whom he got the narration, yet uses a vague word which is [from: 'an   ] followed by a person in the chain higher than one from whom narration is obtained.

Mudd : [مد], volume measure.

Muhkam : [محكم], for a text, when both its authenticity and indication are clear cut.

Muhajir : [P1. Muhajirin مهاجر ، مهاجرين], see immigrants.

Munqati' : [منقطع], see interrupted.

Mursal : [مرسل], in sayings, when a follower drops the name of the companion through whom the saying is received.

Musnad : [مسند], when the chain of the saying is complete to the Prophet (p).

Mustahabb   :   [مستحب], Recommended (or desired), some action graded in *Shari'ah* as desired, a level below required and above permissible.

N.

Nash   :   [نش], a weight measure, equals one half Uqyyah.
(or Nashsh)

Nawah   :   [نواة], a weight measure.

Nisab   :   [نصاب], a minimum amount which determines the *zakatability* of a person. see ... p.... V.1.

Q.

Qafiz   :   [قفيز], a volume measure.

Qirbah   :   [قربة], a volume measure.

Qiyas   :   [قياس], see analogy.

al Qiyas   :   [القياس المرسل]. or (loose analogy), see loose analogy.
al Mursal

R.

Ratl   :   [رطل], a weight measure.

Riba   :   [ربا], any increase in repayment of a loan, generally, interest.

Rikaz   :   [ركاز], burried treasures or sometimes natural ores underground..

S.

Sa' : [صاع], a volume measure.

Sadaqah : [صدقة], charitable donation.
(pl. Sadsqat)

Saying (s) : see Hadith.

Saying critics : [المحدثين] specialists in scrutinizing and determining
(or scholars   their degree of authenticity.
 of sayings)

Second : The generation after the companions. The followers.
Generation

Shafi'i : [شافعي], a follower of the school of jurisprudence
(or Shafiittes)   initiated by al Shafi'i (d 204h) Also, adjective of that school.

Shari'ah : [الشريعة] the total legal system of Islam.

Shi'i (or Shiite) : [شيعي] a follower of the school of thought of those who describe
   themselves as supporters of 'Ali. Also, adjective of that school.

Shuf'ah : [شفعة] right of preference given to neighbour or partner in buying
   a real estate property.

Soft Chain : [sanad layyen سند لين], a chain of a saying which is not strong but
   net yet accused.

Strange : [Gharib غريب], in saying, when the saying is very unfamiliar
(or peculiar)   in its chain or text.

Sunnah : [سنة], path or method. With respect to sayings, it is synonimous to
   hadith.

Sunni   :   [سني], a follower of the school of thought that claims
(or Sunnite)   respect to all companions and moderation toward any extremism. It
                      covers majority of Muslims and Muslim schools of jurisprudence.
                      Also, adjective of that school.

Supporters   :   see Ansar.

Suspended   :   [معلق], for a saying, when it is narrated without any chain (this is
                      especially done sometimes by al Bukhari).

T.

Tafsir   :   [تفسير], with respect to Qur'an, commentary and explanation.

Tawhid   :   [توحيد], Oneness of God.

Tayammum   :   [تيمم], use of regular but clean soil as a ritual substitute of
                      ablution.

Trade inventory :   [Urud al Tijarah عروض التجارة] merchandize acquired
(or trade assets)   for the purpose of resale.

Two correct   :   the two collections of correct sayings of al Bukhari and Muslim.
Books

U.

Unanimity   :   See Ijma'.

Unanimously   :   taken or approved by all scholars.
agreed upon

Unknown   :   [مجهول], with respect to sayings narrators, when no information is
                      available about a narrator.

Uqiyyah   :   [اوقية], a weight measure.

'Urud al Tijarah :   [عروض التجارة], see trade inventory.

'Ushr : [عشر], one tenth, it also refers to the one tenth (or one twentieth) given as *Zakah* in agriculture.

Usul al fiqh : the science of fiqh methodology and axiomatic system.

W.

Wasq : [وسق], a measure of volume used in agriculture.

Wise Successors : see al Khulafa' al Rashidin.

Wudu' : [وضوء], use of water to wash certain parts and members of the body in preparation for prayer. Ablution .

Z.

Zahiri
(or Zahirite) : [ظاهري], a follower or adjective of the school of jurisprudence that puts its main emphasis on the literal meaning of the text.

Zaidi : [زيدي], a follower of the school of jurisprudence initiated by Zaid bin Ali bin al Husain. Also, adjective of that school.

FROM THE ETERNAL DIVINE CHARTER

*"OUT OF THEIR WEALTH, TAKE ZAKAH THAT SO THOU
MIGHTEST PURIFY AND SANCTIFY THEM, AND PRAY ON
THEIR BEHALF, VERILY THY PRAYERS ARE A SOURCE
OF SECURITY FOR THEM AND GOD IS ONE WHO
HEARETH AND KNOWETH."*

AUTHOR INTRODUCTION

Praise be to God and prayer and peace on the messenger of God, his family, his companions, and those who follow his guidance. Out of the five pillars of Islam, *Zakah* is the socio-financial one. By performing *zakah* along with tawhid (belief in the oneness of God) and establishing prayers a person becomes Muslim. As a member of the Muslim community he or she deserves the brotherhood and allegiance of Muslims, as indicated by the Qur'anic verse "but if they repent, establish prayers, and practice *zakah* they are your brethren in faith".

Even though *zakah* is usually mentioned with the methods of worship of Islam, such as prayer, it is in fact a part of the socio-financial system of Islam. For that reason it is always studied under the heading of Financial and Political Issues of the Islamic Society. Therefore, it is no wonder that Muslim scholars are eager to analyze the details of *zakah* from all angles.

Explanatory Issues:

Commentators on the Qur'an study and explain the verses about *zakah* including verse 267 in Sura al Baqarah, verse 242 in Sura al 'An'am, verses 34, 60, and 103 in Sura al Tawbah, and several other verses, Among commentators, those who specialize in ahkam (Injunctions of the Qur'an) such as Abu Bakr al Razi, al Jassas Abu Bakr bin al 'Arabi, and Abu 'Abdullah al Qurtubi, have detail contributions to the explanation of the verses of *zakah.*

Scholars of hadith study the traditions of the Prophet that deal with *zakah.* You will find a chapter on *zakah* in all books of *Sunnah*, especially those sorted according to articles of fiqh such as *Muwatta' Malik, Sahih al Bukhari, Sahih Muslim. Jami 'al Tirmidhi, Sunnan al Nasa'i, Sunnan abi Dawud, and Sunan Ibn Majah.* In *Sahih al Bukhari* alone, the chapter of *zakah* contains 172 sayings attributed to the Prophet Muhammad (P) Muslim agreed with him on All but of the Prophet's sayings. In aslo contains 20 sayings of the companions and the followers.

Jurists study *zakah* in their books as the second major worship in Islam. It is usually listed right after prayers, in line with the sequence found in Qur'an and Sunnah.

Scholars specialized in the financial and administrative issues of Islam look at *zakah* as a component of its socio-financial tem. So we find *zakah* in *al Kharaj* of Abu Yusuf, *al Kharaj* of Yahya bin Adam, *al Amwal*, of Abu 'Ubaid, *al Ahkam al Sultaniyah*, of al Mawardi (Shafi'it), *al Ahkam al Sultaniyah* of abu Ya'la (Hanbalite), and *Al Siyasah al Shar'iyah*, of Ibn Taimiyah.

Since the subject of *zakah* has been extensively researched, and its references are abundant, one may ask, why do we need a new study of *zakah*? Does the contemporary Muslim library need a new work such as the one we are embarking on, (which studies *zakah*, its objectives, its effects on the life of the individual and the society and its status among contemporary socio-financisl systems?) The answer to this question is yes, for the following reasons.

1. This important tenet of Islam needs to be re-examined, combined in one volume and represented in a contemporary style. The authors of old times wrote for their own ages with their own styles. Each era has its own style, as the Qur'an says, "we sent not an apostle except to teach in the language of his own people in order to make things clear to them".

There are two main subject in Islamic economics that deserve to be studied in this time because of their relevance. One is an essential obligation or a pillar of Islam. The other is a prohibition, a major sin. The first subject is *zakah*, the second *riba* (interest). There is no disagreement among Muslims about the obligatory nature of the first, nor the prohibition of the other, for denying this obligation or that prohibition amounts to apostating.

However, the issue of *riba* received more attention of scholars than the issue of *zakah*. Great scholars such as Abu A'la al Mawdudi,[4] Muhammad Abdullah Draz[5] 'Isa 'Abdu, Muhammad Abu Zahrah[7], Muhammad Abdullah al 'Arabi[8], Muhammad Abu Sa'ud[9], Muhammad Baqir al Sadr[10], and Muhammad 'Uzair[11], have written books, papers, and articles on *riba*, whether from a pure Islamic point of view or from a position influenced by the Western capitalistic stance on money and life. In spite of the fact that there is always room for more rigorous and more extensive research, one can note that a reasonable amount of research has emerged on this issue.

As for the issue of *zakah*, there is very little concern for its research by scholars. Such an inportant matter like *zakah* still needs more study and research, especially since it is one of the fundamental obligations of Islam and a cornerstone of its financial, economic, and social systems.

2. Muslim jurists differ on many details of *zakah*. Each has his own opinion and arguments, and there are sometimes contradictions among their interpretations, which leaves the majority of people in chaos and confusion about what opinion to choose.

There is a great need to review these interpretations, opinions, and arguments, to discuss them with certain degree of neutrality, to examine them in the light of the criteria descending from God, and to show which among them is the most worthy.

To this need the late Shiekh Mahmud Shaltut referred' in his book *Islam, Doctrine and Law*[12], saying under the title "*Zakah*, A Principal Religious Pillar".

"In spite of my belief that theoretical differences are indications of thinking vitality and flexibility of the system that accommodates such differences, I feel uneasy when I see the range of difference among the schools of thought on the application of this obligation of *zakah*, as it is exposed in the books of jurisdiction and injunctions. This obligation of *zakah*, that is usually associated with prayer ought to be, like prayers, commonly understood. In prayers we see not much room for differences - just five prayers in the day and night. Unlike prayers, we observe that even the ratio, the exemption, the kinds of wealth that are *zakatable* are subject to differences among scholars. Such differences have serious implications for muslims at large when it comes to their application of the Islamic obligation of *zakah*. For example, some scholars consider the wealth of children and insane individals *zakatable*, others don't. Some scholars consider all agricultural products *zakatable*, others restrict *zakah* to specific kinds only. Some consider debts *zakatable*, others don't. Similar differences exist for business assets and women's jewelry. Some require certain minimum (nisab) for *zakatability*, some don't. etc. The same kind of differences also exist about the disbursement of *zakah*."

The late Shaltut called for a reviw of those differences among schools of thought, which he feared may mar the essence of this obligation. Fuch a review should be based on the ultimate objectives of *zakah* as cited in the Qur'an, so Muslims could understand and apply it on the same level.

3. There are new matters that did not exist in the past and were not known to the ancient jurists. These new matters require new religious injunctions. Today, Mulims ask many questions about *zakah* that must not be left without answers. Questions such as how to consider new forms of wealth other than Iivestock, agricultural produce and fruits. These new forms of wealth include huge buildings for rent, enormous factories and plants, machines and equipment, and all kinds of fixed and circulating capital that provide tremendous flow of income out of their production lines and rental proceeds such as ships, cars, planes and hotels. There are new trading and industrial corporations, the new forms of income of professionals like physicians, engineers, and lawyers and huge numbers of employees receiving wages and salaries. Are all these *zakatable* or not, and if they are *zakatable*, what is the percentage of *zakah* on them? When is it due? And on what basis in *Shari'ah* is it founded.

Many measures and terms mentioned in the texts on *zakah*, such as *al wisq* in agricultural products, *sa'* in the fast-breaking *zakah, darahim* and *dananir* in the *zakah* on money require new definitions and translation into today's measures. Are these quantities given and fixed or can we change them in response to changes in economic and social circumstances, such as a change in the purchasing value of money? There are new taxes with progressive or flat rates imposed by contemporary governments with certain social purposes attached to them. The relation between such taxes and *zakah* should be studied, and the areas of similarities and differences must be pointed out. The substitutability of these taxes and *zakah* must be investigated and their coexistence must also be examined.

Questions like these are waiting for answers and Muslim scholars are looked at to provide such answers. To say that the door of *ijtihad* is closed would incorrectly leave these issues unsettled. None can close the door of *ijtihad* since it was opened by the messenger of God (P).

Reliable scholars of *'usul* (methodology of jurisprudence) are determined that *ijtihad* can be exerted on individual issues, since some people may specislize in certain areas of jurisprudence. In our days this specialized *ijtihad* becomes the comnon rule rather than the exception. Hard work and exerted preparation are required to understand the texts of the original sources of this religion from the linguistic and the religous points of view, and those who have prepared themselves well for *ijtihad* can obviously exercise it.

While I believe that giving fulfilling answers to such questions requires a collective *ijtihad* exercised by a group of muslim schloars, I maintain that individual effort and resarch undoubtedly pave the way for sound collective *ijtihad* until a time comes when Muslim states make it feasible for reliable scholars to work together as teams of collective *ijtihad*.

4. Unfortunately, there are a few misgivings among some Muslims about *zakah*. Some look at it as a very meager amount given by the rich to the poor only to sustain the latter's life and keep him barely at the poverty line, i.e. in permanent need of the condescendent charity of the rich. This picture has no place in the institution of *zakah* in Islam, though it is regrettably practiced by many. We even find some reputable journalists in Egypt writing that *zakah* does not fit our society because the contemporary social and economic systems must be based on work and production instead of charity as if *zakah* were simply a charity for beggars or a support for the idle[14]. Another writer called Islamic social justice "charity socialism"[15]. All this reveals an ill intention to mislead readers or at least an enormous ignorance about *zakah* and emphasizes the need for a new study which I believe is an obligation on Muslim scholars.

Researchers interested in financial and economic issues of Islam have expressed their surprise that the contemporary Mustim library lacks a serious and comprehensive study on *zakah* in spite of its important place in this religion of Islam[16]. The Higher Council of Islamic Affairs in the Ministry of Awqaf in Eqypt felt this need by announcing nine years ago *zakah* as one of few major research areas and allocating prizes to the best research papers written on *zakah*. This need was further stressed by the Congress on Islamic Research held in Cairo, March, 1963, and attended by Muslim scholars from more than forty countries. In their resolution, the conferees declared "The issues of *zakah*, financial resources in Islam, means of investment, their relation to individuals and society, and the private and public rights are the major issues of contemporary concern because these subjects represent the point of convergence in *Shari'ah* of worship and social behavior. For this very reason, the Congress considers these issues as a main theme for its coming session[17]." The present piece of research endeavors to fulfill the following purposes:

A. Gathering the dispersed texts from their original sources in Qur'an, hadith, and commentaries as well as jurisprudence books of all schools of thought, books on financial and religious policies and general books on Islamic culture, and rearrange them in one whole theme that helps to understand *zakah* in Islam.

B. Investigating the differences and disagreements among scholars in an attempt to find the most sound opinions in the light of the evidence in *Shari'ah*, Muslims' needs and their common contemporary interests.

C. Answering questions on *zakah* arising from modern economic practices, questions cannot continue neglecting anymore.

D. Attempting to reveal the nature *zakah* as an Islamic obligation, comparing it with other modern taxes, and showing the similarities and differences between them.

E. Presenting the objectives and goals of *zakah* and its effects on Muslim society in solving problems like poverty, destitution, and begging and in facing socio-economic miseries and showing the precedence of *zakah* with regard to social solidarity and social insurance.

F. Correcting misgivings about *zakah*, which are caused by misunderstanding or erroneous application anl debating objections raised by the enemies of Islam.

Footnotes

1. *Sura at Tawbah*, 9: 11

2. See the conclusion of the book of *zakah* in *Fath al bari* p. 4, al Halabi print, Egypt.

3. *Sura Ibrahim*, 14: 4

4. *Al Riba* published in Arabic.

5. His paper on "*al riba*", read in the conference on Islamic jurisprudence, Paris 1951.

6. His booklet *Why did God Prohibit Riba* published by Maktabah al Manar al Islamiya, Kuwait, under series title, Toward A Sound Islamic Economy.

7. His booklet *Prohibition of Riba. As An Economic Institution* published in the series mentioned in footnote 6.

8. His paper "Private Ownership and its limits in Islam" read at the Congress on Islamic Research, Cairo and published in the first collection of proceedings of the Congress.

9. His book *Outlines of Islamic Economics* and his paper "Is It Possible To Establish an Islamic Bank" published by Makatabah al Manar.

10. His book: *Our Economics,* published by Dar al Fikr, Lebanon; also his book *Interest Free Bank.*

11. His paper "Factors of Success in an Interest Free Eank" published by Maktabah al Manar.

12 *Al Islam, Doctrine and Law*, page 109, Dar al 'Ilm print, Egypt.

13. *Ibid.*

14. He is the socialist writer Ahmad Baha' al Din in one of his weekly editorials in Akhbar Al Yawn Newspaper 1961 Egypt.

15. Khalid Muhammad Khalid in his book *Min Huna Nabda',* from here to there.

16. Mahud Abu Al Sa'ud in an article in the journal *Al Muslimun*, few years back

17. Proceedings of the first session of the Congress of Islamic Research, page 314.

APPROACH AND PLAN OF THIS STUDY

I can define the steps I followed in this study and its plan in the following points.

Depicting References and Gathering Material

The first thing I had to do was to collect relevant material from its sources, that is, texts, injunctions, and opinions of scholars, new and ancient sources, religious texts and books. The Qur'an and Sunnah are the main sources that I relied on in understanding the reality of zakah, its injunctions, objectives, and position in Islam. I found plenty of material in books of commentary from all ages, commentary by narration or commentary by means of explanation, especially the explanation of verses on *ahkam*. Books of *hadith* gave me the second major source. I benefitted from both texts and footnotes, especially from books dealing with *hadith* jurisprudence such as *Muntaqa al Akhbar* and *Bulugh al Maram* and their commentaries. I used books of jurisprudence representing schools of thought as well .as comparative studies, especially those that provide the evidence from *Shari'ah* and debate the objections raised by others, as well as books of jurisprudence methodology and rules (*usul*) and books of financial and administrative jurisprudence such as *al Amwal* by the great jurist Abu 'Ubaid al Qasim bin Sallam. Some material came from modern books and papers that deal with one or more aspect of the social, political, and economic systems of Islam. I also used secondary sources such as books on language, history, bibliographies, encyclopedias, indexes, etc. Quotes from any of those books, ancient or contemporary, are marked to their authors in the text or in a footnote unless the reference is well-known or was mentioned earlier, where I only mention the name of the book. On rare occasions I quote certain statements that are very familiar to scholars without mentioning a specific source for them. In all this I follow our predecessors who said, "It is a blessing for any quote to be attributed to its author". I would like to mention here, that one of the blessings of the present study is that it paved the way for me to get involve in financial and economic readings from which I used to be isolated as a result of my own specialty in *Shari'ah*. Through this new window I came to understand many aspects of the financial and economic system in Islam, its principles and pillars and the kinds of transactions it deals with. This I hope to put in a forthcoming independent study. Furthermore, while working on the present research I was able to put out my study entitled "The Problem of Poverty and its Islamic Solution".

Subdivision and Sequence of the Chapters of this Study

The nature of the subject, interrelation of its parts, and integration of its material determine its structure as well as its organization in such a way that every ingredient requires the other I tried to make it a comprehensive scientific book of reference on *zakah*, which made it rather long. This study is divided into nine parts and a conclusion. The sequence of those parts follows the logical rationale, starting with the obligation of *zakah*, the assets it is required on, its ratios, to whom it should distributed, where it must not be used, means of collection and distribution, objectives and effects of *zakah*, followed by the fast breaking zakah and a discussion of whether there are other financial duties beyond *zakah* and the similarities and differences between *zakah* and contemporary taxes.

Part One deals with the obligation of *zakah*, in which I showed that all religions share in the care for poor and weak members of the society. Islam expressed such concern as early as the Makkan period. This was climaxed by the imposition of *zakah* at the early Madinan period. The system of *zakah* proceeded all similar legislation in the world. Part Two deals with *zakatable* persons. In this part I have detailed the injunctions concerning *zakah* on children and insane persons, and the issue of *zakatablitity* of non-Muslims. Part Three deals with *zakatable* funds and assets and with the ratios of *zakah* - what kinds of wealth are *zakatable* in livestock, in money and currency, in business assets, in agricultural, in minerals, in maritime, ships, vessls, assets, in animal products, etc. In this part I explained *zakah* on buildings for rent, on plants and factories, on income of non-business capital, on salaries and wages, and on the income of professionals. In Part Four I discuss the eight areas of dispersement of *zakah* mentioned in the Qur'an, how much should be appropriated to each category, whether or not all categories should be covered in each distribution of *zakah*, and disqualifications for receipt of *zakah*. Part Five examines with the means of *zakah* payment and collection, its relation to the state, and the prepayment or late payment of *zakah*. It deals also with the issues of transporting proceeds of *zakah* from one country to another and payment in value or in kind. In Part Six I delineates the objectives and the effects of *zakah*. In this part I explain the objectives of *zakah* with reference to the *zakah* prayer, the *zakah* recipient and the whole society. Additionally, this part deals with the role of *zakah* in solving certain socio-economic problems such as unemployment, destitution and begging, natural catastrophe, community disputes and differences, in addition to the major problem of poverty. Part Seven describes fast-breaking *zakah* and its injunctions. Part Eight studies the issue of other duties on wealth besides *zakah*. In this part I discussed the two opposing opinions on the matter, the arguments of each side, and which one is sounder. In Part Nine I compared *zakah* and taxes, and depicted the characteristics of *zakah* as a tax. The principles, objectives and guarantees of *zakah* are discussed in this part, as well as the fact that *zakah* supersedes the contemporary thought on taxation with respect to its principles and regulations. This part also deals with the issue of whether other taxes are allowed in addition to *zakah* or whether *zakah* can be substituted by other taxes. In the conclusion I summarized the institution of *zakah* and gave statements by non Muslims' sholars by writers, Muslim and non-Muslim alike, about *zakah* and its effects in fulfilling justice, equality, and solidarity among the members of a society.

3. Comparative Assessment

Two kinds of comparisons are made in this study: comparison among schools of thought in order to select the opinion that is most supported by evidence in *Shari'ah*, and comparison between *Shari'ah* and other legal systems, divine or not, ancient or new, in order to show the characteristics of this divine *Shari'ah* that came final and perpetual as compared to prior divine laws that *Shari'ah* superseded or man-made systems that are inadequate. While comparing the different views of the Islamic schools I did not limit myself to the four famous schools for this may be unjust to other schools and opinions in Islamic jurisprudence. Since there are views expressed by scholars from among the Companions, the Followers, and the later generations, these views ought not be neglected or disregarded. As for the Companions, there is no dispute about their precedents and their knowledge. Beyond them there are views expressed by great followers such as Ibn al Musayyib, 'Umar bin Abd al 'Aziz, al Zuhri, al Nakha'i, al Hasan, 'Ata', al Sha'bi, Maymun bin Mahran, and many others. Even in the generations after the followers there are great names such as al Thawri, al Awza'i, Abu 'Ubaid, al Tabari, Dawud al Zahiri, and many others. All these views represent in fact a very precious and valuable scientific heritage, the neglect of which would be a great mistake both from the scientific and the religious points of view. Furthermore, I did not limit my study to the Sunnite schools, but expanded it to include schools of Zaidi and Imami. Differences between them and Sunnite schools in the matters of detailed injunctions are trivial and we have seen great scholars such as al San'ani, in his book *Subul al Salam* and al Shawkani in his *Nail al Awtar* mention the views of Zaidis and Imamis, including al Hadi, al Qasim, al Baqir, al Naser, and others. These works circulate among Sunnite scholars without any sort of uneasiness.

As for the comparison between Islamic thinking on *zakah* and systems, it was necessary to compare Islam on zakah with previous religions on charities. It was also necessary to compare *zakah* with contemporary thoughts on taxation and social insurance.

4. Explanation and Reasoning

Throughout the course of this research, I felt it is not sufficient to give the bare *Shari'ah* injunction in each matter. Rather, it is necessary to explain the rationale and the virtues of the rulings and the detriment of what is prohibited. This is in spirit of the approach of the Qur'an itself in providing not just rulings but their rationale, their objectives, and their benefits to mankind, individually and collectively. Qur'an does not merely demand that believers submit to all rulings without knowing the reasoning behind them. If providing the reasoning for *Shari'ah*'s rulings is advisable in general, it is indispensable at this time because there are malicious ideas spread around and misleading pressures from the East and the West. It is no longer sufficient to merely spell *Shari'ah* injunctions and expect believers to cry, "We comply with what we hear!".

5. Weighing Different Opinions

Any research that hopes to dissect and scrutinise all views and opinions from the different sources must also compare them with each other. But if the author himself is subject to one view or biased to certain school of thought, he would do his best to support the view he subscribes to. Therefore, I have freed myself from any such preconceptions or alliance to any specific school of thought. This non-partisan commitment is well appreciated in the tradition of this Muslim *ummah*. Following one jurist in all his opinions, even those that are weakly supported by *Shari'ah* texts amounts to taking that jurist as a legislator or a maker of *Shari'ah* since imitation itself is a form of annulment of mind and its virtue. "The mind is created to think and adore", said Ibn al Jawzi. How could a person who has a candle to shed light put it out and walk in the darkness? Others have said "those who imitate are either insecure or stupid".

I read texts and views as an investigator, an examiner, a researcher who seeks the truth regardless of where or whom it comes from. It may be found with predecessors jurists or with later generations. It may be found in opinionated schools of jurists or in schools of *hadith*, or in the school of *Zahiriyah*. It could be found among the four reputed schools or outside them. I do not subscribe to fanaticism that puts a taboo on all new opinions found after the early four *imams* believing that none are accepted after them, that *ijtihad* came to an end after the first three centuries of Islam and that truth lies only in the writings of those schools and those generations. On the other hand, I would not blindly follow those who claim to be making *ijtihad* without fulfilling all its requirements, those who call frr top to bottom renovation, about whom the late al Rafi'i said in mockery "They wanted to renovate religion, language, even the sun and the moon."

I am committed throughout my research to the principles of no bias, non-partisanship, righteousness, openmindedness to every and all useful renovation and keenness to retain every correct ancient view or opinion. Yellowed and wrinkled pages, bad printing and small script of the old texts did not prevent me from perusing them and extracting their treasures, whether in the original texts, commentaries, or footnotes. Consequently I benefited from old and new without being either cautionary or permissive. I analyzed what I obtained and weighed the arguments of the different opinions and supported the strongest, that is, whose evidence is clearest, without bias to any school. I may take the view of Abu Hanifah sometimes, or Shafi'i, Ahmad, Sufyan, al Awza'i, Abu 'Ubaid, or any other thinker certain other times. I may even leave aside all of them and take instead what is correctly reported from a companion or follower. This is not intermingling ideas together but rather, it is a search for truth and best argument. Only one thing limits all scholars. That is the unmistakable words of the Book of God or the tradition of His Messenger. Ibn 'Abbas, Malik and 'Ata', said, "One may take or leave any opinion from anyone except the Messenger of God (p)".

This approach may allow me to take up an opinion that is otherwise neglected or not to accept an opinion of the majority, since truth does not always accompany great numbers. Even great *imams* sometimes hold to an opinion that is in opposition to the majority. Ibn 'Abbas arguing against following the majority said: "a matter that came neither in the Book of God nor in the judgment of the Prophet (p), yet all people accept it is the inheritance of a sister with a daughter of a deceased." Malik gave his opinion in Shuf'ah on fruits and said "This is something I have not heard anyone else saying." Each one of the great *imams* did not bother that he was alone on certain rulings and opinions. Issues on which *imam* Ahmad differed from the majority were even compiled in a special Vol.ume.

Criteria in Weighing, Arguments and Deductions

I relied on a set of rules that represent the *Shari'ah* basis in pointing out the opinion that overrules others and in deducting new opinions or quasi-new views. These rules can be summarized in the following:

1. Adopting general texts, unless there is an evidence that restricts them. Many texts in our religion are general in form so that they cover multiple cases as well as individual details and ingredients. This in itself is one of the miracles of this religion that equips it to be the final religion and makes it suit all times and places.

Consequently, Qur'anic verses and the Messenger's sayings should be received and taken as general, except when their scopes are narrowed by another text that is correct, authentic and clear in its meaning. In this case, the restriction comes first. I am not among those who reject clear-cut (muhkam) and authentic (sahih) sayings because they oppose general texts in the Qur'an. On the other hand, I do not share the position of those who quickly accept a restriction coming in the *hadith* even though the *hadith* may not be exactly authentic or may not have a clear-cut indication. I do not, for example, subscribe to the position of *Imam* Abu Hanifah in rejecting the saying that "There is no *zakah* in date that is below five wasq" in order to preserve the generality of the text "and of the fruits of the earth which we have produced for you"[3] and the text "in what is watered by the sky there is one tenth", because the first saying is correct and agreed upon. The explanation given by Abu Hanifah that the saying deals with date that is kept for trading is a very weak and heavy-handed explanation. For that reason I go along with the opinion of the two disciples of Abu Hanifah and the majority of scholars that there is *nisab* in the produce of earth, the same as other sorts of wealth.

On the other hand, I fully agree with Abu Hanifah in holding to the generality of the text "and of the fruit of the earth which we have produced for you" and the *hadith* "in what is watered by the sky there is one tenth" and I do not consider this generality modified, by a saying like "There is no *zakah* on vegetables" because this is a weak *hadith*. Of course one can find, a reconciling explanation for this *hadith*, by interpreting it to mean that: Vegetables cannot be collected in payment of *zakah* because they are perishable and cannot be stored for for long. But, if *zakah* is not collected in the form of vegetables, it is still required of their producer on the basis of the generality of these texts.

The generality of the texts of Qur'an and Sunnah must be applied as is until they are modified by another correct and clear-cut text. Consequently, we must observe the general meaning of all verses and sayings that obligate *zakah* on all forms of wealth, such as the verses "Out of their wealth take *zakah*" and "on those in their wealth, there is a well defined right" and the saying of the prophet, (p) "Pay *zakah* of your wealth". These texts do not differentiate between one kind of wealth and another, so we need not make exceptions unless when there are specific texts to support them.

Accepting Consensus or True *Ijma'*

The agreement of all scholars of this ummah, especially in the early generations, on certain issues is an obvious indication that they have based the agreement on strong *Shari'ah* evidence, be it a text, general benefit, or a material fact. Consequently, we should respect such an agreement so that we can preserve the value of *ijma'* in *Shari'ah*, that keeps balance in legislation and prevents chaos and legislative confusion. Examples of this *ijma'* is the agreement of scholars that *zakah* is obligatory on golden assets at the same rate as it is on silver, i.e. one fourth of a tenth, and their agreement that a *mithqal* is one and three sevenths of a dirham.

I mentioned true *ijma'* because some jurists reported *ijma'* on issues that are still controversial. This is because in early generations there were many scholars most of whom were dispersed in several countries, so that it was very difficult to know their stand on certain issues. *Imam* Ahmad went so far as to state "Whoever claims that an *ijma'* on any matter did ever exist is a liar, for how could he know? People may have differed without him knowing. Instead, one may say "To my knowledge there are no disagreements on such an issue' or 'No different opinions have been reported to me'". There are examples of cases in which *ijma'* was claimed or a state of no report of disagreement was mentioned whereas there is concrete evidence that such cases were not agreed upon. Al shafi'i, for example, said about *zakah* on cattle, "On each thirty there is a *tabi* and on each forty there is a *musinnah*, and I know of no difference among scholars on this". It is certain that a difference existed and was reported by Jabir bin Abdullah, Sa'id bin al Musayib, Qatadah, and the *zakah* collectors in Madinah of Ibn al Zubair[4]. Another example is that reported by Ibn al Mundhir, that there was *ijma'* that *zakah* may not be spent on non Muslims while other scholars reported from al Zuhri, Ibn Sirin, and 'Ikrimah, that this is permissible and it seems that this is the view of 'Umar, according to reports from him.[5] Also, Ibn Qudamah in al Mughni said "we know of no disagreement on the view that the clan of Hashim are not allowed to receive *zakah*," This was commented on by al Hafiz Ibn Hajar, in *al Fath*, "But al Tabari reported that Abu Hanifah said that they may receive *zakah* if they were not given the allowance of *dhavi al Qurba* (the close relatives of the Prophet). This is also stated by al Tahawi. Similar views are attributed by some Malikites to al Abhari, a Malikite, and it is an opinion expressed by some Shafi'ites. Abu Yusuf said, "*Zakah* of the clan of Hashim is lawful to members of the same clan." For this special case the Malikites have four different opinions."[6]

Such alleged *ijma'* is not binding because it is not in fact an *ijma'* and one may take a position that opposes it. As for true *ijma'* i.e. *ijma'* that truly has no known opposition, it is an acceptable ruling in *Shari'ah* and I bind myself to following it in spite of objections raised about its binding nature.

Some *usul* scholars say that if Muslims of a certain generation differ on an issue and are divided, for example, into two opinions a later generation may not formulate a third brand new opinion. The argument given is that if there are only two opinions, an implicit *ijma'* to reject a third one must exist. Al Amidi said, if a third opinion contradicts both of the original two then it is not acceptable, while if it coincides with one, or each, of them in certain aspects, then it can be accomodated. Let us take as an example what Abu Hanifah says, i.e. that the one tenth imposed as *zakah* on land is obligated on the landlord. The majority says it is on the tenant. Apparently all agree that the tenth is obligated, so one may say that this tenth is obligated on the tenant on his net agricultural products after deducting the rent which is paid to the owner, and that the landlord is required to pay *zakah* at the rate of 10% on the rent received. Obviously this does not violate the implicit *ijma'* according to Al Amidi. Others believe that the mere fact that scholars of a certain generation differ on an issue and express two opinions is in itself an indication that this issue is controversial in which all can exert effort and apply *ijtihad*. A third and later opinion is merely an outcome of such *ijtihad* and consequently should be accomodated. The followers, as an example, had several third views not known to the companions as it is reported from Ibn Sirin, Masruq, and others[8]." This is the way I see it as long as such *ijtihad* issues are susceptible to new research and efforts.

3. Elaborating An Appropriate Analogy

Analogy means applying to a case the same ruling given to a similar case because of common reason ('illah). It is a matter of natural rationale implanted by God in human minds and, according to Ibn al Qayim, an ingredient of *al Mizan* (right criteria) that descended from God with his Holy Book and made by God a support of the Book. God says: "It is God who has sent down the Book in truth, and the Balance[9]" and "We sent aforetime our apostles with clear signs and sent down with them the Book and the Balance that men may stand forth in justice".[10] The balance is meant here as justice and the criteria and means with which we know justice. Appropriate analogy is the Balance. It is better to give it the noble name that is given to it by God and to recognize that there is an obligation on every Muslim to apply it as much as possible. It is not so with the name "analogy" because analogy may be right or wrong, praised or disclaimed, correct or incorrect. The right and correct analogy is the Balance that God sent along with his Book[11].

Imam Ibn Taimiyah said, "Analogy is an inclusive word. It includes correct analogy and incorrect analogy, but only the correct analogy is accepted in *Shari'ah*. It implies treating similarly, cases that are similar and differentiating between cases that are distinct.. The first application is *called qiyas al tard* (positive analogy) and the second is called *qiyas al 'aks* (negative analogy). Analogy in this meaning is part of justice and balance sent by God with His messenger. Appropriate analogy is one in which the reason on which a *Shari'ah* injunction is based exists in the two cases without anything that opposes it or prevents the application of the same injunction. This kind of analogy is always consistent with *Shari'ah*. By the same token, analogy by disregarding irrelevant differences is also a correct analogy where an acclaimed difference between the two cases is shown as irrelevant. Again this kind of analogy is also consistent with *Shari'ah*."[12]

In brief, if the reason that is common between the two cases, in analogy, is obvious and clear and if there is no relevant difference, apparent or otherwise, nor any factor preventing similarity, analogy should be applied an considered a *Shari'ah* evidence which no one can disclaim. Some object to this on the basis that *zakah* is one of the worships and in worships there can be no analogy. It is agreed upon that matters of pure worship don't have analogy since the true reasons behind them may never be known by human beings and in worships obedience to God is the only rationale. Analogy is not applicable to pure worships such as prayers, fasting, and pilgrimage. This prevents human beings from inventing forms of worships out of their own imaginations, without a clear order from God.

As for *zakah*, it is not purely a worship, for in addition to being a worship it is a defined right of the poor, an established tax, and an ingredient of the social, and economic system of the society. The reasons for enacting *zakah* are, in general, known and clear. Why can we not then use analogy in *zakah*?

The Prophet, (p) collected fast-breaking *zakah* in the form of grains and fruits such as rye, date, and raisin. By analogy, al Shafi'i, Ahmad, and their disciples accept everything that is edible or the common food in that town or (common food) the payer in payment of *zakah*. They did not consider that these special grains and fruits are beyond analogy. On the other hand, the majority of scholars applied *zakah* on different kinds of grains and fruits by analogy to those grains and fruits mentioned by the Prophet, (p)l instead of restricting *zakah* to the items stated in the sayings such as wheat, rye, date and raisin. It is reported that 'Umar used analogy with respect to *zakah* when he ordered *zakah* on horses after he realized that they had become high in value, saying, "Should we only take one sheep out of every forty sheep and leave horses with nothing?" 'Umar was followed in that respect by Abu Hanifah[13].

Because of these precedents, I applied analogy on rented buildings because they are similar to agricultural land, and on wages because they are similar to grants an which Abdullah bin Mas'ud, Mu'a wiyah and 'Umar bin Abdal al 'Aziz used to collect *zakah*. These sorts of incomes and assets are included anyway under the general texts obligating *zakah*. By the same token we apply analogy on silk, milk and other animal products because they are similar to honey, which is mentioned in the Traditions.

However, to emphasize the importance of analogy it may be sufficient to quote *Imam* al Shafi'i in his al *Risalah* about *zakah* on gold: "The Prophet of God ordered *zakah* on silver currency and Muslims after him collected *zakah* on gold. They were either depending on a saying of the Prophet that never reached our times or applying analogy because of the similarities between gold and silver as money, since both were used in several countries as measures and store of value[14]." Imposing *zakah* on gold, especially since gold has become an international reserve for currency in most countries, is not a trivial issue, yet Muslims after the death of the Prophet (p) applied analogy on it and made it *zakatable* for it is very unlikely that there existed a *hadith* about it that did not reach al Shafi'i, Malik, al Bukhari, Muslim and others in spite of their keenness to reach out for all the correct sayings of the Prophet. Malik considers the action of Muslims on this matter to be like Sunnah about which there are no differences. Consequently he said *zakah* is obligated on gold (with a minimum of twenty dinars) the same way it is obligated on silver (with a minimum of two hundred dirhams).

4. Considering the Objectives and Common Benefits

It is established among Muslim scholars that the injunctions of *Shari'ah* are ordained for the benefit of mankind in their earthly living and upon their resurrection after death, whether these benefits are necessities, needed or improvements. *Imam* al Shatibi argued that this can be verified by surveying the injunctions of *Shari'ah* and looking into their supportive evidence, universal or specific. This does not apply only to one case or one text - since all *Shari'ah* is established after this underlying fact.[15] Al Shatibi made the important point that with regard to worship the principle is that people accept and obey without seeking explanation or reasons. As for transactions and interrelations, the principle is to look for meanings, and rationale"[16]. Al Shatibi provides very strong arguments to support this view, but unfortunately they fall beyond the limit of the present work. What should be emphasized here however, is that *zakah*, despite the facts that it is associated with prayers under the label of worships, is in reality not purely a worship. It is closer to being a transaction because it is the major financial institution for Muslims. *Zakah* is a relationship between the state, the wealthy, and the poor. This is perhaps why all works on financial and administrative issues in Islam include a chapter on *zakah* the same way they include chapters on *kharaj*, state revenues, etc. *Zakah* is, as such, a part of the social system in Islam. If we were to re-sort issues of *fiqh* according to contemporary standards, we would classify *zakah* as part of the socio-financial system and not with the pure worships. Similarly, when we talk about law, we talk about *zakah* as part of the financial law of the state.

This does not mean that all the rules of *zakah* are outside the boundaries of worships, Al Shatibi resolves that in transactions that have some characteristics of worship, we should limit ourselves to the texts. This applies not only to *zakah* but also to the requirement of *sadaq* (dowry) in marriage, the distribution shares in inheritance and the number of months in *'iddah*, etc. I add to these the percentages of *zakah* and its minimum exempt (*nisab*) because these are issues defined clearly by texts and Muslims have no disagreement on them through history. So, it is essential to abide by these texts and this *ijma'*. For that reason I disagree with those who claim that the minimum exempt and rates of *zakah* are subject to change with changing time and places on the ground that such changes are in observance to the objectives and common benefits. I believe such changes alter the features of *zakah* and make it a mere civil tax, like other taxes imposed by governments.

The sum up, the objectives of *Shari'ah* are to achieve the common benefit of people and to avoid what harms that benefit. Accordingly, Malik and his disciples went to the extent of considering the achievement of common benefit a *Shari'ah* criterion that should be applied like any other criteria in *Shari'ah*.[17] Ironically, many Hanbalites follow this trend, which is strongly supported by *Imam* Ibn Taymiyah and his disciple Ibn al Qayim. In their writings, they show abundant evidence in the support of this view. Ibn al Qayim wrote a chapter on the principle that religious injunction may be changed in accordance with changes in time, place, conditions, intentions and benefits. At the outset or this chapter he said "This is a great and very useful chapter; ignoring its ideas causes errors in understanding *Shari'ah* and imposes harrassments and unnecessary obligations, which anyone of sense can conclude that this great *Shari'ah* would not accept or bring about. Since the cornerstone of *Shari'ah* is to consider the benefit of people in both earthly life and afterlife *Shari'ah* is most just and all benefit and wisdom for people. In any issue whenever you go from justice to oppression, from mercy to its opposite, from benefit to harm, from wisdom to nonsense, you are going out of *Shari'ah*. *Shari'ah* represents the justice of God among his servants, His mercy on His creatures, His shadow on this earth, His wisdom that leads to believing in Him and in the truthfulness of His messenger, (p). It is the light with which people of sight can see, the guide with which those that are guided can find the truth[18]."

These are words that we must be keen to preserve and make known to all people.

Ibn al Qayim was quite correct in considering religious injunctions or opinions changeable in accordance to changes in time and conditions. It is not the ruling of *Shari'ah* that is changeable, but rather the application of the ruling in time and space and in the specific case that is on hand. *Shari'ah* does not change. What changes is jurisprudence. *Shari'ah* in the final analysis, is the revelation of God; while jurisprudence, religious opinions, and judgments are man-made. For example, 'Umar, (m) refused to give out of *zakah* to people to whom the Prophet had given *zakah* to reconcile their hostility, saying "God has given might and strength to Islam, and we are not in need of them". He did not change a *Shari'ah* ruling, nor did he annihilate the application of the texts of the Qur'an as some people mistakenly think, but rather he changed the religious interpretation in response to the change in time and condition. The specific individuals that used to receive *zakah*, including Uyaynah, and Aqra' were pacified during the early stage of Islam in order to bring their hearts closer. The Prophet (p) did not write perpetual promises to those individuals. It is up to the contemporary ruler to determine who deserves it and if no one fulfills those conditions, at that time, no one would be a recipient of that category of *zakah*. This is not a neglect of texts in the Qur'an. 'Umar as well as all Muslims has no right at all to abandon any texts in the Book of God. But Qur'an found that the common interest of Muslims at his time could best be served by saving those grants. He never thought to abolish the *Shari'ah* ruling about the share of heart softening in *zakah* when need arises. He simply refused to apply it to those ambitious individuals[19].

'Umar also changed the religious application in the case of horses. When some people from Syria asked him to take from them *zakah* on horses, he was hesitant because such a thing had not been done by the Messenger nor by Abu Bakr. 'Umar was reported later to have imposed *zakah* on horses when he found out that horses had become very expensive - as much as one hundred camels for a horse - and he justified it by the analogy mentioned earlier. This is in itself a form of considering the objectives of *Shari'ah* in observing justice and fulfillment of common benefit. Another example of changing religious application to suit current conditions is that of Mu'adh bin Jabal when he was sent by the Messenger, (p) to Yemen. The Messenger ordered him to collect *zakah* from the rich and render it to the poor. He also told him "Take payment in grains out grain holdings, sheep out of sheep holdings, and camel out of camel holdings". Mu'adh understood this saying to mean make it easy for people; take *zakah* out of what is available. When he found out that people liked to pay the value of *zakah* (instead of paying in kind) because it was easier for them he welcomed it. When Mu'adh stood in Yemen, he said "You may give me cloth and fabrics instead of corn and rye as long as it is easier for you and beneficial for the migrants in Madinah."[20]   The consideration of common benefit and the fulfillment of *Shari'ah* objectives in *zakah* is what lead Mu'adh--being one of the most knowledgeable companions, to take *zakah* value in terms of cloth instead of grain, despite what may be thought as a violation of the apparent word's of the Prophet. Mu'adh clearly understood the objectives of the Prophet's command and applied it accordingly. This is why scholars of *usul* require that a *mujtahid* must be quite knowledgeable about the ultimate goals of *Shari'ah*'s rulings their objectives as well as the common interest of people in his time. Whoever obtains theoretical knowledge and means of *ijtihad* but lives isolated in an ivory tower, not knowing the concerns of the society, the ideas and thoughts circulating among people and the desires and incentives of real life, cannot be among those who have the right to give religious opinions on the application of *Shari'ah* rulings.

It is this consideration of common benefit and the general objectives of *Shari'ah* that lead me to accept the religious application given by many companions of the Messenger (p) that there should be no *zakah* on women's jewelry because *zakah* is obligated on growing wealth. Amount of *zakah* collected would generally come out of the growth and the excess, leaving intact the original wealth. Since women's jewelry is lawful, and doesn't grow, it should be considered like clothes or home furnishings, which are not taxable.

The consideration of justice on which all of *Shari'ah* is founded is what leads me to select and accept the view of the of the follower 'Ata' bin Rabah, in deducting the expenses of agriculture out of the gross proceeds and considering only the net as subject to *zakah*. It is the same principle by which I consider that the tenant of the land should pay *zakah* on his net income after deducting all expenses including land rent, and that the landlord should pay *zakah* on the rent he receives.

The Approach of This Book

Our aim in this whole book is to combine easiness for the reader with accuracy of details and to avoid difficult wording and statements. Even when I quote, I try to select the clearest quotations with the simplest words, and at times I try to clarify words in the quotation without affecting its meaning. In my opinion the most successful style is that which puts side by side the accuracy of a scholar and the clarity of a preacher, and I hope I am successful in that.

I should mention that this study was prepared more than six years ago as my PhD. dissertation but I could not then present it because of unavoidable circumstances. The papers remained in my hands and I began reviewing, correcting and editing them until God permitted this work to come out in this form. I hope it will be accepted among non-partisan researchers and that I will benefit from sincere critiques.

I hope Muslims will review the current practices of their religion and will come back to it after long abandonment and make this obligation of *zakah* an important part of their socio-financial institutions. This way they would earn the pleasure of God, solving many social problems and protecting their youth from misleading and deviant ideas.

If I fulfill in this study those objectives, thanks and praise should be to God alone. I intended this effort for Him and He alone is asked to make it benefit people. If it did not reach that goal, it suffices that I exercised my best abilities and I hope God will give me the reward for the effort and good intention, since the reward of every person is in accordance with his intention.

Success can only come from God on whom I depend and to whom I return.
Jumada al Ula, 1389 H., July 1969, A.D.

Yusuf al Qardawi.
Doha, Qatar.

Footnotes

1.   Ibn Hazm; *al Ihkam Fi Usul al Ahkam,* p. 541.

2.   *Ibid,* p. 542

3.   *Sura al Baqarah,* 2:267

4.   Ibn Hazm, *op cit.*

5.   See section on payment of *zakah* to non Muslims in the part of *zakah*'s distribution.

6.   *Fath al Bari* Vol. 3, p, 227, see also the section in chapter 9 on *zakah* distribution.

8.   Al Ahkam, Al Amady, Vol. 1, pp. 137-138.

9. *Sura al Shura*, 42:17

10. *Sura al Hadid*, 57:25

11. I'lam al Muwaqqi 'in Vol. 1, p. 133

12. The paper on analogy by Ibn Taimiyah, Salafiyah Print, 1375 h.

13. Discussed later in this book.

14. Pages 193-4

15. *Al Muwafaqat* Vol.. 2, p. 51

16. *Ibid.* p. 300

17. Al Qarafi said: The common benefit and interest is denied by others while at the same time when they come to deductions of opinions they use benefit or interest in general without obligating themselves to providing proofs of present common benefit. They rather suffice themselves with the usefulness of their deductions. This is in fact the given interest or benefit. See the book *Malik* by Muhammad Abu Zahrah.

18. *I'lam al Muwaqqi 'in* Vol. 3, p.14

19. See later under *zakah* distribution the chapter on those whose hearts are being reconciled.

20. See later chapter on means of *zakah* collection, title Payment in Value.

THE WORDS: *ZAKAH* AND *SADAQAH*

The Meaning of the Word *Zakah* in Language and in *Shari'ah*

Zakah in language is an infinitive of the verb *zakah*. *Zakah* means to grow and to increase. When it is said about a person, it means to improve, to become better. Consequently *zakah* is blessing, growth, cleanliness, and betterment.[1] In *Lisan al Arab* it is said, "The root of the word *zakah* in Arabic means cleanliness, growth, blessing, and praise. All these meanings of the word are used in Qur'an and *Hadith*." It seems to be most obvious according to al Wahidi and others that the root "*zakah*" means increase and growth. For example, with respect to plants it means to grow and with respect to things, it means to increase. But since plants grow only if they are clean of insects and other detrimental things, then the word "*zakah*" implies cleanliness and cleansing. If it is used with respect to persons, *zakah* then means betterment and righteousness. You may say a man is "*zaki*"; that is, he has good character, or you may say that the judge "*zakah*" the witnesses to mean he shows that they are of a higher level in their testimony.

In *Shari'ah* the word *zakah* refers to the determined share of wealth prescribed by God to be distributed among deserving categories. It is also used to mean the action of payment of this share[2]. According to al Nawawi's report from al Wahidi, this share of wealth is called *zakah* because it increases the funds from which it is taken and protects them from being lost or destroyed.[3] Ibn Taimiyah said that the inner soul of the *zakah* payer becomes better, and his wealth becomes cleansed.[4] Growth and cleanliness are not restricted to the *zakated* assets themselves, but reach out to the person who pays *zakah*, in accordance to the verse "out of their wealth take *zakah* that so thou mightest purify and sanctify them".[5] Al Azhari says: it makes the poor grow too, meaning that *zakah* creates psychological and material growth for the rich in his soul and wealth.

Al Nawawi reports that the author of *al Hawi* said: "It should be realized that *zakah* is an Arabic word known before Islam. It is well known that it has been used in poetry". On the other hand, Dawud al Zahiri said this word has no source in the Arabic language before it was used in Qur'an. The author of al Hawi answered "although this is totally wrong, differences about the name do not affect the rulings on *zakah*."

Knowing this, one can find no base for the claims of the Jewish Orientalist, Shacht, who wrote in the Encyclopedia of Islam under the title of *Zakah* that the Prophet (p) used the word *zakah* to mean more than what it meant for the Arabs and borrowed some

of the meaning of the word from Jews that used the Hebrew and Aramaic work *Zakut*."
Schact said: "The Prophet (p), when he was in Makkah, used the word *zakah* and its
derivatives to mean cleansing. This meaning has a close tie to the word *zakah* in Arabic
and in the mind of Arabs but this word and its derivatives are not used except for that
meaning in the Qur'an and this is not an original Arabic meaning: it is borrowed from
Judaism where it means 'fear of God'.[7] Orientalists such as Schact have a fanatic desire
to attribute as much as they can of the Islamic concepts, words, rulings, thoughts, and
ethical values to Jewish or Christian origins or at least to any other origin, be it Eastern
or Western, following only the whims of their own bias. It is sufficient however, to
disprove his claim by stating the following two points:

Firstly, Qur'an used the word *zakah*, in the meaning known to Muslims now, as early
as the beginning of the Makkan period. This is found in Suras: 7:156, 19:31 and 55,
21:72, 23:4, 27:3, 30:39, 31:3 and 41:7. It is undoubtedly known that the Prophet (p) did
not know Hebrew or any other language except Arabic, and that he had no contact with
Jews before migrating to Madinah. When and how could he borrow from Jews and
Judaism?

Secondly, it is mere speculation that violates scientific methodology for anyone to
claim that a language had borrowed a word from another language simply because he
finds the word common to the two languages. Such a common word does not
necessarily mean that one language borrowed it from the other. It is even more
speculative to point out one language as borrowing and the other as borrowed from
without any proof.

The Meaning of *Sadaqah*

Zakah as known in Shari'ah is sometimes called in the Qur'an and Sunnah
"*sadaqah*", to the extent that al Mawardi said "*Sadaqah* is *zakah*, and *zakah* is *sadaqah*.
They are two names for the same thing."[8] God (J) says, "of their wealth take *sadaqah*
that so thou mightest purify and sanctify them"[9] and "and among them are men who
slander thee in the matter of *sadaqat*"[10] and "*sadaqat* are for the poor and the
needy."[11,12] *Hadith* says, "There is no *sadaqah* in what is less than five *Wasq*. There is
no *sadaqah* in what is less than five camels and there is no *sadaqah* in what is less than
five uqiyah."[13] Addressing Mu'adh when sent to Yemen the Prophet (p) said "Inform
them that God has prescribed *sadaqah* on their funds, to be taken from their rich." All
these texts were talking about *zakah* while using the word *sadaqah*, even the *zakah*
collector and distributor is called *musaddiq*. But In the later history of Islam, *sadaqah*
was traditionally used to mean only Vol.untary charitable donations given to beggars
and destitutes. But such a tradition must not be allowed to mislead us and divert us from
the meaning of the word at the time when Qur'an was being revealed. The root of the
word *sadaqah* is the word *sidq*. Judge Abu Bakr bin al 'Arabi, commenting on naming
zakah sadaqah, states that "It is derived from *sidq*. *Sidq* is truthfulness in realizing
declared belief by action. The root *sidq* means realizing and supporting something by
another. The word *sadaq* (Dowry) for women means realizing the lawfulness of
intimacy by the contract and the dowry under specific conditions known in *Shari'ah*.

The root *sidq* has several derivatives. The verb *saddaqa* with respect to statements means to accept and to realize. The verb *tasaddaqa* with respect to funds means gave away, realizing his faith by action. And the verb *asdaqa* means to give dowry in marriage to women. The meaning of *sadaqah* is derived from the root *sidq* because *sadaqah* implies giving away goods and funds for the sake of God in expression of faithfullness and in realization of the belief in ressurection and afterlife."[14] It is for that reason that Qur'an associated giving with affirmation of faith and withholding with rejection of faith, God (s) says, "So he who gives in charity and fears God and in all sincerity testifies to the best, we will indeed make smooth for him the path to bliss, but he who is a greedy miser and thinks himself self-sufficient and gives lies to the best we will indeed make smooth for him the path to misery."[15]

Sadaqah is thus an indication of truthfullness in faith and sincere belief in the day of judgment, Accordingly, the Messenger of God (p) said *sadaqah* is a proof (or evidence),"[16]

Zakah in the Holy Qur'an

The word *al zakah* occurs in the Qur'an thirty times.[17] In twenty-seven of them it is associated with prayers in the same verse. In one place it is mentioned with prayers in the same sequence of verses, this is, "those who humble themselves in their prayers" and "who are active indeed in *zakah*."[18] Surveying these thirty places in the Qur'an shows that eight of them are Makkan verses and the others are Madinan.[19] Some writers claim that *zakah* is associated with prayers in eighty-two places in the Qur'an[20], but this is an obvious exaggeration. Since even if we include such places that have implicit reference to *zakah*, while words like spending, lending or feeding are mentioned, we would not reach that acclaimed number. As for the word *sadaqah*, and its plural, *sadaqat*, it is mentioned in the Qur'an twelve times, all of them in Madinan suras.

Footnotes

1. *Al Mu'jam al Wasit*, Vol.. 1 p. 398.

2. At Zamakhshari said in his *al Fa'iq* Vol.. 1, p. 536, first printing "*zakah* is like the word *sadaqah*. It is a common name" used to refer to a material thing which is the part of the fund paid out in the form of zakah. It also refers to an abstract meaning, the action of sanctification. It was because of lack of knowledge of this latter meaning of the word that some people did not understand the verse, "and those who are active in practicing zakah" thinking of it as a reference to money paid out while it is a reference to the action of sanctification and purification.

3. *Al Majmu'*, Vol.. 5, p. 324.

4. The collection of *Fatawa Shiekh al Islam Ibn Taimiyah*, Vol. 25, p. 8.

5. *Sura at Tawbah*, 9:103.

6. Al *Majmu'*, Vol. 5 p. 325.

7. *Encyclopedia of Islam,* Vol.. 10, pp. 355-6.

8. At Mawardi, *al Ahkam al Sultaniyah*, the beginning of Chapter 11.

9. *Sura at Tawbah,* 9:103.

10. *Sura at Tawbah,* 9:58.

11. *Sura at Tawbah,* 9:60.

12. The late professor Dr. Muhammad Yusuf Musa, commented on, Schact "Qur'an refers first to the meaning of *zakah* using the word *sadaqah*, then used the word *zakah*. But if we look carefully in the Makkan suras of the Qur'an we find the word *zakah* used long before the words *sadaqah* and *sadaqat*. The letters are only used in Madinan suras."

13. Reported by Bukhari, Muslim, and others.

14. *Ahkam al Qur'an* part 2, p. 946, with commentary by al Bijawi.

15. *Sura al Layl,* 92:5-10.

16. Reported by Muslim.

17. We used the word al zakah, with the article al (the) to refer to the word used in the religious meaning. The word zakah, in the pure meaning, is mentioned in two additional places: in sura 18:81, and in sura 19:13.

18. *Sura at Muminun,* 23:2 and 4.

19. See the *Index of the Words of the Holy Qur'an* by Muhammad Fu'ad 'Abd al Baqi, under "*Zakah*".

20. See *al Dur al Mukhtar, al Bahr, al Nahr,* and other books of the Hanifites, Ibn Abideen quoted a correction in his commentary, *Rad al Muhtar*. But the fact is that it came associated with prayer in only 28 places.

FIQH AL ZAKAH
(VOLUME I)

A COMPARATIVE STUDY OF ZAKAH RULES, REGULATIONS AND PHILOSOPHY IN THE LIGHT OF QUR'AN AND SUNNAH

FIQH AL ZAKAH

PART ONE

THE OBLIGATORY NATURE OF ZAKAH AND ITS PLACE IN ISLAM

Condition of the poor classes in ancient civilizations

The care of heavenly religions for the poor

The special attention Islam gives to caring for the poor since the Makkan period Encouragement of *zakah* at large as early as the Makkan period

Zakah in the specific meaning became obligatory in the Madinan period

The place of *zakah* in Islam and the ruling on those who deny it

The difference between *zakah* in Islam and care of the poor in other religions

Discussing the claims of Shacht about *zakah*

INTRODUCTION

Before I delineate the obligatory nature of *zakah* and its position in this religions of Islam, it is useful to examine the position of the poor in the class structures of the societies before Islam, the extent of response to their needs, and the care about their Problems in ancient laws and religions. By so doing, one can show how much Islam superseded other religions in its care of the poor and in the establishment of social justice, social insurance, and social solidarity on the strong basis stated in the Book of God and in the Sunnah of His Messenger, (p).

Poor in Ancient Civilizations

Poverty and destitution are as old as history. It is fair to say that all human communities have some people who call for the care of the poor. Feeling for others' sufferings never ceased throughout the history of humanity and attempts to provide relief and to solve Problems continue in all civilizations. In spite of all that, the situation of the poor has been extremely bad. It has always been a dark spot in human history. All societies had such injustice and did not follow the humanitarian advice of their philosophers and prophets. One historian talks about the relations between the rich and the deprived poor in ancient civilizations in the following way: "In every nation that existed on earth one could easily recognize two classes of people, the rich and the poor. The rich class exercised power and always became richer and inflated while the deprived class was weak and smashed down to earth. With that contradiction the social structure of that civilization would eventually fall apart, with the rich wondering why everything was deteriorating."[1] Egypt in its early history was like a godly paradise on earth, producing all kinds of goods that were more than abundant for its people and at the same time its poor classes could not find even the mere sustenance of food, because the rich class left nothing of substance for them. When the great famine hit Egypt during the region of the XII dynasty, poor people sold themselves as slaves to the rich who made them even suffer more. In ancient Babylon the situation was the same. The poor had no rights to the fruits of their land in spite of huge production. The ancient Persia, Greece, and other kingdoms were also similar. The poor were driven by whips and sticks to lowest jobs an were punished severely and sometimes savagely slaughtered for the slightest errors. In Sparta the rich left for the poor rocky lands that was not fertile, so they lived on suffering. In Athens, the rich used to sell the poor as slaves if they failed to pay tolls imposed on them. In Rome, the source of Western law, the rich ruled over the whole nation, distinct and high-ranked, reducing others to untouchables compared to them. The poor were forced to obey them and this often forced them to escape and find their way out of Rome. As described by Mitchle said about the Roman Empire: "The poor were descending deeper and deeper into poverty while the rich were increasing their wealth. When the Roman empire was abolished and European kingdoms rose in its place, the plight of the poor became even worse. They used to be sold with the land like livestock under the fuedal system of these kingdoms."[2]

The Concern of Religions for the Poor

All religions, including man-made religions, did not neglect this humanitarian social issue, without which brotherhood and quality of life would not be realized. More than four thousand years ago in Babylon, Hamurabi, in introducing the first known recorded law on earth, stated "God's had sent me to prevent the omnpotents from suppressing the powerless subjects and to guide people and secure prosperity for creatures." Thousands of years ago, people, in ancient Egypt, expressed the sentiment that it was their religious duty to give bread to the hungry, cloth to the naked, and passage on their boats to the incapable, or to be father of the fatherless, husband of the widow, and a protector to the outcast in cold winter.[3]

The Concern of the Heavenly Religions

The voice of heavenly religions was louder in calling for care of the poor and powerless than other secular systems, for the former had deeper effects than any human philosophy or man-made law. I cannot believe any Messenger of God to have passed through the world without calling for the care of the poor, which is called in the Qur'an *zakah*. In the Holy Qur'an, which is the most authentic heavenly document existing on earth today, we find mention of the messages of Ibrahim, Ishaq, and Ya'qub. God says: "And We made them leaders, who guide men by our command, and We sent inspiration to do good deeds, to establish regular prayers, and to practice *zakah*, and they constantly served Us."[4] Isma'il's message is described following: "And also mention in the story of Isma'il who was strictly true to what he promised. He was an apostle and a Prophet and he enjoined on his people prayer and *Zakah*, and he was most acceptable in the sight of his Lord."[5] We also see the pledge of bani Isra'il: "And we took a covenant. from the children of Isra'il: worship none but God, treat with kindness your parents and kindred and orphans and all those in need, speak fair to the people, be steadfast in prayer, and practice *zakah*. Then did ye turn back except a few among you, and ye backslide".[6] In another verse this pledge is described "God did afore time take a covenant from the children of Isra'il, and We appointed twelve captains among them and God said I am with you if you establish regular prayer, practice *zakah*, believe in apostles, honor and assist them and loan to God a magnificent loan. Verily I will wipe out from you your evils, and admit you to gardens with rivers flowing beneath, but if any of you after this resisted faith he has surely wandered from the path of rectitude.[7] The message of Jesus Christ is described by his own words as a baby in the cradle "And He hath enjoined on me prayer and *zakah* as long as I live. About the People of the Book in general, God said, "And you have been commanded no more than this: To worship God, offering Him sincere devotion, be true in faith, establish regular prayer and practice *zakah*, and that is the religion right and straight.[9]

In the Old and New Testaments as they exist today, we find many recommendations and directives to have mercy for the poor and to care about the widow, the orphans, and the weak. In the Old Testament, proverbs 22:13 we read "If a man shuts his ears to the cry of the helpless, he will cry for help himself and not be heard. --A gift given in secrecy placates an angry man." In proverbs 22: " The kindly man be blessed for he shares his food with the poor" And in proverbs 27: "he who gives to the poor will never be in need and he who prevents the poor and turns his eyes away from him will have my wrath." And in Deuteronomy 15:7-11 "When one of your fellow countrymen...becomes poor, do not be hard-hearted or closefisted with your countrymen in his need. Be open-handed towards him and lend him on pledge as much as he needs...Give freely to him and do not begrudge him your bounty, because it is for this very bounty that the Lord, your God will bless you in everything that you do or undertake. The poor will always be with you in this land, and for that reason I command you to be open-handed with your countrymen, both poor and distressed, in your own land." In 14:22-29 of the same "Year by year, you shall set aside a tithe of all the produce of your seed, of everything that grows on this land... At the end of every third year, you shall bring out all the tithe of your produce for that year and leave it in your settlements so that the Levites, who have no holding or patrimony among you and aliens, orphans and widows in your settlement may come and eat their fill. If you do this the Lord, your God, will bless you in everything to which you set your hand."

In the New Testament, Luke 13:33 "Sell what you have and give charity" and in Luke 13:10-14 "he who has two garments must give to he who has none. He who has food must do the same." In Luke 11:41 "let what is in the cup be given in charity and all is clean." And in Luke 14:12-14 "Then he said to his host when you are having a party for lunch or supper, do not invite your friends, your brothers, or other relations or your rich neighbors, they will only ask you back again and so you will be repaid. But when you give a party, ask the poor, the crippled, the lame, and the blind and so find hapiness for they have no means to repaying you, but you will be repaid on the day when good men rise from the dead." In Luke 21:1-4, "He looked up and saw the rich people dropping their gifts into the chest of the temple treasury, and he noticed a poor widow putting in two tiny coins, I tell you this, ha said, 'This poor widow has given more than any of them, for those others who have given had more than enough, but she, with less than enough, has given all she had to live on". In Matthew 5:41,42 "Give them what you are asked to to give and do not turn your back on a man who wants to borrow" and in Matthew 6:1-4 "Be careful not to make a sham of your religion by charitable giving before men, if you do, no reward awaits you at your Father's house in heaven. Thus when you do an act of charity, do not announce it with a flourish of trumpets as the hypocrites do in synagogues and in the streets to win admiration from men. I tell you this: they have their reward already. Do not let your left hand know what you right is doing. Your good deed must be secret and your Father who sees what is done in secret will reward you." In Matthew 10:42 "and if anyone gives so much as a cup of cold water to one of these little ones, because he is a disciple of mine, I tell you this: that man will assuredly not go unrewarded."

Notes on the Stand of Religions Towards Poverty

These are supreb examples of the care of previous religions toward the poor and the needy and this was the essence of the message of heavenly scripts before the Qur'an. Some observations, however, must be recorded.

1. These texts do not go beyond recommendations and encouragement to be merciful toward the poor and wary of selfishness and miserlihood. It is a loud call to voluntary and individual charity.

2. These statements on charity do not make it compulsory so that those who abstain from charity do not feel that they have left an essential part of their religion and that they would be punished by God in this life and in the afterlife.

3. It is left to the human conscience to give charity: the state is not given any authority in its collection and distribution.

4. The amount that should be given, the kinds of wealth that are subject to give from and circumstances and conditions of the fulfillment of this charity are not specified. This makes it impossible for state to institutionalize it on any religious grounds.

5. Caring for the poor does not reach the extent of a rigorous attempt to deal with the problem of poverty, to eliminate it, to dry its sources or to transform the poor into property owners and landowners. These calls ended at attenuation of the misery and suffering of the poor.

Consequently, the poor and weak remain at the mercy of the rich and powerful. If the latter are motivated by the love of God, the sense of an afterlife, or their own conscience, then the poor are helped and relieved. But if the faith of the wealthy are wicked, if they love accumulation and exclusive pursuit of their own desires, the poor is left to their suffering without anyone to defend their rights against the rich. This is usual when charity is left voluntary and up to the conscience of individuals.

The Benevolence of Islam in Dealing with Problem of Poverty

Islam is unprecedented in the extent of its care for the poor and its zest to solve the problem of poverty whether through directives and recommendations that exhort Muslims to have mercy on the poor, by means of legislation and laws, or through implementation and application.

The Care Provided in the Qur'an for the Poor in the Makkan Period

It is apparent that as early as the first few months of the Makkan period when Muslims were still a handful of men and women prevented from practicing and calling for this new religion and not constituting a political entity, that the humane social aspect of Islam -- caring about the poor and the destitute, was highly evident. This concept is expressed in the Qur'an as "feeding the poor", "spending of the sustenance that God has provided", "a right to he who asks and to the deprived who does not ask", or "a right to the destitute and the wayfarer", and sometimes, the term "establishing *zakah*", is used.

It suffices to read in the Makkan *suras* the following great verses:

Feeding the Poor is a Requirement of Faith

In *sura* al Muddathir, one of the very early revelations of the Qur'an, we see a scene from the day of judgment. The righteous people in their heavenly gardens inquire of the dis-believers and liars whom the fires of Hell encompasses, what were the reasons for their punishment. Among those reasons are neglecting the rights of the poor, letting him be beaten by hunger, nakedness, and suffering, and turning their faces away from him. God says: "Every soul will be held in pledge for its deeds except the companions of the right hand they will be in gardens of delight. They will question each other and ask of the sinners, 'What led you into hellfire?' They will say, 'we were not of those who prayed, nor were we of those who fed the indigent, but we used to talk vanities with vain talkers and we used to deny the day of judgment.[10] Similar to feeding the poor is clothing, sheltering, and providing necessities for them. In *sura* al Qalam, God tells the story of those who owned a garden and collected its fruits at night in order to prevent the poor and needy that come on harvest day from taking some charity. Because of that God sent to them a quick punishment. The verses read: "Then there came on the gardens a visitation from thy Lord which swept away all while they were asleep so the garden became by morning like a dark and desolate spot whose fruits had been gathered. As the morning broke, they called out one to another, 'Go ye to your tilthe be times in the morning if ye would gather the fruits', so they departed conversing in secret, low tones, saying, 'let not a single indigent person break in upon you into the garden this day?', and they opened the morning strong in an unjust resolve but when they saw the garden they said we have surely lost our way. Indeed we are shut out of the fruits of our labor. Said one of them, more just than the rest, 'Did I not say to you why not glorify God?' They said, "Glory to our Lord, verily we have been doing wrong.' Then they turned one against another in reproach. They said, 'Alas for us we have indeed transgressed. It may be that our Lord will give us in exchange a better garden than this for we do turn to Him in repentance.' Such is the punishment in this life, but greater is the punishment in the hereafter if only they knew."[11]

Encouragement to Take Care of the Indigent

The Makkan verses did not concluded by calling for mercy on the indigents, encouraging and providing for their needs, and making it fearful to neglect or be harsh to them. The Makkan verses went farther, in considering that on each believer there is a duty to the indigent, i.e., believers should urge others to help the poor. The Qur'an considered abstention from encouraging others to aid the needy a feature related to disbelief in God, that implicates His resentmen and punishment in the Hereafter. God (s) says in *sura al Haqqah*, "and he that will be given his record in his left hand will say, 'Oh, would that my record had not been given to me and that I had never realized how my account stood: Oh, would that death had made an end of me. No profit to me has been my wealth, my power has perished from me."[12] And then God, the Lord of the world gives His just judgment in punishment on those who deserve it. "Seize ye him and burn ye him in the blazing fire; further make him march in a chain whereof the length is seventy cubits."[12] The cause of his punishment and humiliation in the sight of witnesses is: "This was he who would not believe in God, most high, and would not encourage the feeding of the indigent."[12] These verses, which promise so strongly the punishment of those who do not encourage the feeding of the indigent, so motivated the companion Abu al Darda' that he said to his wife: Oh, Umm al Darda', God has a chain that has boiled in the blazing Fire since God created hell and it will remain there until it is thrown on the necks of people; God has saved us of half of its pain by bringing us into believing in Him the greatest, so encourage the feeding of the poor, oh, Umm al Darda' (in order to fulfill the other condition mentioned in the verse above)."[13] The world has never witnessed before the Qur'an a script that considers abstention from encouragement to care for the indigent a sin that can send the abstinent to Hell. In *sura* al Fajr, God calls the people of pre-Islam ages who claim to have a religion that brings them close to God and cling to remnants of the religion of Ibrahim: "Nay, but ye honor not the orphans nor do ye encourage one another to feed the poor".[14] Encouraging one another is a call to all of humanity to cooperate and support each other in taking care of the poor. Sheikh Muhammad 'Abduh commented that "Qur'an mentions 'encouraging each other to feed the poor', and not just 'feeding the poor', in order to indicate that members of the community should have solidarity, mercy, and grace toward one another, and should secure one another's needs."[15] In *sura* al Ma'un, God made harshness to the orphan and neglect of the poor signs of disbelief and of denial of the Day of Judgment: "Seest thou one who denies the Judgment? Then such is the man who repulses the orphans with harshness and encourages not the feeding of the indigent."[16] Sheikh 'Abduh said, "It is obvious that he who does not encourage others to feed the poor would not feed them on his own, so the sentence "does not encourage the feeding of the indigent" includes implicitly "not giving anything of his goods to the poor." It is mentioned in this form to show that even one who does not have enough to give the poor is required to call upon others to do so and to encourage all believers to relieve the poor, if it were by collecting funds through, for example, charitable organizations."[17] Sura al Ma'un continues, 'so woe to the worshippers who are neglectful of their prayers, those who want but to be seen by people, but refuse to supply even neighborly needs."[18] Ibn Kathir commented, "This means those do not worship their Lord the right way and do not do good to His creatures even by lending them what they can benefit from without consuming the object lent. People like those benefit not from their prayers, and are not categorized with the believers on the Day of Judgment."[19]

The Right of He Who Asks, He Who Does Not, The Destitute and the Wayfarer

In *sura* al Dhariyat, God mentions sincere believers that deserve the gardens of heaven. One of their most obvious characteristics is "in their wealth there is a right for he who asks and he who is deprived."[20] He who has no wealth of his own, nor means of earning, nor a profession to live on, has also a right. Those sincere believers have realized that their wealth is not only for their own use. They have realized that part of it belongs, in fact to the needy, not as a charitable gift given with condescendence but as a clear-cut right, without humbleness on the part of the receiver or pride on the part of the payer. In *sura* al Ma'arij, this same characterization is repeated with a slight difference in the scene pictured. It came with reference to the characters of the believers who have overcome by the strength of their faith and sense of ethics, the weakness of the human being, "Truly, man was created very impatient, fretful when evil touches him and niggardly when good reaches him. Not so those devoted to prayer, those who remain steadfast in their prayer, and in whose wealth is a recognized right for the needy who asks and he who is prevented."[21] Here the right on their wealth is described as recognized and well-defined. This led some scholars to state that this verse refers to *zakah* because it is the recognized, well-defined right on the wealth of the rich. It is known however that this *sura* is Makkan while *zakah* as defined in *Shari'ah* was prescribed in Madinah, as we shall see later. This recognized and well-defined right could not be anything except a part put aside by the believers out of their wealth to be given to he who asks and to the deprived.[22] The difference therefore, between this right and *zakah* is that this is a portion determined by the believers themselves and put aside by their own action, while *zakah* is defined and determined by *Shari'ah*. In *Suras* al 'Isra God says "And render to the kindred their due rights and also to those in want and to the wayfarer but squander not your wealth in the manner of a spendthrift."[23] And in al Rum "so give what is due to kindred, the needy and the wayfarer. that is best for those who seek the continence of God."[24] By these statements Qur'an instilled in the being of Muslims as early as the Makkan period that kindred and those who are in need have well-defined rights on the believer's funds. It is not a mere voluntary charity which he can pay or refrain from paying according to whim.

The Due Right On Crops at the Time of Harvest

In *sura* al An'am God said, "It is He who produceth gardens with trellises and without, and palm-trees and tilth with produce of all kinds, and olives and pomegranates similar in kind and different in variety, eat of their fruit in their season but render the dues that are proper on the day the harvest is gathered but waste not by excess for God loves not the waster."[25] God brings to the attention of His servants that there is a prescribed right on the fruits of earth. This right should be paid on the day of harvest.

Sa'id bin Jubair noted that "before *zakah* was revealed, a person was required to give out of the crops to orphans and indigents." This is a right that is not determined to be one-tenth or one half of a tenth. It is left to the sincerity of the farmer, and according to the need of the indigents. Later in Madinah the Messenger of God, (p), determined the rate of this right by making it one-tenth or one half of a tenth on crops that are in excess of five *wasq*. Some commentators found in this action of the Prophet an explanation of the dues on crops and fruit as we shall discuss later in this book.

Payment of *Zakah* in Makkah

There are many examples of the provision of the Makkan verses for the poor and destitute in assigning them a recognized right on funds so they may not be lost in the Muslim community. This was crowned by verses offering praise for those who pay it, and vituperation for those who neglect it. In *sura* al Rum, God holds a comparison between the effect of *riba*, which seems to increase wealth while it in fact shrinks it, and the effect of *zakah* which seems to reduce wealth while it in fact, makes It grow best. God says, "So give what is due to kindred, the needy, and the wayfarer. That is best for those who seek the countenance of God and it is they who will prosper. That which you lend in *riba* for increase throughout the poverty of other people will have no increase with God but that which you lay out for *zakah*, seeking the countenance of God, will increase, it is they who will get the recompense multiplied."[26]

At the beginning of sura al Naml, God describes the believers for whom he made his book a guide and a glad tiding as "those who establish prayers and give *zakah* and have full assurance of the Hereafter."[27] In connecting giving *zakah* to establishing prayers one finds a clear indication that what is meant here is the prescribed *zakah* on wealth. At the outset of *sura* Luqman, God says "The Book is a guide and a mercy for the doers of good, those who establish prayer and give *zakah* and have in their hearts the assurance of the Hereafter."[28] In *sura* al Mu'minun He describes the faithful as "and those who are performing *zakah*."[29] In *sura* al A'raf, while telling the story of Musa and his tribe, God says "But My mercy extends to all things. That mercy I shalt ordain for those who do right and practice *zakah* and those who believe in Our signs, those who follow the apostle, the unlettered prophet"[30], and in describing the disbelievers God mentions "those who pay not *zakah* and who even deny the Hereafter."[31]

Some explicators of the Qur'an infer that what is meant by *zakah* here is the sanctifications and purification of the soul from evil and sin, following the idea in *sura* al Shams, "truly he succeeds that purifies it,"[33] (the two verses use the verbs *zakah* and *'tazakka'* for purify). To me, this is only an attempt to escape from the meaning that *zakah* here is the *zakah* on wealth that is prescribed later in Madinah. Ibn Jarir la Tabari holds that *zakah* in those verses means the same *zakah* on funds that is known in *Shari'ah* and says that the word *zakah* was commonly used with regard to wealth. Tabari's view is supported by the fact that the word 'giving' is associated with *zakah*, as giving applies, in the first instance to wealth.

It should be observed that those Makkan verses on *zakah* were not giving commands, and did not clearly indicate the obligatory nature of *zakah* but rather they mention it in an informative manner as a practice essential to the character of sincere believers[35], while not paying it is a characteristic of disbelievers. On the other hand the use of performance of *zakah* as a criterion in classifying believers and unbelievers is itself an implicit reference that *zakah* is obligatory because it is always required to obtain the characteristics of believers and to avoid the characteristics of nonbelievers.

Zakah In The Makkan Period Takes an Undefined Form

The *zakah* which is mentioned in Makkan verses was in the general form of voluntary payments. It did not take the specific definitions as we know it now until it was prescribed in Medina when the rates, minimum exempt, and funds subject to *zakah* were determined. That is when *zakah* collectors and distributors were sent to survey all Muslims and to collect *zakah* and distribute it, and when the state became responsible for *zakah* as an institution. In Makkah *zakah* was left to the faith and the brotherly feelings of individuals, and the amount that was to be paid was not determined.

Some scholars infer from the Qura'nic terms of the Makkan verses like: "destitute's rights", "right for he who asks and he who is deprived", "a recognized right", that in Makkah it was left to the Prophet, (p) to determine the amounts of *zakah* on the funds of Muslims.[36] But such inference is not supported by any reports that the Prophet did so, while there are reports to the contrary.

It seems that in Makkah there was no need for any specific determination because persecuted Muslims were then sacrificing all they had including their own lives. However, the amounts may be determined by the payers of *zakah*, as stated by some commentators. Al Hafiz Ibn Kathir says in his commentary on *sura* al Mu' minin about those who practice *zakah*, "The majority's opinion is that what is meant here is *zakah* on wealth, although the verse is Makkan while *zakah* was prescribed in Madinah in the second year of Hijrah." Apparently, in the second year of Hijrah *zakah* was prescribed in its specific form, with percentages and minimum exempt, while the principle of *zakah* was given in Makkah as in the verse in *sura* al An'am, "and give its right due the day of its harvest."[37] What is found by Ibn Kathir as the obvious meaning is supported by the many verses mentioned earlier.

Zakah in the Madinan Period

<u>In Madina , Muslims community had constructed their own society</u>, political power and a state. This was not so in Makkah. Consequently, Islamic requirements took a new form that was suitable to this stage. These requirements now became specific and well-defined laws and regulations, while they were, in Makkah, general directions and advices. The authority of the state could now be counted on in the execution of these requirements, in addition to the motivation of faithfulness. The characteristics of this new Madinan era are clear in the treatment of *zakah*. The law determines the kinds of wealth on which *zakah* is required, the conditions for its obligation, its percentages and ratios, and the areas of dispersement of its receipts, as well as the institution that organizes and administers *zakah*.

Madinan Verses Impose The Obligation of *Zakah* and Delineate Its Rules

In Madinan *suras*, there is a very clear directive for the payment of *zakah* which is emphasized in different styles as in *sura* al Baqarah, "and establish prayers and practice *zakah.*"[38] Madinan verses on *zakah* are too numerous to list here, therefore I have selected *sura* al Tawbah as an example, a *sura* which is among the latest revelations.

Sura al Tawbah an Example of Madinan Suras About *Zakah*

A. At the outset of this *sura*, the verses speak of fighting unbelievers who broke their covenants with the Prophet, stating "but if they repent and establish prayers and practice *zakah*, then open the way for them, for God is oft forgiving, most merciful."[39] Thus three conditions are set to bring an end to fighting with pagans: Firstly, repentance from paganism. This is, bearing witness that there is no deity but God and Muhammad is the messenger of God. Secondly, the establishment of prayer, which is the characteristic of faith and the greatest pillar of Islam, the criteria on that distinguishes Muslims from non-Muslims, the spiritual bond among all Muslims. Thirdly, the practice of *zakah*, prescribed on the funds of the rich for those who are in need, for the common benefit of the whole community. It is the political, social, and financial bond among all Muslims.

B. After another six verses, God speaks about yet another group of nonbelievers: "But even so, if they repent, establish prayer, and practice *zakah*, they are your brethren in faith. Thus do we explain the signs in detail for those who understand."[40] Conversion from disbelief to become a member of the Muslim community cannot be done without repentance from associating partners with God, establishment of prayer, in which all Muslims share submission to God, and the practice of *zakah*, by which Muslims help one another and establish socio-economic solidarity. Scholars as early as the era of the Companions point out an important issue in the Qura'nic style, that is, the continuous association of *zakah* and prayers. One of them is seldom mentioned without the other. Abdullah bin Mas'ud says: "You are ordained to establish prayer, to practice *zakah*, and he who does not practice *zakah* his prayer is meaningless."[41] Ibn Zaid says: "Prayer and *zakah* were prescribed together. One is not alienated from the other." He read the verse 'But if they repent, establish prayer, and practice *zakah*, they are your brethren in faith', as indication that God does not accept prayer without *zakah*." Ibn Zaid continued, "may the mercy of God be on Abu Bakr for his great understanding"[41], in reference to Abu Bakr's saying that we should not make a distinction between two things God associated with each other.

C. In this *sura*, God refers to those who establish mosques as deserving acceptance by Him. He said, "The mosque of God shall be visited and maintained by such as believe in God and the Last Day, establish prayer, and practice *zakah*, and fear none except God. It is they who are expected to be on true guidance."[42] Establishing mosques and maintaining them is not sufficient for acceptance, there is a need to perform prayer and practice *zakah*.

D. There is a great menace in *sura* al Tawbah to those who hoard gold and silver without paying God's dues. God (s) says, "and there are those who hoard gold and silver and spend it not in the way of God. Announce unto them a most grievous penalty on the day when heat will be produced out of that wealth in the fire of Hell, and with it will be branded their foreheads, their flanks, and their backs. This is the treasure which you buried for yourselves. Take then the treasures you hoarded."[43] Scholars comment that the warning against hoarding money is strong to counteract the instinct of voraciousness for money in most people.[44]

E. Areas of distribution are given in the *sura*. With that, there should be no excuse for those who are eager to take for themselves the receipts of *zakah* without right. God says, "and among them are men who slander thee in the matter of the distribution of *sadaqat*. If they are given part thereof they are pleased but if not, behold they are indingnant. If only they had been content with what God and His apostle gave them, and had said, "Sufficient unto us is God. God and His apostle will soon give us of His bounty. To God we turn our hopes that would have been the right course. Sadaqat are for the poor, needy, and those employed to administer the funds, those whose hearts have been recently reconciled to truth, those in bondage and in debt, in the cause of God, and for the wayfarer. Thus it is ordained by God, and God is full of knowledge and wisdom."[45] With this decisive verse, God left no room for favors in the distribution of the proceeds of *zakah*. He Himself took the issue of determing the eight deserving categories. Who could be more just than God in what He ordained? "But who, for people whose faith is assured, can give better judgment than God."[46] In these verses we find the assertion that there should be a group of workers to administer *zakah*, which indicates that *zakah* should be taken up by the government and not by individuals on their own initiatives.

F. In the *sura*, there are details about the characteristics of the faithful society. God says, "The believers, men and women, are protectors one of another. They enjoin what is just and forbid what is evil. They observe prayer, practice *zakah*, and obey God and his apostle. On them will God pour his mercy, for God is exalted, in power, wise."[47] Thus God made *zakah* one of the main features of communities of the faithful and distinguishes it from that of the hypocrites described in an earlier verse - "the hypocrites, men and women, have understanding with each other, they enjoin evil and forbid what is just and are tight-fisted. They have forgotten God so He has forgotten them. Verily the hypocrites are rebellious and perverse."[48] The hypocrites close their hands in love of money and miserliness, so they deserve being neglected by God, while the believers spread their hands out giving out of faith, so they deserve the mercy of God.

G. In the *sura*, also God instructs His messenger and every head of Muslim state after him: "out of their wealth take *sadaqah*, so thou mightest purify and sanctify them. And pray on their behalf, verily thy prayers are a source of security for them, and God is one who hears and knows."[49] Commentators argue that by saying the word "out" before "their wealth", God meant to include some, and not all of the wealth since *zakah* is not compulsory on all kinds of wealth. Further, the word "wealth" is in the verse in the plural form, so it covers many kinds of wealth. Further, the word wealth, and the pronoun "their" refers to all Muslims according to the majority of commentators. This may be looked upon as proof that *zakah* is obligatory on all Muslims because they are equal in the application of religious ruling.[50] The verse also indicates that *zakah* should be collected by the head of the state or his agents. This, in itself, is confirmed by Sunnah and the actual practice of the Wise Successors (al Khulafa al Rashidin) as we shall discuss later.

At the time of Abu Bakr, some of the rebels that objected to the payment of *zakah* argued that this verse is addressed to the Prophet (p) alone, deducing that *zakah* must not be collected by others. However, it will be shown later in this study, that this interpretation is a false claim. Some scholars say that *sadaqah* in this verse does not necessarily mean *zakah*, since the verse, according to them, refers to those who stayed in the back of the lines and did not go to the battle of Tabuk, those who mixed good deeds with bad. These scholars claim that *sadaqah* should only be taken from those who did join the army, as a matter of compensation for their sins. It is consequently a form of special voluntary contribution, restricted to those individuals as implicated by the context. These scholars continue that this verse, although general in its wording, is not general in its meaning, since *zakah* which is a sign of submission to God and an obligation on all Muslims, cannot be part of the repentance of those individuals that stayed behind.[51] This is the opinion of al Tabari, among others.[52]

Many commentators however, insist that, *sadaqah* in this verse means *zakah*. The majority of scholars in early and late generations used this verse to show the rulings of *zakah*, which means that they understood it as a clear reference to *zakah*, especially that there is no need grammatically or linguistically for this verse to be, necessarily, connected with the verses around it. This understanding is attributed to Ibn 'Abbas, among others. It is also the opinion of 'Ikrimah, as reported by al Qushairi.[53]

At Razi offered an intelligent way of linking this verse to the verses before and after it, without sacrificing the general implication of the verse. He said that *zakah* was not accepted from hypocrites and from those individuals who stayed behind and did not join the army. Upon repentance and acceptance by God, they were given the privilege that *zakah* is taken from them like it is taken from other Muslims.[54] It should be remembered, however, specific causes related to sending down a verse are not taken as restrictions on the general meaning of the words of the verse, as overwhelmingly accepted by scholars of *Usul*. Ironically, those who denied the payment of *zakah* during the time of Abu Bakr used the same verse in their argument that *zakah* should only be paid to the Messenger, without claiming at all that the verse does not make *zakah* obligatory. None of the companions or famous great scholars is reported to have interpreted this verse as referring to voluntary *sadaqah*. All arguments given by Companions and scholars against those who denied the payment of *zakah* to Abu Bakr indicated that the verse is not limited to the Prophet, but general, to any head of state after him.[55]

The interpretation of *sadaqah* in the verse as the obligatory *zakah* is further supported by the saying of the Prophet, to some youth from Bani Hashim who asked him to be employed in the *zakah* fund. The Prophet answered, "It is not permissable to the family of Muhammad, it is the impurities filtered out of people's wealth," This implicitly refers to the verse "So by it you purify and sanctify them." This meaning of the verse is also supported by a report in the Saheeh of Muslim from Abdullah bin Abi Awfa, "Whenever somebody's *sadaqah* is brought to the Prophet, he used to pray for that person. My father brought his *sadaqah* to the Prophet, who then said, "My Lord, give mercy to the family of Abi Awfa." This action of the Messenger is in application of a word in the verse that says "and pray for them". Scholars infer from this verse that the head of the state or his agent who collects *zakah* should pray for its payer.

These are the most important points about *zakah* in *sura* al Tawbah. They represent the general trend of the Madinan *suras* in asserting the obligation of *zakah* and giving its main regulations. A person according to the Qur'an, does not reach righteousness or truthfulness nor does he or she truly fear God, believe in Him - unless he or she practices *zakah* among other things. Without *zakah* a person does not distinguish himself or herself from the hypocrites or the unbelievers. "But My mercy extendeth to all things. That mercy I shall ordain for those who do right, and practice *zakah* and those who believe in our signs."[56] Without *zakah*, a person does not deserve God's mercy, or support and commitment of God, His Messenger, and the believers. Your real supporter is (no less than) God, His apostle, and the believers; those who establish prayers, and perform *zakah*, and they bow down humbly (in worship). As to those who turn (for support) to God, His apostle, and the believers. It is the fellowship of God that must certainly triumph."[57] Without *zakah* a person does not deserve the victory promised by God. God will certainly give victory to those who, if we establish them in the land, establish prayers and give *zakah*, and enjoin the right and forbid wrong. With God rests the end (and decision) of (all) affairs."[58]

Sunnah Affirms Details to the General Directives of the Qur'an

The Qur'an, as the main charter of Islam, and its basic reference, gives usually only the main principles without minute details except in a few areas where there is fear of misconception. Sunnah is the practical manifestation of the Qur'an. It explains, gives details, provides the scope and the specifications of the general verses of the Qur'an, in accordance with the understanding given by God to His Messenger. God says, "And we have sent unto thee the message, that thou mayest explain clearly to mankind what is sent for them."[59]

As far as *zakah* is concerned, Sunnah undeniably asserted its obligation as early as the Makkan period. Ja'far bin Abi Talib, informing the king of Ethiopia about the Prophet on behalf of the Muslim migrants, said, "And he ordains us to pray, pay *zakah*, and fast."[60] This is a reference to the general concepts, and the specific obligated *zakah*. In Madinah, the opportunity was open for Sunnah to give details of *zakah*, its minimum exempt, its ratios, its conditions and its role and importance in the life of Muslims, as well as practical examples of the execution of this major tenet of Islam.

Sunnah Determines Specifications of Zakah

Sunnah gave us that detailed specifications of the kinds of zakatable wealth, the minimum exempt of each of them, and the applicable rates. Sunnah also gave the details of the categories that receive *zakah*."This section is devoted to finding out the history of the obligation of *zakah* as a defined due.

We know that the general principle of *zakah* was prescribed in Makkah without determination of its details. This is what I believe most reasonable and acceptable, in accordance with many scholars, since it is indicated by many verses of the Qur'an and many sayings of the Messenger. Moreover it was shown earlier that Madinan *suras* emphasized this obligation and gave some of the definitions and details of *zakah*. Sunnah took the task of delineating the minute specifications determining *zakatable* kinds of wealth, percentages of *zakah*, and methods of collection. The question of determining the exact year in which *zakah in this specific sense* was prescribed finds an answer during the Madinan period.

It is overwhelmingly recognized that *zakah* was made compulsory in the second year after migration. It is said that *zakah* was prescribed before the fasting of Ramadan was prescribed. Nawawi pointed this out in the chapter on siyar (autobiography) of his book al Rawdah.

On the other hand, it is authentically reported by Ahmad Ibn Khuzaymah, al Nasai, Ibn Majah, and Al Hakim, from Qays bin Sa'id bin Ubadah, that he said: "The Messenger of God commanded us to pay *sadaqah* of al Fitr (fast-breaking *zakah*) before *zakah* was sent down. Later on, the obligation of *zakah* descended." Al Hafiz noted that the chain of this saying is correct. This saying shows that the obligation of fast-breaking *zakah* took place before that of regular *zakah*. Consequently, *zakah* would have been obligated after obligated after the fasting of Ramadan.[62] It is not disputed, however, that Ramadan's fasting was obligated after Hijrah since the verse that talks about it is undisputably Madinan.[62] Ibn al Athir in his *History* states that *zakah* was made obligatory in the ninth year of Hjrrah. This is supported, according to some, by the story of Tha'labah bin Hatib which states, "When the verse of *sadaqah* was sent down, the Prophet, (p), sent a worker to collect *zakah* from Tha'labah. "He answered, this is seemingly nothing but a *jizyah* or the sister of *jizyah*." *Jizyah* was obligated in the ninth year of migration, so *zakah* must be around then. The author of *Fath al Bari* said, "This saying is weak and does not stand in argument."[63]

Al Hafiz argued, however, that *zakah* was made obligatory before the year nine, citing the saying of Anas about the story of Dammam bin Tha'labah (reported in the two correct books) who asked the Prophet (p) in the same of God, to give him the right answer on a few matters. Dammam said "By God, did God order you to take this *sadaqah* from the rich among us and distribute it to the poor among us?" The Prophet answered "yes", Dammam came to the Prophet in the year five after Hijrah[64]. But in the year nine, the Prophet sent, for the first time, *zakah* collectors to collect *zakah*. This implies that *zakah* was made obligatory before that.[64] Additionally, the verse that starts

"*Sadaqat* are but for...," which closed the door in the face of the hypocrites and their ambitions, indicates implicitly that *zakah* was definitely in existence practice and that the Prophet (p) was having *zakah* collected and distributed by his appointed workers at the time of its revelation.

Zakah After Fasting

It seems to be evident from all the sayings together and from the historical development of the legislation on Islamic obligations that the five prayer were the first to be made obligatory. That happened in Makkah on the night of Ascendance, fasting was obligated in the second year after migration, then *zakah* on fast-breaking was also obligated as a purification for the person who fasts and to bring happiness to the indigent on the Day of the Feast: *zakah* on wealth was made compulsory later on. But it is very difficult to find decisive evidence that tells the exact year of its obligation, although the saying of Dammam bin Tha'labah indicates that *zakah* has already been obligated by the year five of hijrah according to al Hafiz Ibn Hajar.

Ibn Muflih mentioned in al Furu' the report of al Walibi from Ibn 'Abbas that: God has sent his Prophet (p) with the testimony that there is no diety but God. When they accepted, they were increased the prayer. When they accepted, fasting was added. After they accepted, *zakah* was added. When they accepted, hajj was added. And when they accepted that, then *jihad* was added, and thus the religion was perfect and completed. And he quoted, "This day have I perfected your religion for you, completed my favor upon you and have chosen for you Islam as your religion...,[65] This is consistent with what Ibn 'Aqil said in *al Wadih,* i.e. *zakah* was prescribed after fasting.[66]

Zakah The Third Pillar of Islam

The Prophet (p) affirmed in Madinah the obligation of *zakah*. He pronounced its importance and rank in the religion as one of the principal pillars. He encouraged its performance, and strongly warned against rejecting its payment. All this came in many sayings and styles. We see it in the reputed saying about when Jibril came to teach Muslims their religion by politely questioning the Prophet: He asked the Prophet (p) "What is Islam? The Prophet (p), answered, "Islam is to testify that there is no diety but God and Muhammad is the messenger of God. to establish prayer, perform *zakah,* fast Ramadan, and make pilgrimage to the House if you can go there." (Agreed upon)* In the famous saying narrated by Ibn 'Umar, "Islam is founded on five: giving witness that there is no diety but God and Muhammad is the messenger of God, establishing prayer, practicing *zakah*, fasting Ramadan, and pilgrimage to the House of God for whoever can reach it" (Agreed upon). In these two sayings and in many others, the Messenger (p) declared that the pillars of Islam are five, among them *zakah* is the third. *Zakah* is declared as the third pillar in Sunnah as well as in Qur'an, without which the structure of Islam does not stand.

---

* i.e. reported by Bukhar as well as by Muslim.

In some sayings the Prophet (p) only mentioned some of those pillars, but he always mentions prayer and *zakah* in the forefront of what he calls for and takes covenant on. An example is the saying narrated by Ibn 'Abbas in the two correct books (of *hadith*, i.e. the compilations by Bukhari and Muslim). The Prophet (p), when he sent Mu'adh to Yemen told him,[67] "You are going to folks from the People of the Book. Call upon them to testify there is no diety but God and I am the messenger of God. If they obey you in that, inform them that God prescribed upon them five prayers every day and night. If they obey you in that, inform them that God obligated them to practice *sadaqah* to be collected from their rich individuals and rendered to their poor individuals. If they obey you in that, then carefully avoid their other wealth and valuables. Be very fearful of the prayer of an oppressed person since there is no barrier between such a prayer and God." The *hadith* mentions only prayer and *zakah* in order to show how much special importance God has given to them, especially when the matter is the call to Islam. These two tenets, along with the declaration of faith, should be sufficient indication of Islam, as it is, in the verse "But if they repent, establish prayer and perform *zakah* they are your brethren in religion." (This saying also indicated the assignment of workers to collect and distribute *zakah* and that payment and distribution of *zakah* is not left to the individuals' initiative.)

Bukhari reports from Jabir bin Abdullah, "I gave pledge to the Prophet (p) to establish prayer, perform *zakah*, and give sincere advice to each Muslim".

Ibn 'Umar narrates in the two correct books (of *hadith*) that the messenger of God (p) said, "I am commanded to fight disbelievers until they testify that there is no diety but God and Muhammad is the messenger of God, and establish prayer and practice *zakah*"... This saying talks, in principle, about the Arab pagans. God wanted Arab land to be sanctified for Islam and cleansed from all remnants of paganism, blind ignorance, and oppression.

There is a saying reported by al Bazzar from Anas: The messenger of God (p) said "He who dies having sincere faith in God, worshipping Him without partners, establishing prayer, and practicing *zakah*, he finishes with the pleasure of God." Anas said: "This is the religion of God for which messengers are sent, They reveal it to people from the Lord. It was there long before vain talks and differences of whims. There he quoted the verse: "But if they repent and establish prayer and practice *zakah* then open the way for them, and said: "Repentance is by their dissociation of ideals, by the worship of God alone, by the practice of prayer and by the performance of *zakah*,"and Anas quoted another verse: "But if they repent, establish prayer and practice *zakah* they are then your brethren in religion."[69]

Strong Warning Against Rejection of Payment of *Zakah*

Several sayings mention the warning the Messenger (p) gave to those who reject the payment of *zakah*. Warning of severe punishment in the hereafter is aimed at awakening dormant hearts and shaking miserly souls to give by both positive encouragement and fear of punishment. If they do not perform this duty with awakened consciouses, the power and authority of the state is used to collect *zakah*.

Punishment In The Hereafter

Bukhari reported from Abu Hurairah, "The messenger of God, (p) said: "He who is given wealth by God but he does not pay its *zakah*, that wealth is made for him, on the Day of Judgment, the form of a huge bald serpent with two horns, encircling that person and squeezing him all day, then holding him by lips telling him, 'I am your wealth, your treasure that you hoarded'. Then the Prophet quoted the verse, 'and let not those who covetously withhold the gift that God hath given them of His grace, think that it is good for them. Nay, it will be the worse for them. Soon shall the things which they covetously withheld be tied to their necks like a collar on the Day of Judgment'.[70] In another saying, Muslim reports that the Prophet (p) said: "He who owns gold and silver and does not pay the dues on them they will be made, on the Day of Judgment, like sheets heated by the fire of Hell. His front, back and sides will be ironed with these sheets on a day which is as long as fifty thousand years, until judgment is given to all human beings and he will be shown his way to the Garden or to the Fire. He who owns cattle or sheep and does not give their dues, they will be brought on the Day of Resurrection to stamp an him with their hoofs and pinch him with their horns. When the last one finishes with him the first will be brought again to continue that stamping and pinching until God gives judgment to all his servants, on a day that is as long as fifty thousand years of yours. Then he will be shown his way to the Garden or to the Fire."

Punishment In This Life to Those Who Reject The Payment of *Zakah*

The Sunnah did not merely threaten of punishment in the Hereafter for those who do not pay *zakah*, but went on to warn them of a punishment in this life, punishment from God and a penalty from the State. A *hadith* states, "There is no people, who do not pay *zakah*, left without being made to suffer by God through disasters, or famine or drought."[71] In another saying, "Any people who do not pay *zakah* on their wealth, verily they will be prevented rain from sky except for animals and livestock."[72] And also, "*Zakah* is never intermingled with any amount of wealth without destroying and rotting it."[73] This saying has two meanings according to al Mundhiri: Firstly, that whenever due *zakah* is not paid it will be a cause for ruining that wealth. This meaning is upheld by another *hadith* that states "Whenever any amount of wealth is destroyed in the land or in the sea it could be because its *zakah* was not paid."[74] Secondly, if a person who takes *zakah* as recipient without deserving that *zakah* and mixes it with his wealth, that will be a reason for rotting all his wealth, according to Imam Ahmad.[75]

Legal Penalty for He who Does Not Pay *Zakah*

The legal penalty is mentioned by the Prophet, (p): "He who pays it seeking the reward from God will be rewarded and he who refuses to pay it, we shall take it from him, along with half of his wealth, and by the authority given to us by our Lord. The clan of Muhammad are not allowed to take anything of its proceeds."[76] This saying includes a few important principles.

Firstly, *zakah* is, in principal, paid out of sincerity on the part of the believer for the sake of pleasing God and seeking reward from Him, since a Muslim is ordained to worship God by paying *zakah*.

Secondly, He who is overcome by his miserliness and refuses to pay *zakah* is not left without payment being extracted from him anyway. *Zakah* is a legal institution that is supported by the law-enforcement power of the state. The state must use its authority to collect *zakah* in addition to the penalty, (equal to half the wealth of the hoarder) imposed by God and His Messenger. Some say that this penalty was levied only at the beginning of Islam but was annuled later.[77] There is no evidence whatsoever of this annulment and I feel that the state can impose this penalty in order to prevent people from abusing this tenet of Islam.

Thirdly, the strong penalty imposed on those who reject paying *zakah* shows the extent to which Islam cares about the rights of the poor and the other deserving categories. As for the Prophet, (p) all members of his family, and his descendants, they are not allowed to receive any of the proceeds *zakah*; it is made unlawful to them no matter under what title, in contrast with charity in Judaism, where one-tenth of it is assigned to the Levites, the descendants of Harun, and part of it used to be spent for other religious leader.[78]

Fighting the Rejecters of *Zakah*

Those who refuse to pay zakah on their wealth are fined as above. But if it so happened that a group of people refused to pay *zakah* collectively, that group should be fought by the Islamic government because this represents a rebellion against the state and Islam. Although fighting implies as we know, bloodshed, and destruction of property that Islam aims to avoid, but fighting becomes legitimate and permissible when it is done for the establishment of justice on earth. As for the rejecters of *zakah*, they have lost the respect and protection of their lives and property by declaring their rebellion against God and His apostle by rejecting this basic pillar of Islam. This matter of fighting rebels against *zakah* is affirmed by correct sayings and the unanimous stand of the Companions. Bukhari and Muslim reported from Abdullah bin 'Umar that the messenger of God (p) said: "I am commanded to fight unbelievers until they testify there is no diety but God and Muhammad is the messenger of God, establish prayer and practice *zakah*. If they do all that, their blood is protected except by the due course of Islamic law and to God is left their reckoning," They also reported from Abu Hurairah "The messenger of God (p) said, 'I am commanded to fight unbelievers until they testify there is no diety but God and believe in me and in what I brought. If they do so, then they have protected their blood and property except by due course of law, their reckoning is left to God". And a similar saying is reported by Muslim and Nasa'i from Jabir bin Abdullah.[79] These sayings clearly indicate that rejecters of *zakah* payment must be fought until they pay. It may be that these sayings were not known to Abu Bakr and 'Umar when they argued whether it is lawful to fight those who reject *zakah* without denying the other pillars of Islam, such as prayer and fasting.[80]

After the death of the messenger of God, several Arab tribes rebelled and rejected the payment of *zakah* though they continued their regular prayer and they declared faith in God. There were also totally rebelious tribes that turned back from Islam and claimed false prophets such as Musailamah the Liar, Sajah, and Tulaihah al Asdi and their clans. Abu Bakr then took an historical stand. He refused to acknowledge any differentiation between the bodily worship (prayer) and the financial worship (*zakah*). He rejected the reduction of what used to be paid to the Messenger of God, no matter how small such a reduction may be (a baby goat or a camel's tether), He was not weakened in the face of the danger of apostates invading Madinah, on the hesitation of some Companions to fight the rebels.

Abu Hurairah describes this historical stand: When the Messenger of God (p) died and Abu Bakr came to power, many Arabs turned back as apostates. 'Umar said by what virtue should we fight those people, knowing that the Messenger of God, (p) said, 'I am commanded to fight pagans until they witness that there is no diety but God. Once they say that, they have protected their blood and their property, except by due course of justice, and their reckoning is left to God". Abu Bakr answered, 'By God I shalt fight them who differentiate between prayer and *zakah*. Zakah is the right due on wealth. By God, if they refuse to give me one baby goat they used to give to the Messenger of God as *zakah*, I shall fight them for it. 'Umar said, "And by God, it was not until I realized that God had opened the heart of Abu Bakr to fighting that I knew it was the truth." Reported by all except Ibn Majah. (In another version Abu Bakr said "A tether of a camel" instead of a "baby of goat".)[81] "Umar took the words of the saying of the prophet literally to mean the declaration of faith alone is sufficient to protect the pagans, without attention to the essential implications of that declaration, without which the declaration itself is merely vain talk.

On the other hand, Abu Bakr brought out some basic points. Firstly, the text of the saying itself suspended protection by the condition of "due course of Law." *Zakah* is the dues on wealth under Islamic law, 'Umar did not disagree on this point. Secondly, there is an analogy between *zakah* and prayers, as two sisters always associated together in the Book of God and the tradition of His messenger. The conclusion of the argument of Abu Bakr and 'Umar was that the Companions were unanimously agreed that those who refuse to pray must be fought, including those who were hesitant at first. 'Umar realized that Abu Bakr was correct, and accepted his argument and his evidence.[82]

This is what was done by the first caliph Abu Bakr the Truthful, with regard to those Arab clans that insisted on rejecting the payment of *zakah* after the death of the Messenger of God. Consequently, fighting the rejecters of *zakah* has become a matter of *ijma'* that cannot be altered. *Imam* Nawawi said, "If a person or a group of people refused to pay *zakah*, and resist the law enforcement of the state, the state must fight them, because it is authentically reported in the two Correct Books* from Abu Hurairah that the companions, after an initial debate, realized the value of the opinion given by Abu Bakr and the strength of its supportive evidence and agreed with him in making the ruling on fighting *zakah*'s rejecters unanimous among Muslims.[83] It should be pointed

---

*   of *hadith*, compiled by Bukhari and Muslim respectively. that the speech is addressed to

out that for the first time in the history of humanity a state, that is, the Islamic state of Abu Bakr, fights for the purpose of protecting the right of the poor and the weak sections of society. Most states stand in support of the rich and strong. Abu Bakr and the Companions rejected the idea that *zakah* should only be paid to the Prophet (p) and after his death no one has the right to collect *zakah*, claiming that verse 103 of *Sura* Tawbah gives the right to collect *zakah* to the Prophet alone. The judge Abu Bakr bin al 'Arabi said about this claim, "These are words of a person who is totally ignorant of the Qur'an, who does not know how *Shari'ah* rulings are derived, who wants to tamper with religion and whose viewpoint is falling apart on its own.[84] The verse is addressed to every head of state after the Prophet, though it speaks to him at that particular time. It is not addressed to the personal affairs of the Prophet, like the verses that speak about his family life or his personal prayers.

Al Imam al Khattabi said "The address of speech in the Book of God is of three kinds: one, a general address such as the verse, "Oh, you who believe, when you stand for prayer wash your faces..,; two, an address specifically to the Prophet, (p) alone. This is clearly indicated in the verse itself such as, "and pray in the small hours of the morning an additional prayer for thee" and "this is only for thee and not for all the believers", And three, there is the address to the Prophet, (p), and with him all his followers, such as in the verses, "Establish prayer at the sun's decline till the darkness of the night". "When thou doest read the Qur'an, seek Cod's protection,"Of their wealth take *zakah*."Such verses are not restricted to the Prophet alone. They are in fact addressed to him and to all Muslim nation together. It should be mentioned the Messenger of God (p), because he is required to preach and explain God's commandment and he is an example for all Muslims to follow.

Verse 103 of *sura* at Tawbah mentions that the Prophet, (p) should pray for those who give *zakah*. However, no one can make the claim that only the Prophet (p) should pray for *zakah* payers. All *zakah* collectors are also addressed with this verse. The payment of *zakah* itself is related in the verse to sanctification and purification of the payers. Muslim scholars comment that purification, sanctification, and prayer for *zakah* payers are consequences of their obedience to God, and His messenger in practicing *zakah*, and every reward for good deeds that is mentioned with respect to the time of the Prophet, (p) remains in effect after his time for all doers of such good deeds without interruption until the Day of Judgment.[85]

Zakah Is Part of What is Recognized in Religion

It is important lastly to point out that *zakah* as a pillar of Islam, is among those principles that, are necessarily known to be part of religion. It was instituted by clear verses in the Qur'an by abundant sayings of the Prophet and has been affirmed by the *ijma'* (Unanimity) of Muslims, generation after generation.[86]

Denying *Zakah* Equals Denying Faith

We have shown how important *zakah* is in Islam and how high it is ranked among Islam's obligations, It is now time to mention that scholars have established that the denial of its obligation is equal to disbelief and apostating from Islam. Nawawi said, "Anyone who does not pay *zakah* on the basis of denying its obligation is considered a disbeliever except if that person is new in Islam or has lived all his or her life far from sources of information (in an isolated desert, for example). Then he or she should first be made aware of the importance of the obligation of *zakah*. If he or she insists on denying it, then that is disbelief, because the obligation of *zakah* is basic to this religion, without which Islam becomes annulled. That who denies this obligation denies the words of God and His Messenger, and therefore is a disbeliever. This ruling is also established by Ibn Qudamah and other scholars.[88] With this unanimous ruling we should realize the low rank in the eyes of God those, who deny *zakah* or ridicule it assume.

The Main Differences Between Zakah in Islam and Zakah in Other Religions

Firstly, *zakah* in Islam is not a mere charity left to the righteousness of individuals, as part of their good deeds. It is rather an essential pillar of this religion, one of its major rituals and the second of its main four forms of worship. Not paying it is like going astray. He who denies its obligation is considered disbeliever, It is an obligation supported by the ethical values of Islam as well as by the power of law in the Islamic state.

Secondly, *zakah* is a right to the poor in the wealth of the rich, a right decided by the true Owner of wealth, God and imposed on those who have bean given control of that wealth by Him. *Zakah* thus does not humble or humiliate the receiver nor does it make the rich get a higher rank, ethically or socially.

Thirdly, *zakah* is a recognized and defined due, determined by *Shari'ah* so that Muslims may know with clarity the ratios, conditions, and exemptions of this due.

Fourthly, the Islamic state is charged with the responsibility of collecting *zakah* and distributing it. *Zakah* is in this respect like a tax that must be collected and not like a contribution that is granted. The Qur'an states, "Take out of their wealth *sadaqah*" and the Sunnah says, "to be taken from the rich".

Fifthly, the state has the right to penalize that who refuses to pay *zakah*. This penalty may include a fine of as much as half the assets as mentioned in the saying, "we shall take it along with half the wealth of the rejecter".

Sixthly, any group of people that thinks of using force in resisting the payment of *zakah* would be fought by the Islamic government. War is declared on them until they accept to pay the due on their wealth, imposed by God, to the poor.

Seventhly, the individual Muslim is called upon to establish this essential obligation of Islam even if the state does not collect it, since the payment of *zakah* is in itself a worship that a Muslim offers to his Lord. If the government does not require its collection, it is required by the faith and by the Qur'an. Each Muslim should know of all the rulings of *zakah* so he or she may pay it according to the conditions stipulated in *Shari'ah*.

Eighthly, the proceeds of *zakah* are not left to government or to religious leaders or priests to determine their distribution. The distribution of *zakah* and the deservant categories are determined in this religion in the verse "*sadaqat* are only for the poor, the needy,..." Sunnah brought the details of distribution. It is known from human experience that righteousness is not achieved by merely collecting the right dues. The dispersement of the proceeds is even more important, so the messenger of God (p) announced that neither he nor any member of his family and descendents were allowed to take any part of the proceeds of *zakah*. *Zakah* is taken from the rich in every area and rendered to the poor in that same area.

Ninthly, *zakah* is not merely temporary relief to the immediate needs of the poor and to attenuate his misery, leaving him in the long run to his poverty. *Zakah* aims at eliminating poverty and making the poor at least self sufficient, helping them with sufficient financial means to enable them to work and produce for their own sustenance, *zakah* is a periodical due repeated each year, aimed at raising the level of living of the poor.

Tenthly, *zakah* in its dispersement aims at achieving several spiritual, moral, social, and political purposes. For that reason, it may be spent for the reconciliation of hearts, for the liberation of slaves, for those who are in debt, and for the sake of God in the widest meaning of the word.

With these characteristics of *zakah* that are so distinct from alms in other religions, we realize that *zakah* is an institution unique in its characteristics and features. It is different from taxes and other dues in as much as it is different from alms known in other religions.

Disproving The Claims of Schacht About The Nature of *Zakah*

It may be useful to go throgh the biased claims of some who assume the position of knowledge in the West without exhibiting the necessary honesty that is required for any scientific research. Schacht said under the title 'Zakah' in the Encyclopedia of Islam,[89] "The tradition of the Prophet includes cases where *zakah* is obligated which are not in consistency with the institution of *zakah* as it came to be known later. In all cases, the nature of *zakah* at the time of the Prophet, (p) was still ambiguous and it was not one of the taxes required by religion. That is why many Arab tribes refused to pay it after the death of the Prophet (p). They considered that their covenant to pay it with the Prophet came to an end at his death. Some believers, including 'Umar bin al Khattab, were inclined to accept that view." (p 358).

Schacht did not mention which sayings of the Prophet he referred to so we can discuss his unfounded claims. Additionally, his words "the institution of *zakah* as it came to be known later" imply that this system of *zakah* was fabricated by Muslims some time after the era of the Prophet: that is, it is not a system revealed from God but it was created by the conditions and the human experience that Muslims gained from the Persians and the Romans. This, in itself, is an old falsehood with which Schacht and other Orientalists have long been branded. The truth that is confirmed by verses of the holy Qur'an, correct and good sayings of the Messenger, and the heritage of the

Companions and the Wise Successors (Al Kulafa" al Rashidin) is that *zakah* is a pure Islamic system. It is a unique and unprecedented institution which any person who is not ridden by prejudice would agree that it is a tint from God; who has better tint than God?

The claim of ambiguity of *zakah* at the time of the Prophet is even more ridiculous. I wonder how a person who claims to be a researcher with insight into Islamic jurisprudence and *Shari'ah* could prove this statement of his that *zakah* at the time of the Prophet was ambiguous and was not a religious requirement, especially since we have shown the sayings of the Prophet (p) that determine kinds of assets that are *zakatable* which includes all kinds of growing wealth known to the Arabs in the Prophet's era, such as livestock, agricultural products, and gold and silver. The percentages and ratios of *zakah* are also determined in a clear manner in the sayings, ranging from ten percent to five percent to two and a half percent on different kinds of wealth. The tradition of the Prophet also defined the time of payment and the pattern of periodicity of *zakah*. The destinations of *zakah* are also well defined in the Qur'an and in more detail in Sunnah. Sunnah also determined methods of collection and administration of *zakah*, called in the Qur'an the commissioners of *zakah*. Accordingly the Prophet (p) sent his commissioners and collectors to different regions and tribes and ordered them to collect and distribute *zakah*. Can anyone, after all these details, claim an ambiguity about the nature of *zakah* during the Prophet's era?

Even more surprising is Schacht's claim that *zakah* was not a due required by religion, when on the contrary, we find the Prophet always listing *zakah* as one of the pillars and essential obligations of Islam, to the extent that some sayings mention prayer and *zakah* immediately after the declaration of faith and leave out fasting and pilgrimage. We have quoted earlier the saying that requires Muslims to fight those who refuse to pay *zakah*, such as the sayings narrated by Ibn 'Umar, Abu Hurairah, and Jabir. We have noted that the Prophet (p) put a clause on prayer and *zakah* in every treaty he concluded with any tribes that were entering into the religion of Islam. We have seen *zakah* mentioned in every letter he sent with his commissioners and deputies in the different regions or with the delegations that used to come and visit with him. It is obvious that the importance of prayers and its ranking in this religion of Islam is not denied by Schacht and his colleagues. How could he then throw any doubt on *zakah*? The Prophet's messages put down in detail the ordinances about *zakah* and its ratios, leaving no room for any ambiguity or doubt. For those who would like more references may I mention the collection of Political documents of the time of the Prophet and the Wise Successors by Dr. Muhammad Hamidullah.[90]

Schacht used the rejection of payment of *zakah* by some Arab tribes to imply that *zakah* was ambiguous. Those tribes who refused to pay *zakah* fell in several categories. Some denied Islam in total and followed individuals who falsely claimed prophethood, such as Musaylamah, Sajah, al Aswad, and Tulayhah. Others denied the whole of Islamic *Shari'ah* including prayers and *zakah*, but Schacht did not use this to claim that prayer was also ambiguous. Some other tribes accept prayer and the rest of Islamic *Shari'ah* and raised objections on *zakah* as we studied earlier. Most of these were either very new in Islam, and unversed in it, while some of them did not even deny the payment of *zakah* but like Bani *Yarbu'* were rather prevented by their leaders from paying *zakah* to Abu Bakr.[91] Muslim scholars such as Imam Abu Sulaiman al Khattabi did not consider this category apostates. He only considered them rebellious because their denial of the payment of *zakah* was caused mainly by their lack of comprehension and understanding of the religion and its obligations. About this latest category, 'Umar debated with Abu Bakr, but it is obvious from studying the story that 'Umar was convinced by the evidence provided by Abu Bakr and it became unanimous among all the companions that even this last category of Arab tribes must be fought.

Schacht claimed that the stand of Abu Bakr toward those who refused to pay *zakah* was responsible for giving *zakah* its obligatory nature. But he forgot that Abu Bakr gave his proofs and evidence from the verses of the Qur'an and the sayings of the Prophet and was not bringing any new argument from his own mind but rather following the Messenger of God. In his statement "by God I shall fight them if they refuse to pay me any portion of *zakah*, be it as little as a baby goat, that they used to pay to the Messenger of God". Abu Bakr was only following the tradition of the Messenger (p). 'Umar, on the other hand, thought that they could accept prayers now from those tribes and wait on the matter of *zakah* until the Muslim government in Madinah was strongly established, because of the dangers he anticipated from the apostates.[92] Abu Bakr was more convincing even to 'Umar himself because he had undeniable evidence from the Qur'an and Sunnah: "But if they repent, establish prayer, and practice *zakah*, they are then your brethren in religion."

Footnotes

1. The late scholar Muhammad Farid Wajdi, author of the *Encyclopedia of the Twentieth Century* and for many years editor of the *al Azhar Review*. His book *Islam a Universal and Eternal Religion*, is quoted above, pp 179-181, first print.

2. *Ibid.*

3. from a lecture by Dr. Karl Schobens in the Seminar on Social Studies, third session, p. 546.

4. *Sura al Anbiya'*, 21:73.

5. *Sura Maryam*, 19:54.

6. *Sura al Baqara*, 2:83.

7. *Sura al Ma'idah*, 5:12.

8. *Sura Maryam*, 19:31.

9. *Sura al Bayinah*, 98:5.

10. *Sura al Muddaththir*, 74:38-46.

11. *Sura al Qalam*, 68:19-33.

12. *Sura al Haqqah,* 69:25-29 and 30-34.

13. *Al Amwal,* p. 350.

14. *Sura al Fajr,* 89:17-8.

15. The commentary on part 30 of the Qur'an, p.83, Misr Press.

16. Verses 1-3 of the *sura.*

17. Commentary on part 30 of the Qur'an, p. 162.

18. *Sura al Ma'un,* 107:4-7.

19. Commentary of *Ibn Kathir,* vol 4, p. 555, al Halabi Print.

20. *Sura al Dhariyat,* 51:19-20.

21. *Sura al Ma'arij,* 70:19-25.

22. See *Ibn Kathir,* Vol 4, p. 234.

23. *Sura al Isra',* 17:26.

24. *Sura al Rum,* 30:38.

25. *Sura al An'am,* 6:141.

26. *Sura al Rum,* 30:38-9.

27. *Sura al Naml,* 27:1-3.

28. *Sura al Luqman,* 31:4

29. *Sura al Muminun,* 23:4.

30. *Sura al A'raf,* 7:156-7.

31. *Sura Fussilat,* 41:6-7.

32. *Sura al Shams,* 91:9.

33. *Sura al A'la,* 87:14.

34. *Tafsir al Tabari,* vol. 24, p. 93, al Halabi Print.

35. Except what came in the last verse of *sura* al Muzzammil "read ye therefore as much of the Qur'an as may be easy for you and establish prayer and give *zakah.* " This is on the assumption that that *sura* is all Makkan which is the view of some scholars. Others say the last verse as Madinan because it is different in style and content from the rest of the *sura.*

36. Muhammad Izzat Darwazah Autobiography of the Messenger as derived from the Qur'an, vol. 2, p. 341.

37. Commentary of Ibn Kathir, vol 3, pp, 238 and 239.

38. *Sura al Baqarah*, 2:110.

39. *Sura at Tawbah,* 9:5.

40. *Sura al Tawbah*, 9:11.

41. Commentary of At Tabari, vol 14 p. 153, al Ma'arif Print.

42. *Sura at Tawbah,* 9:18.

43. *Sura at Tawbah*, 9:34 and 35.

44. Abu Bakr bin al 'Arabi, *Ahkam al Qur'an.*

45. *Sura at Tawbah*, 9:58-60.

46. *Sura al Ma'idah*, 5:53.

47. *Sura at Tawbah*, 9:71.

48. *Ibid,* 9:67.

49. *Ibid*, 9:103.

50. See the commentary of Tubrusi: *Majma'al Bayan* under the verse mentioned.

51. *Al Rawd al Nadir*, vol 2, p. 410.

52. Commentary of al Tabari, vol. 14, pp. 454-456.

53. *Commentary of al Qurtubi,* vol. 8, p. 244 sea also *Ibn Kathir,* vol. 2 pp. 385-386 and *Ahkam al Qur'an* of Ibn al 'Arabi, pp 997-998 and *al Tafsir al Kabir'* of al Fakhr al Razi, vol. 16, p. 177 and following pages, also al Qasimi, *Mahsin al Ta'wil,* vol. 8 p. 3253.

54. See commentaries of al Razi and al Qasimi, *Ibid.*

55. See commentaries of Ibn Kathir and al Qasimi, *Ibid.*

56. *Sura al A'raf,* 7:156.

57. *Sura al Ma'idah*, 5:58 and 59.

58. *Sura al Hajj,* 22:40 and 41.

59. *Sura al Nahl,* 16:44.

60. Reported by Ibn Khuzaimah In his correct collection as narrated from Umm Salamah.

61. *Fath al Bari,* vol. 3, p. 171.

62. *Ibid.*

63. In Takhrij al Kashshaf, p 77 the author said the saying is very weak.

64. Fath al Bari, vol. 3, p. 171.

65. *Sura al Ma'idah,* 5:3.

66. Al Furu', in Hanbalite Fiqh, vol. 2, pp. 217 and 318, second printing.

67. Al Shawkani said: he was sent in the year 10 just before the Prophet (p) went for pilgrimage as reported by Bukhari at the end of the chapter on "travels and battles of the Prophet." some said he was sent in the year 9 upon returning from the Battle of Tabuk. Others said he was sent the same year of opening Makkah in the year 8. It is agreed on, however, that he stayed in Yemen until after the death of the Prophet and his succession by Abu Bakr. There are also differences on whether he was sent as a governor or only as a judge. Ibn Abd al Barr believes the latter while al Nasa'i confirms the former. See *Nayl at Awtar,* vol. 4 p. 115, 'Uthmaniah Misriah Print.

68. Poor alone are mentioned because they are the most important and common category of recipients and also for contrast between the payer (rich) and receiver (poor).

69. Commentary of Ibn Kathir vol. 2 pp 235-238.

70. *Sura Al 'Imran* 3:180.

71. Reported by al Tabarani in his *al Awsat,* with a trustworthy chain of narrators and by al Hakim and al Bayhaqi, but the latters' words were "whenever any people refuse to pay *zakah* God would verily withhold rain from them". Al Hakim said it is correct according to the criteria of Muslim. See *al Targhib wa al Tarhib,* vol. 1, p.270, print of al Numairiah, and *Majma al Zawa'id,* vol. 3, p. 96. 72.

72. Reported by Ibn Majah, al Bazzar and al Bayhaqi from Ibn 'Umar, same source as in n 71. It is also reported by al Hakim who branded it as correct and he was followed agreeably by al Dhahabi. This saying has also other narrations that support it, see the series of correct sayings by al Albani, text number 105.

73. Reported by at Bazzar and al Bayhaqi as in *al Targhib.* In *al Muntaqa* it is said reported by al Shafi'i and al Bukhari in his *History* and al Humaidi, the letter added that if *zakah* has become due but was not paid out so the whole asset is ruined. See Nail al Awtar, vol. 4, p. 126.

74. It is said in *Majma'al Zawa'id,* vol. 3, p. 93: reported by al Tabarani in *al Awsat* in the chain there is 'Umar bin Harun and he is weak.

75. *Al Targhib wa al Tarhib, op. cit.*

76. Reported by Ahmad, al Nasa'i and Abu Dawud from Bahz bin Hakim from his father from his grandfather. It is also reported by at Bayhaqi in his *Sunan,* vol. 4 p. 105, al Bayhaqi continued, "this is a saying reported by Abu Dawud, it was not reported by Bukhari and Muslim because they have the condition that the Companion or the

Follower should have more than one narrator of the next generation in order to put the saying in their correct collections. The grandfather, in this saying, is only narrated by his son. Ibn al Turkumani followed in his *al Jawhar al Naqi* that this was not a universal condition of Bukhari and Muslim, See the note on this saying in *Nail al Awtar* vol. 4 p. 132.

77. This is stated by al Shirazi in his *al Muhadhdhab*, See *al Majmu'*, vol 5, pp. 332 and 334.

78. Abu al Hasan al Nadwi, *al Arkan al Arba'ah,* p. 129.

79. *Nail al Awtar,* vol 4, p. 121.

80. This is not surprising. It may happen that some Companions did not hear from the Prophet what some others heard. An example is the statements of 'Umar about the saying narrated by Abu Musa on seeking permission: I missed it by getting busy with my trades in the markets. It is possible also that Abu Bakr knew that saying since he used its meaning in his argument with 'Umar.

81. *Nail al Awtar*, vol. 4, p. 119.

82. *Ibid,* p. 120, see also *Ma'alim al sunan*, vol. 2, p. 165.

83. *Al Majmu'*, vol. 5, p. 334.

84. *Ahkam al Qur'an*, vol. 2, p. 995.

85. See al Khattabi, *Ma'lim al Sunan*, vol. 2, p. 165, *Ahkam al Qur'an*, part. 2, pp. 994-996 and Nail al Awtar, vol. 4, pp. 102-103, al Halabi Print, 1347 H.

86. Some scholars said that its obligation is also deducted by rational thinking of Muslims. The author of *al Bada'i'*, vol. 3, p. 3, said the following reasons are used to rationalize the obligation of *zakah*: 1- the payment is a help and relief to the poor, the incapable and the needy, it helps him to support his own life and to perform his prayers and other worships; 2- *zakah* purifies the soul of the *zakah* payer from sins, trains him to become generous and helps him avoid misery. This training is very useful to each soul and 3- the payment of *zakah* is an expression of thankfulness to God by the rich individuals who are granted their wealth as a bounty from God.

87. *Al Majmu'*, vol. 5, p. 334.

88. *Al Mughni*, vol. 2, p. 573, al Manar printing.

89. Vol. 10, p. 58 of the Arabic translation.

90. See documents carrying the following numbers in the third edition, 1969, Beirut: 56, 59a, 66, 66a, 72a, 77, 78, 78a, 81, 82, 84, 85, 87, 90, lO4a, 104b, 104c, 104d, 105, 106d, 109, ll0c, 110d, 111, 112, 117a, 120, 121, 133, 141c, 152, 157, 165, 173, 174, 177, 184a, 186, 188, 189, 190, 191, 192, 193, 194, 195, 196, 197, 216, 233, 234, 242a.

91. *Nayl at Awtar*, vol. 4, p.102.

92. Ahkam al Qur'an, part two, p. 995.

FIQH AL ZAKAH

PART TWO

ON WHOM IS *ZAKAH* OBLIGATORY

Exemption of Non-Muslims from Zakah

Zakah on Funds of Children and the Insane

This part contains one chapter with two sections. Section One will discuss that *zakah* is not required from non-Muslims and Section two will discuss the *zakah* requirement on funds of children and the insane.

SECTION ONE

ZAKAH IS NOT REQUIRED FROM NON-MUSLIMS

There is an agreement among Muslim jurists that *zakah* is obligatory on the Muslim who has reached puberty, who is sane, who is free, and who owns the minimum assigned, *nisab*, according to the conditions in *Shari'ah*.[1] We have previously discussed the clear texts of the Qur'an and authentic sayings of the Prophet that indicate this obligation. All these texts necessarily imply that *zakah* is an obligation. This has been inherited by Muslims generation after generation, and is overwhelmingly reported in both theory and application as a well known tenet of Islam. He who denies this obligation, without an excuse of being new in Islam and not having had a chance to study it, is a dis-believer, since such a denial amounts to apostating from Islam.

Muslims have also agreed that *zakah*, as an obligation of Islam, is not required from non-Muslims because it is a part of this religion of Islam and could not be expected of he who does not believe in Islam. By the same token, *zakah* will not be considered due for the past period of disbelief for a person who converts to Islam. Muslim jurists point to the *hadith* narrated by Ibn 'Abbas in the two correct books of hadith: Bukhari and Muslim:

> The messenger of Allah (p) when he sent Mu'adh to Yemen told him: 'You are going to folks who are of the people of the Book. The first thing you call them to should be to testify that there is no god but God and that Muhammad is the Messenger of God. If they accept that, tell them that God has made it obligatory on them to pray five times every day and night. If they accept that then tell them that God has imposed *zakah* on them, to be taken from the rich among them and given to the poor among them.'[2]

This saying indicates, according to al Nawawi and others, that all obligations in Islam come only after the declaration of faith. That much is universally agreed upon.[3]

"And because *zakah* is one of the pillars of Islam," said the jurists, "it is not required from a disbeliever," In that sense, it is similar to prayer and fasting. There is another reason for the exemption of disbelievers from payment of *zakah*, mentioned by al Shirazi and approved by at Nawawi of the Shafi'ites. They both contend that *zakah* is an obligation that is not binding on disbelievers because they did not accept it to start with,[4] be they from the people of war or the people of pledge. Consequently, a disbeliever is not obligated to pay it while he remains a disbeliever, and if he converts to Islam, should not be asked for any past dues of *zakah* for the period of disbelief.[5]

Not only is *zakah* not required from non-Muslims, it is also not acceptable from them as a form of worship, since the prerequisite for its acceptance is the declaration of faith in Islam. God says: "We shall turn to whatever deeds they do (in their lives) and We shall make such deed floating dust scattered about."[6] But it should be added that good deeds reduce the severity of punishment in the hereafter, since punishment has degrees just as enjoyment has degrees.

All this applies to the born disbeliever. As for he who turns back from Islam to disbelief, *zakah* shall not be waived if it had already become due while he was Muslim. *Zakah* is a direct responsibility on Muslims and tampering with one's faith by apostating does not waive this responsibility, just as financial responsibilities and due fines may not be waived. This is the Shafiite opinion, which contradicts Abu Hanifah.[5]

As for *zakah* due on the period of apostatehood, Shafiite jurists have differences among themselves. Some say *zakah* is due for that period. I agree with them, since it is a right of the poor and other deservants and should not be waived by apostatehood. It is similar to due fines and financial responsibilities.

Why Did Islam Exempt Non-Muslims from Paying *Zakah*?

A question may occur to us when we consider that Islam has made bountiful provisions for the people of the Book and other non-Muslims, providing them with the pledge of God and the pledge of his Messenger that their lives, properties, and liberties be protected under the Islamic state and that they have the same rights and obligations as Muslims. So why then did Islam make the difference with respect to *zakah* between Muslims and non-Muslims minorities that live under the Islamic state, despite the fact that *zakah* is a social obligation and a financial due, whose proceeds help the economically weak and needy citizens of the state?

To answer this question, we should point to two considerations. The first consideration is that *zakah* is a social duty, a defined right of the needy and destitute, a financial tax obligated by God to be taken from the wealthy in the nation and rendered to its poor in fulfillment of the right of brotherhood, the right of society, and the right of God.

The second consideration is that *zakah* is a form of worship in Islam and one of the five pillars on which Islam is established. In this way, *zakah* is similar to the declaration of faith, establishment of prayers, fasting during the month of Ramadan, and pilgrimage to Makkah.

We have shown in previous pages that *zakah* is associated with prayers in tens of verses in the Qur'an. In other verses it is related to repentance from the belief in partnerships with God. Knowing that establishment of prayers is the symbol of becoming Muslim and deserving the brotherhood of other Muslims.

Additionally, some of the proceeds of *zakah* shall be spent for the support of Islam, for raising high its banner, and. for the general interests of its message and state. This is the part known as "for the sake of God." Another portion is spent on reconciling hearts with Islam and establishing them on its path. The justice of Islam, its sensitivity in dealing with non-Muslims, and its respect of their beliefs precludes obligating them to pay a due that has clear religious character to the extent that it is one of the major symbols of Islam, one of its four principal forms of worship, and one of its five tenets.

Can An Equivalent of *Zakah* Be Taken from Non-Muslims as a Tax?

After settling that *zakah* is not required religiously from non-Muslims because it is a form of worship, the question arises: Is it permissible to take an amount equal to *zakah* in the form of a regular tax from wealthy non-Muslims to be rendered to the poor? Hence for Muslims what is paid is an obligation and a form of worship while for non-Muslims it is a simple tax. By so doing we avoid differentiating between citizens of the same state by imposing a financial burden on Muslims that has no equivalent on non-Muslims, and creating technical and administrative difficulties inherent in applying different rules on Muslims and non-Muslims.

This is a new matter which needs collective *ijtihad* of capable Muslim jurists.[8] But until this is achieved, I find no reason why I should not put forward my opinion based on my research and my understanding of the subject, believing that such individual exertion of effort could open the way for a sound collective *Ijtihad*. If this opinion is correct, God alone deserves praise and if it is wrong it is I who should be blamed. What appears to me after research is that there is no reason why an equivalent to *zakah* should not be taken from the people of the pledge in the form of a tax if it is so decided by the proper authorities. The following points elaborate upon this assertion.

1.   When Muslim jurists state that *zakah* is not required from non-Muslims, they are speaking of the religious kind of requirement which is related to reward and punishment in the hereafter. There is nothing, however, that prevents its establishment as a political requirement by the proper authorities, based on public need as perceived by legislators.

2.   The reason jurists give for not obligating non-Muslims to pay *zakah* is that it is a duty to which non-Muslims did not commit themselves.[9] This means that if non-Muslims accept such a duty there is no reason why it may not become mandatory.

3.   The people of the pledge in Muslim lands used to pay a financial due to the Islamic state called by the Qur'an "*jiziah*" as a contribution towards the public expenditure of the state that provides them with protection, defense, social security, and disability, old age, and poverty insurance, like Muslims. This is clear in the action of Omar, who made these provisions when he saw some elderly jews begging at doors. The reality in Muslim countries today is that the people of the Book do not pay *jiziah* and reject the word itself. Is it thus possible that they should pay a substitute tax calculated like *zakah* but without the label of *jiziah*?

Historians, compilers of *hadith*, and jurists specialized in Islamic finance report that 'Umar bin al Khattab provided us with a precedent in this matter in his stand with the Christians of *bani Taghlib*. Abu 'Ubaid reports that al Nu'man bin Zar'ah asked 'Umar bin al Khattab about the question of *bani Taghlib*. 'Umar was about to collect *jiziah* from them, which would drive them to disperse in the land. Al Nu'man bin Zar'ah told 'Umar, "Oh Leader of Believers, *bani Taghlib* are Arabs. They are dismayed at the word *jiziah*. They don't own cash funds. They are people of agriculture and cattle and they can be instigated by our enemy. Please do not help your enemy by drifting them away." Then 'Umar reconciled with them on the condition that they pay double the amount of *zakah*.

Al Baihaqi reported from 'Ubadah bin al Nu'man, in a long saying, that the tribe argued, "We are Arabs. We don't pay what the non-Arabs pay. Take from us as your people take from each other", meaning *zakah*. 'Umar said, "No. This is an obligation on Muslims," They replied, "Impose whatever you want, but under that name, not under the name or *jiziah*." He agreed, and then they settled on doubling the amount due from them. In some versions of this saying 'Umar said, "Call it whatever you like."[10]

Imam Abu 'Ubaid comments on the action of the Leader of Believers, 'Umar, with bani Taghlib by saying, "In my opinion 'Umar used the word *zakah* and left the word *jiziah* because he noticed their abhorrence and rejection of the word *jiziah*. He feared that they would join and aid the Romans against Muslims, and realized that no harm would be done to Muslims by leaving aside that word as long as what needed to be collected was collected. So he agreed to collect the dues under the name of *zakah*, thus reconciling them with the state while still collecting their dues. He was correct in so doing, especially since it is reported in a saying from the Prophet (p) that God has put truth in the mouth and heart of 'Umar. Abdullah bin Mas'ud said, 'I have not seen 'Umar except as if an angel were on his forehead between his eyes holding him straight.'Ali is reported as having said, 'It was not unrealistic to say that wisdom always came from 'Umar's mouth,' and 'Aisha said, 'He was of a unique nature, as if he had prepared, for all difficulties, solutions that are exactly what is needed."

Abu 'Ubaid added, "What he did with *bani Taghlib* was one of those exact solutions and one of those uncountable good deeds of 'Umar."[11] So 'Umar did not see any wrong in collecting a due from Christians under the name of *zakah,* because of their dislike of the title *jiziah*, and doubled the amount of *zakah* owed by them through mutual agreement. For that reason al Zuhri said: there are no financial dues on the livestock of the people of the Book except the Christians of *bani Taghlib* or Christian 'Arabs, for whom livestock is the major part of their wealth.[12]

What 'Umar did was approved by other companions. So why can we not make a tax on the people of the pledge in Muslim countries today in place or the *jiziah* levied on them by the Islamic system. This tax would be in substitution for two mandates on Muslims, that of *jihad*, in which they sacrifice their own blood, and that of *zakah*, in which they sacrifice part of their wealth. Why could we not legislate such a tax after consultation with prominent figures, Muslim and Non-Muslims? This tax need not even be called *zakah* I believe that the act of 'Umar is an enlightening precedent for those who would like to take such an approach in contemporary circumstances with relation to problems of our age.

Shafiites and Hambalites have said, "If a group of non-Muslims was potentially powerful and refused to pay *jiziah* except with an agreement similar to that of *bani Taghlib*, and there was danger in not accepting its demand, and the Imam agreed to accept it to prevent such danger, it is permissible to do so if the amount collected from them is equal to or greater than jiziah."[13] Undoubtedly this is a sound opinion that has strong support in the action of 'Umar regarding *bani Taghlib*.

There is no doubt that *zakah* on all growing forms of wealth is much more than *jiziah*. *Jiziah* is a small due exacted from men who are capable of carrying weapons, while *zakah* is imposed on men, women, children and insane individuals according to the view of the majority of jurists. However, doubling the amount of *zakah* on the people of the people of the pledge is not necessary. 'Umar did that with *bani Taghlib* only because it was a condition of an agreement they signed and accepted. Such a matter depends on the religiously conducted political decisions and on the public interest as well as that of the state and religion.

Ibn Rushd correctly raised this question under the title of "*Zakah* on the People of the Pledge," saying, "As for the people of the pledge, the majority's view is that they are not compelled to pay zakah. The only exception is the view of some scholars concerning doubling *zakah* on the Christians of *bani Taghlib*. Shafi'i, Abu Hanifah, Ahmad, and al Thawri offered such opinions too. However, it is not reported that Ma'lik expressed such a view. The formers refer to the action of 'Umar bin al Khattab as applicable only to that specific case since it does not seem to fit with the basic rules of *Shari'ah*."[14]

I may add that we have previously quoted Abu 'Ubaid's explanation of 'Umar's move. It was not in violation of the basic rules of *Shari'ah*. Rather, it was a realization of the interests of Muslims and the removal of a potential threat to them. This means that there is no reason why it should be applicable only to that specific incident, especially in light or Prophet Muhammad's command to follow the tradition of his wise successors (al Khulaf' al Rashidin).

4. Our stance is supported by a precedent mentioned by Muhammad bin al Hasan, a disciple of Abu Hanifah. He said, "If a Muslim sells his *zakatable* land ('ushri) that is not Kharajable to a person of the pledge, that person becomes liable to the *zakah* on the land ('ushr). Being *Zakatable* is a description of land that does not change because of a change of ownership. It is not permissible to let the person of the pledge use the land without paying any dues.[15]

5. The people of the Book are ordained in their religion to perform *zakah* and to care for the poor. We have quoted earlier the verses of the Qur'an which point to this ordinance, such as the verse: "And they have been commanded no more than this: To worship God, offer Him sincere devotion, be true (in faith), to establish regular prayer, and to practice *zakah* and that is the religion right and straight."[16]

We have also quoted from their books as they exist today. Both Old and New Testaments have many statements that call for, and encourage, caring for the poor. So if the people of the Book are called to implement *zakah*, they are asked for something which has its seed in their own religion.[17] The only new issue being the estimation of the amount due and its compulsory character.

6. It is narrated from 'Umar bin al Khattab and some Followers that spending the proceeds of *zakah* on the people of the pledge is permissible. This will be discussed in detail in the part on the dispersement of *zakah*. If it is permissible to spend on them *zakah* that is collected from Muslims, why should it not be permissible to take *zakah* from their wealthy members and render it to their poor? This fulfills the social solidarity that must exist among all Muslims and non-Muslims who live under the Islamic state. In such a case, this duty may be called "tax of social insurance" or "tax of caring" or any similar name that distinguishes it from the Islamic *zakah*, so as not to disconcert their consciences or those of Muslims. The dispersement of the proceeds of each of these taxes should be distinctly separate. They are similar in ratio, rate, conditions, and the assets taxed, but they are different in name and dispersement since they have two different natures and are mandated by different authorities.

SECTION TWO

ZAKAH ON CHILDREN AND THE INSANE

Jurists who agree that *zakah* is compulsory on the funds of sane Muslims after puberty, disagree on whether it is compulsory on the funds of the child and the insane individual. There exist two contrasting points of view. The first is that *zakah* is either not obligatory at all or only mandatory on specific kinds of wealth of children and the insane, and the second asserts that *zakah* is obligatory on all of their assets.

Those Who Do Not Consider *Zakah* Required

A. Abu 'Ubaid reports from Abu Ja'far al Baqer and al Sha'bi that there is no *zakah* on the funds of the orphan.[18] Ibn Hazm mentions a similar view from al Nakh'i and Shuraih.[19]

B. It Is reported from al Hasan that there is no *zakah* on the wealth of the orphan except on agricultural products and livestock.[20] Ibn Hazm reports in *al Muhalla* that Ibn Shabrumah had a similar view.[21]

C. In *al Amwal*, Mujahid is reported as saying that any form of wealth of the orphan that has growth potential such as livestock, agricultural products, and business funds, should be zakated, and any kind of wealth that is stagnant is not *zakatable* until the orphan reaches puberty, and should then be given to him.[22] Al Lakhmi,, a Malikite jurist, stated that foregoing *zakah* on a child whose wealth does not grow is like the case in which the owner cannot make the wealth grow, e.g. buried treasure whose whereabouts are unknown, or an inheritance not know to the heir. Ibn Bashir explains that incapacitation in the case of the child is related to the nature of his ownership. There is no disagreement that for the person who must pay *zakah*, inability to invest his wealth is not sufficient reason to waive *zakah* except for the case where the property is of a stagnant Character. Ibn al Hajeb contends that the argument of al Lakhml is weak.[23]

D. Abu Hanifah and his disciples argued that *zakah* is obligatory on agricultural products only, all other assets are exempt.[24] Ibn Hazm commented that he knew of no one who preceded Abu Hanifah with such a distinction. But the author of *al Bahr al Zakhkhar* of the Zaidi school reported it from Zaid bin 'Ali and Ja'far al Sadiq,[25] contemporaries of Abu Hanifah.[26] However, it seems incredible that this view of Zaid, al Sadiq, and al Naser, who are of Ahl al Bait contradicts what is correctly reported from 'Ali. 'Ali used to pay *zakah* on funds of Abu Rafi's children, who were orphans. When Zaid was asked about this he replied, "We of Ahl al Bait deny this report."[27]

Evidence Supporting This Group of Scholars

A. This group of scholars looked mainly at the second consideration mentioned earlier, i.e. that *zakah* is a pure worship, which requires intention. Children and the insane cannot fulfill this requirement. They are not, therefore, addressed with the command of worship. Prayer is not required from them, and for the same reason, *zakah* should not be.[28]

B. This opinion is supported by *sunnah*. Prophet Muhammad (p) said, "The Pen is suspended from three: The child until puberty, the sleeping until awakening, and the insane until recovery.[29] Suspension of the Pen stands for cessation of the recording of sins and for the release from obligations, since obligation applies only to those who understand the address of God. Childhood, insanity, and sleep prevent that understanding.

C. Their stance is also supported by the holy verse, "of their goods, take *zakah* that so thou mightest purify and sanctify them."[30] Purification is needed from sins and evil. The child and the insane have none of these, and need no purification or sanctification, so they should not be among those from whom *zakah* must be taken.

It is ironic to notice that these three arguments do not stand in support of the Hanafite stance that *zakah* is obligatory on some kinds of the child's wealth and not others. On the other hand, these arguments may bolster the view of al Baqir, al Sha'bi, al Nakh'i and Shuraih since they perceive *zakah* as not required on all kinds of wealth belonging to the child and the insane.

D. The well-being of the child and the insane demands that their wealth stay intact and not be used up by *zakah* payments. Growth is not realized in the assets of the child and the insane because of their weakness and inability to sustain their matters. There is always the fear that the repetitive collection of *zakah* over years may consume all their wealth and leave them poor and in need.

This may be the reason behind the opinion of Mujahid that *zakah* is mandatory on that kind of wealth of the child and the insane that grows of its own such as agricultural products and livestock, and wealth that grows by action such as money used in business. It could also be the reason for the report that al Hasan al Basri and Ibn Shabrumah only excluded the child's gold and silver from *zakah*. As for fruits, produce, and livestock, they have considered them *zakatable* since growth is realized in them, whereas money, gold and silver do not grow except through business ventures and investment. The child and the insane cannot engage in such ventures, so they are exempt from *zakah* on this kind of wealth.

Those Who Consider *Zakah* Obligatory on the Wealth of Children and the Insane

This opinion is expressed by 'Ata', Jabir bin Zaid, Tawus, Mujahid, and al Zuhri, all of them are Followers. Of the Second Generation, Rabi'ah, Malik, al Shafi'i, Ahmad, Ishaq, al Hasan bin Saleh, Ibn Abi Laila, Ibn 'Uyainah, Abu 'Ubaid, and Abu Thawr agreed. This view is expressed by al Hadi and al Mu'ayad Billah of the Shiites; it is also the view of the Companions 'Umar, his son, Ali, 'Aisha, and Jabir. These did not make any exceptions like those made by Mujahid, al Hasan, Ibn Shabrumah, and Abu Hanifah.

The Arguments Forwarded by This Group

1. They argue that the verses and authentic sayings about the mandate of *zakah* on the assets of the wealthy are general. They do not exclude children or the insane. Take as an example the verse "Of their wealth take *zakah* that so thou mightest purify and sanctify them." Ibn Hazm explains, "and see how general it is. It includes the child, the adult, the sane and the insane. All these are in need of purification and sanctification of God. They are all believers." Similarly, the Prophet told Mu'adh before he left for Yemen: "And inform them that God imposes on their funds a *zakah* to be taken from the wealthy and rendered to the poor among them." Children and the insane receive *zakah* if they are poor, so they must pay it if they are rich. Ibn Hazm continues, 'This general text is addressed to all wealthy Muslims, including the child and the insane.'[31]

2. Al Shafi'i reported from Yusef bin Mahak that the Messenger of God, (p) said: "Invest the fund of the orphans so they may not be used up by *zakah*." The chain of narrators of this saying is correct, as confirmed by al Baihaqi and al Nawawi. But Yusef is a Follower who never met the Messenger of God (p) so his saying is *mursal*. However, al Shafi'i says that this *mursal* saying is supported by the general implication of other texts and by what is authentically reported from the Companions that *zakah* is compulsory on the assets of orphans.[32]

Al Tabarani reported in his *al Mu'jam al Awsat* from Anas bin Malik that the Messenger of God (3) said. "Make trading with the funds of the orphans so the funds may not be consumed by *zakah*." Referring to al Hafez Zain al 'Iraqi, al Haitami said in Majma' al Zawa'id[33], "I was told by my teacher and shiekh that the chain of this saying is correct.[34] Al Tirmidhi reported from 'Amr bin Shu'aib from his father from his grandfather from the Prophet (p) "He who is a guardian of an orphan should make business for the orphan and not let his assets be used up by *zakah*." The chain of this *hadith* is controversial but its meaning is reported authentically as being said by 'Umar bin al Khattab. Al Baihaqi reported through Sa'id bin al Musayyib that 'Umar bin al Khattab said, "make business with the funds of the orphans so they may not be consumed by *zakah*." Al Baihaqi found the chain to be correct and bolstered by other reports.[35] Accordingly, these ordinances of the Prophet (p) indicate that *zakah* is compulsory on the wealth of orphans since the guardians are not permitted to make any voluntary contributions out of such wealth because these contributions make the orphans unnecessarily poorer[36]. God ordained in the Qur'an that guardians must not use the funds of orphans except for the latter's best interest, until orphans reach puberty.[37]

3. The views that, are authentically reported from the Companions also support this group. Abu 'Ubaid, al Baihaqi, and Ibn Hazm report that 'Umar, Ali, Abdullah bin 'Umar, 'Aishah, and Jabir bin Abdullah said that *zakah* is obligatory on the assets of children.[38] There is no report that any Companion (m) opposed this view, except for a report from Ibn 'Abbas, which is too weak to use in argument.[38]

4. It is argued that the purpose of *zakah* itself supports this view. The intent of *zakah* is to satisfy the needs of the poor from the assets of the affluent, as a sign of thankfulness to God and purification of these assets. The fund of the child and the insane can accomodate *zakah*, just as they accomodate other financial responsibilities or fines.[40] It is argued that guardians are responsible for paying *zakah* from the funds of the two categories the same way sane adults pay it. Guardians act on behalf of the child or the insane. This is required from, them, and must be fulfilled. The intention of the guardian can substitute for the intention of the owner of the funds.[41]

Some Malikites say the guardian must only pay *zakah* for the child if he were assured that what he was doing would be later approved by the child, but if not, he is not obliged to pay. When the guardian pays *zakah* his action should be witnessed, but Ibn Habib says that if he is trustworthy, his word alone is accepted.[42] On the other hand, if the guardian fears that the child, after puberty, or the insane after recovery, would not approve that payment and ask him for compensation, the guardian, according to some Malikites should seek a ruling from a judge who believes *zakah* is mandatory from children and the insane in order to protect himself against and future liability.[43]

Weighing the Two Arguments

The evidence provided by those who regard *zakah* as mandatory on funds of children and the insane seems to outweigh that of the other view. It is the stance of the majority of scholars from among the Companions, the Followers, and later generations.

A. The universality of the texts and their covering of children and adults, sane and insane is a sound argument that should not be underestimated. God made *zakah* a right of the poor, the needy, and other deservants on the affluent. These texts did not make special provisions regarding the age or sanity of the rich, in spite of special attention *Shari'ah* gives to preserving the funds of orphans. Those who want to exclude children and the insane from *zakah* are called upon to furnish evidence from Qur'anic texts or from *hadith*.

B. The saying reported by Yusef bin Mahak commanding the investment of the funds of orphans in order not to let *zakah* payment wear them out is an authentic one. Though it is *mursal*, it has corroberating reports and it is within the general trend of the texts. Additionally, it is supported by sayings of the Companions, as well as the saying of Anas reported by al Tabarani and confirmed by al Haitami and al 'Iraqi.

C. There is no doubt that the agreement of many Companions such as 'Umar, 'Ali, ' Aisha, Ibn 'Umar, and Jabir has great importance in such an issue of public concern and frequent occurrence, especially in a society in which martyrs and orphans were plenty. No scholar would dare to neglect this agreement in understanding especially since these Companions lived at the same time as the Messenger, and were fully aware of the warnings to those who wasted the assets of orphans. It is significant that there is not a single report from any Companion to the effect that *zakah* is not mandatory on the funds of orphans. What is narrated by Ibn Mas'ud and Ibn 'Abbas is weak to the extent that it could not stand critical analysis.[44]

D. If we look carefully at the objective of *zakah* we may come to the conclusion that funds of a wealthy child or insane person should be covered by *zakah*, like other financial responsibilities on their funds. There is no doubt that *zakah* is a right of other people. It is covered by the verses, "and in their wealth, there is a defined right for he who asks and he who is destitute" and "*zakah* is only for the poor, the needy,...etc." This was the perception of the First Successor as seen in his saying to 'Umar: "By God I shall fight he who differentiates between prayer and *zakah*, since *zakah* is the right on wealth." This is reported in the two correct books (of *hadith*). There is universal agreement among scholars that the assets of the child and the insane are subject to the right of other people. Childhood and insanity do not preclude financial liability to others, including fines, due expenses, and other contractual responsibilities.[45]

Consequently, we come to the conclusion that *zakah* is binding on the wealth of children and insane individuals under the same conditions as applied to wealth of other people. With this conclusion we see that the views of the three major schools of jurisprudence outweight the view of the Hanafi school. The Hanafi School itself made *zakah* on breaking the fast and 'ushr (*Zakah* on land) obligatory on the child or the insane, so why exclude them from other forms of *zakah*? If *'ushr* is obligated, *zakah* should be. There should be no distinction between *'ushr* that is made necessary by the verse, "and give its dues the day of its harvest" and *zakah* that is made necessary by the verse,"'and in their wealth there is a right for he who asks and the destitute". Similarly, there is no justification for making a distinction between the saying there is *'ushr* (ten percent) in what is watered by the sky" and his saying, "There is one fourth of ten percent in silver currency." Therefore, the Hanafite's distinction between fruits and produce on one hand and other kinds of wealth on the other, based on the claim that the formers are provision for sustenance unlike the latter, is not justified rationally or by reference to texts. Hence Ibn Hazm came down hard against this distinction, saying, "I wonder about such acclaimed difference between *zakah* on produce and fruits and *zakah* on livestock, gold, and silver! If someone reversed it i.e., obligating *zakah* on the latter and exempting the former, would it not be as arbitrary?" Ibn Rushd said, "I am aware of no rationale for those who differentiate between produce of the land and other funds or between apparent and non-apparent assets.

Refuting the Arguments of Those Who Believe *Zakah* Is Not Obligatory

A. Those who do not obligate *zakah* on the child and the insane claim that they are not covered by the verse, "of their wealth take *zakah* that so thou mightest purify and sanctify them" because purification means cleansing from sins and the child and the insane are not sinful. However, the fact that purification is not merely removal of sins should be emphasized. Purification includes moral uplifting, psychological growth, and training to be helpful and merciful; it also means purification of the assets themselves. Even if we accept purification to be only for sins, the meaning of the verse need not be limited, according to al Nawawi.[47] *Zakah* is not only purification. It is undisputed that there is another reason for *zakah*, i.e. fulfillment of the needs of Muslims. The child and the insane, as Muslims, can share in such a fulfillment.

B. As for the saying, "The Pen is suspended from three,,,etc.", it means according to al Nawawi that those three may not be held sinful. No one claims that they are sinful. No one says *zakah* must be payed by them personally. My opinion is that *zakah* is obligatory on their assets. Their guardians are required to pay it just as they are asked to dispose of other financial responsibilities.[48] The suspension of Pen from them does not imply waiving their financial responsibilities toward others, such as wives and other relatives. Why should the responsibilities toward the needy and the wayfarer be abandoned?

C. There is the argument that *zakah* is a form of worship just like prayer and requires intention. Since the child and the insane are not liable to having intentions, they should not be required to pay *zakah*. The reply to this is that we all agree that *zakah* is a worship, the twin of prayer and one of the pillars of Islam, but it should be added that *zakah* is a distinct worship because of its financial and social character. It is a financial worship that can be done by proxy. Rules applicable to rights of others (huquq al 'ibad) apply to it. According to the Hanafites, a person of the pledge can be assigned to pay it on behalf of the *zakah* payer. Ibn Hazm adds, it is true *zakah* needs intention, but Muslims and Muslim governor are ordered to collect *zakah* by the verse, "take *zakah* out of their wealth." Therefore, if the *zakah* collector has that intention, he can take it from the funds of the absentee, the person who is in coma, the insane, and the child, without any need for their own intention.[49]

In summary, *zakah* is a financial worship that can be done by proxy, and the guardian, as an operator on behalf of the child or the insane, can fulfill it. It is unlike bodily worship such as prayer and fasting that need to be done by the person himself. Exempting the child and the insane from prayer does not mean wavering *zakah*, because each is an obligation independent from the other. God did not ordain all obligations as a package deal, so that if one become compulsory the other does, and vice versa.[50] If prayer is forgone for certain reason, *zakah* need not be abandoned. An obligation ordained by God or His Messenger can be waived only in accordance with the text from God or His Messenger. It may not be neglected without texts of the Qur'an or Sunnah because another obligation is relaxed.[51]

The statement of Abu 'Ubaid in this respect was most brilliant: The obligations of Islam must not be taken merely by analogy of one another since each of them is basic, independent and essential, each of them is performed in accordance with the way it is ordained in to Qur'an and Sunnah."[52] "Prayer is a right to God (s) on all His servants. *zakah* is a right given by God to the poor from the funds of the wealthy."[53]

The special interests of the child and the insane are to be balanced against the special interests of the poor and needy as well as those of the state and religion, and by imposing *zakah* on children and the insane their interests are not sacrificed. *Zakah* is taken from assets that grow actually or potentially. It is only obligated on properties that are in excess of essential needs. Some *hanafi* jurists went as far as considering *zakah* not obligated on money saved for necessary expenditure even if it were above the minimum assigned i.e. *nisab*. This will be discussed in Part Three,[54] and is what I see applicable on child and the insane that own only liquid funds saved for necessary expenditure, until puberty, or the expected life-span of the insane.

Three points of importance should be mentioned before we come to the conclusion of this section.

Firstly, *zakatable* children are not necessarily orphans. They may have inherited their wealth from their mother's side or from someone other than their parents. The proper title for this section should be *Zakah on the Assets of Children* and not as very often cited, *Zakah on the Assets of Orphans*. This way we can eliminate a sentimental aspect of the issue. Let us not forget that a child's wealth may come to hundreds of thousand of dinars.

Secondly, there are sayings that instruct the guardians to invest orphans' assets so such assets will not be used up by *zakah*. An example is the saying of 'Amr bin Shu'aib from his father from his grandfather that "the Messenger of God (p) gave a talk to some people saying, 'For those who guard orphans, they should make business ventures with their funds on their behalf and not leave the funds idle to be consumed by *zakah*,"[55] and the saying of Yusef bin Mahak that "the Messenger of Allah (p) said "seek investment of the funds of the orphans so they may not be used up by *zakah*."[56] Guardians of orphans are obligated to invest these funds the same way they are required to pay *zakah* out of them. It is true that there is some weakness in the chain of these two sayings but they are strengthened by the following facts:

a. The meaning is reported through other chains that support each other.[57]

b. Similar statements are correctly attributed to some Companions.

c. The order to invest orphans' funds is in line with the verse, "and feed them and clothe them therewith"[58], because the verse does not say "and feed them out of their funds" but rather "therewith", which implies the idea of using their funds for growth and investment and feeding them from the proceeds.

d. This kind of investment is well suited within the general approach of Islam in economic matters, i.e. the preference for investment and the prohibition of hoarding.

The ordinance (in the above sayings) is addressed to orphans' guardians in specific, and to the Muslims community and authorities in Muslim countries in general. It is therefore mandatory for the Muslim society and its government to preserve the funds of orphans, to see that they are invested and to provide necessary guarantees and detailed legislation to serve this purpose.

Thirdly, the Islamic society provides guarantees for orphans and the economically weak, so there should be no fear that orphans would be lost if their assets were *zakatable*. Wealthy relatives are required, legally, to guarantee the sustenance of their orphaned relatives. Orphans are also insured by the state. God said, "they ask thee what they could spend in charity. Say: Whatever thee spend that is good, is for parents, and children, and orphans, and those in want, and for wayfarers, and whatever thee do that is good, God knows it well."[59] "It is not righteousness that thee turn thy face toward east or west, but it is righteousness to believe in God, and the Last Day, and the angels, and the Books, and the Messengers, to spend of your substance - in spite of your love for it - for your kin, for orphans, for the needy, for the wayfarer, for those who ask and for the ransom of slaves."[60] "And know that out of all the booty that theee may acquire in war, a fifth share is assigned to God, and to the apostle, and to the relatives, and to the orphans, and to the needy and the wayfarer."[61] "What God has bestowed on His apostle and taken away from the people of the township belongs to God, to His apostle, and to kindred, and to orphans, and to the needy, and to the wayfarer, in order that it may not merely make a circuit between the wealthy among you."[62] Consequently, in the assets of all individuals, there exists a share for the orphans: it may be under the name of *zakah* or not. A part of the revenues of the state is assigned to orphans as ordained by God. The Prophet (p) said, "I am the guardian of every Muslim. He who is deceased and leaves behind wealth, it belongs to his heirs; if he leaves debts or children in need of care, they belong to me and my duty."[63] Therefore, if the well-being of orphans is guaranteed by the Muslim society, there is no room for fear that they may be neglected or lost if they are not wealthy.

Conclusion

Zakah is obligatory on the property of children and the insane. It is a right on those assets that is not waived by young age or insanity. It makes no difference whether those assets are in the form of livestock, agricultural produce, fruits, business assets, or money, except for liquid cash earmarked for future necessary expenditure, whereby it is not considered in excess of essential needs. The guardian of the child or the insane is required to pay *zakah* on their behalf. It is preferred, according to some Malikites, that a court order be sought so the guardian can protect himself against future claims based on Hanafite's viewpoint.

Footnotes

1. Jurists cite several studies about the obligation of *zakah* on slaves. I did not discuss this use because of its irrelevance to our time. Those who wish to study it may refer to *al Majmu'* Vol. 5, pp. 326-7, *al Mughni* with *al Sharh al Kabir* p. 494, *Rad al Muhtar*, Vol. 2, p. 5, *Bulghat al Salik*, p. 206, *Bidaiet al Mujtahid*, Vol. 1, p. 209, (al Halabi Print). The latter provides a good summary of the opinions of different schools of jurisprudence along with their supporting arguments.

2. See *Fath at Bari,* Vol.3, p. 229.

3. There is here a question of principle; Are disbelievers addressed with the detailed requirement of *Shari'ah*, so their punishment would increase in the hereafter because of lack of performance? The majority view is that they are addressed, in opposition to the Hanafites' view. However, I do not intend to discuss this side issue any further, as this is not a suitable place for it.

4. This justification brings a new issue, i.e. if the people of the pledge accept to pay *zakah* like Muslims the same way they accept nowadays military service, would it be possible to extend the rules of *zakah* to cover them, since military service for Muslims is *jihad*, which is, like *zakah*, a form of worship.

5. *Al Majmu'*, Vol. 5, pp. 327-8.

6. *Surah al Furqan*, 25:23.

7. *Al Majmu'*, Vol. 5, pp. 327-8.

8. See the article of His Eminence Professor Mustafa al Zarqa about *"Collective Ijtihad."*

9. *Al Majmu'*, Vol. 5, pp. 327.

10. *Al Amwal*, p. 541, and its footnote, p. 28-9. Ibn Hazm considered weak the story of *Bani Taghlib* (see *al Muhalla*, Vol. 6, p. 111), but it is well known, and has been reported by Ibn Abi Shaibah and Abu Yusef in *al kharaj*, p. 143 (Salafiyah Print), Yahya bin Adam in *al Kharaj*, p. 66-7, and al Balazari in *Futuh al Buldan*, p. 189 (Egypt Print 1319h). Ahmad Shakir comments on the story of *bani Taghlib*, "It is narrated by many chains of narrators so one feels satisfied of its authenticity."

11. *Al Amwal*, p. 541.

12. *Al Kharaj* by Yahya bin Adam, p. 65 (Salafiyah Print).

13. *Ahkam Ahl al Dhimmah Wal Musta'minin* (Rules of People of Pledge and Non Citizen Residents) by Dr. 'Abd al Karim Zaidan, p. 149, as quoted from *al Mughni*, Vol. 8, p. 526, and *Matn al Minhaj*, Vol. 4, p. 261.

14. *Bidaiet al Mujtahid*, Vol. 1, p. 209 (Halabi Print).

15. *Bada' i'al Sana'i'*, Vol. 2, p. 54-5, *al Hidayah* and its commentary *Fath al Qadir*, Vol. 2, p. 10. Muhammad bin al Hasan stands in opposition to the opinion of Abu Hanifah and Abu Yusuf on this matter. Abu Hanifah says the buyer is obligated by *al Kharaj* and the land becomes Karajable. Abu Yusuf says the land remains 'Ushri land but 'Ushr should be doubled as with *bani Taghlib*.

16. *Sura al Bayinah*, 98:5.

17. See Part One of this book under "The Heavenly Religions' Care of the Poor".

18. *al Aawal.* p. 453.

19. *Al* Muhalla, Vol. 5, p. 205.

20. *Al Aawal*, p. 453.

21. *Al Muhalla*, Vol. 5, p. 205.

22. *Al Amwal*, p. 453.

23. *Sharh al Risalah* by Ibn Naji, Vol. 1, p. 328.

24. *Bada'i 'al Sana'i'*, Vol. 2, p. 142 (al Sa'adah Print 1948.

25. Zaid was killed in 122h and Ja'far died in the year 148h. About the tatter Abu Hanifah said, "I haven't seen a person who has better understanding". Abu Hanifah died in 158h.

27. *Al Rawd al Nadir*, commentary on *Majam' al Fiqh al Kabir*, Vol. 2, p. 416.

28. *Rad al Muhtar*, Vol. 2, p. 4.

29. Al Nawai said this is a correct saying. It is reported by Abu Daud al Nasa'i in *Kitab al Hudud* in their respective books, as narrated from 'Ali bin Talib with an authentic chain. It is also reported by Abu Daud in *al Hudud*, al Nasa'i and Ibn Majah in *Kitab al Talaq* as by 'Aishah with a good chain. See *al Majmu'* Vol. 6, p. 253.

30. *Sura al Tawbah*, 9:103.

31. *Al Muhalla*, vol 5, pp, 201-2.

32. *Al Majmu'*, Vol. 5, p. 329, *al Sunan al Kubra*, Vol. 4, p. 107, and al Rawd al Nadir, Vol. 2, p. 417.

33. Vol. 3, p. 67.

34. Al Suyuti in *al Jami' al Saghir* (Halabi Print with commentary: *Faid al Qadir*) referred to it with a "correct" mark. But it seems that this mark was not the original of the author. The commentator al Kanawi said that al Suyuti marked it with the sign "correct" in his book Jami' al Jawami', while here he only marked it with "good". However, al Hafez Ibn Hajar supports the good marks only. *Faid al Qadir*, Vol. 1, p. 108.

35. *Al Sunan al Kubra*. Vol. 4, p. 107. See also *al Majmu'*, Vol. 5, p. 329.

36. *Muqaranat al Madhahib fi al Fiqh* by Mahmud Shaltut and Muhammad al Sayes, p. 48 (1953); also *al Mughni* (Printed with *al Sharh al Kabir*) Vol. 2, p. 493.

37. As in verse 152 of *Sura al An'am* (5) and verse 34 of *Sura al Israa'*.

38. See *al Amwal*, p. 448, *al Sunan at Kubra*, p. 107, *al Muhalla*, Vol. 5, p. 208, *Musannaf Ibn Abi Shaibah*, Vol. 4, pp. 24-5, and *al Talkhis by Ibn Hajar*, p. 176. Al Nawawi added in *al Majmu'*, Vol. 5, p. 329, al Hasan bin Ali too. He did not add Ibn Mas'ud because the report from him is weak as stated in *Sunan al Baihaqi, al Majum',* and *al Talkhis*. Al Nawawi's opinion if that the guardian should keep a record of all *zakah* due on the assets of the orphan. When the latter reaches puberty he should be informed and it is up to him to pay *zakah*.

39. *Al Muhalla*, Vol. 5, p. 330.

40. *Al Mughni*, Vol. 2, p. 494.

41. *Sharh al Risalah*, Vol. 1, p. 329.

43. *Hashiyet al Sawi Ala al Dardir*, p. 206.

44. See *Mura'at al Mafatih* by al Mubarakburi, Vol. 3, p. 25.

45. *Bada'i 'al San'i'*, Vol. 2, p. 4-5, and *Rad al Muhtar*, Vol. 2, p. 4.

46. *Bidaiet al Mujtahid*, Vol. 2, p. 209 (Halabi Print).

47. He said in *al Majmu'* that most likely it is a purification but this is not a condition since we agree that *zakah* of al fitr and al 'Ushr are obligatory on their funds, even though originally all these are purifications. Vol. 5, p. 330.

48. *Al Majmu'*, Vol. 5, p. 330, *al Mughni,* Vol. 2, pp. 493-4, and *Muqaranet al Madhahib*, p. 49.

49. *Al Muhalla'*, Vol. 5, p. 206.

50. *Al 'Umm* by al Shafi'i, Vol. 2, p. 24 (Bulaq Print).

51. *Al Muhalla*, Vol. 5, p. 206.

52. *Al Amwal*, p. 454. Abu 'Ubaid made a full account of the differences between the two obligations.

53. *Al Amwal*, p. 455.

54. In Chapter I under the title "Excess Over Essential Needs."

55. Reported by al Tirmidhi and al Daraqutni.

56. See footnotes 34 above.

57. Al 'Iraqi considered some versions of its chain correct.

58. *Sura al Nisa'*, 4:5.

59. *Sura al Baqarah*, 2:215.

60. *Sura al Baqarah*, 2:177.

61. *Sura al Anfal*, 8:41.

62. *Sura al Hashr*, 59:7.

63. Agreed upon.

FIQH AL ZAKAH

PART THREE

ZAKATABLE WEALTH IN TERMS OF ITS AMOUNT AND RATIOS

1. Assets that are *zakatable*

2. *Zakah* on livestock.

3. *Zakah* on gold, silver currency and jewelry.

4. *Zakah* on commercial assets.

5. *Zakah* on agriculture.

6. *Zakah* on honey and animal products.

7. *Zakah* on mining and fishing.

8. *Zakah* on rented buildings, plants, and fixed capital.

9. *Zakah* on salaries, wages, and professional incomes.

10. Other *zakatable* items (bonds, stocks, and shares).

CHAPTER ONE

ZAKATABLE ASSETS

The Qur'an does not give the definition of *zakatable* wealth nor does it provide the required percentages in *zakah*. It is left to Sunnah to give, by example or by directives, details of the general Qur'anic command and to convert the theoretical axioms of the Qur'an into a living reality in human life. The Prophet (p) was assigned this responsibility and he is the one who knows most about what God ordains in His Holy Book. God says, "And we have sent down unto thee the message that thou mayest explain clearly to people what is sent for them and that they may give thought."[1] It must be realized, however, that the Qur'an mentions a few kinds of *zakatable* assets, such as (1) gold and silver, in the verse "and there are those who hoard gold and silver and spend it not in the way of God. Announce unto them a most grievous penalty."[2] (2) crops and fruits that are refered to in "Eat of their fruit in their season, but render the dues that are proper on the day that the harvest is gathered,"[3] (3) earnings of trade and other business enterprises, refered to in the verse, "0 ye who believe, give of the good things which ye have earned,"[4] and (4) what is drawn from beneath the earth, "And of that which we have produced for you from the earth,"[5]

Except for these items, the Qur'an mentions *zakah* in general and the word *amwal* [assets or wealth] in its plural form, such as in the verse, "Out of their wealths take *sadaqah* so by it you purify and sanctify them,"[6] and "In their wealths and properties is the right of the poor, he who asks, and he who is deprived."[7]

The Meaning of Amwal in Arabic and in *Shari'ah*

The word *amwal* [meaning: wealth, property, goods, possessions] that is mentioned in the Qur'an is the plural of the word *mal*. *Mal* meant in the minds of Arabs at the time of the Qur'anic revelation all things that people like to acquire and own, including, for example, camels, cows, sheep, land, palm orchards, gold, and silver, Arabic dictionaries such as *al Qamus* and *Lisan al Arab*[9] defined the word *mal* as all things one owns, knowing that bedouins use the word more in reference to their livestock and urban dwellers us it in reference to gold and silver, despite the fact that all are *mal*. Ibn al 'Athir says the original meaning of the word *mal* refers to owned gold and silver, and was then generalized to include all material things that are obtained and owned.

Jurists express several opinions on the meaning of the word *mal* in *Shari'ah*. Hanafite jurists say *mal* is everything that a person acquires and usually uses, so there are two conditions for anything to be *mal*: The possibility of acquiring it, and the possibility of using it in general. Consequently *mal* includes all that is owned--land, animals, furniture, equipment, and money. As for things that are not actually acquired or usually used, if there exists a possibility of obtaining and using them, then they are considered *mal*, such as lawful things like fish in the sea, birds flying in the sky or wild usable animals in the wilderness. Things that cannot be acquired are not considered *mal* even though they may be useful, such as sunlight and heat. By the same token, things that are usually not usable but can be obtained, such as a handful of soil, a drop of water, one bee, or one grain of rice are not *mal*. This definition implies that *mal* must be a material thing, because non-material things cannot be obtained. Consequently, services are not *mal*, such as inhabiting a house, riding car, or wearing a garment, because these are not acquirable. Similarly, rights , like custodianship and guardianship rights are also not mal.

Shafi'ite, Malikite, and Hanbalite jurists consider services as *mal*. According the them the possibility of acquisition is not a condition; rather, the condition is the possibility of obtaining the source of *mal*. Since the car can be acquired physically, its utility is considered a *mal*. Scholars of man-made laws consider both utilities and rights such as authorship rights and patents as *amwal*. This means that *mal* in human-made laws includes more than what it includes for the jurists.[10] My opinion is that the definition of the Hanafites seems to be closer to the linguistic meaning given in dictionaries, and more sensible to the application of the texts on *zakah*, since it is material assets and not services that can be *zakatable*. *zakah* cannot be collected from utilities and distributed to the deserving categories. Ibn Nujaim in his *al Bahr* states that *mal* is what can be obtained and saved to be used at the time of need, and this can only be applied to material things, excluding utilities. The author of *Kashf al Kabir* says *zakah* can only be fulfilled by giving the recipient a material thing that has value, so if a poor person was allowed to inhabit free of charge the house of a *zakah* payer, this would not fulfill the responsibility of the payment of *zakah*, since this utility is not a material thing that can be acquired. Ibn Nujaim continues, "This is one opinion. The other is, however, that the utility is also a *mal*. But when the word *mal* is used, without any specification, it applies to material acquisitions only."[11] For the purpose of this book, *mal* means material things, and that is where *zakah* applies.

Conditions for *Zakatability* of a *mal*

If we agree that all obtainable and owned materials are *mal*, is *zakah* required on all kinds of *mal*, no matter how little it may be or how much the owner is in need of it? A house inhabited by the owner is a *mal*, as are clothes worn and books used and tools of professionals who work with their hands. Is *zakah* required on all these ? Is a bedouin who owns only two she-camels or a few sheep, from which he derives his essential food, *zakatable*. How about a peasant whose crop is only a small quantity that can barely satisfy the food needs for his household, or a businessman who has inventory and cash funds, but at the same time is overridden by debts that are in excess of his business assets? Are all these *zakatable*? Justice in Islam and easiness in *Shari'ah* would not allow such people to be burdened by what brings great difficulty and uneasiness into their lives. Consequently, it is important to define the conditions of *zakatable* assets as in the following sections:

1. Undivided and absolute right of ownership

All *mal* in the ultimate analysis belongs to God. He is the creator of it, He is the one who gives it for human sustenance. Qur'an repeatedly refers to this final reality, either by attributing *mal* to God, such as in "And give them out of the wealth of God that He has given,"[12] and "0 ye who believe, spend out of the bounty We have provided for you"[13] and refers to "those who covetuously withhold of the gifts which God has given them of His grace."[14] Qur'an also refers to humans as only vicegerents or agents with regard to the wealth they own, such as in the verse, "And spend out of the sustenance whereof He has made you vicegerent."[15] God, although He is the true owner, honors His servants with the privilage of authority over the bounties He bestows on them, and holds them responsible and accountable for what they control. It is like when a father gives his child some of his property in order to make the child experience his or her independence and test him or her with that. It is no surprise, therefore, that Qur'an mentions wealth (*amwal*) as attributed to people: "0 ye who believe, let not your riches. . .."[16] "Your riches and your children are only a trial,"[17] "thinking that his wealth would make him last forever,"[18] "No profit to him from all his wealth and all his gains,"[19] "And in their wealth there is a right of the needy, he who asks, and he who is deprived,"[20] "Out of their wealth take *sadaqah*,"[21] "Let not their wealth nor their sons dazzle thee,"[22] and "Then release their wealth to them,"[23] "Eat not up your wealth among yourselves in vanities,"[24] etc.

God highly honors humans by sometimes using the phrase "borrowing from people " those assets, although they are in fact bestowed by God upon His servants. God says, "Who is he that will loan to God a beautiful loan which God will double unto his credit and multiply many times,"[25] "Who is he that will loan to God a beautiful loan, for God will increase manyfold his credit and he will have a liberal reward,"[26] "And loan to God a beautiful loan,"27. "God hath purchased of the believers their persons and their wealth, for theirs in return is the Garden."28 Al Hasan comments that here God "buys" persons that he created and wealth that he bestowed.

Ahmad bin 'Abd al Rahim al Dahlawi, the philosopher of Islam in India, comments on the verses that attribute ownership to human beings, "When God made it permissible for people to use what He created for them in and on the earth, people got greedy about things, so there was a need to establish a rule based on the priorities of acquiring things. So all land is for all human beings, but those who come first are served first. Consequently, the human ownership of these created things depends on the priority of extracting utilities and usefullness."[29]

However, it should be pointed out that by titling this section "undivided and absolute right of ownership" I do not mean the ultimate ownership which belongs to God alone. What is meant here is the right of control of assets and material things as attributed to humans in the above-mentioned verses.

After this rather lengthy introduction, we will define what is meant by "undivided and absolute ownership." This is a jurist's term that is composed of two factors, *milk* [ownership] and absoluteness of ownership. *Milk* [ownership] is the noun from the root *Malaka* [to own] which means to obtain and have control and authority of disposition of, as stated in *al Qamus*. In *al Mu'jam al Wasit*, the verb "*malaka* means obtain and have exclusive right of disposition over. This linguistic meaning is included by the meaning in *Shari'ah,* as defined by jurists. Al Kamal bin al Humam, in his *al Fath*, defines ownership as the power of disposition which is original and not derived from another person.[30] Al Qarafi in his *al Furuq* defines ownership as "A *Sahri'ah* conjunction on material things or on their utilities which allows the person to whom things belong to utilize them and/or their services, or to exchange them for a substitute, except when lawful obstacle [that prevents the exercise of such authority] exists."[30] Sadr al *Shari'ah,* in his commentary on *al Wiqayah*, defines the right of ownership as a legal relation between a person and materials whereby the person is absolutely authorized to use the material, an authorization that prevents others from having any power on that thing.[31] All these definitions include the idea of exclusiveness that is refered to in Arabic dictionaries. Experts in law have similar definitions. For them, ownership is an "authority that enables the owner to use the owned thing and get the benefit of all its utilities in a perpetual and exclusive manner,"[31]

The meaning of absoluteness and undividedness of the ownership is that the owned material is exclusive to the owner.[32] No one else has any share in it, nor does the owner's right to use it depend on authorization from others.[32] For that reason, it is said that whenever the right of ownership is not absolute, such as merchandize purchased but not yet received, *zakah* is not obligated. Nor is *zakah* obligated in the case in which the asset is used as a lien and held by the lien holder, or the asset is stolen and actually in the possession of the thief.[34] Jurists express the condition of absoluteness of ownership by the ability to dispose of the asset, as is known among the Zaidis: Zaidis require for *zakatability* that the owner must have authority of disposition over *nisab* throughout the whole year, or at least that the owner has sufficient reason to hope that if he so wishes he can have total authority of disposal, such as if he has funds deposited with others. Zaidis say if the owner does not have that power of disposal or sufficient reason for hope of having it at his wish, then *zakah* is not required on that *mal*.[35]

The rationale of this condition

Private ownership is a great bounty from God. It is one of the fruits of freedom and of humanity itself. Animals do not own; humans do. Ownership gives the feeling of authority and power and satisfies the acquisitive desire. Complete ownership enables people to extract benefits of owned materials, as well as putting assets to growth. The grace from God should be recognized by people. The payment of *zakah* is an expression of thankfulness to God and recognition of his bounty.

The proof of this condition

This condition is justified by two major points. Firstly, the fact that assets and wealth are attributed to people in Qur'an and Sunnah implies that *zakatable* individuals must have owned these assets. This general form of ownership requires owning in an exclusive manner. Secondly, the performance of *zakah* requires that the recipients such as the poor and destitute, should become owners of what is given them. They cannot be made owners if the *zakah* payers do not have complete right of ownership on what they are paying.

Imliplications of this condition

1. The case of assets that do not have a specific owner

This condition Implies that assets that do not have a specific person as owner should be *unzakatable*, such as the state's revenue collected from taxes, *zakah*, and other sources. These are not *zakatable* because they are not owned by a person and the right to them belongs to the whole society, including the poor and needy. Additionally, the government is the agency that collects *zakah* and there is no reason that it should collect from itself. Scholars have said, "There should be no *zakah* on state resources like fai' [taken from enemies without fighting] or on the government's share of *ghanimah* [gained as a result of lawful war with enemies] because these revenues belong to all Muslims and are spent for their benefits."[36] In general, all publicly owned property is not *zakatable*.

2. Property in public trust

Property put in public trust for, say, the poor, mosques, orphans, schools, fighters for the sake of God, etc., are not *zakatable*. On the other hand, property of private trusts that are withheld for the benefit of an individual or a group of beneficiaries, such as children's trusts, are *zakatable*, since the right of private ownership is transferred on these properties to the benefit of the children, although they cannot, for some time, dispose of the property themselves.[37] This is more similar to privately owned things than to public trusts, since the most important element of private ownership is the exclusivity of benefit of the property and this feature exists in private trusts. Some jurists, however, consider *zakah* obligated on all trusts, public and private. Ibn Rushd says, "it seems that imposing *zakah* on public trusts designated for the benefit of the indigent is meaningless, for two reasons. One, their ownership is incomplete, and two, they are not *zakatable* but rather recipients of *zakah*."[38]

3. Unlawful wealth

This condition excludes from *zakatability* wealth acquired by unlawful means, such as theft, counterfeiting, bribery, interest, monopoly or cheating. This may include the most part of the wealth of autocratic rulers, interest financiers, thieves, etc. Such individuals do not indeed own the stolen properties which are in their hands, although they might have mixed them with property obtained by lawful means. Scholars declare that evil wealth is not *zakatable* because all such wealth must be returned to its true owner if known, or to his or her heirs, and if not, then to the poor and needy. It is not sufficient that only a small part of such assets is given out as *zakah*.[39] The authentic saying speaks for itself: "God does not accept *sadaqah* from stolen property."[40]

Jurists justify the un*zakatable* of such wealth by the fact that it is not owned by those who have actual control. Therefore, the latter has no authority to pay *zakah* or to make any other disposal except rendering it to the lawful owner.[41] Thus a person whose methods of gain are unlawful is not considered rich in *Shari'ah* even though ha might control huge wealth. Some Hanafite jurists, including al Sarakhsi, go to the extent of permitting giving charity to dictators on the grounds that they are in fact poor, although they unlawfully dispose of the riches of the whole country.[42] Such bold opinions mean to us that unlawfully acquired wealth cannot be owned or transferred to heirs or any other recipient.[43] On the other hand, giving charity, per se, to such oppressors is not acceptable because, although they are legally poor, they use their holdings to oppress people and for other evil purposes. The rule is that even a poor person should not be given *zakah* if it is known that he uses such income for disobedience of God.[44]

4. *Zakah* on debts

Another implication, of this condition relates to *zakah* on debts. Who should pay such *zakah*, the creditor, the debtor, or both? None of the jurists would say both. 'Ikramh and 'Ata are reported to be of the opinion that both are not *zakatable*, on the basis that the debtor does not own it while the creditor does not have control of it.[45] Ibn Hazm reports from 'Aishah, the Mother of the Faithful, "There should be no *zakah* on debts," This means that both parties are not *zakatable*. Ibn Hazm and his Zahiri colleagues support this opinion on the grounds that the right of ownership of each of the debtor and the creditor is incomplete. The debtor does not own borrowed property although he makes use of it, while the creditor does not have control over the debt and does not extract benefit from it. The author of *al Amwal* attributes to al Nakha'i that "unreasonably delayed debts are *zakatable* by debtors."[46] This opinion is a violation of the condition of completeness of ownership which is almost unanimous among all jurists.

The majority of jurists since the era of the Companions distinguishes between two kinds of debts. One is a debt whose creditors hope to receive it back, meaning debts on parties who are capable of payment. *zakah* is obligated on this category of debts yearly, as if they were property under control. Abu 'Ubaid reports this opinion from the Companions 'Umar, 'Uthman, Ibn 'Umar, and Jabir, and from the Followers Jabir bin Zaid, Mujahid, Ibrahim, and Maymun bin Mahran.[47] Second, doubtful or dead debts, which are debts on individuals who are incapable of repayment or are denied by debtors, There are three views about *zakah* on these debts, (a) the creditor must pay *zakah* for all past years upon receiving the debt back if ever. This is the opinion of the Companions 'Ali and Ibn 'Abbas, (b) the creditor, on receipt of the debt must pay *zakah* for only the last year. This is the view of al Hasan, and 'Umar bin 'Abd al 'Aziz. It is also the view of Malik on all debts,[48] and (c) the creditor does not owe any *zakah* whatsoever and the debt when paid back starts a new year of *zakatability*, which is the view of Abu Hanifah and his two disciples.[49] Abu 'Ubaid selects the opinion that if the creditor hopes to got back the debt, it should be *zakated* as if the debt was part of the current assets, in accordance with 'Umar, 'Uthman, Jabir, and Ibn 'Umar. However, Abu 'Ubaid cautiously allows deferring the payment of *zakah* until the receipt of the amount of the debt, provided that *zakah* is paid strictly for all preceeding years. As for doubtful and dead debts, Abu 'Ubaid selects the opinion of 'Ali and Ibn 'Abbas, payment of *zakah* by the creditor for all past years upon receiving the amount of the debt back. He argues that since the right of ownership on the debt is not annuled by the doubtfulness, then the right of God should also remain.[50] I agree with Abu 'Ubaid on the first case, but I differ with him on the case of doubtful and dead debts, because the right of ownership on such debts is not complete, since the creditor has no hope of extracting benefit and of disposing of the debt.[51] This is also the argument of Abu Hanifah and his two disciples. That is, all assets whose owner is not capable of extracting benefit from them should be excluded from *zakatability*, since such an owner is not rich and *zakah* is only imposed on the rich.[52] I agree with Abu Hanifah that all doubtful and dead debts are, like assets whose owner is incapable of benefiting from, *unzakatable* for all past years. But when the debts is received, it should be treated as a newly earned asset, although I prefer that the creditor, upon receipt of the debt, pay *zakah* for one year only, like on any other newly earned asset.

5. Grants and savings of employees

A common question arises at this time about the retirement savings and grants that are retained by governments, employers, or any independent agency without giving the employee direct access to the fund, except upon retirement or termination of employment. The *zakatability* of such funds is determined by whether they can be defined as completely owned by the employees. Can they dispose of them at will or not? Are these funds the right of the employees or mere grants whose amounts and eligibility requirements will be determined at the time of retirement? If they are purely grants or gifts, they accrue only to the employee at the time of receipt. But if they are part of what the employee has access to and may dispose of at will, then they should be treated like debts whose debtors are capable and ready to pay, i.e. they are *zakatable* every year, once they reach the minimum for *zakatability*, as will be discussed later.[53]

6. Growth

The second condition for *zakatability* is that wealth must either be actually growing or have the potential for growth. Growth means something that provides the owner with profit and benefit. Or the asset itself should be the result of growth, being surplus or a newly accrued item. "This has been established by Muslim jurists in a clear and specific manner. Linguistically, "growth" is any surplus. In *Shari'ah*, growth has two meanings, actual and potential growth. Actual growth is the increase by Genetic or business reasons. Potential growth is when the asset can increase if it is used properly for that purpose. This implies the availability of the asset for potential use.[54]

The rationale for this condition

Ibn al Humam writes, "*zakah* is legislated to help and relieve the poor without impoverishing the rich, by having the rich pay from their surplus, taking a little from the plenty. Imposing *zakah* on wealth that does not, be definition, grow, reverses this purpose, since *zakah* is paid year after year, in addition to living expenses."[55] This condition of growth applies the saying of the Messenger of God (p) "Wealth never decreases as a result of *sadaqah*,"[56] since the payment of a small fraction as *zakah* out of growing wealth does not make the wealth decline. What is important, however, is the growth potential of the assets and not actual growth, because actual growth can hardly be measured and is subject to differences in measurement.

According to the author of *al Mughni*, it is mentioned in *al Bada'i'* that "the very naming of *zakah*--as growth or increase--is not realized except in growing assets. It is not necessary, however, for wealth to actually grow, but the ability to grow through business, animal breeding, or seed planting, is sufficient, since growth by reproduction, profit, and multiplicity is realized by those means. The possibility of using the means is alone sufficient. This is similar to traveling, which allows the traveler to reduce prayer even if he can pray without hardship."[57] On the other hand, the asset itself may be a result of growth, as in crops and fruits. In this case, *zakah* is only obligated after growth has happened.

The proof for this condition

This condition is derived from the spoken and practiced tradition of the Prophet (p), which was sustained in application by his successors and Companions. The Prophet (p) does not obligate *zakah* on assets which are obtained for personal use, as indicated by the correct saying, "A Muslim is not *zakatable* for his [or her] mare or for his [or her] servant."[58] Al Nawawi' says, "This saying plants the seed for the principle that assets obtained for personal use are not *zakatable*." The Prophet did not impose *zakah* except on growing and producing assets, of which Arabs at his time had several kinds:
- Livestock such as camels, cows, and sheep
- money, gold or silver used as cash business assets and as savings
- crops and fruits, especially basic foods, such as wheat, barley, date, and raisin. Honey goes with this category.
- treasures hidden underground by ancients and minerals stored by ancients and minerals stored by God inside and on the surface of the earth.

About the dispersement of the proceeds of dues on this last category, there are two opinions. One is that it should be treated like *zakah*, and the other is that it should be treated like fai [property taken from enemies who surrender without fighting].

Jurists who believe that rulings of *Shari'ah* are always justifiable-- and they are the majority-- have agreed that the justification for *zakatability* on the above mentioned assets is actual or potential growth. Livestock physically grows by weight increase, reproduction and milk production. Business assets also grow; they are there to make profit and bring return. This growth is not simply natural like that of animal and agricultural wealth, but is caused by the action of people. Since it is considered lawful in Islam as well as in all heavenly and earthly religions and laws, business growth is put in the same category as natural growth. Money also grows, because it is the means of exchange and the measure of value as a substitute of goods. When money is used in industry and trade, it brings income, which is what is meant by growth in this section. If money is hoarded and prevented from fulfilling its role in circulation and production, the hoarder is held responsible for leaving it idle. He is not by that action exempt from *zakah*, but rather, *zakah* gives him the signal to utilize his money in growth and useful business, otherwise it will perish. Crops and fruits are themselves the result of growth, being produced by the process of agricultural reproduction. Honey, discovered treasures, and minerals are similar.

This condition is founded by jurists on the basis of the guidance of the Messenger of God and the practice of the Wise Successors. It is also consistent with the meaning of *zakah* itself, since one of the meanings of the word "*zakah*" is growth. What is being paid as *zakah* is given this name because it brings blessing and growth, in accordance with the promise of God "and nothing do ye spend in the least in His cause but He replaces it,"[59] and "that which ye lay out for *zakah* seeking the countenance of God, will increase. It is these who will get a recompense multiplied."[60] Giving the name *zakah* for what is paid in fulfillment of the requirement of *zakah* may have yet another meaning, according to some scholars. That is, the amount paid is called *zakah* because it comes out of surplus or excess that is the result of the process of growth,. Consequently, *zakah* is obligated on growing assets, and not on assets held for personal and family use.[61] In application of this condition, Muslims since the early stages exempted animals used for personal transportation, homes inhabited by the owner, tools of professionals, and household furniture from *zakah*. Also exempted are assets that cannot be made to grow, such as assets unlawfully controlled by others.[62]

On the other hand, it is because of this condition that scholars declare that *zakah* on crops and fruits does not repeat every year. Once the ten percent *zakah* is paid on them, no more *zakah* is imposed even though these crops and fruits may remain owned in storage by the same owner for several years, because crops and fruits after being harvested do not grow anymore, and *zakah* is repeated yearly only on growing assets. In contrast, livestock is *zakatable* every a year because of its continuous growth.[63] It should be pointed out that the school of Malik extends the application of this condition more than other schools. One of these applications is related to debts. Since all kinds of debts do not grow, they are, according the Malikites, *unzakatable*, but once they are paid back, the creditor must pay *zakah* on debts for the last year only. Similarly, *zakah* on lost property is only due once the property is found, and for one year only. According to Malik, this applies to all debts, whether good or bad, except for strong debts owed to non-monopolistic businesses, which are *zakatable* as part of the net worth of businessmen.[64]

According to Malikites, the exemption of all debts from *zakah* is simply an application of this condition for growth. Additionally, Malik goes as far as exempting monopolistic traders (who keep their inventory for years) from *zakah* on the basis that inventory does not increase during this period. This is assuming that inventory shows an increase only at the time of selling. Malik says, at that time, inventory is *zakatable* for the past year only.[65]

Assets whose owners are not able to invest

Since growth, actual or potential, is a requirement for *zakatability*, what should be the status of wealth whose owner does not make it grow?

A distinction must be drawn between two cases of idleness from growth of an asset: idleness implied by the nature of the asset such as hopeless debts and stolen property, and idleness caused by the owner. In the former case, the asset is not *zakatable*, but once the owner becomes able again to make it grow, such as lost/found treasure, then the asset is *zakatable* only from that year on. On the other hand, if the incapability of investment is caused by the owner, i.e. if the owner withholds his wealth from investment, then he is not excused from the yearly payment of *zakah*. It is assumed that Muslims would do their best to invest their assets.

Incapability to make one's assets grow is not an excuse for exemption from *zakah*.[66] Inability to invest is rather blameable because it indicates lack of will or means on the part of the owner. Against this kind of incapability, the Prophet (p) strongly warned and he reprimanded those who have it. He used to pray, "My Lord, I seek your protection from incapability and laziness."[67] Abu Hurairah narrates from the Prophet, "Be keen to hold to what benefits you, seek the help of God, and do not stay incapable or stand still,"[68] and the Prophet once told a man, "God verily reprimands for incapability."[69]

All growing assets are subject to *zakah*

This condition of growth for *zakatability* can be used as a criterion for determining kinds of wealth that are subject to *zakah*, even if they were not specifically mentioned by the Prophet (p), as long as they are covered by the general texts of Qur'an and Sunnah. This is not accepted by some jurists who restrict *zakah* to those items mentioned by the Prophet (p). Ibn Hazm, for example, restricts *zakah* in his *al Muhalla* to eight kinds of wealth: camels, cows, sheep, wheat, barley, date, gold, and silver.[70] For him even raisin is not *zakatable*, nor is livestock other than camels, cows, and sheep. The same applies to agricultural crops except wheat, barley, and date, and to minerals and currencies except gold and silver. Moreover, according to him, there should be no *zakah* on business assets. Jurists differ on the extent to which *zakah* is obligated as far as the different kinds of wealth are concerned. While some are very restrictive, others are liberal. Abu Hanifah is one of those who extend *zakatability* to most kinds. For example he considers *zakatable* all that is produced by the land, without any minimum; he includes horses with livestock in *zakatability*; he obligates *zakah* on jewelry. On the other hand, *zakah* in his view is not required from all minors and insane individuals, nor does he require the tenth on the output of *kharaji* land owned by Muslims.

The theory of Ibn Hazm, and those who restrict *zakatability* along with him, such as Shawkani and Siddiq Hasan Khan, is based on two principles: That a Muslim's wealth is protected and must not be taken, so nothing must be imposed on it without virtue of a text; and that *zakah* is a religious obligation. Thus, in order to prevent anyone from incorporating in religion anything that God does not ordain, it is necessary that people must not be obligated without a text. Analogy should especially not be used in the area of *zakah*.

My theorem is exactly opposite. It is based on other equally important principles in *Shari'ah*:

1. The general texts of Qur'an and Sunnah confirm that there is a right, a *sadaqah*, or a *zakah*, on all wealth. The verse, "and those on whose wealth there is a recognized defined due," and "Out of their wealth take *sadaqah*," and the saying of the Prophet "Inform them that God prescribed on them in their wealth a *sadaqah*, taken from the rich among them to be rendered to the poor among them," and "Pay the *zakah* on your wealth." These texts do not distinguish between kinds of wealth. We know that the word *'amwal*" in Sunnah means growing assets and not those things designated for personal use. It is not allowed to exclude some kinds of wealth from this *zakah* or *sadaqah* without clear evidence. Alas, there is no such evidence.

2. Each rich person is in need of purification and sanctification--sanctification through giving for the sake of God and purification from miserliness, selfishness, and overwhelming desire for money. God says, "Out of their wealth take *sadaqah*, so thou mightest purify and sanctify them." It is unreasonable to think that peasants who own wheat and barley should be purified and sanctified while owners of large orchards or landlords of luxurious high-rises or owners of factories are not in need of that purification and sanctification. The return on the latter's property is manifold that on wheat and barley.

3. Wealth of any kind is in need of purification, since it may have been mixed with some sort of unlawfulness in the process of its generation and earning. Purification of wealth can only be done by the payment of *zakah*, and it is authentically reported from Ibn 'Umar that "God has verily imposed *zakah* as a purification of wealth." It is also reported in some sayings, "If you pay *zakah* on your wealth, you would have removed its evil."[71] It does not seem rational to restrict such purification to the eight items mentioned by Ibn Hazm and to exclude the bulk of the other kinds of wealth which are nowadays the backbone of private and public wealth since all kinds of wealth are in need of purification.

4. *zakah* is ordained in order to satisfy the needs of the poor, the destitute, and the wayfarers, and to pay for the fulfillment of some public affairs of the Muslim community, such as *jihad* for the sake of God, reconciling hearts to Islam, and helping those who carry disproportionately large burdens of financial responsibility in the public interests of Muslims. The satisfaction of these needs and the achievement of those interests is a duty of all rich individuals. It is unthinkable that *Shari'ah* meant to throw this burden on those who own five camels or forty sheep or five *wusq* of barley and exempt big businessman who own factories, buildings, and other businesses, or professionals, such as physicians, lawyers, executives, etc., who earn in one day much more than five camels or forty sheep. According to this religion of Islam, riches are in reality the property of God, humans being only vicegerents or agents. The right of poor

brethren who are in need is established on these riches because they are dependent on God. By the same token, the public interests of the nation also have rights on those riches. Every rich person must share this responsibility, whether he or she invests in agriculture, industry, business, or professional services.

5.   Analogy, as was shown earlier, is one of the essential axioms of *Shari'ah*, according to the majority of scholars, despite the disagreement of Ibn Hazm and other Zahiris. Consequently, I say that every growing wealth is *zakatable* by analogy to those items mentioned by the Messenger, We are certain that *Shari'ah* does not treat differently those who are similar, nor does it treat similarly those who are different, thus we can use analogy in the matter of *zakatability*. This cannot be tagged as addition to religion, which is not allowed by God, especially since *zakah* is not a pure worship but an essential component of the socio-economic system in Islam as well.

6.   No one would disagree with the postulate that "the wealth of a Muslim is protected, and he/she has a right to private ownership." But it can be shown that the right of God, the right of the community, and the right of those who are in need of *zakah* are also well established by the texts themselves. Ibn Hazm agrees with this principle because he believes that on assets of individuals there are rights besides *zakah*. He further gives authority to the government to force the rich to pay for the support of the poor, and even says that the poor have the right to revolt until their needs are satisfied. Ibn Hazm would have been more sensible had he imposed *zakah* on all items of wealth before talking about additional dues to satisfy the needs of the poor. After the complete practice of *zakah* on all items of wealth, if there is still need for more funds, additional dues can be imposed.

At last I should address myself to the allegation that *zakah* should not be extended to items from which the Prophet did not take *zakah*. Two points should be raised with this regard: Firstly, the growth of such items was very negligible in his time, so he did not consider it. Secondly, he left *zakah* on such items to the individual practice and the conscience of the owner. If the Messenger of God did not collect *zakah* from certain items, this does not necessarily mean that they are not *zakatable* on the initiative of individuals, especially if the latter are informed as to the requirement of zakah and the need of all items to be purified.

3.   Reaching the minimum For *zakatability*.

Islam does not impose *zakah* on all amounts of growing wealth. There is a minimum required for *zakatability*, which is called among jurists "*nisab*". Sayings of the Prophet (p) exempt anything that is less than five camels, forty sheep, two hundred dirhams of silver, or five *wasq* of grain, fruits, or agricultural crops.[72] Shaikh al Islam al Dahlawi says about the rationale of these quantities,[73] "Five *wasq* of grain or date is considered minimum because that much would be the minimum required for sustaining a household for a year, a household composed of three people. On the average, people ate one *ratl* or *mudd* of grain per person per day. Five *wasq* would therefore be sufficient for three people for a whole year, and a small extra quantity would be left as a provision for emergencies. For silver, the minimum required for *zakatability nisab* is two hundred dirhams, because this would be sufficient for the same household for one full year, at prices similar to those prevailing at the time of the Prophet. Five camels are the minimum for *zakatability*, and *zakah* on them is one sheep. In principle, *zakah* is collected from the same kind of the *zakatable* asset, but camels were exchanged for sheep at the time of the Prophet at the rate of eight to one, ten to one, or twelve to one, as reported in many sayings. One camel out of five would be too much, so one sheep is considered the amount of *zakah* due on five camels, since five camels would be at the least equal to forty sheep, on which the *zakah* due is one sheep."[74]

The condition of *nisab* for *zakatability* is agreed upon among scholars, except in the case of crops, fruits, and minerals. Abu Hanifah considers anything that comes out of the earth *zakatable*, no matter how little it may be. The *zakah* on it is ten percent. Also, a report from Ibn 'Abbas, 'Umar bin 'Abd al 'Aziz, and others says "There is on each ten bundles of parsley one bundle as obligated *sadaqah*." The majority of scholars see in *nisab* a necessary condition for *zakatability* on all kinds of wealth, whether it comes from the ground or not. They argue that there is a saying, "There is no *sadaqah* on what is less than five *wasq*." This argument is supported by analogy, since other kinds of wealth have *nisab* of their own.

The rationale behind this condition is very obvious. *zakah* is a due on the rich to relieve the poor and to share in the expenses for common interest to Islam and Muslims. It can only be taken from those who can afford it. It is meaningless to take *zakah* from those who are themselves in need of help, knowing that the Prophet (p) says, "There is no *sadaqah* except from richness."[75]   It is on the same grounds that contemporary taxation systems tend to exempt those with limited resources from taxes, in consideration for their inability to pay. It is worth registering that the *Shari'ah* of God precedes those system by fourteen hundred years.

4.   Excess above essential needs

Some jurists add to the condition of growth another condition. That is, *nisab* must be in excess of basic needs of the owner. Hanafites, in most of their literature, tend to establish this principle on the basis that richness itself is not realized without this condition, since if the person who owns the assets needs them for essential necessities, he/she is not considered rich, nor would such a person like to sacrifice anything of what he/she owns for the payment of zakah. The Prophet (p) says, "Pay *zakah* on your wealth with your hearts willing and pleased."[76] Some other jurists feel that the condition of growth is alone sufficient since things needed to satisfy basic needs are not usually growing or designated for growth, as in the case of homes inhabited by owners, personal transportation animals, personal clothing, personal arms, books for personal study, and handicraft tools. All these satisfy basic needs and at the same time are not growth assets. These jurists argue that true personal need is something very subjective and usually cannot be recognized positively by others. Consequently, what is in excess of those needs cannot be known, so instead of the condition of excess above personal needs, we can use a recognizable condition, like designation of the assets for business and growth purposes.[77]

In fact the condition of growth does not cover all the cases of the condition of excess above essential needs. Money, for example, is considered a growth asset, because it is created for circulation and investment, even if the owner does not actually use it for growth. Without the condition of being in excess of needs, an amount of money that is equal to *nisab* is *zakatable* even if it were designated for providing food, clothing, shelter, or medical care for the owner and his household. It is known among the deeply involved scholars that assets designated to satisfy basic needs are treated as non-existent from the point of view *zakatability*.

We should, however, note that this condition refers to essential or basic needs. People have an infinite amount of needs, especially in this time of ours, when many goods that used to be considered luxuries have become a basic need, since if the son of Adam had two valleys full of gold, he would want to obtain a third one. Basic needs are those human beings cannot survive without, such as food, shelter, clothing, and items needed for a job, such as books for study and tools for work. Some Hanafite scholars define essential needs in an accurate and scientific manner, as "those things that are used to avoid the realized or potential destruction of humans; realized such as expenses for living, clothing, personal weapons, and potential such as the need to pay one's debts, tools for handicraft, home furniture, personal transportation animals, and books for study because ignorance is like destruction. If a person has money that is designated for such needs, it is considered non-existent with regard to *zakah*. This is similar to the case of someone who has no water except that designated for drinking. This water is considered non-existent with regard to making abolution [*wudu'*], and one is allowed to make ritual abolution [*tayammum*]."[77] It should be gratefully and proudly recorded that our scholars consider knowledge like life and ignorance like destruction, consider what prevents ignorance an essential need just like food that prevents hunger or cloth that prevents nakedness, and consider freedom like life and imprisonment like destruction. It should be noted, however, that the essential needs of human beings evolve and change with time and circumstance, so determining them should be left to those of understanding and to the exertion of best effort [*ijtihad*] of the proper authorities in the Islamic state. Basic needs include the needs of the *zakah* payer, his household, and all family members whom he is required by *Shari'ah* to support.

This condition in Islamic jurisprudence precedes the latest theories in taxation that call for exempting a certain minimum for living from taxes and puts an end to the materialist theory that taxes all assets, regardless of the circumstances of the owner, his or her business, and family needs. Modern theorists take consideration of the personal circumstances of the taxpayer as a sign of advancement in taxation thought and legislation. Unfortunately, much of the legislation does not actually apply this principle in levying taxes. For example, sometimes tax laws exempt a minimum for living expenses for the taxpayer alone, regardless of the number of mouths he or she has to feed.

Evidence from Qur'an and Sunnah supporting this condition

1. Ahmad, in his *Musnad* reports from Abu Hurairah that the Prophet (p) said, "*Sadaqah* is only taken out of richness," and in another version, "There should be no sadaqah taken except out of richness."[80] Al Bukhari mentions this saying as suspended [waithout chain] in the chapter on advice and wills in his correct collection. He makes it a title of a section in the chapter on *zakah*, "Section: There is no sadaqah except out of richness; he who gives *sadaqah* while he or his family are in need or while he is under the burden of debts should first pay his debts out of what he would give as *sadaqah*." Al Hafiz comments on Bukhari's title, "It seems that al Bukhari wants to explain the above mentioned saying by stating that it is a required condition for *sadaqah* that the payer or his family must not be in need."[81] There is no doubt that *zakah* is *sadaqah* as expressed in Qur'an and Sunnah.

2. In the Qur'an, God says, "They ask thee what they are to spend. Say, what is beyond your needs."[82] Ibn 'Abbas is reported to have said, "This means what is in excess of yours family's need."[83] Ibn Kathir says "This is also reported from Ibn 'Umar, Mujahid, 'Ata'" , 'Ikrimah, Sa'id bin Jubair, Muhammad bin Ka'b, 'Ata', al Hasan, Qatadah, al Qasim, Salem, 'Ata' al Khurasani, al Rabi' bin Rabi' bin Anas, and several others. They say, what is beyond the need is what is in excess."[84] This means God, His wisdom be glorified, makes subject to spending only what is in excess of basic needs, i.e., the needs of the person, his family, and all those he is required to support. The needs of the person and his family have priority, for himself, over the needs of other people, so *Shari'ah* does not ask him to sacrifice his own needs to which his heart is attached in order to satisfy other people's needs. Al Hasan is reported to have commented on the preceding verse, "That is so as not to extinguish your wealth so you go begging people."[85]

3. Ibn Kathin says that this condition is also supported by what is reported by Ibn Jarir, narrated through his chain to Abu Hurairah, "A man said, 'O Messenger of God, I have one *dinar*.' The Messenger said, Spend it on yourself.' The man said, 'I have another one.' The Messenger replied, 'Spend it on your wife,' whereupon the man said, 'I have a third one.' Spend it on your children,' the Messenger said. The man then said, 'I have a fourth,' and the Messenger answered, 'you know [your needs] better.'" This saying is also reported by Muslin in his correct collection. It indicates that the needs of the person, his wife, and his children have priority over the needs of others. Muslim reports also from Jabir, "The Messenger of God (p) said to a man, 'Start with Your self, give it charity. If anything is left, give it to your family, If anything is left after your family, give to your relatives, and if anything is left after your relatives, then give this way and that way." Some of those sayings are about charity and not obligated one, but in all cases they indicate the intention of *Shari'ah* on spending, which is that all spending, voluntary and obligatory, should come out of the surplus. The surplus, as understood by the majority of scholars, and as defined by Ibn Kathir, is the excess after satisfying needs.

5. Freedom from debt

That *nisab* should be free of debt is in fact an implication of the first condition, i.e. completeness of ownership, and of the excess above essential needs. If the owner is burdened by debts that exceed *nisab* or that reduce the assets net worth to below *nisab*, *zakah* is not obligated. Jurists have varying opinions on debts, especially those debts that are related to apparent assets [assets that can be detected by *zakah* collectors]. The reason for this variety of opinion is that they do not agree on the classification of *zakah* as mentioned by Ibn Rushd as a worship or a financial right due to the poor. Those who see *zakah* as a right to the poor consider that the person who is burdened by debts in a manner that reduces his current assets to below *nisab* is not *zakatable*, since the right of the creditors preceds timewise the right of the poor, because the creditors are the true owners of that asset. Those who see zakah as a form of worship say that such a person is *zakatable*, because the condition for *zakatability* is the presence of assets above *nisab*; no mention of debts is made. They add that there is in this case a conflict between two rights, the right of God and the right of a person, the creditor, and the right of God has priority.[86] Ibn Rushd remarks, "What seems to be more consistent with *Shari'ah* is waiving *zakah* on the debtor."[87] It should be added, however, that what is selected by Ibn Rusad is what can be derived from texts of *Shari'ah*, its spirit, and its major principles concerning all kinds of assets. This can be shown in the following:

Firstly, the ownership of the debtor is in fact weak and incomplete, because of the authority the creditor has on his due debts in asking for payment, to the extent that the creditor may take back the lent asset if it is still in the debtor's hands, even without the consent of the debtor, according to the Hanafite school and others.[88] The first condition for *zakah* is that the right of ownership should be complete.

Secondly, the creditor is required to pay *zakah* for the loan, being the real owner, according to the majority of scholars. If the debtors is also asked to pay *zakah* on that same debt, then there will be a double *zakah* on the same asset. This duality is prohibited by *Shari'ah*.[89]

Thirdly, a person who is overwhelmed by debts that exceed what he owns, or at least reduces it to below nisab, can be a recipient of *zakah* on the grounds of being poor or of being overwhelmed by debts. How could he be a *zakah* payer and a *zakah* recipient at the same time?!

Fourthly, *zakah* is only legitimately taken out of richness, as mentioned in the sayings. The debtor who needs to pay back his debts is not rich. Moreover, he is under stress caused by the debt.

Fifthly, *zakah* is legislated to relieve those who are in need. The overwhelmed debtor is in need of paying his debts. He is like the poor. It is not rational to leave the needs of the debtor unsatisfied in order to provide for the needs of others,[90] knowing that the Messenger (p) said, "Start with yourself, then with whom you are responsible for."

Sixthly, Abu 'Ubaid reports from al Sa'ib bin Yazid, "I heard 'Uthman bin 'Affan saying, 'This is the month of your *zakah*; you who are under debt should pay back your debts, so you can start paying zakah on your assets."[91] In another version reported by Malik, "He who is under debt should pay back his debt and then pay *zakah* on the rest of his assets."[92] A version is reported by al Baihaqi from al Sa'ib, who heard 'Uthman bin 'Affan giving this speech from above the *minbar* [The podium of the speaker in Friday prayer] of the Messenger of God (p). 'Uthman said, "This is the month of your *zakah* . . ." etc. This last version means that 'Uthman said that in the presence of many Companions, and none of them disagreed, meaning they all knew and accepted that opinion.[93]

It is for those reasons that the majority of jurists hold the view that debts prevent *zakatability*, or at least reduce *zakatable* assets by the amount of the debts, in non-apparent assets, money and business assets. This is the opinion of 'Ata , Sulaiman bin Yasar, al Hasan, al Nakha'i, al Laith, Malik, al Thawari, al Awza'i, Ahmad, Ishaq, Abu Thawr, Abu Hanifah, and his disciples. Only Rabi'ah, Hammad bin Salman and Shafi'i in his new opinion, disagree.

As far the apparent assets-- livestock and crops-- some jurists say that debt does not prevent *zakatability*, differentiating between these assets and the former ones because these items are more seen by the poor and they feel envy in their heart about them. This may be confirmed by the fact that *Shari'ah* instituted sending collectors to collect *zakah* on those assets since the time of the Prophet (p) and his Successors. Abu Bakr fought those who refused to pay *zakah* on these assets, while it is not reported that *zakah* payers were forced to pay *zakah* on non-apparent assets, nor that collectors were sent to count the non-apparent assets and collect their *zakah*.[94] This is the view of Malik, Awza'i, Shafi'i, and a version from Aamad.[95] On the other hand, Abu Hanifah believes that debts are a reason to waive *zakah* on all assets except crops and fruits.[96]

Ibn 'Umar and Ibn 'Abbas have two different views with respect to debts on a person who owned crops. Ibn 'Abbas says the debtor should take out an amount equal to the debt used for farming expenses, then pay *zakah* the residual. Ibn 'Umar says the debtor should deduct an amount equal to the debt that is spent on farming expenses or on himself and his family, and pay *zakah* on the residual. It seems to me, however, that the distinction between apparent and non-apparent items of wealth is unclear, since those are relative matters that change from time to time. For example, in our times, business assets are apparent and very visible by the poor, much more than livestock and crops. I do not see in the above-mentioned reasoning anything that stands against the opinion given earlier which indicates that the presence of debts waives *zakatability* on all assets. We should remember also that *Shari'ah* tends always to make things easier on debtors in order to help them by all means to rid of the burden of debt. This approach obviously contradicts forcing the debtor to pay zakah. This is the view of 'Ata' , al Hasan, Sulaiman, Maimun bin Mahran, al Nakh'i, al Thawri, al Laith, Ishaq, and a version from Ahmad.[97] Abu 'Ubaid reports it from Makhul, and continues, "It is also reported from Taus."[98] Abu 'Ubaid, however, chooses the following stand: If the debt is certain, it waives *zakah* in the case of plants and livestock, in the footsteps of the Prophet's tradition, which ordered *zakah* be collected from the rich and rendered to the poor, How can *zakah* be collected from the debtor, since he or she is a recipient of *zakah* on two grounds, being in debt and being poor?[99] This is if the debt is certain and known. In the case then the debt is not known and not certain, collectors of *zakah* are not supposed to accept the claim of the debtor, and should collect *zakah* on all present crops and livestock, because *zakah* on those items is a very obvious obligation, binding the owner, while the claimed debt is unknown. This is similar to a case where a person has definite obligations that are known and claims to have paid them without having sufficient evidence. His, or her word is not sufficient as proof.[100] Apparently, Abu 'Ubaid is making the certainty of the debt a condition in order to take it into consideration in wavering *zakah* or deducting the amount of the debt from *zakatable* assets. This is a sound position which protects the right of God and the poor.

Conditions of deductible debts

For debts to waive *zakah* completely, the amount of the debt should be large enough to cover all present assets, or at least bring them down to below *nisab*. For example, if the amount of debt is ten *dinars* and the taxable person has thirty *dinars*, then what is left after the debt is still *nisab*, which is *zakatable*. But if the amount of debt is more than ten *dinars*, then this person is not *zakatable*.[101]

For deferred or immediate debts that are due in either a long or short period it seems that this makes no difference in its effect on *zakah*. The selected view is that all debts, immediate and deferred are deductible from *zakatable* asset. Some scholars, however, hold to the view that deferred debts are not deductible.[102] One of the common deferred debts could be part of the wife's *mahr* [dowry given by the husband] that is deferred until death or divorce. Some scholars argue that this deferred *mahr* is not deductible, while others consider it deductible like other debts.[103] All money for an ex-wife or for children in the custody of their mother are deductible debts. There is a discussion also about debts that belong to human beings. Al Nawawi, a Shafi'ite, says if debts are deductible, then, this applies to all debts, whether they are God's or a person's.[105] Hanafites say only debts to people are deductible because people seek payment and are protected by the judicial system. Debts to God, such as pledges and *kafarat* [recompense for a break in some religious obligation such as fasting] are not deductible. It should be noted, however, that past due *zakah* is considered like debts to other people. It is deductible because the state is authorized to collect it on behalf of the recipients.[106]

The view of the Hanafites is also my choice on this issue; if the Islamic state takes the responsibility of collecting *zakah* this rule shuts the door on false claims of pledge to God and *kaffarat* made in order to reduce the amount of *zakah*, since there are no accessible means of verifying those pledges and *kaffarat*. If the state does not collect *zakah* and individual Muslims pay *zakah* or their own and make their own calculations, those debts to God can be deductible, because the texts are general, such as the saying, "but the debt to God deserves priority in payment."[107]

6. The passage of a year

Twelve full lunar months should pass from the beginning of ownership, or past due date of *zakah*, for *zakah* to accrue again on assets. "This condition is restricted to livestock,, money, and business assets. It does not apply to crops, fruits, honey, extracted minerals, found treasure, etc., where there is no condition of one year on the grounds that *zakah* on those items is a sort of *zakah* on income.

The value of this condition for certain assets

Ibn Qudamah expresses his opinion on the essence of distinction between *zakatable* items as far as the passage of a year is concerned. "Items for which the passage of a year is considered necessary are those designated for growth, such as business assets, or as storage of value, such as money, because it is of the nature of being used for growth, so that *zakah* would be paid at the end of each year out of their profits and income. As for crops and fruits, they themselves are the income, and *zakah* is taken out of them. Once they are produced they obviously do not grow. Extracted minerals are considered similar to plants and fruits."[108]

Reasons for this condition

Ibn Rushd states,[109] "The majority of jurists believes that this condition is required for the *zakatability* of gold, silver, and livestock. It is confirmed that the four *Khulafa'* applied this condition, and it is commonly known among the Companions, which means that all these people would not agree on such a mater without knowing that the Prophet had said something about it. It is reported from Ibn 'Umar that the Prophet (p) said, "There is no *zakah* on an asset until a year has passed."[110] This is agreed upon among jurists in all countries, and there is no dispute about it in the Companions' generation except a report from Ibn 'Abbas and Mu'awiyah. It seems that the reason for that exemption is the lack of an authentic saying.[111]

Variations among Companions and Followers on this condition

Ibn Mas'ud, Ibn 'Abbas, and Mu'awiyah are reported to have the view that *zakah* is due on assets when acquired, without needing the passage of a year, if that earned asset reaches *nisab* on its own or after being added to what was in possession before its accrual.[112] Some of the Followers also take this view.

What is agreed upon about the passage of a year

There is no disagreement among scholars, both predecessors and latecomers, that *zakah* on capital assets such as livestock, money, and business inventory, is required only once a year. Ibn Abi Shaibah reports from al Zuhri, "Nothing reached us from any ruler of this nation who was in Madinah-- Abu Bakr, 'Umar and 'Uthman-- to the effect that they were collecting *zakah* twice. They sent collectors every year, fertile or barren. Collecting it this way in accordance with the tradition of the Messenger of God (p)."[113]

This shows the justice of Islamic *Shari'ah*. The periodicality of *zakah* is not left to rulers and governments to impose at will, or to the desire and miserliness of individuals. The year is considered the pattern of repetition because it is the cycle of all season, and it is long enough for growth and profitability to accure[114] Ibn al Qayim says about the guidance received from the Messenger (p) on *zakah* "He [the Prophet] obligated it once every year. He made the time of accrual of *zakah* on crops and fruits the time of ripening and harvest. *zakah* is an expression of the utmost justice, because had it been obligated every month or every week, it would have heavily burdened the rich, but if it were made once in a lifetime, it would not have satisfied the needs of the indigent. The best way was to make it once every year."[115]

Variation on the issue of accrued assets

Accrued assets or goods include regular income, periodical salaries and wages, grants, windfall profits, gifts, etc. Some of those accrued goods, such as crops, fruits, honey, found treasures and extracted minerals, are *zakatable* once acquired if they reach the amount of nisab. That much is not disputed. There is, however, a difference of opinion on the *zakatability* of capital assets, like money, business inventory, and livestock, that are acquired during the year. Are they *zakatable* at the time they are possessed? On this we should bring forth some details mentioned by Ibn Qudamah in *al Mughni*, which distinguish between three cases:

1.   If acquired assets are the result of already owned capital, such as profit on business assets and the offspring of already owned livestock, they are *zakatable*. This income should be added to the original assets in calculating *zakah*. Ibn Qudamah says, "I am aware of no dispute on this. It goes by the year of its principal and is like continuous growth, such is the increase in the value of inventory."[116]

2.   The second case is then the accrued asset as not of the same kind of capital a person already owns, such as a person who owns *nisab* of camels and is given a gift of cows.   According to the majority of scholars, this acquired asset is not added to the capital he or she owns, but rather starts a new year and a new *nisab* of its own. If it is below *nisab*, the new asset is not *zakatable*. There is, however, a report from Ibn Mas'ud, Ibn 'Abbas, and Mu'awiyah that these are *zakatable* once they are earned. Ahmad says it should be *zakated* upon receipt. Ahmad reports via his own chain from Ibn Mas'ud, that 'Abd Allah used to deduct *zakah* when he gave us the grants." Al Awza'i is reported as saying, about the case of a person who sells his home or slave, "He should pay *zakah* on the price once he receives the money, unless he has already established an accounting month for *zakah* payment; in which case he may delay payment until the last month of his accounting year.[117] Supporting evidence for this opinion shall be presented later in the section on *zakah* on salaries.

3.   The third case is if the acquired asset is the same kind as already-owned assets that have reached *nisab*, and have started the year of *zakatability*, but acquiring the new assets is completely independent of the already-owned assets. For example, someone owns forty sheep and during the year is given as a present another twenty. Those new

sheep are not *zakatable* in that year, according to Aamad and al Shafi'i'. Abu Hanifah says it should be added to what he already owns and *zakah* is due on the total at the end of the *zakah* year, except in the case when this new asset is merely a substitution of an older one that is being *zakated*. Abu Hanifah argues that what is obligated should not be divided and there should be no different times for *zakatability* on different sections of the same kind of asset that is owned the same group. Because this creates accounting and collection difficulties, it should be avoided, in accordance with the verse, ". . . and has imposed no difficulties on you in your religion."[113] *Shari'ah* always considers the removal of difficulties, such as in the case of taking one sheep on each five camels because a camel is indivisible. Also adding profits to original capital, in *zakatability*, is of that same easiness. Malik agrees with Abu Hanifah in the case of pastured livestock, while in money he tends to agree with Ahmad and al Shafi'i' because according to him, the above mentioned difficulty does not arise.[119] The author of *al Mughni* argues against the Hanfi point of view, but it seems that the latter is definitely simpler in application and much less complicated and for that reason I tend to agree with it.

Footnotes

1. *Sura al Nahl,* 16:44.

2. *Sura at Tawbah* 9:34.

3. *Sura al sura Baqarah,* 2:267.

4. *Ibid.*

6. *Sura at Tawbah,* 9:103.

7. *Sura al Dhariyat,* 51:19.

8. *Al Qamus al Muhit,,* Vol. 4, p. 52.

9. *Lisan al 'Arab,* chapter on the letter *lam* section on the letter *mim.*

10. See Shaikh 'Ali al Khafif, *Ahkam al Mu'amalat al Shari'ah,* pp. 3.4.

11. *Al Bahr al Ra'iq,* Vol. 2, p. 217.

12. *Sura al Nur,* 24:33.

13. *Sura al Baqarah,* 2:254.

14. *Sura 'Ali 'Imran,* 3:180.

15. *Sura al Hadid,* 57:7.
16. *Sura al Munafiqun,* 63:9.

17. *Sura al Taghabun,* 64:15.

18. *Sura al Humazah*, 104:3.

19 *Sura al Massad*, 111:2.

20. *Sura al Dhariyat*, 51:19.

21. *Sura al Tawbah*, 9:103.

22. *Sura al Tawbah*, 9:55.

23. *Sura al Nisa'*, 4:6.

24. *Sura al Nisa*, 4:29.

25. *Sura al Baqarah*, 2:245.

26. *Sura al Hadid*, 57:11.

27. *Sura al Muzzammil*, 73:20.

28. *Sura at Tawbah*, 9:111.

29 *Hujjat Allah al Balighah*, vol 2, pp. 640-641.

30. Shaikh 'Ali al Khafif, "Al Milkiyah al Fardiyah wa Tahdiduha fi al Islam," in the proceedings of the first conference of the Islamic Research Congress, p, 99.

31. *Ibid.*

32. *Al Bahr al Ra'iq*, Vol. 2, p. 218.

33. *Matalib Uli al Nuha, Sharh Ghayat al Muntaha*, Vol. 2, p. 16.

34 *Al Bahr al Raiq, op. cit.*

35. *Sharh al Azhar*, Vol. 1, pp. 452-453.

36. *Matalib Uli al Nuha*, Vol. 2, p. 16.

37. Al Nawawi, *al Majmu'* , Vol. 5, pp. 339-340.

38. Ibn Rushd, *Bidayat al Mujtahid*, Vol. 1, p. 239.

39. *Al Bahr al Ra'iql*, by Ibn Nujaim, and its commentary by Ibn 'Abidin, Vol. 2, p.121. It should be noted that Abu Hanifah thinks that a person who takes by use of unlawful force, money from another and mixes it with his own, is considered as changing its nature. He becomes a guarantor of the stolen money to its owner, and the total that the thief possesses becomes his property. On the other hand, Abu Yusuf and Muhammad do not agree on the guarantee, or on attributing ownership of stolen property to the thief.

40. Reported by Muslim.

41. *Fath al Bari*, vol, 3, p. 180, al Halabi print.

42. Mentioned by Ibn al Humam in *Fath al Qadir* from *al Mabsut*. He also reports from Qadi Khan that he said in *al Jami' al Saghir*, "If he made a last will of one third of his wealth to the poor, and that third was given to an oppressing ruler, the will is satisfied. See *Fath al Qadir*, Vol. 1, pp. 513-514. These kinds of religious opinions are in fact written protests against oppressive rulers.

43. *Ibid*. See also *al Bahr*, Vol. 2, p. 240.

44. *Al Muhlla*, Vol. 2 p, 101. It is narrated from Ibn al Qasim, a disciple of Malik, that wealth taken from its owner by force is guaranteed by the thief from the time of theft; consequently, the latter must pay *zakah* on it. Some Malikites apply that only to the case in which the thief has other property that can be used to satisfy the guarantee. If not, they say there is no *zakah* on stolen wealth. In the commentary of al Dusuqi, it is mentioned that materials stolen by force must be *zakated* by the thief every year as long as they remain in his possession. This is done without affecting the obligation of the owner in paying *zakah* the moment he gets his stolen property back. This means *zakah* may be paid twice on such stolen property, once every year by the thief, and when it is returned, by the owner. The thief has no right to claim any liability on the owner for the amount of *zakah* paid by him. See *al Sharh al Kabir* and its commentary by al Dusuqi, Vol. 1, pp. 456-457.

45. *Al Muhalla*, Vol. 2, p. 101, and al Baihaqi says in his *sunnan* Vol. 4, p. 150, "It is mentioned by Ibn al Mundhir from Ibn 'Umar and Aishah".

46. *Al Amwal*, p. 432. A similar report is narrated from 'Ata. However, the contrary is also reported from them.

47. *Ibid*, p. 430.

48. Debts are *zakatable*, according to Malik, for one year only from the time they are paid back, even if the debt is for many years. Once the creditor receives the debt back, he should pay its *zakah* for one year, provided it is equal to *nisab*. This is certainly if the delay in getting the debt back was not merely to avoid accrual of *zakah*. If for that reason only, it is *zakatable* every year. On the other hand, if the debt results from a gift or charity, i.e. a gift is pledged but not surrendered to the gifted by the giver, *zakah* is not obligated until the passage of one year from the time of acquiring it physically. Debts that are expected to be paid back and those that are not, are the same in this regard, except for business credit , which is *zakatable* by the creditor in calculating his or her business assets. Business credit is the loan that results from sales. See *al Sharh al Kabir* and *Hashiat al Dusuqi,* Vol. 1, p. 466.

49. *Al Amwa'l*, p. 434-435.

50. *Ibid*.

51. *Matalib Uli al Nuha*, Vol. 2, p. 14.

52. *Badai' i' al Sana'i'*, Vol. 1, p. 9.

53. Malik's view on debts is that they are not *zakated* until received back, then *zakah* is due on them for one year.

54. *Hashiat Ibn 'Abidin,* Vol. 2, p. 7, as quoted from *al Bahr.*

55. *Fath al Qadir*, Vol. 1 1, p. 482.

56. Reported by al Tirmidhi from Abi Kabshah al Anmari. Al Tirmidhi says it is good correct.

57. *Bada'i' al Sana'i'*, Vol. 2, p. 11.

58. *Sahih Muslim*, with commentary of al Nawawi, Vol. 7, p. 55.

59. *Sura Saba',* 34:39.

60. *Sura al Rum,* 30:39.

61. *Al Muntaqa*, a commentary on al Muwaata' by Abu al Walid al Baji, Vol. 2, p. 9.

62. *Al Bahr al Ra'iq*, Vol. 2, p. 222.

63. Al NawawI, al Majmu, Vol. 5, p. 569.

64. Al Sharh al Kabir with commentary of' al Dusuqi, Vol. 1, p. 457.

65 *Ibid*, p. 473.

66. Some jurists expand the use of incapacitation as an excuse to the extent that they exempt the lender from *zakah* on debts, even if payment is expected, because it is not growing and its ownership is not complete. They also exempt from *zakatability* the assets of the child and the insane persons, because they are incapable of making assets grow.

67. Reported by al Bukhari from Anas.

68. Reported by Muslim from Abu Hurairah.

69. Reported by Abu Daud from 'Awf bin Malik.

70. *Al Muhalla*, Vol. 5, p. 209.

71. Reported by Ibn Khuzaimah and al Hakim from jabir, linked to the Prophet as well as not linked. Al Hakim says, "It is correct according to the criteria of Muslim;" This is uphed by al Dhahabi in *al Talkhis*. But in his al *Muhadhdhab*, he says "The most correct is that which is not linked to the Prophet." See *al Faid*, Vol. 1, p. 253.

72. This will be detailed in the following chapters.

73. He is the great scholar and renovator of the practice of Islam in India, the late Ahmad

bin 'Abd al Rahim, known as Shah Waliyu Allah, born 1114 H, died 1176 H, author of *Hujjat Allah al Balighah*, and several other valuable books. See his autobiography in detail in *Nuzhat al Khawatir*, by al Sayed 'Abd al Hay al Hasani, Vol. 6, pp. 398-415, autobiography no. 760, and also in The History of the *Call for Islam in India* by Mas'ud al Nadwi, p. 129-plus, and in *A Brief History of the Renovation and Revivication Movements of Religion*, by Abu al A'la al Mawdudi, pp, 101-121, and in *al A'lam* by al Zirkili, Vol. 1, pp, 144-145.

74. *Hujjat Allah al Balighah*, Vol. 2, p. 506.

75. Reported by al Bukhari as suspended, and by Ahmad as linked. We shall discuss this in the next section.

76. *Badai'i' al Sana'i'*, Vol. 2, p. 11. The saying is reported by al Tabarani from Abu al Darda. It is weak.

77. *Ibid.*

78. Ibn 'Abidin, commentary on *al Durr al Mukhtar*, Vol. 2, P. 6.

79. *Ibid*, and *al Bahr al Ra'iq*, Vol. 2. p. 222, as quoted from Ibn al Malik in his *Sharh al Majma'*.

80. Saying number 7155 in *al Musnad*. Ahmad Shakir comments, "Its chain is correct." See commentary in Vol. 12, *al Musnad*. See also *Fath al Bari,* Vol. 3, p. 189.

81. *Fata al Bari*, Vol. 13, p. 189.

82. *Sura al Baqarah,* 2:219.

83. *Tafsir Ibn Kathir*, Vol. 1, p. 256.

84. *Ibid.*

85. *Ibid.*

86. *Bidayat al Mujtahid*, p, 328.

87 *Ibid.*

88. *Al Majmu* , Vol. 5, p. 46, and *al Bahr*, vol, 2, p. 219.

89. *Ibid.*

90. *Al Mughni,* Vol. 3, p, 41.

91 *Al Amwal*, p. 437. The above mentioned month is said to be Ramadan or al Muharram.

92. In his *al Talkhis*, p. 178, al Hafiz says it is reported by Malik in *al Muwatta'* and by al Shafi'i from Malik from Ibn Shihab from Sa'ib from 'Uthman.

93. *Al Mughni, op. cit.*

94. *Al Mughni,* Vol. 3, p, 42-43.

95. This is similar to what is known in contemporary taxation in the matter of real estate taxes levied on real estate properties, which is usually taken from the income of the property, regardless of the tax payer and his or her circumstances. The same thing applies to stocks and interest income in many countries. See *Taxation Legislation* by Dr. Muhammad Hilmi Murad, Vol. 1, p. 78, first edition.

96. *Al Mughni,* Vol. 3, p, 42.

97. *Ibid.*

98. *Al Amwal,* p. 510.

99. *Ibid.*

100. *Ibid.*

101. *Al Mughni,* Vol. 3, p. 43.

102. Ibid.

103. *Al Bahr al Ra'iq,* Vol. 2, p. 216.

104 *Ibid.*

105. *Al Majmu',* Vol. 5 p. 345.

106 *Al Mughni,* vol, 3, p. 45. See also *al Hidayah* and its commentaries, Vol. 1, pp. 486-457.

107. Al Bukhari and others.

108. *Al Mughni,* Vol. 1, p, 625, third printing of al Manar.

109. *Bidayat al Mujtahid,* Vol. 2, pp. 261-262.

110. Al Hafiz in *al Talkhis,* p, 175, says "This saying is reported by al Daraqutni and al Baihaqi from Ibn 'Umar. In its chain is Isma'il bin Ayash, whose narration from other than people from Syria is weak. Some narrators report the same saying as a statement by Ibn 'Umar, and not linked to the Prophet (p). Al Daraqutni an *al 'Ilal* views the non linked version as correct. The saying, however, is unanimously graded weak. Variation on this issue is known since the time of the Companions and Followers. This is stated by Ibn Rushd from Ibn 'Abbas and Mu'awiyah in correct reports. The report from Ibn Mas'ud is also correct.

111. *Bidayat al Mujtahid, op. cit.*

112. *Al Muhalla,* Vol. 6, pp. 83-85, *Nail al Awtar,* Vol. 4, p. 148, *al Raud al Nadir,* Vol. 2, pp. 411-412, and *Subul al Salam,* Vol. 2, p. 129.

113. *Kanz al Ummal,* Vol. 6, p. 294, which also reports similar statements from al Shafi'i and al Baihaqi, in *al Sunan* as a narration from al Zuhri.

114. *Bidayat al Mujtahid,* Vol. 1, p. 261-262.

115. *Zad al Ma'ad,* Vol. 1, p. 307.

116. *Al Mughni,* Vol. 2, p, 626.

117. *Ibid.*

118. *Sura al Hajj,* 22:78.

119. *Al Mughni,* Vol. 2, p, 617.

CHAPTER TWO

ZAKAH ON LIVESTOCK

The animal kingdom has many species. Mankind has made use of only a few of them. This is what is known by Arabs as *al an'am*. Camels, cows, buffalo, sheep, and goats, are all part of what God bestowed on His servants. Their benefits are mentioned in several places in His Holy Book. In *sura al Nahl* - sometimes called *sura al An'am* (livestock) - God says "and cattle He has created for you, from which ye derive warmth, and numerous benefits, and of their meat ye eat. And ye have a sense of pride and beauty in them as ye drive them home in the evening, and as ye lead them forth to pasture in the morning, And they carry your heavy loads to lands that ye could not otherwise reach except with souls distressed, for your Lord is indeed most kind, moat merciful,"[1] Also "and buried in cattle will ye find an instructive sign, from what is within their body between excretions and blood, we produce for your drink, milk, pure and agreeable to those who drink it,"[2] "and made for you, out of the skins of animals, tents for dwellings, which ye find so light and handy when in travel and when ye stop, and out of their wool, and their soft fibers, and their hair, furniture and articles for all convenience to serve you for a time"[3]. In *sura Yasin*, "See they not that we have created for them among the things which our hands have fashioned, cattle which are under their domination. And that we have subjected them to their use: of them some do carry them and some they eat, and they have other profits from them besides, and they get milk to drink. Will they not then be grateful?".[4] God fashioned this livestock for mankind, and He subjects then to humans to ride and to make use of their skin and hair. It is not surprising that God asks people to be thankful.

The most obvious and practical thankfulness urged by the Holy Qur'an and the purified tradition of the Prophet (p) is the obligation of zakah. Its *nisab* and rates are determined, collectors are sent every year to owners of cattle, and warning to those who refuse its payment is put forth. Livestock, especially camels, were the most useful asset for the Arabs at the time of the Prophet (p). Consequently, Sunnah determined their nisab and rates very clearly. In many countries today especially Muslim countries, livestock still represent one of the most important national assets and source of income. The following sections attempt to provide full account of zakah on livestock.

SECTION ONE

GENERAL CONDITIONS FOR *ZAKAH* ON LIVESTOCK

Zakah is not imposed on livestock of all quantity and kind. There are certain conditions that should be fulfilled for the zakatability of livestock which are ennumerated here:

1. The minimum for *zakatability* (*Nisab*)

The first condition is nisab, since zakah is only on the rich, and not every owner of livestock is rich. There always should be a limit above which persons are considered rich. This limit is nisab. It is five camels by unanimous agreement of Muslims for centuries. There is no obligated zakah for anything below five camel, nisab for sheep is forty sheep, also unanimous. *Nisab* is determined by sayings of the Prophet (p), by his actual practice and by the application of his successors. Nisab for cows varies from five to thirty-two to fifty, depending upon the school of jurisprudence one adopts.

2. The passage of a Year (Annual)

This is reported authentically from the Prophet (p) and his successors. They used to send zakah collectors once every year to take the count on livestock. It was shown in the previous chapter that the condition of the passage of one full lunar year for non-earned assets is accepted unanimously. One can add here that the majority who assert this condition on earned income do not require it on the offspring of livestock that result from reproduction during the year, and accept the zakatable year for offspring to be that of their mothers.

3. They should be pastured naturally

Pastured livestock are those that are grazed on natural and cost-free pasture land during the major part of the year for the purpose of breeding, milking, and putting on weight.[5] The opposite of natural grazing is buying feed.

The condition is satisfied if livestock is pastured naturally most of the year. Pasturing should be made for the purpose of growth, reproduction, and milking; thus if it is made for the purpose of personal riding or eating, these animals are not zakatable, since such allocation removes animals from being growth assets and put them in the category of personal use which is not zakatable as shall be shown in the next subsection.

The reason for this condition is that zakah is obligated on the surplus, what is easy for persons to pay, in accordance to the verse, "take the surplus"[6] and the verse "when they ask you what to spend, say the surplus"[7], that is, on what does not cost much and grows rapidly. This can only be fulfilled if the animals pastured cost-free, since artificially fed animals have high cost, which makes it hard for people to give then away as zakah.

This condition is derived from what is reported by Ahmad, al Nasa'i, and Abu Daud from Bahz bin Hakim from his father from his grandfather, who said: I heard the Messenger of God (p) saying about naturally (cost-free) postured camels, for each forty, there is one as zakah ... etc. "This saying is graded correct by a group of leading scholars. The adjective "naturally, cost-free pastured" here implies that artificially fed camels are not subject to zakah; otherwise adding such an adjective becomes meaningless, and the Prophet (p) does not speak in vain. It is obvious from this saying that camels characterised, as naturally, cost-free pastured are unlike those that are not. Al Khattabi comments, "When something may have either of two characteristics, and a ruling of Shari'ah is applied to one of them, then the opposite ruling applies to the other characteristic, by implication".[8] It is also accepted by scholars of the methodology of jurisprudence that giving a specific characteristic in a ruling implies that when the characteristic is absent the ruling does not apply[9] i.e., camels fed by purchased feed are treated differently.

This saying is further supported by a report is the correct collection of al Bukhari and others from Anas, that "if sheep are naturally (cost-free) pastured, and reach 40 in number, there is one sheep as zakah". If the condition of natural free pasture is required on sheep it should also be, by analogy, required on camels and cows, since there should be no distinction between them. Sayings without such restriction should be taken with reference to those that came with the restriction of natural free grasing.

This is the opinion of the majority of scholars, Rabi'ah, Mlaik and al Layth differ on that. They obligate zakah on manually fed livestock the same way it is on naturally pastured, as implied by the sayings that do not have the restriction. Their explanation of the restricting sayings is that the word "natural or cost-free pasture" is a general description because this was a common adjective of livestock at the time of the Prophet (p).[10]

4. Zakatable livestock should not be working animals

This is the fourth and last condition for zakatability of livestock. It means that they should not be used for cultivation, carrying water or loads or riding, etc. This condition only applies to camels and cows. Abu Ubaid reports from 'Ali, that " There is no sadaqah on working cows."There is also a report that Jabir bin 'Abd Allah said "Animals working in cultivation are not zakatable."[11] Abu Daud, in his *Sunan*, reports from Zuhair "We are told by Abu Ishaq from 'Asem bin Damurah and al Harith from 'Ali, (Zuhair said "I think from the Prophet") that he said, "Bring me one-fourth of a tenth, i.e. on each forty dirhams one dirham..." and he continued, "and there is nothing due on working animals." This is reported also by Ibn Abi Shaibah linked to the Prophet, and by 'Abd Al Razzaq, in his Musannaf, via al Thawri and Mamar as from 'Ali only.[12] Similar reports exist as coming from Ibrahim, Mujahid, al Zuhri, Umar bin 'Abd al Aziz, and some other Followers.[13] It is also the view of Abu Hanifah, al Thawri, al Shafi'i, and the Zaidis. It is the opinion of al Layth as far as cows are concerned.

Two things support these narrations and this point of view. The first is the principle that assets designated for personal use and service are not zakatable, and by the same token livestock designated for cultivation, or personal transportation should not be zakatable. It is apparent that such animals are not part of the assets invested for growth.[14] Secondly, the report of Abu 'Ubaid from al Zuhri, that cows and camels used for carrying riders are not zakatable, and neither are cows used for cultivation.[15] All these are like tools for agriculture, Sa'id bin Abd al Aziz al Tanukhi says "Cows used in cultivation are not zakatable, because the grain produced is being zakated, and it involves the work of cows.[16] If animals used in the process of farming were to be zakated, zakah would then be double on agriculture, taken once on the means of production and again on the produce, as rightly stated by Abu 'Ubaid. Malik disagrees with the majority on this ruling, and according to him zakah is obligated on cows and camels, working or not, naturally pastured or not. When the view of Malik was mentioned to al Thawri he replied "I did not think that anyone would say that".[17] In fairness, one should add that some Malikite jurists lean toward the view of the majority. Ibn Naji quotes lbn 'Abd al Salam as saying "In this regard, the view of the majority is the one that one feels more comfortable with." Abu 'Umar bin 'Abd al Barr shows that Maliketes' view on working animals is in conflict with their position on jewelry designated for personal use; the latter is not zakatable, according to them.[18]

SECTION TWO

ZAKAH ON CAMELS

The unanimous agreement of Muslims, as well as several correct sayings of the Messenger of God (p) and reports from his Companions indicate *nisab* of camels and the rates of *nisab* on them are as follows:

Number of Camels		Amount Due as *Zakah*
From	**To**	
5	9	1 sheep
10	14	2 sheep
15	19	3 sheep
20	24	4 sheep
25	35	female camel between 1 and 2 years old
36	45	female camel between 2 and 3 years old
46	60	female camel between 3 and 4 years old
61	75	female camel between 4 and 5 years old
76	90	2 female camels between 2 and 3 years old
91	120	2 female camels between 3 and 4 years old

There is *ijma* on this schedule,[19] except for a report from 'Ali that on 25 camels there is five sheep and on 26 camels there is one female camel between one and two years old.[20] Ibn al Mundhir says. The unanimity is net broken, because what is reported from 'Ali is not authentic. The saying of Anas on these quantities and amounts is correct and there is a unanimous agreement on its content.[21] For more than 120 camels the majority's view is that for each additional 50 camels the additional amount of *zakah* is a female camel between three and four years old while on each additional 40 camels the additional amount of *zakah* is a female camel between two and three years old.[22] This is shown in the following table :

From	**To**		**Amount of** *zakah*
121	129	Camels	3 female camels, 2 to 3 years old
130	139	Camels	1 female camels, 3 to 4 years old and 1female camels, 3 to 4 years old
140	149	Camels	2 female camels, 3 to 4 years old and 1female camels, 2 to 3 years old
150	159	Camels	3 female camels, 3 to 4 years old
160	169	Camels	4 female camels, 2 to 3 years old
170	179	Camels	1 female camels, 3 to 4 years old and 3 female camels, 2 to 3 years old
180	189	Camels	2 female camels, 3 to 4 years old and 2 female camels, 2 to 3 years old
190	199	Camels	3 female camels, 3 to 4 years old and 1 female camels, 2 to a years old
200	209	Camels	4 female camels, 3 to 4 years old or 5 female camels, 2 to a years old

It is seen from the table that for big numbers, an increase of less than ten camels does not affect the amount of *zakah*. Once it is increased by ten, then you go one step higher in the amount of *zakah* due according to the same rule mentioned above. It is obvious from these two tables that if the number of camels owned is less than five then there is no *zakah*. Once they reach five , the amount due is one sheep. The author of *al Mabsut* quotes a scholar as saying, "this means that the value of the livestock is considered. Camels between one and two years old used to be priced at forty *dirhams* and a sheep at five *dirhams*, so five camels equal 200 *dirhams* also equal 40 sheep. This implies that the minimum for *zakatability* of camels, sheep, and silver money is the same. Ibn al Humam in *al Fath* and Ibn Nujaim in *al Bahr* reply, there is a saying that states "Whoever is obliged to give as *zakah* a camel of a certain age group, but does not own any in that age, can pay in substitution on the average of 10 *dirhams* for a sheep, if he does not have a sheep. This is an explicit text that contradicts the explanation of al Sarakhsi.[24] The saying referred to is reported by *al Bahr* from Anas.

Shari'ah obligates sheep as *zakah* on camels if the number of *zakatable* camels is lees than 25, though usually *zakah* is paid out of the same kind of the *zakated* assets. The reason is obviously that the amount due is less than one camel, but at the same time *Shari'ah* considers five camels to sufficiently define who is rich.[25]

Numbers and amounts in the above two tables come from the actions of the Messenger of God (p). Al Nawawi in *al Majmu'* says that the quantities and amounts of *zakah* on livestock come from the two saying narrated by Anas and Ibn 'Umar.[26]

Fiqh al Zakah (Vol. I), Dr. Yusuf al Qaradawi

Anas narrated that Abu Bakr, the Truthful wrote this message when he sent him to Bahrain:

In the name of God, most merciful, most gracious. This is the obligation of *sadaqah* imposed on Muslims by the Messenger of God (P), as ordained to him by God. Whoever is asked to pay it according to these rules must give it, and whoever is asked to pay more should refuse. On each 24 camels or less, *zakah* is due in sheep. On each five camels, one sheep is required. Once they reach 25 and up to 35 one female camel, one to two years old, is required. From 36 to 45, there is one she-camel two to three years old. If they reach 46 to 60, there is one she-camel three to four years old due, one that can be bred. If they reach 61 to 75, one she-camel four to five years old is due. If they reach 76 to 90, there is two she-camels two to three years old due. If they reach 91 to 120, there are two she-camels, three to four years old due. If they are more than 120, for each 40 there is one she-camel two to three years old, and for each 50 there is one she-camel three to four years old. A person who owns [up to] four camels is not *zakatable* unless he volunteers, but if they reach five camels, one sheep is due on them as *zakah*. In the *sadaqah* on sheep, if they are naturally, cost-free pastured, and number between 40 and 120 sheep, there is one sheep due. For more than 120 and up to 200, there are two sheep. For more than 200 up to 300 there are three sheep. For more than 300, the amount of *zakah* is one sheep for each 100 or a fraction therein. If a person owns less than 40 naturally cost-free pastured sheep, there is no *sadaqah* unless the person wishes to volunteer. On mint currency there is one-fourth of one-tenth due . If a person own only 190 *dirhams*[27] there is nothing on them except by the voluntary initiative of the owner". The letter further states, "The person whose *zakah* is a female camel, one to two years old, and who has none of that age , but one in the next higher age bracket, it is acceptable, and the *zakah* collector returns to him the difference, twenty *dirhams* or two sheep. If he owes a she-camel one to two years old but does not have it, a male camel between two and three years old is accepted in its place. A person who owes as *zakah* one she-camel four to five years old and has none in that age group, but has a she-camel one year younger, may pay the younger along with two sheep if available, or twenty *dirhams*. A person who owes as *zakah* one female camel three to four years old and does not have any in that age bracket can pay one female camel in the next higher age bracket and the collector then returns to him 20 *dirhams* or two sheep. Nor a person who is required to pay *sadaqah* in the amount of one female camel three to four years old and has only a female camel in the age group of two to three years old, it can be accepted from him, along with two sheep or 20 *dirhams*. For a person whose *sadaqah* should be one female camel two-three years old who has one a year older, it is an acceptable substitute the *zakah* collector returns to him 20 *dirhams* or two sheep. If a person *sadaqah* is one female camel two to three years old and he does not have it, but has one a year younger, it is acceptable as *zakah* along with 20 *dirhams* or two sheep.[28] An old, damaged or defected animal is not accepted as *zakah*, nor should the collector take a ram unless it is volunteered as extra *sadaqah* by the *zakah* payer. What is divided should not be added together, and what is together a *zakatable* unit must not be divided in order to avoid *zakah*.[29] For cattle owned by partners,[30] partners would settle the account among themselves in proportion to their shares. Al Nawawi says "this letter is reported by al Bukhari in his correct collection, scattered throughout the chapter on *zakah*. I put it back together."[31] It is also reported by Ahmad, 'Abu Daud, al Nasai and al Daraqutni. The latter adds "The chain is correct and the narrators are all trustworthy," as in al Muntaqa.[32] Al Shaukani says "It is also reported by al Shaukani, al Baihaqi, and al Hakim, Ibn Hazm says this message is maximum in correctness. It is also graded correct by Ibn Habban and others.[33]

The saying from Ibn 'Umar, is narrated by Sufian bin Husain from al Zuhri from Salim from his father, 'Abdullah bin 'Umar: The Messenger of God (p) wrote the message on *sadaqah* but did not send it to his commissioners until he died. He tied it to his sword, and when he died, Abu Bakr applied it until he died, and then 'Umar, until he died. The letter contains "For five camels there is one sheep due, for ten, two sheep.."etc, continuing with the same rates listed in the saying from Anas. Al Nawawi said it is reported by Abu Daud and al Tirmidhi, who marks it a good saying.[34] Al Shaukani adds "This saying is reported also by al Daraqutni, al Hakim and al Baihaq".[35]

Ibn Hazm says in his commentary on the saying from Anas "This saying is maximum in correctness. The Truthful Abu Bakr applied it in the presence of all the Companions, and none of them is known to have disagreed at all, although *ijma'* is usually claimed in much lees unanimitty than this."[36] The great majority of scholars of this nation have received these messages with acceptance, and practically apply them, although some of the leading scholars of *hadith*, such as Yahya bin Ma'in hesitate in considering them correct, in consistency with his special approach in scrutinising narrators and the links among them.

It seems that the Orientalist Schacht abuses the stand of Ibn Ma'in in order to shed doubt on all the sayings on *zakah* and the whole institution itself. He claims that the jurists' opinions on the issue have their stamp on the saying itself, and adds "we note, in this respect, that the detailed system of *zakah* commonly attributed to Abu Bakr is sometimes attributed to the Prophet (p), to 'Umar bin al Khattab, or 'Ali bin Abi Taleb".[37] Schacht is known for his hostility toward the traditions of the Prophet (p). Very often he fabricates reasons to shed doubt on them and to disorient the reader about them. In his books he collects all the misinterpretations and misleading statements and the fabricated and false misrepresentations against the Sunnah. I thank God that my dear and respected colleague, Dr. Muhammad Mustafa al Azami threw these falsehoods back in the face of their author in his extensive study on *hadith* in English, which was submitted to Cambridge University as his Ph.D. dissertation.[38] It showed that to be fair and reasonable, the Orientalist should have realised that it is extremely unlikely that the Prophet (p) would leave such an important issue like *zakah* on camels, sheep, etc., without determining its minimums and its rates, since this was where the majority of the wealth of the Arabs at his time lay. The *zakah* collectors and commissioners were sent by him to oasis and deserted areas to collect and distribute *zakah* every year from the scattered tribesman. There are many reports about sending those collectors and the way they were told to treat *zakatable* individuals, what to take, what not to take, what the response of cattle owners should be and how they should treat the collectors. No fair and reasonable researcher can claim that all these sayings are fabricated on behalf of the Messenger (p).

It is no surprise that the Prophet (p) sent instructions determining *nisabs* and rates of *zakah* on cattle and other growing items of wealth that were most dominant at his time and within his environment. This is testified by the message of instruction of Abu Bakr as well as in that of 'Umar, and both of them are linked to the Prophet (p). It was shown in the previously quoted message of Abu Bakr that "This is the obligation of *sadaqah* that the Prophet of God (p) imposed on Muslims..,". The letter written by 'Umar, and narrated by his son, Abd Allah reads "Verily the Messenger of God (p) wrote the letter of instructions on *sadaqah*..." As for the letter of inetruction of 'Ali bin Abi Talib, there is no agreement among scholars about whether or not it was linked up to the Prophet (p). This anyhow is not as famous as the letters of Abu Bakr or 'Umar, nor does it have the same strength of chain they do. It should be noted that these were not the only letters of instructions that provide details of *zakah* on livestock, There are several other messages, such as that of 'Amr bin Hazm which was addressed to the people of Najran, about the details of obligated *zakah*, and ransoms compensating accidental deaths or the loss of parts of the body. We have also the message of Mu'adh that delineates *sadaqah* on cows, and several other letters.

It is worth observing that all these instructions do not differ on certain major points, such as:
1. There is no *zakah* obligated on anything less than five camels.
2. There is no *zakah* on any number of sheep lees than 40.
3. There is no *zakah* on less than 200 *dirham* of silver.
4. The amount of *zakah* that is obligated on less than 25 camels is calculated in sheep.
5. *Zakah* on up to 25 camels is one sheep for each five camels.
6. They agree on the ages and number of camels due as *zakah* on the wealth of 25 to 120 camels.
7. They also agree on the rate of *zakah* on sheep from 40 to 300, and that the rate afterward is one for each 100.
8. The rate on silver and silver money is one-fourth of one-tenth.
9. Both damaged animals and the top quality animals are not taken as *zakah*. What is required is animals of about average quality.

Those instructions do not agree, however, on certain minute and secondary details such as the rate on camels after 120. The instructions of Abu Bakr put the rate at one female camel two to three years old for each 40, and one female camel three to four years old for each 50, while the instructions in the letters of 'Ali and Amr bin Hazm start again with the same rate as that between five and 125. Also, these instructions do not mention some other items of wealth, such as gold money and cows. It seems to me that this itself provides us with some additional proof that these texts are rightly attributed to the Prophet (p), and that they were not influenced by the jurists' opinions as Schacht claims, because many detailed thoughts of jurists do not appear in these instructions. The Prophet (p) was writing practical instructions to different people according to their needs and circumstances, he did not mention gold money because Arabs of his time did not frequently use it and did not mention cows because they were not common in Madinah. Only in his instructions to Mu'adh, who was being sent to Yemen, did the Prophet mention cows, because they were common in Yemen.

Variance on the Rates after 120 Camels

I pointed out earlier that there are varying views among jurists on *zakah* on above 120 camels. Malik, Shafi'i, Ahmad, and the majority consider the rate to be one female camel, three to four years old for each additional 50, and one female camel, two to three years old, for each additional 40,[39] as mentioned in the message of Abu Bakr and 'Umar narrated successively by Anas and Ibn 'Umar. The same also appears in the messages of Ibn Hazm and Ziad bin Labid to the people of Hadramut,[40] in the words of the Prophet (p) "If they exceed 120, then for each 40 one female camel two to three years old, and for each 50 one female camel three to four years old". Some versions of the last saying are summarized by that narrator, as "In each 50 one female camel ..." without mentioning the rate for each additional 40, but the different versions complete each other.

Abu Hanifah's view

Al Nakha'i, Al Thawri, and Abu Hanifah[41] say that "for what is above 120, we start the rates from the beginning, i,e., for an additional five to 24 camels, the rate is one sheep for each 5 camels, and for an additional 25 camels *zakah* due is one female camel, one to two years old, etc."The following table shows the amount due according to this opinion:

Number of Camels	The Rate		
	Female Camel 3 to 4 years old	Sheep	Others
125	2 +	1	
130	2 +	2	
135	2 +	3	
140	2 +	4	
145	2 +	0	1 (female camel 1 to 2 years old)
150	3 +	0	
155	3 +	1	
160	3 +	2	
165	3 +	3	
170	3 +	4	
175	3 +	0	1 (f.c. 1 to 2 years old)
186	3 +	0	1 (f.c. 2 to 3 years old)
196	4		
200	4		or 5 (f.c. 2 to 3 years old)

After 200 the rate repeats itself, one sheep for each additional five camels, and each time the additional *zakatable* camels reach fifty, the amount of *zakah* due on it is one female camel three to four years old.

The Hanafites argue that Abu Daud reports as *mursal* [saying in whose chain the name of the reporting Companion is not mentioned], Ishaq in his *Musnad* and al Tahawi in his *Mushkel* from Hmmad bin Salamah, who said, "I told Qais bin Sa'd to get me the message of Mohammad bin Hazm, so he gave me a letter which he said he took from Abu Bakr bin Mohammad bin Hazm, who said that the Prophet (p), wrote it to my grandfather. I read it and found in it the rates of *zakah* on camels... " and he narrated the saying until, "Once they exceed 120 make due on each 30 one female camel three to four years old. For the increments, restart the rates from the beginning, and for what is less than 25 camel increments, the amount of *zakah* is due in sheep, one sheep for each five." This is reported in *Nasb Al Rayah* by al Zaila'i.[42] A similar version is narrated by 'Asem bin Damurah from Ali, linked to the Prophet as well as ending at 'Ali,[43] and Ibn Mas'ud is reported to have said similar things. The Hanafites are said by Ibn Rushd to have argued that such a thing cannot be decided but by instructions from the Prophet, because it is not anything that can be deducted by analogy.[44]

The majority of scholars disapprove of the arguments of the Hanafites and see weakness in their findings. Al Baihaqi shows that whatever is reported from Ibn Mas'ud in this matter is not correct.[45] The version of the saying of 'Ali which is linked to the Prophet (p) is also incorrect, and there are also differing opinions on the version that is attributed to 'Ali. In one version it is reported in a consistent manner with the letters of Abu Bakr and 'Umar, while in another version it is reported differently. The usual applicable rule in such a case is that we give more weight to the version that is consistent with other correct sayings which are not disputed. This was noted by al Hazimi.[46] Moreover, the same version of the saying (from 'Asem) contains a sentence all scholars agree to disregard because of its weakness. That is the statement that for each 25 camels the *zakah* due is five sheep instead of a one to two years old she-camel. On the other hand, it is possible to interpret those differing versions in a way that make then consistent with the other correct sayings.

As for the saying of Ibn Hazm, some scholars interpret the starting over of the rates as a reference to the calculation of the rates on additional 40 or 50 camels as mentioned in the two sayings of Abu Bakr and 'Umar.[47] However, the majority of scholars are of the opinion that this version is weak because of the following reasons:

A. It contradicts what came correctly in an exact saying from Anas.

B. It is in opposition to other versions of the same saying, and those other versions are consistent with the two letters of Abu Bakr and 'Umar. Those other versions are sustained by al Baihaqi and others.[48]

C. This differing version is not consistent with the general rule in *zakah* collection, that *zakah* is due in the same kind of the *zakatable* asset except out of necessity. The case of camels below 25 is an obvious necessity, but it is not necessary to take sheep when the number of *zakatable* camels is above 120. Another inconsistency in this version is that the increase of five camels from 145 to 150 requires an increase in *zakah* from a one to two years old female camel to a three to four year old female camel, which makes the rate at this level more than the ratio at other levels.[49]

Other scholars consider the report of lbn Hazm superseded by those of Abu Bakr and 'Umar. Ibn Taimiyah supports this last view an the basis that Ibn Hazm was given these instructions when he was appointed governor of Najran, some time before the death of the Prophet (p), while the message of Abu Bakr the truthful was written by the Prophet (p), just before he died, and since he did not have a chance to send it to his governors it was sent by Abu Bakr after he succeeded him.[50] Thus it seems that Ibn Taimiyah tends to go along with these who consider the instructions of Ibn Hazm cancelled by the later instructions of Abu Bakr and 'Umar, since it is known that the former preceded chronologically the latter.

The view of majority, including; Ahmad, al Shafi'i and al Awza'i, is much stronger and better supported by proofs than that of the Hanafites. Some fair Hanafites even give more weight to the majority view, such as the late 'Abd al 'Alyy al Laknawi, known as the "Ocean of knowledge", from India. In his *Rasa'il al Arkan al Arba'ah*, pp, 170-171, he says: "What seems to be stronger is the view of al Shafi'i and Ahmad.[51]

The view of Al Tabari

Abu Ja'far al Tabari expresses a third, reconciling view, stating that both opinions are acceptable, and it is up to the *zakah* collection agency to select which view to apply.[52] In my opinion this is a better approach, since one should not consider the content of a saying superseded and annulled if there is the slightest chance of a reconciliation of all the reports from the Prophet (p). The reconciliation proposed by al Tabari is undoubtedly acceptable if we keep in mind that the determination of ages and quantity of camels due as *zakah* is meant to facilitate *zakah* calculation, payment, and collection, and to simplify the procedures so that the *zakah* collecting agency can exercise some discretion.

The slight differences in the letters of *zakah*

Looking at the different versions of messages about *zakah* reported from the Messenger of God (p), and his Wise Successors, one would find some minor differences. An example is whether the difference in value between different age camels is ten *dirhams* (or two sheep) or twenty *dirhams* (or two sheep)[53]. How can the difference between the letter of 'Ali and those of Abu Bakr and 'Umar be explained? It is known that the report of 'Ali is incorrect as linked to the Prophet (p), but it is also known that the version stating that it is a saying of 'Ali himself is correct. How could 'Ali differ with the letter of the Prophet (p)? How could he, who lived the era of Abu Bakr and 'Umar not be aware of their letters and application? Did he believe that he had information which superseded that contained in the other letter?

In my opinion all these questions are answered negatively and it seems to me that another interpretation of those minor differences is due. I believe that some of these equalities, like the value of sheep in silver, are given by the Prophet (p), in his capacity as the head of the state. Their prices at his time were such that a sheep equaled approximately ten *dirhams*. It is known that prices vary from time to time, and when the

Prophet (p), gave the ratio as twenty *dirhams* for two sheep he was quoting his period's current prices. At the time of 'Ali's caliphate, prices of sheep were different, and his quotation of those prices were ten dirharms for two sheep. This is not a violation of the Prophet's saying, but rather an application of the rule used by the Prophet (p), to what suits the time of 'Ali. This interpretation is, in my opinion, better than any attempt to disregard any of the differing texts, like what Yahya bin Ma'in did in claiming that nothing correct is reported on the determination of rates and quantities of *zakah*.[55] Ibn Hazm came down very hard on such a claim and asked how a person like Ibn Ma'in could state such a thing without even the slightest supporting evidence.[56] An Orientalist like Schacht abuses to the utmost that claim in his attempt to reject all the correct sayings on *zakah*.

SECTION THREE

ZAKAH ON COWS

Cows, used by mankind for land cultivation, meat and milk, are another bounty of God on His servants. The usefulness of this species was so great at times that some peoples, such as the ancient Egyptians and contemporary Hindus worshiped this animal. Buffalo is counted with the cows by all Muslim jurists, as stated by Ibn al Mundhir.

Zakah on cows is obligated by *Sunnah* and *Ijma*. Bukhari, in his correct collection, reports from Abu Dharr "I came to the Prophet (p)[58] and he said 'I swear by He who holds my soul in His hand,' or 'I swear by the one beside whom there is no God. No man who has camels, cows or sheep and does not pay their right due but on the Day of Judgement will be trampled by them at their largest and heaviest. They will be stepping on him with their hooves and ramming him with their horns, and when the last one is done with him the first is brought back until judgement has been given to all people." Imam al Bukhari said "It is also narrated by Bakir from Abu Saleh from Abu Hurairah from the Prophet (p). The "right due" mentioned in the saying means *zakah* before any other thing. *Zakah* is the right due on wealth as defined by Abu Bakr at the time of fighting those who rejected *zakah*, this definition was approved by 'Umar and all other Companions, (reported by al Bukhari and Muslim). In the version reported by Muslim the word "*zakah*" is used in place of the word "right due", moreover, Muslims through all generations have unanimously confirmed that *zakah* is obligated on cows. Not a single scholar disagrees.[59] There are however, differences in determining nisab and *zakah* rates on cows.

Nisab and rates of *zakah* on cows

There is no correct saying that provides us with the *nisab* and rates of *zakah* on cows as we have seen on camels. This may be because cows were rare in the area of *Hijaz* (around Makkah and Madinah); it may be also because cows are close in size and value to camels, so the Prophet did not determine their rates on the assumption of their obvious similarity. But the fact that there is no correct saying on the issue left the jurists with varying views on the determination of *nisab* and rates.

The popular opinion: *Nisab* **is 30 cows**

The reputed position upheld by the four schools of jurisprudence is that *nisab* is 30 cows, and there is no obligated *zakah* on less than 30 cows. For 30 cows, a one-year old cow is due, and for 40 to 59 cows there is one cow, two years old, due. For 60 cows, two one-year-old cows are due; for 70 cows, a one-year-old and a two-year-old; for 80 cows, two two-year olds; for 90 cows, three one- year-olds; for 100 cows, one two-year old and two one-year-olds; for 110, two cows two year olds and one cow one year old, and for 120 cows, three two-year olds or four one-year olds.

This opinion relies on the saying reported by Ahmad and the four books of Sunan al Tirmidhi, al Nasa'i, Abu Daud and Ibn Majah from Masruq from Mu'adh bin Jabal who said "The Messenger of God, (p) sent me to Yemen. He instructed me to collect on each 30 cows, a one year-old cow, and on each 40 cows one two-year-old"[60]. This saying is graded as good by al Tirmidhi and as correct by Ibn Habban and al Hakim, Ibn 'Abd al Barr comments "Its chain is correct, continuous and authentic" and similar statement is made by Ibn Battal. Ibn Hajar said in *al Fath* "We need to scrutinise any ruling about the correctness of this saying, because Masruq [The follower] did not meet Mu'adh." al Tirmidhi considers it good because there are other sayings that testify with it, such as the one in *al Muwatta*, from Taus from Mu'adh, but Taus did not meet Mu'adh either.[61] Abu Daud has a similar saying from 'Ali.[62] Ibn al Qattan comments on the narration of Masruq from Mu'adh, "It is probable; it should be considered connected in accordance with the majority's view.[63] Ibn Hazm first considered this saying weak on the ground that Masruq did not meet Mu'adh, but he later corrected himself and said. "I found that Masruq merely mentioned the practice of Mu'adh in Yemen regarding *zakah* on cows; there is no doubt that he lived in Mu'adh's era, witnessed his governorship, and recognized his well-known practices. Consequently his quotation of Mu'adh is accepted, because he is quoting many people that witnessed the same practice, a practice that reflected the instructions of the Messenger of God (p), so we must accept that report"[64]. Al Hafiz Ibn Hajar in his *al Talkhis* quotes Ibn 'Abd Al Barr from the latter's *al Istidhkar*, "There is dispute among scholars that the tradition about *zakah* on cows is what exists in the saying from Mu'adh. That is the agreed upon *nisab*"[65]. The saying of Mu'adh is supported by the letter of the Prophet (p) to 'Amr bin Hazm, which says "and on each 30 cows, one cow one-year-old is due, and on each 40 cows, one cow is due". Several scholars of *hadith* consider this last one good.[66]

It should be noted, however, that both of these sayings do not explicitly set the minimum for *zakatability* at 30, and that the wording of these two sayings does not prevent the possibility of imposing *zakah* on less than 30 cows. Thus any claim of *Ijma* as that of Ibn 'Abd al Barr is rejected, because it is known that Ibn al Musayyeb, al Zuhri, Abu Qulabah, al Tabari and others disagree, as will be shown later. Ibn Hajar quotes al Hafiz 'Abd al Haqq as saying "There is no saying, about *nisab* of cows on whose correctness there is agreement."[67]

The saying of Mu'adh also indicates that there is no additional *zakah* on between 40 and 59 cows, and this is also supported by the report that Mu'adh was brought additional *zakah* on cows and refused to take it on this number, as mentioned in *al Muwatta'* and other works. This is the opinion of the three schools of jurisprudence, Abu Yusuf, Mohammad, and the majority of scholars. Abu Hanifah disagrees and expresses the view that what is above 40 cows is *zakatable* at the rate of two-and-half percent of the price of a cow, two years old, for each additional cow above 40. Al Hasan has another report from Abu Hanifah that additional amounts of *zakah* are due only when the number reaches 50, whereby one-and- one-quarter cow becomes the due *zakah*. There is still a third report from Abu Hanifah that goes along with the majority's view.[68]

The view of al Tabari that *nisab* is 50

Ibn Jarir al Tabari argues that *nisab* must be 50 cows, that if is undoubtedly unanimous that for each 50 cows there is an obligatory *zakah* of one cow. Anything below 50 is controversial and not supported by a clear text.[69] Ibn Hazm in *al Muhalla* supports this opinion on the same grounds as al Tabari. He comments "Anything that is controversial and on which there is no text making it obligatory must not be imposed on people, because it means confiscating a part of a Muslim's wealth without being certain about its requirement by virtue of a correct text from God or His messenger (p).[70] He went on to quote, through his own chain, from 'Amr bin Dinar, "The commissioners of Ibn al Zubair as well as Ibn 'Auf used to collect one cow from each 50 cows,[71] 2 cow from each 100 and for more than that, the rate was one cow out of each 50.[72] These commissioners were performing their duties in the presence of many, many Companions in Madinah, and this performance was not objected to.

But one may disprove this opinion on two grounds:

A. From the point of view of the text. The long saying of 'Amr bin Hazm on *zakah* says "and from each 30 cows, take one cow one-year-old, and from each 40 cows, one cow". This saying is graded good by a handful of leading scholars and it was used by al Tabari against the view of Taqiy al Din bin Daqiq al 'Id in his book *Al Imam*.[73] Additionally, the saying of Mu'adh according to which *zakah* should be collected on 30 and 40 cows is graded correct by a group of the leading scholars. It is by virtue of this saying that Ibn Hazm corrected himself and reverted to the view of the majority.[74]

B. From the point of view of the rationale. It is very unlikely that *Shari'ah*, which is most just and wise, would obligate *zakah* on only 5 camels or 40 sheep and leave the minimum for *zakatability* on cows to be 50. Cows may not be as huge as camels, but they certainly are bigger, more useful, and more valuable than sheep.

The opinion of Ibn al Musayyeb and Al Zuhri

Two leading scholars, Said bin al Musayyeb and Muhammad bin Shehab al Zuhri, along with Abu Qulabah and others view *nisab* on cows to be the same as *nisab* on camels, and the *zakah* rate of camels to be the same for cows with only a minor change, that is, disregarding the ages of camels. A similar opinion is reported as a version of the letter of 'Umar bin Al Khattab on *zakah*, from Jabir bin 'Abd Allah and others who paid *zakah* at the time of the Prophet (p). Abu 'Ubaid reported from Mohammad bin 'Abd al Rahman that the instructions 'Umar bin al Khattab wrote on *zakah* included "from cows one should take the same as from camels." Abu 'Ubaid continues "Others were asked about *zakah* on cows and the answer was it is the same on camels".

Ibn Hazm reports with his own chain from al Zuhri and Qatadah, both from Jabir bin 'Abd Allah his saying that "in each five cows there is one sheep due, in ten two sheep, in 15, three sheep, and in 20, four sheep due." Al Zuhri says "*zakah* on cows is like *zakah* on camels except for the ages. That is, if the number of cows were between 25 and 75 the amount of *zakah* due on it is one cow, between 76 and 120 two cows. Above 120, for an additional 40 cows there is one additional cow. We were told that the statement 'in each 30 cow there is one cow due one year old, and in each 40 cows there is due one cow ' was only a simplification and reduction in the rates for the people of Yemen which was disregarded later."[76] It is also reported from 'Ikrimah bin Walid his saying: later I was commissioned on the *zakah* of 'Ikk and I met some old people who paid *zakah* at the time of the Messenger of God (p). They disagreed: some of them said make *zakah* on cows like *zakah* on camels, and some said from each 30 cows you take one cow, one year old, while yet some others said from each 40 cows you should take one two-year-old cow."[76] Ibn Hazm reports through his own chain from Ibn al Musayyib, Abu Qulabah, and another scholar a view similar to that of al Zuhri. He also report from 'Umar bin 'Abd al Rahman bin Khildah al Ansari, "*Zakah* on cows is the same as *zakah* on camels except for the ages.[77]

Evidence supporting this view

A. This opinion is supported by a report of Abu Ubaid with his own chain from Muhammad bin 'Abd al Rahman, "It is in the Prophet's letter on *zakah* and in the letter of 'Umar bin al Khattab that from cows, one should take the same as from camels."[78] Also, this view is supported by what is reported by 'Abd al Razzaq from Ma'mar, who said, " Sammak bin al Fadl gave me a letter from the Prophet, to Malik bin Kuflanis Al Mus'abiyn, in which I read, 'and on cows is due the same as on camels.'"[79]

B. This is confirmed by what is mentioned by al Zuhri that it was the latest report from the Messenger of God (p), and that taking a one-year-old cow of each 30 cows was, at the beginning, a matter of favor for the peoples of Yemen. This report is *mursal*, but it is supported by the previous saying and by statements from some Companions. Ibn Hazm comments "If a *mursal* saying would be accepted from anyone, it deserves to be accepted from al Zuhri because he was well versed in Suunah and met a number of the Companions".[80]

C. This view is also supported by the general rule implied in the saying mentioned at the beginning of Section 3 "And for anyone who owns cows and who does not pay their right due, he would be laid down for the cows to trample on the Day of Resurerction" It is argued that this is a general text that includes cows of any number except for restrictions brought in by a text or any *Ijma'*. It is further argued that the saying stating that there is one cow, one year old, due, on each 30, and a two-year-old due on each 40 also supports this opinion because it does not waive *zakah* from cows below 30. It is only a statement of the rate of *zakah*.

D. It is further argued, by analogy, that cows are similar to camels. In 'Id sacrifice, for example, a cow is sufficient for seven individuals, just as a camel. Also in the gifts of thanks to God after pilgrimage , the rate of camels and cows is the same, so *zakah* on cows should be like that on camels.[81]

However, Ibn Hazm disproves these arguments on the basis that the sayings attributed to the Prophet (p) are not completely linked to him and one can only give as evidence a saying whose chain is completely linked to the Prophet. He notes that the argument that the saying about *zakah* on cows is general for any number of cows is binding only an the Hanafites and Malikites who obligate *zakah* on business assests by generality of texts alone, but not those who require specific text for obligating any ruling in *Shari'ah*. As for the argument that *zakah* on cows should be similar to that on camels by analogy, I say that if analogy is accepted as a tool in deducting rulings in *Shari'ah*, then this application of it is a correct one, since I am aware of no agreed-upon difference between camels and cows. Thus, this conclusion must be binding to those who accept analogy--the Hanafites, Malikites and Shafi'ites, but I do not.[82]

On the other hand, scholars of the known schools of jurisprudence argue that *nisab* should not be deducted by analogy; *nisab* should only come from a text, and it is evident that there is no text on *nisab* of cows. Ibn Qudamah adds that such an analogy is incorrect, since in sacrifice and pilgrimage, 35 sheep equal five camels, but 35 sheep are not *nisab* in *zakah*.[83]

A fourth opinion

Ibn Rushd gives yet another opinion without providing the name of its author nor its argument: On each ten cows there is one sheep due, until they reach 30 cows, on which there is a one-year-old cow due.[84] I find that Ibn Abi Shaibah attributes this view to Shahr bin Haushab in his *al Musannaf*. The latter says "*zakah* should be one sheep due on each ten cows, two sheep on each twenty cows, and one cow, one year old, on 30 cows."[85] This means that *nisab* of cows is ten as compared to five in the previously mentioned opinion. No evidence of support is given by Ibn Abi Shaibah. It may come to mind that this argument can be supported by the saying that estimates the compensation for the loss of life at 100 camels or 200 cows. This is reported as said by 'Umar, as well as linked to the Prophet (p).[86] This implies that one camel equals two cows. If *nisab* for camels is five, that of cows must be ten, and if for each five camels the amount of *zakah* due is one sheep, there should be one sheep due for each ten cows.

Analysis and weighing

After listing all these opinions,[87] it seems to ms the view of the majority about the rate on each 30 and 40 cows is the one that carries more weight, on the basis of the saying of Mu'adh and Amr bin Hazm. However, it is notable that these two sayings do not give information about what is below 30 cows, whether negative or positive, but only determine the rate of *zakah* rather than its *nisab*, except by contrast. Interestingly enough, the saying of Ibn Hazm goes on to state, "And on each 40 dinars (of gold) there is due one dinar". The majority of jurists agree that *nisab* on gold is 20 dinar and not 40, which indicates that this saying was given to determine the rate of *zakah* and not necessarily its *nisab*, since the rate on gold is two-and-half percent or one-fortieth.

It is possible to combine this opinion with that of Ibn al Musayyib, al Zuhri and their group of followers in putting *nisab* on cows at five, especially since it is put at five in a version of 'Umar's letter on *zakah*, as a report from Jabir bin 'Abd Allah, a Companion, and is sometimes attributed to the letter of the Prophet (p). Abu 'Ubaid comments that this opinion was not known by people, but it was shown earlier that it was in fact known to a number of Companions and Followers. Additionally, one can argue that the analogy of cows and camels is a strong one and the objection of Ibn Hazm can be disregarded as based on his personal view that all analogy is invalid. The majority of scholars are in accord on the principle that the correct analogy is a source of deduction in *Shari'ah*.

God knows best, but it seems to me that the Messenger of God (p), intentionally left certain issues in *zakah* undefined and undetermined in order to make its application flexible with changing circumstances. It is left to the Islamic state and its *zakah* institution to draw up those details from time to time. Cows may become more expensive and useful than camels. In this case *nisab* may be set at five, and the rate of one sheep for each five cows could be applied, and when they number 30's and 40's, the saying from Mu'adh could be applied. This opinion may become more practical and clear when cow raising becomes big and profitable business. In some countries or times, cows may carry lesser value than camels, to the extent that five of them would not be such substantial wealth as to stand as a minimum *zakatable*, in which case *nisab* could be put at 30. This flexibility has its root in the comment of al Zuhri that 30 cows as *nisab* was made only to make things easier for the people of Yemen. Given what al Zuhri said, the sequence in time between letters setting the *nisab* at 30 and at five does not necessarily imply that the latter annuls the former, but can be interpreted as different applications in two different circumstances by the Prophet (p), in his capacity as head of state and not just as a Messenger. Consequently, for different circumstances he may have even another opinion.[89]

SECTION FOUR

ZAKAH ON SHEEP

Zakah on sheep is obligating by virtue of *Sunnah* and *Ijma'*. In *Sunnah*, Anas narrates in the letter of instruction of Abu Bakr mentioned earlier that "As for *sadaqah* on sheep, naturally cost-free pastured, out of each 40 there is one sheep due, up to 120. If the number increased, then two sheep are due up to 200, and if the number increases by one up to 300, there are three sheep due. If it is above 300,[90] then one sheep is taken for each additional 100. If naturally, cost-free pastured sheep are less than 40, even by only one, there is no obligatory *sadaqah* on it unless the owner wishes to volunteer, As *zakah* one should not accept the old, the damaged, or the ram except when volunteered by the owners." Similar statements appear in the saying from Ibn 'Umar and in several others.

Jurists unanimously agree that *zakah* is obligatory on sheep. There is also unanimous opinion that the word "*ghanam*" includes both sheep and goats in such a way that they are combined together as one item.[91]

According to this saying the following table can be drawn:

Number of sheep		Amount of *zakah* (in sheep)
From	to	
1	39	Nothing
40	120	one
121	200	two
201	300	three
301	400	four
401	500	five

and so on.

We will discuss in section 6 the description of what animal should be taken as *zakah* as for its size, age and sex.

Discussion of the rate on sheep

It is notable that *Shari'ah* reduced the rate on sheep as their number increases. From the previous schedule it is observed that as the number grows above 120 the rate stabilizes at one percent in contrast with the usual two-and-half percent on business assets, money and other assests. What is the rationale for this reduction? Some contemporary researchers[92] attempt to explain this reduction with the argument that *Shari'ah* intends to encourage animal breeding by this reduction, since the rate on 40 sheep is two-and-half percent and it regresses at 200, going clean to one percent. But one wonders, if this explanation is correct, why the same is not applied on *zakah* on other kinds of livestock. The rate on both camel and cows stabilizes around two-and-half percent on big numbers, which is consistent with the general rate of *zakah*. If the above-mentioned interpretation is correct, it should apply to other animals as well.

The way I see it --God knows best-- is that once the number of sheep grows, the total assests of sheep shall contain many baby lambs because most sheep give birth more than once a year, These babies are counted in the number of sheep but not accepted as payment of *zakah*, as shall be shown in the following two sections. It seems to me that the justice requires certain reduction in the rate for this reason. If the rate is kept at one out of each 40 while the herd contains many babies, the actual rate becomes much higher. As for the first 40, the rate is two-and-half percent because it is expected that babies would not be counted in the first 40, as will be explained in Section five.

This shows that the rate of *zakah* is in fact about constant, not progressive or regressive, which will be discussed at length in the last part of this book. In the commentary on *al Risalah*, the late Malikkite Sheikh Zarruq writes on the declining rate of *zakah* on sheep between 40 and 200" once the numbers of sheep grows their cost increases, and the desire for accumulation increases too, therefore, the rate on cash assets is as low as one fourth of ten percent, while it goes up to ten percent on other assets."[93] I could not appreciate this argument because when wealth increases its costs decline. This is perhaps why owners of cattle like to pasture together on a large scale, to diffuse the cost of shelter and shepherding. This is known now as the economy of large scale. If the explanation given by Zarruq is correct it should have applied to all cattles but we see the rate not reduced for large quantities of camel and cows.

SECTION FIVE

ARE BABY ANIMALS *ZAKATABLE* ?

Ahmad, Abu Daud, and al Nasa'i report from Suaid Bin Ghaflah that "the *zakah* commissioner of the Messenger of god (p), came to us. We sat close to him and I heard him saying 'In my instructions it is pleased that I should not take from nursing animals'.[94] This indicates that baby livestock are not *zakatable*, and this is the opinion of a group of leading scholars. But the chain of this saying is contested. On the other hand, Malik in *al Muwatta* reports that 'Umar told his commissioner, Sufian bin 'Abd Allah al Thaqafi, to "Count the babies in them, even those carried by the shephered in his hands, but do not accept them in payment."[95] This is also reported by al Shafi'i and 'Abu Ubaid.[96] This report of 'Umar contradicts the previous report and indicates that baby animals are counted in *nisab* and consequently *zakatable*. This is what a group of jurists adopt, to the extent that if all the *zakatable* animals were babies, one of them would be acceptable as payment,"[97] though others say the owner should be asked to buy an older animal from outside to fulfil the payment of the *zakah*.[98]

Some scholars attempt to reconcile the report of 'Umar with the saying of Suaid by not obligating *zakah* on baby animals if they comprise the entire *zakatable*, saying that is where the saying of Suaid applies, while counting baby animals if they are with their mothers. However, some jurists consider that baby animals are counted in the total number of the *zakatable* herd only if older animals make up the *nisab* required for *zakatability*. This is the view of Abu Hanifah, al Shafi'i, Ibn Hazm and others.[99] It is, in my opinion, the closest to Islamic justice and it seems to outweigh other views. It violates the principle of justice to exempt from *zakah* a person who owns, for example, four old camels and collect it from a person who owns five baby camels or four baby lambs, since the latter is less rich than the former. Once *nisab* is fulfilled by counting adult animals alone, then baby animals can be counted in determining the total number subject to *zakah*. For larger quantities, the rate structure itself is flexible because it takes stratas of quantities and applies the same rate on the lower and the higher ends of each layer. Thus five camels are *zakatable* at the rate of one sheep, the same as nine camels. It seems to me that this was purposefully set up by the Prophet (p) in order to give leeway for the presence of baby animals. It seems that this becomes more apparent in sheep, especially goats, which give birth more than once a year. This is perhaps why the rate of sheep is lower at larger quantities, and becomes one percent after the sheep reach 200 in number.

SECTION SIX

CONDITIONS OF ANIMALS GIVEN AS *ZAKAH*

A few conditions are required of the animals that can be paid as *zakah*, which include:

1. Free of defects and damage. The animal should be free of illness, bone fracture, old age, or birth and accidental defects or damages. The Qur'an says "and do not aim at getting anything which is bad, in order that out of it ye may spend "[100] and the Prophet (p) states "and one should not give an old or defective animal, nor should a collector accept a ram unless the payer wishes to volunteer it". This is part of the saying from Anas. Accepting damaged animals as *zakah* payment is not fair to the poor and other deserving recipients; it is a bias in favor of the owner, which is improper.

As for the definition of defect or damages, the majority are of the view that it is the same definition used in sales contracts, though some say that anything not accepted for sacrifice is not accepted as *zakah*.[101] One should mentions unique case where a defected or damaged animal is accepted as *zakah*, which is if all the animals being *zakated* have the same defect or damage, such as a common disease. This is because the ordinance of *zakah* asks payment from what the *zakatable* person owns without forcing him or her to purchase from outside a good animal only for the payment of *zakah*.[102]

2. Specification of the animal's sex, The animal given as *zakah* must be a female of the species. This applies only to camels, except in the cases mentioned in the saying from Anas, whereby a male of a higher age group is accepted instead of the due female. Hanafites accept the payment of male animals on the basis of estimating their value,[103] because according to them, the value of the due item can be paid instead of it as shall be discussed, God willing, in Part Five.

As for cows, the text requires male or female, one year old, out of each 30, which is not disputed. However, there is a variation on whether to accept a two-year-old male cow, out of each 40. The majority do not approve of that, while the Hanafites accept it on the grounds that male and female cows are similar in value. Hanafites are also supported by a saying reported by al Tabarani from Ibn 'Abbas "For each 30 cows there is due one cow one year old, and for each 40 one older, male or female".[104]

With regard to sheep, Hanafites do not distinguish between male and female because of the similarity in price and use and also because the text mentions a sheep due, without distinguishing between male and female.[105] Malikites go along with the Hanafites on *zakah* on sheep, while the Hanbalites do not approve of taking the male sheep as *zakah* as long as there are females in the herd. This is taken in analogy to camels.[107] Furthermore, Malik and al Shafi'i leave it to *zakah* collectors to select the male or the female animal, depending on which is better for *zakah* recipients.[108] Al Nawawi writes, "If the male sheep is given as *zakah*, it is alright, according to the majority of Shafi'ites "It is also Shafi'i's opinion himself. Some Shafi'ites do not approve of this view because of 'Umar's report mentioned earlier, which states "and take the female sheep more than one year old".[109] After presenting the different opinion, I select the Hanafite's view with regard to cows and sheep because I think it carries more weight and has more convincing evidence than the others.

3. Age requirement. Sayings give specific ages for *zakah* on camels and cows which must be complied with, on the ground that taking less or more is unfair with either payers or recipients of *zakah*. This is agreed upon. As for sheep, there is a variation of opinion. According to Malik, sheep accepted in *zakah* should be at least one-year-old sheep or goat, in compliance with the saying "our right is at the least one-year-old sheep or goat". Shafi'i and Ahmad believe that what is paid as *zakah* should be at least one year old for goats and six months old for sheep. This is also reported by Abu Daud and Muhammad, while Abu Hanifah agrees with Malik, although he allows giving of six-month-old sheep on the basis of value.[112] I select the view of Ahmad, al Shafi'i, Abu Yousuf and Muhammad, because it has strong proofs.

If the age necessary for payment is not available and other ages are available, how should *zakah* be paid? Ibn Rushd summarizes the several opinions, "according to Malik the *zakah* payer is required to buy the necessary animal. Others say the payer should pay a lower-age animal plus compensation at the rate of 20 *dirhams* or 2 sheep for each one year difference in the age of camels, as mentioned in the letter of Abu Bakr on *zakah*, and there should be no differences about it. This is also the view of al Shaifi'i and Abu

Thawr. Some jurists say that payment must be made of the available age and a compensation for the difference should be paid.[113] According to Abu Hanifah, the value of the necessary animal is due. It seems to me, however, that Abu Hanifah's view is also consistent with the saying, because the Prophet (p) estimated the difference in age in his capacity as head of state rather than as religious ordinance, and such estimation varies with time. 'Ali estimated sheep at different prices than the estimation of the Prophet (p).[114]

4. The average

The *zakah* collector should not take the best or the worst in quality, but the average of the animals owed. Ibn 'Abbas narrates that the Prophet (p) said to Mu'adh, "Avoid the best of people's wealth, and be fearful of the prayer of the oppressed, for there is no curtain between it and God." Ibn Abi Shaibah reports that the Prophet (p) saw among the camels collected as *sadaqah*, an excellent she-camel. He was furious at the collector and said, "What is this?" The collector answered "I exchanged it for two lesser quality camels". The Prophet said, "Then it is all right."[115]

This is essentially because *zakah* is based on fairness to the two parties, payers and recipients, and taking the best or the worst means favoring one of them. However, it is obvious that the worst or the best can be taken on the basis of value at the option of the livestock owner. Abu Daud reports, through his own chain, from the Prophet (p) "There are three things, which whoever fulfills them will taste the sweetness of faith: to worship God alone, realizing that there is no deity but God, to give *zakah* on your wealth with your soul pleased at paying it year after year... and to give not the old, or the ill or the baby, or the defective animal that give little milk, but to give from the average of your wealth. God does not ask you to give the best of it, nor does He ordain you to give the worst of it."[116] As *zakah* payment, the collector must not take the animal that nurses babies, nor pregnant animals, nor the ram out of sheep, nor the animal that is meant to provide meat for the household of the *zakah* payer.[117] Malik reports in *al Muwatta* from 'Aishah that 'Umar bin al Khattab passed by the sheep taken as *sadaqah*, and saw one with big udders and asked, "What is this sheep? "He was answered, "One taken as *sadaqah*." He replied, "Its owners did not give it pleasantly, so do not force people to turn back, and do not take the best of the wealth of Muslims."[118]

As an application of this condition, baby animals are not accepted as *zakah*. When 'Umar bin al Khattab commissioned Sufian bin 'Abd Allah al Thaqafi on *zakah*, he started counting the baby sheep and was asked "Are you counting these babies while you don't accept them in payment? "When he came back to 'Umar and told him that, 'Umar said, " Yes, count baby sheep, even those which are so young that they must be carried by the shepherd, but do not accept them in payment, nor should you take that which is meant for meat of the household, nursing mother sheep, pregnant sheep, nor the ram. Take only sheep or goat which are one year old." Ahmad, Abu Daud, and al Nasa'i report from a person named Si'r from the two men commissioned by the Messenger of God (p) to collect *zakah*. They said "The Messenger of God (p) prevented us from taking a pregnant animal". And from Suaid bin Ghafalah "A *zakah* collector sent by the

Messenger of God (p) came to us end I heard him saying 'In the pledged instructions given to me it was written I should not count baby animals'.. and when a man wanted to give him a pregnant she-camel, he refused to accept it".[120]

SECTION SEVEN

THE EFFECT OF MIXING AND PARTNERSHIP ON *ZAKAH* ON LIVESTOCK

It is common for livestock owners, to put together their cattles in order to save on overhead expenses. Should all gathered livestock be treated as one unit in determining the *nisab* and rate of *zakah*? or should they be considered for each owner alone?

To deal with this question one should note that there are two leading forms of collective breeding. One involves keeping the ownership separate and sharing in certain expenses, and the other is when the cattle is owned commonly among the partners. In the latter form, the share of each owner is not determined in number but only as a proportion of the total, whereas in the former each person's own animals are distinguished. These two forms of investing together need not have the same effect on *zakatability*.

Ibn Rushd in *Bidayat al Mujtahid*, summarizes the views of jurists according to the following:

Most jurists view mixing animals as affecting the *zakatability* except for Abu Hanifah and his disciples, who believe that mixing together of animals does not have any effect on *nisab* or on the applicable rate. Malik, al Shafi'i, and most jurists agree that the group of breeders who mix their cattles together are treated as if they were one owner. Those jurists however differ in two areas: the determination of *nisab* and the definition of effective mixing together.

It should be noted that the reason for these different opinions is the different interpretation of the saying of the Prophet (p). In the letter on *sadaqah* the Prophet (p) said, "What is separate should not be counted together, and what is together may not be counted separately in order to avoid *sadaqah*, and as far what belongs to two persons, they must settle their account in proportion to their ownership". Those who say that mixing together does not affect the *zakah* interpret this to mean that the *zakah* collector should not divide herds owned by one person in such a way that would increase *zakah*. For instance, 120 sheep owned by one person should not be divided into three groups of 40 to make *zakah* three sheep instead of one. They also say that what is owned by one person should not be added to what is owned by another in order to make *nisab*, such as grouping the herds of two peoples, each with 20 sheep, to make them *zakatable* as *nisab*. Al Shafi'i and his disciples interpret this saying to mean that cattle put together are treated as if they were owned by one person, both in the application of *nisab* and in the determination of the *zakah* rate. On the other hand, Malik and his students interpret it to mean that if each owner alone has the minimum of *nisab* then the applicable rate is that of the total and not that which applies on what belongs to each owner alone.[122]

As for the variation on the definition of mixing together, al Safi'i is of the opinion that mixing animals together means in pasturing, milking, sheltering and watering, to the extent that putting animals together is like partnership. Accordingly, *nisab* is applied on the total and not on each owner alone. Malik sees effective mix together as where watering, pasturing, sheltering and shepherding are common.[123]

Ibn Hazm in *al Muhalla* strongly criticizes the opinion that mixing animal, together affects *zakah*, on the grounds that this ends up in fact violating the essential texts of *zakah*. For example, a person who owns less than *nisab* is exempt from paying *zakah*, so how could such a person be *zakated* if he puts his cattle with others? This, according to Ibn Hazm, contradicts the principle of individual responsibility and private ownership, making one person's property affect other persons duties and obligations. This is a violation of the Qur'an and *Sunnah*.[124] It should be noted at last that the view of the Shafites has widest concept of the effect on *zakah* of mixing the wealth of several owners. They go as far as affecting *zakah* not only on livestock but also on crops, fruits, silver, and gold money that are mixed.[125] This view may serve as a basis for the treatment of contemporary corporations as the *zakah* agency may find best, because it provides for simplicity in procedures and thrift in collection expenses.

SECTION EIGHT

ZAKAH ON HORSES

Horses used for personal transportation and fighting are exempt from *zakah*.

It is agreed upon among Muslims that horses owned for the purpose of personal riding, carrying personal loads, and fighting for the sake of God are exempt whether they are naturally pastured or fed in ranches, because they are for personal and household use and are not growing assets in excess of personal needs.[126] On the other hand, all Muslims except Zahirites have agreed that horses used as business inventory owned by horses' merchants, are *zakatable* whether they are naturally pastured or manually fed on the grounds that horses designed for business inventory are commodities, like other business asset.[127] It is also agreed upon that horses that are fed by owners most of the year, which are not owned for any of the previously mentioned purposes, are exempt from *zakah*, because natural free pasturing is a condition for *zakatability* of animals, according to the majority of scholars.[128]

Zakatability of naturally pastured horses designated for breeding

There are two opinions on the *zakatability* of naturally cost-free pastured horses that are designated for breeding and growth. Abu Hanifah believe they are *zakatable*, provided that not all horses owned are males since in this case they cannot breed.[129] The majority of jurists consider these horses exempt from *zakah*, and this is narrated by Ibn al Mundhir from 'Ali, Ibn 'Amr al Sha'bi, 'Ata, al Husain al Abdi, 'Uamar bin 'Abd al Aziz, al Thawri, Abu Yusuf, Muhammad (the two disciples of Abu Hanifah) Abu Thawr, Abu Khaithamah, and Abu Bakr bin Shaibah. Others attribute this opinion to 'Umar, Malik, al Awza'i, al Laith and Daud.[130]

Evidence of the majority for the non-*zakatability* of horses

1. It is reported in the two correct books and in others from Abu Hurairah that the Prophet (p) said " There is no *sadaqah* obligated on Muslims on their slaves and mares."[131] This exemption includes all horses, naturally pastured or not, female or male because it is general.

2. The report of Ahmad, Abu Daud, and al Tirmidhi from Ali from the Prophet (p) "I waived for you *sadaqah* on horses and slaves. Pay *sadaqah* on silver money, one dirham for each 40."[132]

3. The actions of the Prophet (p) did not include collecting *zakah* on horses, even though it was collected on camels, cows and sheep. The Messenger is the one who gives the details of the obligation outlined in the Qur'an, and his word and deed indicate that horses are not *zakatable*.

4. They also argue that livestock that are *zakatable* are obviously very different from horses and that horses cannot be made *zakatable* by analogy because of the basic differences in use and in the purpose of owning these different kinds of animals. Horses are obtained for use in fighting, in establishing this religion, and in defense against enemies, so people should be encouraged to obtain them and keep them for such purposes. God says "Against them make ready your strength to the utmost of your power, including seeds of war.[133] Horses of war are fighting equipment, like weapons and like other fighting tools are not *zakatable* as long as they are not used as a commodity for trade.[134]

Abu Hanifah's opinion and its supporting evidence

Abu Hanifah, who believes that naturally pastured horses are *zakatable*, provides the following arguments:

Firstly, al Bukhari reports in his correct collection from Abu Hurairah that the Prophet (p) said "Steeds are for a person a source of reward, for another they are a source of sustenance, and for yet another they are a source of sin. He for whom they are a source of reward is the man who owns horses for the purpose of fighting for the sake of God, to ride it in battle or to give it to someone else to ride in battle. That is why they are a source of reward. For one who keeps horses for personal transportation so he does not need others, and does not forget God's right on the horses or the right of people to be given lifts on their backs, they are source of sustenance. And for the person who keeps steeds as a matter of pride and to fight against the people of Islam, they are a source of sin."[135] This saying indicates that there is a right of God on horses, *zakah* and giving lifts on their backs.[136] Other jurists argue that what is meant by the right on horses is the use of horses in fighting.[137]

Secondly, it is reported from Jabir from the Prophet (p), "On each naturally pastured mare there is due one diner or ten *dirhams*." It is reported by al Daraqutni and al Baihaqi, and they grade it weak. For this reason, the majority of jurists argue that it can not stand against the correct saying of *zakah* waiving off horses." There is no *zakah* on the slaves and mares of Muslims."

Thirdly, by analogy to camels, both are growing and useful animals, and in both the condition for *zakatability*, natural cost-free pasturing, is fulfilled. The claimed differences between horses and other livestock are no more than those among the other kinds of livestock, since each animal has its unique characteristics. There are many differences between camels and sheep yet both are *zakatable*. Abu Hanifah holds to this argument on the basis that the reason for the obligation of *zakah* is a matter that can be rationalized and not a matter of worship only. This reason is growth or growth potential and once growth exists in another asset *zakatability* must be extended to it.

Fourthly, al Tahawi and al Daraqutni report, with a correct chain, from al Sa'ib bin Yazid "I witnessed my father evaluating his horses and paying its *sadaqah* to 'Umar bin al Khattab,[138] 'Abd al Razzaq and al Bai'aqi report from Ya'la bin Umayah that 'Abd al Rahman, brother of Ya'la, bought a mare from a man in Yemen for the price of 100 camels. The seller felt sorry and went to 'Umar complaining "Ya'la and his brother forced me to sell my mare. 'Umar asked Ya'la to come and meet with him, and he gave 'Umar the true story. 'Umar wondered "Would a steed reach that high a pries in your area? I never realized that a mare would reach that value. Would it be just to take one sheep out of each 40 and not take anything from horses? Collect one *dinar* per horse". He then imposed *zakah* on horses at the rate of one *dinar* each.[139] Ibn Hazm reports, with his own chain, from Ibn Shihab al Zuhri that al Sa'ib bin Yazid told him that he used to bring 'Umar bin al Khattab *zakah* on horses. Ibn Shiab adds, "'Umar used to collect *zakah* on horses."[140] Anas bin Malik narrates that "'Umar used to collect ten *dirhams* on each mare and five on each male horse.[141] Zaid bin Thibit had similar views to that of 'Umar. During the reign of Marwan bin al Hakam, jurists disputed the *zakatability* of naturally cost-free pastured horses, and when Marwan consulted the Companion, Abu Hurairah, he narrated the saying "There is no *sadaqah* on one's slave and one's mare." Marwan turned to Zaid bin Thabit and asked "What do you say, O Abu Said?" Abu Hurairah said, "I wonder at Marwan. I tell him the saying of the Messenger of God (p) and he asks 'What do you say O Abu Sa'id?" Zaid answered "The Messenger of God (p) verily said the truth, but he meant the horse of a fighter for the sake of God. For a merchant who keeps horses for breeding, they are *zakatable*." Marwan asked

"How much?" He replied "One *dinar* or ten *dirhams* on each horse".[142] Ibn Zanjawaih in *Kitab al Amwal* reports with his chain from Taus "I asked Ibn 'Abbas, 'are horses *zakatable*?' and he answered "There is no *sadaqah* on the horse of the fighter for the sake of God,"[143] which implies that other horses are *zakatable*. Ibrahim al Nakha'i, a Follower, had the same view as 'Umar and Zaid. He said "Naturally pastured horses raised for breeding are *zakatable* at one *dinar* or ten *dirhams* on each horse, or else evaluate them and pay ten *dirhams* for each 200 *dirhams* of their value." Mentioned by Muhammad in al 'Athar, Abu Yusuf reports a similar statement,[144] also from Hamad bin Abu Sulaiman that he said and horses are *zakatable*."[145]

Nisab and rates of *zakah* on horses

Abu Hanifah does not determine a *nisab* for horses. The author of *al Durr al Mukhtar* writes "It is best known that Abu Hanifah does not estimate *nisab* for horses; we have no report from him about that."[146] Ibn 'Abidin in his commentary quotes al Qahastani as saying "Some indicate *nisab* at three and others indicate it at five."[147] It seems that the estimation of five is mare correct because of its similarity to that of camels. The number five is often used in *nisab* . *nisab* is five camels, five *'uqiyyah* of silver [equals 200 *dirhams*] and 5 wasq of grain.

The rate is explained by Ibn Abidin from Abu Hanifah: Owners of Arabian horses are given the choice of paying one *dinar* on each or evaluating their horses and paying 5 *dirhams* for each 200 *dirhams* of value - the rate is just two-and-half. For non-arabian horses, only the value is considered.[148]

Analysis

After discussing the two arguments, it seems to me that the Messenger (p) did not negate the existence of *zakah* on horses in a clear way, but neither did he obligate it clearly. The saying from Abu Hurairah, "There is no *sadaqah* on a Muslim's slave and mare" does not touch on anything other than the horse used for personal transportation and as a mount for war. This explanation is supported by the interpretation from Zaid bin Thabit and 'Abbas, correctly reported to him. The very words "His slave and his mare" in the saying seem to indicate this meaning. Also, that it is unanimous by *Ijma'* among jurists -- except Zahirites-- that *zakah* is obligatory on horses and slaves when they are part of business inventory. Abu Hurairah was inclined to hold to the letters of texts, and was known among the Companions for his precise memory, and did not have a reputation of analyzing and elaborating like Zaid and Ibn 'Abbas. The saying from 'Ali, "I have waived for you the *sadaqah* on horses and slaves" is noted by al Daraqutni as correct when it ends at 'Ali and is not linked to the Prophet. It is well known that al Daraqutni is the expert on such matters. However the words "waived for you" imply that these assets should be in principle *zakatable* but the Prophet (p) waived the *zakah* are them for certain reason.[149] This could be the desperate need for steeds of war or the fact that horses were not a substantial item of wealth in Arabia.

Anyhow, the lack of a text clearly obligating the *zakah* on horses does not necessarily mean that they are not *zakatable*. The Prophet (p) is not reported to have said anything about obligating *zakah* on gold. It is apparent that most coins used at his time were silver and the ruling on gold is derived by analogy because of the apparent similarity in use of the two metals. The story of 'Umar with Yala bin Umayah has, in my opinion, extremely important weight. The action taken by 'Umar indicates that analogy and *ijtihad* have an important position in *zakah*. The fact that the Prophet (p) took *zakah* from certain kinds of assets does not mean that Muslims after him may not take it from other kinds that are similar. In fact every substantial growing asset must be *zakatable*. The rates, wherever there is no text, are subject to *ijtihad*.

The majority of jurists consider the action of 'Umar as his own *ijtihad*, which is not binding. They also argue that 'Umar obligated *zakah* on horses after it was requested from him by a group representing the people of Syria who said to him, "We have acquired certain wealth, including horses and slaves, and we would like it to be purified and sancitified." "Umar replied "How could I do a thing which was not done by my two predecessors before me!" He consulted the Companions of Muhammad (p). 'Ali suggested, "It is a good idea as long as it does not become a regular due enforced by rulers after you."[150] It seems to me that this incident preceds the above-mentioned story about the people from Yemen. The story of Yemen explains the reasoning of 'Umar, which was spurred by the high prices horses had assumed in Yemen. His words were, "Should we take one sheep out of each forty and take nothing on horses?" What seems reasonable is that the story with the Yemenites took place after that with the Syrians, since with the latter he was hesitant and consulted the Companion, while with the Yemenites he was determined because he had already made up his mind after consultation.

On the other hand, the rate imposed by 'Umar (one *dinar* per horse) does not seem to be binding on us because of changes in the purchasing power of the *dinar* as well as in the prices of horses in both time and place. I prefer at our time to revert to the opinion of al Nakha'i and Abu Hanifah, who suggest the evaluation of horses and the application of the rate 2.5%. Obviously, this is the required rate on money and business assets, it also approximates the rate on livestock. It seems most likely that the Prophet (p) intentionally left certain undetermined areas in *zakah* in order to make things more flexible for Muslims after him, and in order to leave the freedom of decision to the proper *zakah* authority.

Digression: **The distinction between orders of the Prophet as a messenger of God orders as a temporal head of state.**

The previous discussion leads us to devote a few paragraphs to deal with this important point. One should always look at the circumstances that surround a statement made by the Prophet (p) and the subject matter of the saying to see whether it relates to temporal, political, economic, military, or administrative affairs, or to the principles of the Islamic way of life. There may exist sometimes another text that indicates the enduring principle of a special temporal application, or similar events may have been differently treated, which indicates this treatment may be temporal rather than religious. An example is give by al Qarafi in his *al Ihkam* about the saying "One who kills an enemy soldier shall have his personal property". Malik says this is a decision by the Prophet (p) as a head of state and is not a general rule. If the leaders of the Islamic state declare such a regulation at the beginning of a war, then it should apply, but otherwise, the general principle that war booty is distributed according to the text of the Qur'an in *sura* eight (*al Anfal*) remains applicable. Malik gives the following arguments to support this view:

1. The verse about the distribution of war booties in *sura* (*al Anfal*) contradicts this saying.
2. Such a regulation may interfere with, and divert the intentions of the fighters from being for the sake of God to being the desire for the enemy's property.
3. The reason why this saying was given by the Prophet (p) was to encourage the fighters in a particular battle.[151]

The late Shaikh al Dahlawi in *Hujjah Allah al Balighah*[152] mentions that what is reported from the Prophet (p) is of two categories. The first is what he said as a Messenger to explain the message of God, according to the verse "So take what the Apostle assigns to you and deny yourself that which he withholds from you"[153] This category includes all sayings about the unseen. The second category includes what he said in his capacity as a human being and a head of state, as he himself stated: "I am only a man. If I ordain something as your religion, you should take it: If I give you something as my personal opinion, then I am merely a man."[154] Part of this category are his sayings on medicine, because they are based on experiments and customs of his time, and are not a form of obedience to God or worship. Also in this category is what he did by chance and accident and not by intention and determination. Dahlawi continues that also in this category are those sayings that reflect temporal concerns which do not relate to all generations of this nation, such as the commands he gave in preparing armies and selecting emblems. Many sayings that contain regulations of this kind are considered in this category, such as his sayings" One who kills an enemy soldier shall have his personal property,"[155] and, "One who revives a dead land shall own it."[156] According to Malikites, the soldier that kills an enemy does deserve his property unless Muslims leaders prohibit that before or during the battle, and according to Hanafites, the rejuvenation of dead land requires prior permission from the Islamic government.

It seems to me that the waiver the Prophet (p) gave of *zakah* on horses--if correctly reported--is also part of this category, because it is related to temporal benefit, i.e. the encouragement of owning steeds for fighting for the sake of God. The very words of that waiver also indicate that it may only be temporal, because they imply that *zakah* should have been there but was waived "for you". This means that the Islamic state has the choice of imposing *zakah* on horses or not according to the public interests. If horses represent substantial wealth, they may be *zakated* in order to apply *zakah* on all those who are wealthy, while if they are not an important item of wealth they may be exempted. This interpretation reconciles the action of 'Umar with the saying of the Prophet (p), and God knows best in all cases.

SECTION NINE

OTHER NATURALLY PASTURED DOMESTIC ANIMALS

This section deals with the general case of naturally cost-free pastured domestic animals maintained for profit. Can we generalize the case of *zakah* on all such animals or not? In other words should *zakah* be restricted to the four previously mentioned species or should it include all domestic animals? Some of today's leading professors of Islamic studies, including Muhammad Abu Zahra, 'Abd al 'Wahab Khallaf, and 'Abd al Rahman Hasan, deduct from the practice of 'Umar that one can apply analogy on *zakah*. 'Umar bin al Khattab obligated *zakah* on horses by analogy, on the grounds that horses were becoming valuable assets. This is upheld by Abu Hanifah, the master in the application of analogy. Those who do not obligate *zakah* on horses do not do so in denial of analogy, but because they consider the edible character of livestock an important reason for their *zakatability*. Since horses are not edible, they refuse to extend *zakatability* to horses. The author of *al Mughni* writes "The analogy of horses and livestock is incorrect, because the latter are growing wealth that is used for milking and meat and can be used for sacrifice." The majority of scholars does not consider the character of growth alone the reason for *zakatability*.

These three professors add: If the Wise Successor 'Umar considered growth the essential requirement for *zakatability*, and was followed Abu Hanifah, then we can extend their application to other animals and declare that all animals that are growing and naturally, cost-free pastured are *zakatable*, if they reach the minimum for *zakatability* (*nisab*), which equals twenty *dinars*, at the rate of 2.5%. *Nisab* is estimated in relation to gold, because 'Umar accepted the principle of evaluating horses to determine *zakah*, and value is currently estimated in gold.[158]

This is supported by the fact that the Messenger (p) when asked about *zakah* on donkeys did not negate the obligation of *zakah* in a clear statement but said "God did not send upon me anything on this matter except this comprehensive and precise verse 'Then shall anyone who has done an atom's weight of good see it, and anyone who has done an atom's weight of evil see it'.[159] The ratio of 2.5% is supported by the saying from Bahz bin Hakim from his father from his grandfather that the Prophet (p) said "Out of all naturally pastured camels, on each forty there is due one camel, two-three years old". This is a general rate for camels exceeding 130 and for cows exceeding 40. Applying this rate on all other animals acquired for breeding for profit is undoubtedly a correct *ijtihad*, based on analogy between similar growing assets. Consequently, mules, reindeers, and other animals would be included in this concept.

I disagree with these professors on the estimation of *nisab* on these animals at 20 gold *dinars*, on the basis that the equalization of *nisab* on animals and *nisab* on money is not, in my opinion, valid. I have quoted earlier from *al Mabsut* that five camels equal 40 sheep equal 200 dirham, and noted that Ibn al Humam and Ibn Najaim object to this equation because there are correct saying indicating that two sheep equal 20 dirham, which means that 40 sheep = 400 *dirhams*, i.e. the *nisab* on livestock is twice as much as the *nisab* on money. Thus, if we take *nisab* on money as a reference, *nisab* on animals should be estimated at twice as much as that on money, since money owners have more freedom of choice than animal owners.

I prefer to determine *nisab* on animals as growing assets on two grounds: Firstly, that this number should not be less than five, because *Shari'ah* does not obligate *zakah* on any amount less than five camels, five *wasq* of grain, or five *uqiyyah* of silver currency. This indicates that five should be the lowest quantity considered for *zakatability*. Secondly, that the value of *nisab* should equal that of five camels or 40 sheep in an area where prices are close to average. Estimating value on the basis of the value of camels or sheep is better than estimating on the basis of money, because (a) the purchasing power of money is usually volatile, and (b) it is much more correct to draw an analogy between two animals than between animals and money; likewise it is better to estimate *nisab* on new animals with reference to old animals than with reference to money.

SECTION TEN

GENERAL PRINCIPLES DERIVED FROM THE PREVIOUS SECTIONS

The discussion in the previous sections of this chapter has been lengthy because *Shari'ah* itself dictates many principles and rulings about *zakah* on livestock that may not be as detailed in other areas of *zakah*, and because the lengthy analysis of this issue uncovers important principles that will be of great benefit in understanding the essence of *zakah* in general. Among these principles are the following:

1. *Zakah*, although a worship, is also a public institution supervised by the Islamic state. Appointing and sending *zakah* commissioners is the duty of the Islamic state.

2. *Zakah* regulations balance the concerns of the poor on one hand and the interests of the rich on the other hand, so that small quantities of wealth are exempted from *zakah* and average quality assets only are accepted as *zakah* payment.

3. The expensive upkeep of an asset reduces *zakah* or waives it on that asset. For that reason, the majority of leading jurists consider manually fed animals exempt from *zakah* on the ground that they cost as much as they profit the owner.

4. A transformation of a growing asset from its use for profit to personal use exempts it from *zakah*, according to the majority of scholars with regard to cows and camels used for watering, cultivation, and carrying personal loads.

5. *Shari'ah* treats the common property of partnerships as one unit, which may constitute a foundation for handling contemporary corporations.

6. *Shari'ah* refuses to accept any loopholes in *zakah* and does not allow the combination or separation of assets for the purpose of decreasing *zakah*.

7. Analogy can be used in *zakah* because its rulings have rational reasoning behind them. If these reasons exist in another asset, *zakah* can be extended. That is why 'Umar obligated *zakah* on steeds. I advocate obligating *zakah* on all naturally, cost-free pastured animals, even though they may not have been known at the time of the Prophet or the Successors.

8. Some rulings given by the Prophet (p) can be categorized as regulations coming from the head of the Islamic state and not religious principles coming from within his capacity as a Prophet. These two types of rulings must be clearly known and distinguished. This, for example, explains the slight differences among the letters of instructions given by the Prophet (p) and his Successors.

9. *Nisab* for animals is twice as much as *nisab* for money. In correct saying , two sheep are estimated at 20 *dirhams*, so 40 sheep equal 400 *dirhams*. It is unamiously known that *nisab* for money is 200 *dirhams*.

10. *Zakah* -- even on livestock -- is a proportional due. It is not regressive as wrongly understood by some contemporary writers. The reduction of the rate for larger quantities of sheep is done for a specific reason explained earlier.

11. The rate of *zakah* on animals is approximately one-fourth of one-tenth (2.5%) as is obvious in the case of camels and cows and taking into consideration the explanation given earlier in the case of sheep. The rate of *zakah* on animals is similar to that on money and business asset.

These principles are worthy of being remembered, for they will help, God willing, the understanding of the following chapters.

Footnotes

1. *Sura al Nahl,* 16:5-7.

2. *Ibid.*

3. *Ibid.*

4. *Sura Yasin*: 36:71-73.

5. *Al Durr al Mukhtar* and its commentary, *Rad al Muhtar*, Vol. 2, p. 20-21.

6. *Sura al A'raf,* 7:199.

7. *Sura al Baqarah,* 2:219.

8.. *Al Rawd al Nadir*, Vol. 2, p. 399.

9. *Ibid*, p. 400.

10. *Ibid*, p.399.

11. *Al Amwal*, p. 380.

12. *Nasb al Rayah*, Vol. 2, p. 360.

13. *Al Amwal*, pp. 380.382, and *al Rawd al Nadir*, Vol. 2, p. 408.

14. *Al Rawd al Nadir, Ibid.*

15. *Al Amwal*, p. 381.

16. *Ibid*, p. 382.

17. *Ibid*, p. 381.

18. Ibn Naji, *Sharh al Risalah,* Vol. 1, p. 335.

19. This *ijma'* is quoted by Ibn al Mundhir and al Nawawi in *al Majmu'*, Vol. 4, p. 400, and also by Abu 'Ubaid in *al Amwal*, p. 363, Ibn Qudamah in *al Mughni*, al Sarakhsi in *al Mabsut*, and by al 'Aini. See *al Mirqat*, Vol. 3, p. 49.

20. *Al Majmu'*, Vol. 5, p. 400. Al Nawawi comments, "It is supported by a saying from 'Asim bin Damurah from 'Ali, linked up to the Prophet (p), but its weakness is agreed upon."

21. *Ibid.*

22. Hanafites, al Nakh'i and al Thawri are exceptions, as will be shown later.

23.. Al Sarakhsi, in *al Mabsut*, Vol. 2, p. 150.

24. *Al Bahr al Ra'iq*, Vol. 2, p. 230, and *Fath al Qadir*, Vol. 1, p. 495.

25. *Al Mabsut*, Vol. 2, p. 156.

26. *Al Majmu'*, Vol. 5, p. 382.

27.   See later, chapter or, *zakah* on money.

28.   Al Nawawi says in *al Majmu'*, Vol. 5, p. 409, quoting al Khattabi, "It seems that the Prophet (p) made two sheep or 20 *dirhams* equal the difference in one year of age for camels, because of the difficulty of going to court or to appraisers to determine the exact worth of different age camels in the remote places where *zakah* was collected on camels. The Prophet (p) did not want to leave this value for the *zakah* collector to decide. Al Khattabi thinks that this estimation of two sheep or 20 dirhams is binding, like a religious rule. This is the opinion of al Shafi'i, Ahmad, and the school of *hadith*. The author of *al Fath* writes that it is reported from al Thawri that the difference is ten *dirhams*; a version is also reported from Ishaq. Al Shawkari quotes Zaid bin 'Ali as saying, "The difference of one year of age equal one sheep or ten *dirhams*." According to Malik, the owner of camels is required to buy a camel of the necessary age to fulfill *zakah*, while according to Abu Hanifah, they should resort to evaluation. See *al Fath*, Vol. 4, p. 62, al Halabi Print, and *Nail al Awtar*, Vol. 4, p. 109, al Halabi Print.

29.   Al Hafiz quotes Malik in *al Muwata* as saying, "The meaning of this saying is that if you have three people, each owning forty sheep, they are *zakated* in the amount of one sheep each, but if they add their herds together, there will be only one sheep due on the 120. Also, when two individuals together own 202 sheep, they are *zakated* the amount of three sheep, but if they divide the herd into two halves, each one of them is *zakated* in the amount of one sheep." According to this interpretation, this saying is addressed to the *zakah* payer. Al Shafi'i, on the other hand, considers this saying addressed to both payers and collectors; each of them is ordered not to combine or separate assets in order to influence the amount of *sadaqah*. The payer would be interested in reducing it, while the collectors would like to increase it. It seems more logical that the words of the saying are addressed to the payer, but God knows best. See *al Fath*, Vol. 4, p. 26.

30.   See Section seven of this chapter.

31.   *Al Majmu'*, Vol. 5, p. 383.

32.   *Nail al Awtar*, Vol. 4, p. 107.

33.   *Ibid.*

34.   *Al Majmu'*, Vol. 5, pp. 383-383.

35.   *Nail al Awtar*, Vol. 4, p. 112.

36.   Ibn Hazm upholds that all narrators of this saying are trustworthy, and criticizes the view of Yahya bin Ma'in as weak, commenting, "The words of Yahya bin Ma'in or other may be accepted when they tell about narrators who are not commonly reputed for their trustworthiness. But his claim that a saying whose narrators are trustworthy is weak, unbacked by proof, is rejected for lack of evidence. God says, "Say, bring your proof if you are truthful." See *al Muhalla*, Vol. 5, p. 20-21. The affirmation of Ibn Hazm is accepted under two conditions. One, that all narrators are well-reputed for their honesty and precision, and two, that the saying must not have a strong reason for being rejected. In the above-mentioned saying, we have 'Abd Allah bin al Muthanna,

who is disputed by critics. He is described once by Yahya bin Ma'in as righteous, and once as "nothing." Abu Zar al Hatim, and al 'Ujali consider him a strong link, while al Nasa'i says he is not very reliable. Al 'Aqili comments, "most of what he narrates has no witnessing chain (other chains supporting his narration)." Al Hafiz Ibn Hajar says, "He is followed in this saying by Hamad bin Salamah, who narrates from Thumamah that the latter gave the former a letter, claiming that Abu Bakr wrote it for Anas and it has the seal of the Messenger (p) on it. This is the report by Ahmad in his *Musnad*: "I am informed by Abu Kamil who is informed by Mammad, who said, "I took this letter from Thumamah bin 'Abu Allah bin Anas, from Anas, that Abu Bakr . . .'" and he narrates the saying. Ishaq writes in his *Musnad*, "Al Nadr bin Shumail told me that Hammad bin Salamah told him "I took this letter from Thumamah, narrating it from Anas from the Prophet (p), and repeated the whole saying." Al Hafiz says, "It is obvious Hammad heard it from Thumamah and read the letter, so the claim that it was only transmitted in writting and the claim that 'Abd Allah bin al Muthanna was not supported by other chains are both refuted." See *Fath al Bari,* chapter on *zakah*, section on *zakah* on sheep, Vol. 4, p. 59. This saying is also supported by the fact that it quotes a famous letter preserved by the descendents of Anas bin Malik, sealed with the seal of the Messenger of God (p) reported by al Bukahari in his collection through a chain of the descendants of Anas.

37.   *Encyclopedia of Islam*, Vol. 10, p. 258, Arabic Translation.

38.   Published by the Catholic Press in Beirut.

39.   There is a slight difference on the quantity between 121 and 129. According to Malik, the collector has a choice of taking two camels that are three years old, or three camels that are two years old, while according to Shafi'i it must be three of the two year old camels only, A third view given by Ibn al Majashaw, a disciple of Malik, is that the collector must only take two camels that are three to four years old. Once the camels reach 130 in number, all agree on the rest of the table. See *Bidayat al Mujtahid*, Vol. 1, p. 221, and *Bulghat al Salik* with commentary, Vol. 1, p. 208, and *al Mirqat* on *al Mishkat*, vol, 3, p, 49-50. 40

40.   Al Zaila'i, in *Nasb al Rayah*, gives ull account of these letters, Vol. 2, pp. 535-345. The first three are reported by al Daraqutni, pp. 208-210, and al Hakim in *al Mustadrak*, vol, 1, pp. 390-397, and al Baihaqi in his *Sunan*, Vol. 4, pp. 85-92. See *al Mirqat*, commentary on *al Mishkat*, Vol. 3, p. 50.

41.   It is narrated also by al Mahdi in *Al Bahr*, from 'Ali, Ibn Mas'ud, Hammad, al Hadi, Abu Talib, al Mu'ayad bin Allah, and Abu al 'Abbas. See *Nail al Awtar*, Vol. 4, p. 109, and *al Majmu'*, Vol. 5, p. 400, *al Hidayah*, with commentary, Vol. 1, p. 495, and afterword, and *al Durr al Mukhtar* with its commentary, *Radd al Muhtar*, Vol. 2, pp. 22-23.

42.   *Al Mirqat*, Vol. 3, p. 51, *al Sunan al Kubra*, Vol. 4, p. 94, and its commentary by Ibn al Turkumani, and *al Muhalla*, Vol. 6, pp. 33-34, with commentary by Ahmad Shakir on pp. 34 and 36.

43.   *See al Sunan al Kubr*a, Vol. 4, pp. 92-94, and *al Muhalla*, Vol. 6, pp. 38-39, and al Mirqat, Vol. 3, p. 52.

44. *Bidayat al Mujtahid*, Vol. 1, p. 222.

45. *Al Mirqat,* vol, 3, p. 52, and *al Muhalla*, Vol. 6, p. 42.

46. *Ibid.*

47. *Nail al Awtar*, vol, 4, p, 109, and *al Muhalla,* Vol. 6, pp. 37-38.

48. *Al Sunan al Kubra*, Vol. 4, pp. 89-90.

49. *Al Mughni* with commentary, Vol. 2, p. 452.

50. *Al Qawa'id al Nuraniyah*, p. 87.

51. *Al Mirqat*, Vol. 3, p. 51.

52. *Al Majmu'*, Vol. 5, pp. 400-401.

53. *Al Muhalla*, Vol. 6, p. 39.

54. Among these slight variations, one may include the differences about quantities above 120 camels, that is, whether we start the rate again as if it were from five camels, or we follow the table on page 178.

55. Ibn Hajar, *al Talkhis*, p. 143.

56. *Al Muhalla*, Vol. 6, p. 21.

57. *Al Mughni,* Vol. 2 p. 594.

58. This is the way it is recorded in *al Bukhari* and in the copy with commentary by al Qastallani, whereas in the copy printed with the commentary of Ibn Hajar, it reads as follows: He said, "I came to him," i.e. al Ma'rur talked about Abu Dharr, which implies the saying ends at Abu Dharr and is not linked up to the Prophet (p). However, it is confirmed by Muslim and al Bukhari himself that the saying is linked up to the Prophet (p). See *al Fath*, Vol. 4, pp. 66-67.

59. *Al Mughni,* Vol. 2, p. 591, and *al Amwal*, p. 379.

60. *Al Mughni*, with commentary, Vol. 2, p. 463.

61. Al Shafi'i says, "Taus was well aware of Mu'adh action, even though he did not meet with him, because he met many people who knew Mu'adh." This is not--to the best of my knowledge--disputed with anyone. Al Baihaqi says, "Taus did not meet Mu'adh, but as a Yemeni he was very familiar with details about the biography of Mu'adh, which is commonly known in Yemen." See *al Mirqat*, Vol. 3, p. 71.

62. *Al Fath*, Vol. 4, pp. 65-66, *Nail al Awtar*, Vol. 4, p. 122, 'Uthmaniyah Print. *Nasb al Rayah*, Vol. 2, p. 346, and afterword. This saying has supporting follow-up other than that from 'Ali. Among them are reports from Ibn Mas'ud, Ibn 'Abbas, and Anas, and

also the long saying from 'Amr bin Hazm. See *Sunan al Baihaqi*, vol, 4, pp. 98-99, and *Mirqat*, Vol. 3, p. 71.

63. Because according to the majority of critics it is not necessary that a report must exist to the effect that a narrator met the person from whom he narrates. Information of them being contemporaries and the possibility of having met together is sufficient. See *Nail al Awtar, Ibid*, and *al Mirqat, Ibid*. On the other hand, al Bukhari, along with his teacher, Ibn al Madini, require the knowledge that narrators have met at least once. This is the reason why al Bukhari does not report in his correct collection anything about *nisab* of cows. This is quoted from Zain bin al Munir. See *al Fatah*, Vol. 4, p. 65.

64. *Al Muhalla*, Vol. 4, p. 65.

65. *Nail al Awtar*, op. cit.

66. *Sunan al Baihaqi*, Vol. 4, pp. 89-90, and *Majma' al Zawa'id*, Vol. 3, p. 72.

67. *Nail al Awtar*, op. cit., and *al Talkhis*, p. 174.

68. *Al Mirqat*, Vol. 3, p. 70.

69. Mentioned by al Hafiz in al Talkhis, p. 174.

70. *Al Muhalla*, Vol. 6, p. 16.

71. He is Talhah bin 'Abd Allah bin 'Awf, nephew of 'Abd al Rahman bin 'Awf, and is one of the leading Followers in Madinah, according to Ibn Hazm, *al Muhalla, Ibid*.

72. *Al Muhalla, Ibid*, pp. 7-8.

73. As in *al Talkhis, op. cit.*, and *Nail al Awtar*, Vol. 4.

74. As at the end of his section on *zakah* on cows. See *al Muhalla*, Vol. 6, p. 16.

75. *Al Amwal*, p. 379, and a*l Muhalla* Vol. 6, p.2.

76. *Al Muhalla*, vol, 6, p, 3.

77 *Ibid*.

78. *Al Amwal*, p. 379, and *al Muhalla*, vol, 6, p. 4.

79. *Al Muhalla, Ibid*.

80. *Al Muhalla*, Vol. 6, p. 9.

81. *Al Muhalla*, Vol. 6, p.

82. *Ibid*, p. 8-11.

83. *Al Mughni*, Vol. 2, p, 468.

84. *Bidayat al Mujtahid*, Vol. 1, p. 223.

85. *Al Musannaf,* Vol. 3, p. 221, Hyderabad Print.

86. Reported by Abu Daud in his *Sunan,* chapter on ransoms, section on the amount of ransom. From 'Amr bin Shu'aib, from his father his grandfather, who said, "The ransom used to be at the time of the Messenger of God (p) 800 *dinars* or 8000 *dirhams* . . . this remained in effect until 'Umar took over as Khalifah, and he announced, Camels have become expensive, then 'Umar ordered ransoms to be 1000 *dinars* of gold or 12000 *dirhams* of silver, or 200 cows or 2000 sheep or 200 garments . . . " Abu Daud reports from 'Ata bin Aba Rabah, "The Messenger of God (p) gave his judgement on ransome. For those who own camels it is 100 camels, for those who own cows, it is 200 cows, . . " etc. This is *mursal* [the name of the Companion does not appear in the chain]. In another version, 'Ata narrates from Jabir bin 'Abd Allah, "The Messenger of God imposed . . .etc.

87. Schacht mentions in the *Encyclopedia of Islam,* vol, 10, p. 359, Arabic translation, that *nisab* is 20 cows. I am aware of no place where he might have got this figure from.

88. *Al Amwal,* p. 379.

89. We shall return to this issue at the end of section eight of this chapter.

90. The author of *Sharh al Sunnah* writes, "This means increase of another 100 until the number of sheep reaches 400. Then four sheep are required." This is the opinion of the majority of jurists. Al Hasan bin Saleh indicates that if the quantity becomes 301, then four sheep are required. This is also the view of al Nakha'i. See *al Mirqat,* Vol. 4, pp. 144-145, Multan Print.

91. See the chapter on *zakah* of sheep in *al Majmu* , Vol. 5, p. 417, and afterward, *al Mughni,* Vol. 2, p. 472, and afterward, *Bidayat al Mujtahid,* Vol. 1, p.. 224, and *Sunan al Baihaqi,* Vol. 4, p. 99, and afterward.

92. He is Shawqi Isma'il, in an article titled, "The Accounting System of *Zakah*" in *al Iqtisad wa al Siyasah fi Daw' al Islam,* a review published by the Faculty of Commerce at the University of Cairo more than 15 years ago.

93. *Sharh al Risalah,* Vol. 1, p. 337.

94. Mentioned in *al Muntaqa.* Al Shawkani comments, "Reported by al Daraqutni and al Baihaqi, Hilal bin Khabbab is one of the links of the chain, and he is graded trustworthy by more than one scholars, while some speak critically of him. See *Nail al Awtar,* Vol. 4, p. 133.

95. *Al Muwatta,* Vol.1, p. 265, al Halabi Print.

96. *Nail al Awtar,* Vol. 4, p. 134.

97. Al Shawkani comments, "This is done on the basis that restricting the meaning of a text is validated by the opinion of a Companion, but this is an incorrect basis." *Ibid.*

98. *Bidayat al Mujtahid,* Vol. 1, pp. 252-254.

99. *Al Muhalla,* Vol. 5, p. 274 and afterword.

100. *Sura al Baqarah,* 2:267.

101. *Fath al Bari,* Vol. 4, p. 63.

102. *Al Mughni,* Vol. 2, p. 473.

103. "*Al Bada'i,* Vol. 2, p. 33.

104. The author of *Majma' al Zawa'id,* Vol. 3, p. 75. writes "Laith bin Abu' Salim is in the chain, and he is trustworthy but mudallis [he may intentionally delete some name in the chain].

105. *Al Badai', op. cit.*

106. *Bulghat al Salik,* Vol. 1, p. 209.

107 *Al Mughni,* vol, 2, pp. 473-474.

108. *Ibid.*

109. *Al Majmu',* Vol. 5, p, 397. The statement of 'Umar is reported by Malik with a correct chain as quoted by al Nawawi. We will discuss it in detail latter in this section.

110. *Al Mughni,* Vol. 2, p. 479.

111. *Al Durr al Mukhtar* with its commentary *Radd al Muhtar,* Vol. 2, p. 25.

112. *Ibid.*

113. *Ridayat al Mujtahid,* Vol. 1, pp. 222-223.

114. This is the opinion of al Thawri. It is also attributed to Ishaq, as in *al Fath,* Vol. 4, p. 62.

115. *Nasb al Rayah,* Vol. 2, p. 361.

116. The same is reported by al Tabarani too, who grades its chain good. See *Nail al Awtar,* Vol. 4, p. 114.

117. *Al Bada'i, op. cit., al Mughni,* Vol. 2, p. 476, and *al Muhadhdhab* and its explanation, *al Majmu',* Vol. 5, pp. 426-427.

118. *Al Muwatta*, Vol. 1, p. 267, chapter on zakat, section on preventing embarrassing people in *sadaqah*.

119. *Nail al Awtar*, Vol. 4, p. 133.

120. *Ibid.*

121. *Al Rawdah*, Vol. 2, p. 170.

122. *Bulghat al Salik*, Vol. 1, pp. 210-212.

123. *Bidayat al Mujtahid*, pp. 254-256.

124. *Al Muhalla*, Vol. 6, pp. 51-59.
125. *Al Rawdah*, Vol. 2, pp. 172-173.

126. *Al Bada'i*, Vol. 2, p. 34.

127. *Ibid.*

128. *Ibid.*

129. *Radd al Muhtar*, Vol. 2, pp. 25-26.

130. *Al Majmu'*, Vol. 5, p. 339.

131. The author of *al Muntaqa* is quoted by al Shawkani, "This is reported by all the group." See *Nail al Awtar*, Vol. 4, p. 156.

132. *Ibid*, p. 137. Al Tirmidhi mentioned that al Bukhari grades this saying correct, al Hafiz grades it good, and al Daraqutni says "The correct version ends at 'Ali."

133. *Sura al Anfal*, 8:60.

134. *Al Rawd al Nadir*, commentary on *Majmu' al Fiqh al Kabir* on comparative Zaidi jurisprudence, Vol. 2, pp. 408-409.

135. These are the words of al Bukhari in the chapter on sharing water, section on drinking from rivers by people and Livestock. *Al Bukhari*, with commentary by al Sindi, Vol. 2, p. 33. The saying is also reported by Ahmad and Muslim. See a*Nail al Awtar* Vol. 4, p. 117.

136. *Al Mirqat*, Vol. 4, p. 122.

137. *Al Muhalla* Vol. 5, p. 228, and *Nail al Awtar*, Vol. 4, p. 118.

138. *Nasb al Rayah*, Vol. 2, p. 359.

139. *Ibid.*

140. *Al Muhalla*, Vol. 5, p. 227.

141. *Ibid*, p. 226.

142. *Nasb al Rayah, op. cit.*

143. *Ibid*, p. 357. The commentator notes, "Al Hafiz in *al Dirayah* says that its chain is correct.

144. *Ibid*, p. 359.

145. *Nail al Awtar*, Vol. 4, p. 136.

146. *Radd al Muhtar*, commentary on *al Durr al Mukhtar*, Vol. 2, p. 26.

147. *Ibid*, p. 25.

148. *Ibid*.

149. Al Tibi explains, "I waived' means, I removed or over-looked from taking *zakah*, refering to the fact that it should originally have been *zakatable*." Al Qari comments, "It implicitly means that the matter was left to the Prophet (p)." See *al Mirqat*, Vol. 4, p. 149.

150. Reported by Ahmad and al Tabarani in al Mu'jam al Kabir. The author of *Majma' al Zawa'id*, Vol. 3, p. 69, says, "Men of its chain are trustworthy." See also *Nail al Awtar*, Vol. 4, p. 156.

151. *Al Ihkam* by al Qarafi, pp. 106-108.

152. *Hujjat Allah al Balighah*, Vol. 1, pp. 271-272. See also Shaikh Mahmud Shaltut, *al Islam 'Aqidah wa Shari'ah*, Part Three, section entitled "Sunnah, a Legislation and Not a Legislation."

153. *Sura al Hashr*, 59:7.

154. Reported by Muslim.

155. Reported by Bukhari, Muslim and other from Abu Qatadah al Ansari: The Prophet (p) said this in the battle of Hunain.

156. Reported by Abu Daud and al Tirmidhi, who grades is good.

157. For details, see al Qarafi, *al Ihkam fi Tamyizal Fatawa min al Ahkam*, question number 25 and its replies, pp. 86-108. At the end of his discussion, he comments, "There are several other cases similar to these in *Shari'ah*. One should search of them, for once found, they are abundant source of knowledge and depth for those who exert their efforts."

158. Seminar on social studies, Third Section, pp. 246-247.

159. Reported by Ahmad and Muslim. See *Nail al Awtar*, Vol. 4, p. 117.

CHAPTER THREE

ZAKAH ON GOLD AND SILVER

Gold and silver are useful precious metals. Many nations have used gold as money and a measure of value. *Shari'ah* considers gold and silver growing wealth by definition, and they are *zakatable* whether they are used in the form of coins or bullion, or even as ornaments and decorative materials. However, they carry a different ruling when they are used as women's ornament and jewelry. This chapter will have two sections, one devoted to *zakah* on money and another to *zakah* on jewelry and ornament.

SECTION ONE

ZAKAH ON MONEY

The role and development of money

Barter was the method of exchange for primitive tribes. Once society and trade grew, barter could not satisfy all transactions because of the difficulty of finding another party that wants to exchange exactly what the first party wants. God guided humanity to use money as a medium of exchange and a measure of value in order to facilitate exchanges and transactions.[1] Man used many items as money until the rise of precious metals. Gold and silver dominated international and national trade for centuries because of the natural physical characteristics God implanted in them.[2]

Money used at the time of the Prophet Muhammad

When the Messenger (p) was receiving revelation, Arabs used these two metals as money. Gold was used in the form of the coin *dinar*, and silver in the form of the coin *dirham*. *Dinars* and *dirhams* came to Arabia from the neighboring kingdoms, gold mainly from the Byzantines and silver mainly from the Persian Empire. *Dirhams* had different weight, heavy and light, and so pre-Islamic Makkans used silver *dirhams* by weight and not by number, as if they were not minted. They had their weight measure system, which is composed of *ratl* (equals twelve *uqiyyah*), *uqiyyah* (equals 40 *dirhams*), nash (equals 20 *dirhams* or one-half *uqiyyah*), and *nawat* (equals five *dirhams*).[3] The Prophet (p) said "The weight [measurement system] is that of the Makkans."[4] He obligated *zakah* on *dirhams* and *dinars*, as we will see. This gave gold and silver recognized status as currency in Muslim lands. They have come to be subject to many *Shari'ah* rulings in transactions related to civil and commercial matters in addition to *zakah* and they are used as measures in determining many values, such as dowries, ransoms, and *nisab* in *zakah*.

Evidence for the obligation of *zakah* on money

The obligation of *zakah* on money is confirmed by the Qur'an, Sunnah, and *ijma'*. God says, "and there are those who hoard gold and silver and spend it not in the way of God. Announce unto them a most grevious penalty on the day when heat will be produced out of that wealth in the fire of Hell and with it will be branded their foreheads, their flanks, and their backs. This is the treasure which ye hoarded for yourselves. Taste ye then the treasure ye buried."[5] These two verses indicate--with a strong warning--that there is a right for God on gold and silver. The words "and do not spend it" refer to the monetary character of gold and silver, since money can be spent. The verse says "do not spend <u>it</u>" instead of "them" because "it" refers to money, while the pronoun "them" could have been used to refer to gold and silver. These verses indicated also that there is grevious penalty promised for two evil actions, hoarding and abstention from spending for the sake of God. No doubt non-payment of *zakah* is the most obvious sort of abstention from spending for the sake of God.

Sunnah gives some details of these verses, Muslim reports from Abu Hurairah that the Messenger (p) said "No one who owns gold or silver and does not pay their due, but will have his wealth on the Day of Resurrection made into sheets of fire, heated in the fire of Hell, and with it will be branded his forehead, his flanks, and his back. The moment they cool off they are heated again, during a day the length of which is fifty thousand years, until judgement is given to God's servants, and he will then be shown his way to the Garden or to the Fire."[6] All this warning is for non-payment of dues on gold and silver. Another version of this saying provides the meaning of this due as *zakah*: "No one who owns a treasure and does not pay its *zakah* but will have it heated in the fire of Hell . . . ." etc.[7] In the saying from Anas that gives the instructions of *zakah* that were ordained by God to His Messenger, as written to Anas by Abu Bakr when sent to Bahrain,[8] "And on silver, in each two hundred *dirhams*, the due is one-fourth or a tenth. If there are only one hundred and ninety *dirhams*, they are not *zakatable* unless the owner volunteers to pay."

As for *ijma'*, Muslims, unanimously agree throughout all generations that *zakah* is obligatory on these two currencies.

The reason for the zakatability of money

Money should always be circulating; hoarding money diffuses its usefulness and leads to stagnation in business, the spread of unemployment, and regression in economic activity in general. Hoarding can become epidemic sometimes, and it is feared by economists to the degree that some propose the issuance of currency that has a determined expiration date and thus cannot be hoarded. They call this kind of currency "melting money".[9] Some Western economists experiment with another idea to discourage hoarding, by cutting off monthly vouchers from paper currency, in order to reduce its value and prevent its hoarding.[10] These means aim at enhancing circulation and penalizing hoarding, but they are surrounded by complexities and practical difficulties; however, they all reaffirm the Islamic point of view against hoarding. By imposing a due of two-and-a-half percent every year, Islam encourages people to invest money , for otherwise *zakah* payments year after year will use up all the capital. Thus the Prophet (p) urged the guardians of orphans to invest the funds of orphans in order that they would not be consumed by *zakah*.[11] This urging comes for investment of the funds of orphans since it is expected that adults would not neglect to invest their own wealth, because of the inner impulse to be richer, while orphans do not have control over their own wealth.

The rate of *zakah* on money

There is unanimous agreement among Muslims that the rate of *zakah* on money is two and a half percent. The. author of *al Mughni* says, "I am aware of no dispute among scholars that *zakah* on gold and silver is one-fourth of a tenth." This is authentically reported from the Prophet (p): "On, silver, one-fourth of a tenth is due."[12] It is apparent that *Shari'ah* makes the rate of *zakah* low on money, because it is calculated on both principal and accumulated profit. This rate is much lower than the one-tenth or one-twentieth imposed on crops and fruits, but crops and fruits to land are like profit to capital. *Zakah* on fruits and crops is calculated only on the profit, while *zakah* on money is taken from the capital itself, whether it actually grows or not and whether it has made profit during the year or not.

Is it possible to increase this rate today?

Some non-specialized writers argue that the proceeds of *zakah* as regulated in *Shari'ah* may not be sufficient to satisfy all the complex needs of today's life, especially with changing economic circumstances, so there is a need for revising the regulations of *zakah* and possibly raising the rate of *zakah* on money.[13]

I reject this proposal on the following grounds:

1. It contradicts clear and authentic texts from the Sunnah of the Messenger of God and his Wise Successors. We are ordained to hold strongly to this Sunnah and are warned by God about the consequences of deviating from it. God says, "Then let those

beware who withstand the Apostle's order, lest some trial befall them or a grevious penalty be inflicted on them."[14]

2. It is in opposition to the *ijma* of all Muslims throughout fourteen centuries, during which many social and economic changes took place and many internal and external political situations changed. Needs arose for additional funds and the state treasury emptied many times, but in spite of all that, not a single Muslim scholar suggested a change in the rate of *zakah*.

3. This *ijma* is supported by the fact that Muslim scholars have always thought of additional dues besides *zakah* . If the rate of *zakah* is changeable, why should they have brought about additional levies? The very discussion of additional taxes indicates that the rates of *zakah* are fixed.

4. Jurists accustomed to applying analogy, such as the Hanafites, argue that rates of *zakah* cannot be derived by analogy, because their determination comes only from the Legislator, and has been given and done with. If these rates cannot be derived by analogy, how could a rate fixed by texts and *ijma'* be changed?

5. *Zakah* is, before anything else, a religious obligation , fixed and eternal, one of the pillars of Islam, and one of its great institutions. Allowing its rates to change according to changing circumstances is equal to removing this sacred character of *zakah* and putting it in the hands of governments and rulers to tamper with. One time they may make it 20% and another time they may make it 30% or a progressive tax. This pillar of Islam symbolizes the unity of all Muslims by the fact that Muslims in all places under all governments are required to apply the same rates.

6. Moreover, if *zakah* rates are allowed to increase, they should also be allowed to decline or to he eliminated. If a time of prosperity comes to Muslim land with huge resources (such as oil), those who call for its increase today may then call for its reduction or complete elimination. *Zakah* loses its validity as a given worship and becomes a tool in the hands of the state.

7. The allowance of any change in the rates of *zakah* would pave the way for changes in other areas of *Shari'ah*. If today's society needs more resources, we can impose other taxes in addition to *zakah*, to the degree that is needed. We need not change *zakah*.

Nisab of money

The agreed-upon saying states, "There is no *sadaqah* on anything less than five *uqiyyah* of silver currency."[15] *uqiyyah* equals 40 *dirhams*, according to many texts and *ijma*, as quoted be al Nawawi.[16] Thus five *uqiyyah* equals 200 *dirhams*. It seems, however, that silver currency was predominantly used by Arabs at the time of the Prophet (p),[17] so the sayings determine *nisab* and rates on silver currency. These are not disputed by Muslim scholars.[18]

As for gold currency (*dinar*) we have no sayings determining its *nisab*, or at least not as strong and commonly known sayings as those about silver. Hence the *nisab* of gold is not agreed upon unanimously, but the great majority of scholars are of the opinion that *nisab* on gold is 20 *dinars*. It is reported from al Hasan al Basri once that it is 40 *dinars*, and once that it is 20 *dinars*.[19] *Nisab* on gold is independent from that on silver, except according to Taus, who evaluates gold by silver. Hence, according to him, an amount of gold whose value is 200 *dirhams* is the *nisab*.[19] A similar view is also reported from 'Ata al Zuhri, Sulaiman bin Harb, Ayub and al Sakhtiani.[20]

The opinion of the majority is supported by the following points:

1. A few sayings, none of the free from criticism, but when taken together are strengthened by each other, include (a) Ibn Majah and al Daraqutnii (p. 199) reporting from Ibn 'Umar and 'Aishah that the Prophet (p) used to collect half a *dinar* on each 20 *dinars*,[21] (b) al Daraqutni (p. 199) reports from 'Amr bin shu'aib, from his father from his grandfather, from the Prophet (p), "There is no [obligated *sadaqah*] on any less than 20 *mithqal*. [*dinar*] of gold or 200 *dirhams*,"[22] (c) Abu 'Ubaid--with his own chain-- reports from Muhammad bin 'Abd al Rahman al Ansari, a Follower, that in the letter of the Messenger of God (p) and in the letter of 'Umar on *sadaqah* it is written, "From gold, nothing must be taken until it reaches 20 *dinars*. Once it is 20 *dinars*, then on it there is one half *dinar* due,"[23] (d) Abu Daud reports from 'Ali, linked up to the Prophet, "If you have 200 *dirhams*, and a year passes on them, there must be five *dirhams* [taken as *zakah*]. You are not obligated to pay anything [on gold] until you have 20 *dinars*. If you have 20 *dinars* and a year passes on them, there is a half *dinar* due on it [as *zakah*]." Some hafizes [*hadith* critics] grade this good. Al Daraqutni considers it correct when it ends at 'Ali.[24]

Those jurists who view the quantities as given by *Shari'ah* and not deducted through reasoning, like the Hanafites,[25] say, "If it is authentically reported from 'Ali that the *nisab* of gold is 20 *dinars*, then this has the same authority as if it were linked up to the Prophet (p)", because 'Ali would not say it from his own opinion.

2. It is known historically that, at the time of the Prophet (p), one *dinar* equalled ten *dirhams*.[26]

3. Muslims since the time of the Companions practiced *zakah* on gold on the basis of this *nisab*, by which an *ijma'* has been established after the era of al Hasan [who had a different view according to a version of a report from him]. From the time of the Companions we have a report from Anas bin Malik that "I was commissioned by 'Umar to collect *sadaqah*. He instructed me to take from each 20 *dinars* one-half a *dinar*, and from more than 20 at the rate of one *dirham* from each four *dinars*."[27] 'Ali says, "There is nothing due on less than 20 *dinars*, on 20 *dinars* there is one-half *dinar* due, and on 40 *dinars* there is one *dinar* due."[28] This is part of the saying that is linked up to the Prophet by some narrators. Ibrahim al Nakha'e says, "The wife of Ibn Mas'ud has a necklace that contained 20 *mithqal*. Her husband instructed her to give five *dirhams* as its *zakah*."[28] That on each 20 *dinars* there is due one-half *dinar* is also reported from

leading Followers, such as al Sha'bi, Ibn Sirin, Ibrahim, al Hasan, al Hakam bin 'Utbah, and 'Umar bin 'Abd al 'Aziz.[29] Abu 'Ubaid and Ibn Hazm report from Zuraiq bin Habban, "'Umar bin 'Abd al 'Aziz wrote me to look for Muslims who pass by you, and take out of their apparent wealth and what they conduct of trade, one *dinar* out of each 40 *dinars*, and apply the same proportion for what is less than that until you reach the amount of 20 *dinars*, Once it is less than 20 *dinars*, even by one-third of a *dinar*, leave it intact."[30]

On this estimation of s*nisab, zakah* application stabilized and has continued since the time of 'Umar bin 'Abd al 'Aziz. No variation or dispute is mentioned, and some leading jurists consider this a virtual unanimity. Malik relies on such an established practice, especially among Madinans. In affirming this ruling is his *al Muwatta'*, Malik writes, "The undisputed Sunnah, in my opinion, in that *zakah* is obligatory on 20 *dinars* of gold as it is on 200 *dirhams*."[31] Al Shafi'i in *al Umm* says, "I know of no controversy that there is no *sadaqah* on gold until it reaches 20 *dinars* and once it does, then it is *zakatable*,"[32] Abu 'Ubaid comments in *al Amwal* on the saying from 'Amr bin Shu'aib that *nisab* on gold is 20 mithqal, "There is no controversy about this among all Muslims. If a person owns at the beginning of a year what is *zakatable*, i.e. 200 *dirhams*, 20 *dinars*, five camels, 30 cows, or 40 sheep, and continues to own it until the end of the year, *sadaqah*. is obligatory on him indisputably among all people."[33] 'Iyad says, "*Ijma'* is relied upon in determining the *nisab* of gold, although a disregarded deviant view is reported."[34]

Many leading scholars have established that if all Muslims embrace a saying, even if it were criticized from the point of view of the chain, this embracing raises it to the degree of acceptance, as in the case of the saying, "There must be no last will to an heir." This principle is supported by al Shafi'i, al Hafiz Ibn 'Abd al Barr, Ibn al Humam, Ibn Hajar, Ibn al Qayyim, and many others. On this ground we notice that al Tirmidhi may sometimes report a saying about which he expresses doubt or weakness, with the qualifier that it is accepted among scholars. Also, Ibn 'Abd al Barr says that a saying sometimes is correct because scholars espouse it, or that the people's *ijma'* on the meaning of a saying renders any criticism of its chain obsolete.[35]

However, this principle must not be applied indiscriminately. I think it is only applicable if the saying is not extremely weak, if the acceptance is expressed by the generation of the Companions and Followers, and not only by later generations, and lastly, if the saying does not stand in opposition to a well established principle or ruling in *Shari'ah*. These three conditions are satisfied in the case on hand about *nisab* of gold. The chains of narrators in the above mentioned sayings are close to being accepted. Companions and Followers practiced *zakah* on gold in accordance with the meaning of these sayings, and there is no ruling in *Shari'ah* that opposes them. In fact there is a ruling which supports their meaning, that 20 *dinars* equal 200 *dirhams*.

Disproving an objection

Some argue that al Hasan's opinion according to one version of the report from him--that *nisab* is 40 *dinars*, may be supported by the saying from 'Amr bin Hazm that the Prophet (p) wrote for him. That letter continues, after the mention of the *nisab* of silver, "and on each 40 *dinars* there is due one *dinar*."[36] One can easily disprove this argument by the very text cited, which talks obviously about the rate of *zakah* and not about *nisab*.

Dirhams and *dinars* in *Shari'ah*

It is essential in order to complete the picture of *zakah* on gold and silver to find out how much, exactly, is the *dirham* of silver and the *dinar* of gold worth today. We can then determine the current equivalent of *nisab*. Many scholars early and late, have attempted to find out the exact quantity of the *dirham* and *dinar*. They include Abu 'Ubaid in al Amwal,[37] al Baladhari in *Futuh al Buldan*,[38] al Khattabi in *Ma'alim al Sunan*[39], al Mawardi in *al Ahkam al Sultaniyah*,[40] al Nawawi in *al Majmu'*[41], al Maqrizi in *Ancient Islamic Currencies*,[42] Ibn Khaldun in the Introduction,[43] and several others. Ibn Khaldun summarizes, "One must realize that it is unanimously agreed upon since the early ages of Islam, the era of the Companions and Followers, that the *dirham* in *Shari'ah* is that ten of which equal in weight seven *mithqal* of gold. *Uqiyyah* is 30 *dirhams*. Consequently, the weight of a *dirham* of silver equals seven-tenths the weight of a *dinar* of gold. One *dinar* of pure gold equals 72 grains of rye of average weight; thus, one *dirham* weighs fifty-five grains. All these measures are affirmed by unanimous agreement."

The *dinar* [which is the same as a *mithqal*] did not change from the era before Islam. However, Muslim currencies, at the above mentioned weights, were used in a wide area, since the time of Ummayad caliph 'Abd al Malik bin Marwan. At this time, there were different *dirhams* with different weights, and he unified them, in accordance with the above ratios. Changes were incorporated in later minting of *dirhams* and *dinars* after 'Abd al Malik in several countries, so the above-cited definition by Ibn Khaldun became only theoretical, and people had to find out the proportion between their local currencies and those definitions in determining *nisab* and other *Shari'ah* quantities.

The Prophet (p) guides us to a very useful practice, in unifying measures and quantities all over the country. He said, "Weight measures are those used by Makkans, and volume measures are those used by Madinans." Makkans were people of trade, accustomed circulating *dinars* and *dirhams* by weight, and they wore more precise in their weight measurements. Madinans were cultivators of crops and fruits, and they were more accurate in using volume measures, such as *al Wasq,* al Sa', and *al mudd*. It was hoped that all Muslim countries would unify and standardize their measure of weight and volume, in accordance with those of the Makkans, and Madinans, in order to make the application of quantities mentioned in *Shari'ah* easier. Unfortunately, Muslims have not given sufficient attention to that useful directive of the Prophet (p). They have differences in their measures of weight and volume from one country to the other, and we came to see *ratl* defined differently in Baghdad, Madinah, Egypt, and Syria, the same way the *dirham* and *dinar* were given different weights in different countries. All this makes our task of finding the exact equivalent of the *dirham* and the *dinar* today even more difficult. Those grains that were used in defining the *dirham* and the *dinar* are not themselves precise, which adds yet another difficulty to the problem on hand. Yet we must determine the exact weight of the *dirham* and the *dinar* in order to define *nisab* of gold and silver in our days.

'Abd al Rahman Fahmy, secretary of the Islamic Art Museum in Cairo, after a thorough examination of the tools used for minting, and many historical coins, comes up with the estimation that a *dirham* equals 3.104 grams of silver in his book on coin minting in the early ages of Islam.[44] Ibn 'Abidin, after narrating several views of the Hanafites, comes up with a conclusion that it is very difficult to find an agreement on the exact weights of *dirhams* and *dinars*.[45] A more recent researcher, using al Maqrizi's writings and comparing Greek and Islamic weights for the *dirham* and *dinar*, concludes that the *dirham* should be 3.12 grams of silver, which is close to Fahmy's figure.[46] But it seems that the latter study does not distinguish between the *dirham* that used to be a unit of weight and the *dirham* that was used as a unit of silver currency. Al Maqrizi himself quotes from al Khattabi that there used to be several *dirhams*, one a weight unit and another a currency unit.[47] Some other studies depend on actually weighing coins that were saved from the early Islamic eras and preserved in museums throughout the world. It seems, however, that the *mithqal*, which is the same as the *dinar*, is more constant and stable than the *dirham*. If we can determine the weight of a *mithqal*, then the weight of a *dirham* can easily be derived. Fortunately, several *dinars* that were minted at the time of 'Abd al Malik have been preserved. Some European scholars and the Egyptian 'Ali Basha Mubarak,[48] in separate studies, take the weight of several Islamic *dinars* that exist in London, Paris, Madrid, and Berlin. They come to the conclusion that the *dinar* of 'Abd al Malik weighed 4.25 grams. The *Encyclopedia of Islam* cites this as the same weight of the Byzantine *dinar*.[49] Thus the *dirham* would be 4.25 x 7/10 = 2.975 grams.[50] This is supported by many contemporary researchers, Arab and European,[51] including the Orientalist Zembaro, who writes in the *Encyclopedia of Islam*, Arabic translation, vol. 9, p. 226, under the title "*Dirham* and *Dinar*," that "Historians differ greatly on the exact weight of the *dirham* and *dinar*. But they agree that ten *dirhams* equal seven *dinars*, which is the same as seven *mithqal*. The *mithqal* of the of the Makkans equals 4.25 grams. This means that a *dirham* is 2.97 grams, which coincides with the weight of coins minted at the time of al Muqtadir (the years 295-320 H / 903-932 AD) discovered by Roger in al Fayum, Egypt. It seems that 'Umar was the first to stabilize the legal weight of the *dirham*, and later 'Abd al Mllik unified all coins on that legal weight, 2.97 grams." Zembaro continues, "Historians are unanimously of the opinion that 'Abd al Malik in his currency reform did not alter the weights of gold coins. The weight of gold coins can easily be determined by weighing the existing *dinars* in museums. The exact weight of the *dinar* is 4.25 grams. This is also equal to the actual weight of the Byzantine *dinar*."

It seems that the survey of preserved coins is the most accurate means of determining the exact weight of the *dinar* and the *dirham*. The *nisab* of silver must then be 200 x 2.975 = 595 grams, and the *nisab* of gold should be 20 x 4.25 = 85 grams of gold.

Nisab of non-metal money

Paper currency is now predominantly used in transactions in all countries, and gold and silver have disappeared from circulation as currencies. What is, then the *nisab* of paper money? Is it that of silver or gold? It is apparent that 20 *dinar* of gold (85 grams) and 200 *dirhams* of silver (595 grams) are no longer equal in value to each other as they were at the time of the Prophet (p).

It is expected that since this is a matter of human reasoning, some scholars will be inclined to consider the *nisab* of silver most appropriate for non-metal money because it is determined explicitly by Sunnah and *ijma'*, and it is the smaller amount of the two in today's value, so using it as *nisab* would be of more benefit to the poor. This is perhaps why it is commonly used in countries like Egypt, Saudi Arabia, the gulf states, India, and Pakistan.[52] Other scholars tend to consider the *nisab* of gold more appropriate because the value of gold did not change through the centuries as much as did the value or silver.[53] Scholars favoring gold *nisab* include the late Abu Zahrah, Khallaf, and Hasan.[54] This view can be supported by comparing *nisab* on gold with *nisab* on camels, sheep, and crops, because one finds that under today's prices, the *nisab* of gold is more comparable to *nisab* on other items of wealth than the *nisab* of silver. Five camels or 40 sheep are a value that is very close to 85 grams of gold, while the 595 grams of silver may not equal the price of one camel. Waliyullah al Dahlawi in his *Hujjat Allah al Balighah*, says, "*Nisab* on silver was estimated at five *uqiyyah* because that was sufficient for the smallest household to live on for one year, under reasonable prices and with average dietary habits."[55] Can we find any country today in which the value of 595 grams of silver would be sufficient for one year's expenses for a small household? In fact, that much silver would hardly be sufficient for one month or even one week. It is much better to determine the *nisab* on money today at the equivalent of that on gold, i.e. the value of 85 grams of gold, because doing it otherwise would inflict great injustice on *zakah* payers.

Can we find a stable, permanent *nisab* for money?

The value of money is not fixed; it goes up and down from time to time in accordance with many variables. The real value of money is its purchasing power,[56] and the only reason paper currency could succeed was because it has purchasing power. We noted that silver money decreased in value to the extent that made silver *nisab* extremely low, compared to *nisab* on other items of wealth. That is the reason I prefer to use the equivalent of the *nisab* on gold for paper money. What would happen if the value of gold declined drastically? Can we discover a standard and stable measurement that can be used as a *nisab* for money? Some may look to *nisabs* applicable on other items, such as animals, crops, or fruits, whose value may be more stable than that of money.

Can we use *nisab* of crops and fruits?

The immediate observation on *nisab* of crops (five *wasq*) is that its current value is very low in relation to *nisab* on livestock. This may be explained by the following points: First, the bounty of God is more apparent in agriculture, where the human role is relatively less than in generating other forms of wealth. God says, "that they may enjoy the fruits of this artistry. It was not their hands that made this; will they not then give thanks?"[57] Second, humanity cannot survive without what comes out of the soil as crops and fruits the way they can do without animals for food. *Nisab* on crops is made low in order to provide larger proceeds of *zakah* to benefit the needy. Third, crops and fruits are to land as profit is to capital. While *zakah* on cows, camels, and sheep is obligated on the capital and profit together, *zakah* on crops and fruits is only taken from the profit. To compensate for that difference, *nisab* is made low and the *zakah* rate is made high.

Can the livestock *nisab* be used?

If *nisab* on crops is not adequate approximation, then the *nisab* on livestock may be another alternative. To start with, the *nisab* on cows must be disregarded because it is not obligated by a clear-cut text. *Nisab* on camels and sheep are obligated in non-controversial texts and are confirmed by *ijma'*. Can we take the value of five camels or 40 sheep as the *nisab* on money?

To answer this question we must first consider whether the *nisab* of camels and sheep equalled the *nisab* of silver money at the time of the Prophet (p). A leading scholar, al Sarakhsi, in *al Mabsut*, argues that the answer to this question is affirmative. A one-year-old she-camel used to be valued at about 40 *dirhams*, and one sheep at five *dirhams*. Thus, five camels should equal 200 *dirhams* of silver.[58] But we mentioned earlier that Ibn al Humam in *al Fath* and Ibn Nujaim in *al Bahr* both critically investigate the argument of the author of *al Mabsut*. They contrast it with a saying reported in the correct collection of al Bukhari, which indicates that the difference in value of one year of age in camel is estimated by the Messenger (p) at 2 sheep or 20 *dirhams*. This is an explicit text that contradicts the calculation of Sarakhsi.[59] According to this authentic saying, 40 sheep equalled at the time of the Prophet (p) 400 *dirhams*, that is, twice as much as the *nisab* of silver money.

It seems, however, that the *nisab* of silver was intentionally made lower than *nisab* of livestock for a special reason in *Shari'ah*. Owning money enables the owner to select from a wide range of uses, certainly many more choices than owning camels or sheep presents. Money is a liquid asset, while camels and sheep are not. Holding on to money for one full year, despite all temptations to spend it, is more of an indication of richness and ability to save than retaining livestock for a year. There is an implication, especially according to Hanafites, who even make it an explicit condition, that this money is above and beyond the basic needs of the owner. These reasons may have been considered by the Legislator in determining *nisab* of money as below that of livestock.

Thus, if we decide to determine a *nisab* for paper money that can be stabilized and used as a standard when the purchasing power of money drastically varies, this *nisab* should be equal to one-half the value of five camels or forty sheep in an average country. I suggest an average country in order to avoid the two extremes, lands where these two animals are very expensive, and lands where they are very cheap.

Types of paper money

Paper money is fiat money, printed by the government or a government-authorized body and circulated among people for use in their transactions. This kind of money is commonly used all over the world, via which many national and international transactions take place. Paper money is used as a means of exchange, a store of value, a measure of future values, and a means of evaluating financial transactions.[60]

Paper money evolved through time from obligatory convertibility to non-convertibility. In its early stage, paper money took the form of I.O.U's issued by banks, that guaranteed their substitution for fixed amount of gold or silver. Banks were obliged to convert these I.O.U.'s into gold or silver on demand. As time went on, the banking machinery was able to influence the government and gain permission to hold only partial reserves of gold and silver against issued I.O.U.'s. Governments themselves went into the business of producing paper money because it seemed lucrative. At first governments issued paper money on partial precious metal reserves to the system of government authorizations given to central banks to issue a certain quantity of paper money. Thus we entered the phase of non-convertibility, where national currencies become compulsory and non-convertible to gold or silver within the borders of each country.[61]

Zakatability of paper currency

Obviously, we do not expect to find any opinion about the *zakatability* of paper money in the early generations of Islam because paper money is an invention of the last few centuries. Contemporary scholars look at this money from different angles and express different opinion about its *zakatability*. Shaikh 'Alaish, a Malakite in Egypt, says paper money is unlike *dinars* and *dirhams* and consequently not *zakatable*.[62] Some Shafi'ites add a condition for the *zakatability* of paper money, the actual conversion of paper money into gold and silver.[63] The group of scholars who authored the book *al Fiqh 'ala al Madhahib al Arba'ah* write:[64]

1.   Shafi'ites consider paper money to be drafts representing debts of the issuing banks. Since the bank is fully capable of payment, the rules of *zakah* on debts apply. This draft is *zakatable*.

2.   Hanafites consider paper money to be claims on the bank that circulate among individuals. They are *zakatable*.

3.   Malikites find in these bank notes a means of exchange, representing gold and silver, convertible into these metals on demand. They are *zakatable*

4.   Hanbalites consider paper currency not *zakatable* until it is converted into gold or silver, and then the conditions of *zakatability* of gold and silver apply.

It is apparent that all these views are based on the principle of obligatory convertibility, whereas the latest development in paper currency makes it non-convertible at all, which means that these views, even those that count paper currency *zakatable*, should be revised according to this reality.

We should recognize the fact that paper currency is now the backbone of transactions. Gold and silver are used only exceptionally. Paper currency, issued and guaranteed by the state, is the measure of current and future values. Laws provide for its acceptability and enforce its non-convertibility. Paper money is used to perform all the activities and functions of monetary gold and silver. It is true, however, that the precious metals have value of their own, which may at times be different from their monetary value, a value that is determined by the supply and demand for these two metals, merely on the grounds of their industrial and commercial value. It is imposed on gold and silver in consideration of their characteristics as growing assets used as a measure of value. That is perhaps why gold and silver are usually called in jurist literature "the values" or "the two currencies." It is not fair or acceptable for anyone to claim that some schools of thought do not consider paper money t*zakatable* or to attribute such a owing to the schools of Ahmad, Malik, or al Shafi'i, simply because paper money is a new invention and was not in existence at the time of these leading scholars.

One should feel proud of what is written by the late scholar, Muhammad Hasanain Makhluf al 'Adawi in his booklet titled *al Tibyan fi Zakat al Athman*. He comments on those who consider paper currency as representing bank debts:

> It is obvious that there are essential differences between paper currency and I.O.U.'s. I.O.U.'s are not growing assets. Paper currency is a growing asset, used for obtaining goods and services. *zakatability* of debts is based on the ability of debtors to pay back, knowing that debts do not grow, while the *zakatability* of money is derived from its use as a means of exchange. The fact that paper currency is not any kind of debt known to jurists means it must be *zakatable* because it is completely substitutable for other wealth. If we look at paper currency, regardless of any consideration of reserves, we find in it a measure of value. Paper money is perhaps the only measure of present and future values in most countries, especially with the government taking full responsibility for issuance. As such, paper currency is similar to gold and silver, and it is *zakatable* because the reason for the *zakatability* of gold and silver is their use as measures of value.

> Paper money is *zakatable* on four rounds: (1) It represents funds deposited in the bank, which is similar to present disposable assets, (2) it represents the stock of gold or silver in the vaults of the bank, (3) it is a debt on the bank, which is fully capable of payment, and (4) it is a measure of value acceptable in transactions, so it is also *zakatable* like coins and other things used as currency.

This last consideration of Shaikh al Makhluf is, in my opinion, the most relevant one today, because of the prevalence of non-convertability of paper currency. In the early use of paper currency, people differed because of its vagueness and unknown future,[65] but now paper money has become well-established, so we must be certain about its *zakatability*. Besides, money is anything used as a measure of value and a means of exchange, regardless of what material it is made from. This form of money is used for all the monetary functions of gold and silver as known in *Shari'ah* and must likewise be *zakatable.*

Conditions for the *zakatability* of money

Four conditions are required for the *zakatability* of money:

1. *Nisab*

The first condition is that the amount of money should be at least equal to *nisab.* Anything that is below *nisab* is exempted from *zakah,* since the owner is not considered rich. *nisab* on gold is the equivalent of 85 grams of pure gold, which equals 20 *dinar.* On silver, *nisab* is 595 grams, which is equal to the 200 *dirhams* mentioned in the saying, and *nisab* on paper currency was discussed in the previous subsection.

Is it necessary that the owner be one person?

Take the example of a partnership or a corporation, in which the owners are several individuals and the company has cash assets of more than *nisab,* but the share of each partner of the cash money is lass than *nisab.* According to Abu Hanifah and Malik, partners are *zakatable* only if the share of each one alone is *nisab* or more. Al Shafi'i treats this common property as one unit and considers it *zakatable* if the total is at least *nisab.* The reason for this difference in opinion is the general terminology of the saying of the Prophet (p), "On that which is lass than five *uqiyyah* there is no sadaqah due." This text leaves undetermined whether these five *uqiyyah* (200 *dirham*) belong to one owner or more, but I may add that the very reason for which *nisab* is a condition of *zakah* is to exempt owners of small quantities. This may indicate that *nisab* should perhaps be applied to one owner, since otherwise it loses its virtue.

Al Shafi'i look at the similarity between common property in a partnership and mixing cattle together in grazing, but here again the same difference in views appears with respect to the effect of mixing cattle in grazing.[67] The majority's view is based on the assumption that since *zakah* is an obligation on the rich only, a partnership may contain some poor partners, and why should these poor fellows become a*zakatable* simply because of their association with the rich? On the other hand, al Shafi'i's view appears to be simpler in application in a time when corporations have become of major importance in the business world. However, it could be suggested that part of the proceeds of *zakah* taken from corporations be distributed among the poor shareholders or partners of that corporation.[68]

2. The passage of a year

The second condition is that a full lunar year must have passed on the ownership of *nisab. zakah* on money is a yearly obligation, and cannot be imposed at shorter intervals. Hanafites require that *nisab* at least exist at the beginning and end of the year. If the amount of money owned declines from *nisab* during the year, and increases again at the year's end, *zakatability* is not affected.[69] The other three schools of jurisprudence require that *nisab* stay in ownership during the whole year. They argue that the Prophet's saying, "There is no *zakah* on an asset until a year passes on It."[70] Implies that the year should pass on it all and it is not sufficient that the amount of *nisab* exist only at the beginning and end of the year.[71]

All this applies on money as a stock asset. Earned money, such as salaries, wages, awards, professional income, and the rental proceeds of leased buildings or cars, are all disputed. The majority of jurists require that a year must pass on every amount of money, stock or flow, for *zakah* to be obligatory. Abu Hanifah suggests adding the flow to the stock and making *zakah* due on the total at the end of the year that started on the stock. An exception is made in the case where the flow of cash is a substitution for an asset whose *zakah* was already paid.[72] It is authentically reported from some Companions that such flow of money is *zakatable* at the time of its receipt. We shall study this issue in detail in chapter nine.

3. Money should be free of debt

The third condition is that the owned *nisab* must be free of any debt whose liability would reduce the amount of money to below *nisab*. Debts that prevent *zakatability* are those that prevent liability toward other human beings, including personal debts and past due *zakah*,[73] while debts that belong to God are not deductible, such as the cost of making pilgrimage.[74] According to some scholars, deferred debts do not prevent the *zakatability* of present sums of money.[75] Al Nawawi summarizes the Shafi'ite view, "If debts prevent *zakatability*, then debts due to God and debts due to others should be treated the same."[76]

4. Excess above basic needs

Some leading Hanafite jurists require that *nisab* be counted only above the satisfaction of basic needs of the owners. According to Ibn Malik,[77] basic needs are those that prevent the destruction of a person and his dependents; such as food, shelter, defence tools, clothes that protect from cold and heat, money to pay back debts, furniture, utensils, basic transportation, and books of knowledgs. According to Hanafites, ignorance and demoralization are like personal destruction.[78] If a person owns an amount of money that is above *nisab* but needs it for any of the above expenses, he or she is not considered *zakatable*[79] on the grounds that this person is not rich and *zakah* is collected only from the rich. The Prophet (p) proclaims that "There is no sadaqah except out of richness," and "Start with those whom you support."

SECTION TWO

ZAKAH ON GOLD AND SILVER JEWELRY, ORNAMENTS, AND ANTIQUES

In order to complete our study of *zakah* on gold and silver, we must understand *zakah* on utensils, ornaments, decorative objective, statuery, and men and women's jewelry made of gold and silver.

Gold and silver utensils and ornaments are *zakatable*

It is not disputed among Muslim scholars that whenever gold and silver are used in a forbidden manner they are subject to *zakah*. Authentic and correct sayings are reported which forbid the use of gold and silver as kitchen and dining utensils because that is a feature of a lavish and ostentatious way of living and constitutes a form of hoarding.[80] The author of *al Mughni* explains, "Whatever is prohibited for use is also prohibited for decoration," no matter whether such utensils and decorative objects are owned by men or women. Women's jewelry is allowed on the grounds that women wear it for their husbands. This need cannot be extended to utensils and other ornaments. Additionally, statues are prohibited regardless of the metal or stone they are made from. If they are made of gold or silver, the grounds for their prohibition is doubled. Ibn Qudamah adds, "Once this is realized, ornaments and utensils are indisputably *zakatable*, if they reach nisab either alone or when added to other owned gold and silver."[82] The author of *al Mughni* attributes an opinion to some Hanbalites that the market value of such items should be considered and not only their weight, because of the high artistic value incorporated in them.[83]

Men's Jewelry is *zakatable*

Men are forbidden to wear jewelry made of gold, silver, or any other substance, except for a plain silver ring which is permissible.[84] Men's jewelry is thus subject to *zakah* if it reaches nisab, because the use of jewelry by men is not considered a satisfaction of a natural need like that of women.[85] *Zakah* is obligated on men's jewelry as a reminder of the error of owning and of the need to put its value back into productive use. As for the use of gold by men, it is prohibited completely, except for such necessities as its use as caps for teeth, tooth filling, or as a substitute for a broken nose or a cut ear.

Abu Daud reports from 'Abd al Rahman bin Tarafah that "the nose of his grandfather, 'Arfajah bin Sa'd, was severed the day of al Kilab. He got an artificial nose made of silver, but it got rotten and smelly. The Prophet ordered him to get a gold nose." Ahmad says, "It is all right in cases of necessity to tie the teeth with gold thread, if it is feared the teeth may fall out." Any other use of gold by men is forbidden and is subject to *zakah*. We should recognize, however, that it is preferred to consider value and not only weight in the case of men's jewelry, because of the value added by the artistic labor. Once the value of this jewelry reaches the equivalent of 85 grams of gold, it becomes *zakatable*.

Pearls, precious stones, and women's jewels are not *zakatable*

Women's jewelry made of other than gold and silver, such as pearls, diamonds, and other precious stones and metals are not *zakatable*, because they are designated for personal and lawful use by women, as determined by God, "And that ye may extract therefrom ornaments to wear,"[86] and are not considered growing assets. Some leading Shi'ite scholars of Ahl al Bait disagree and consider any women's jewelry that reaches *nisab* in value is subject to *zakah* on the grounds that are jewels valuable items of wealth, and God says, "Out of their wealth take a *sadaqah*." They indicate that the words "their wealth" in this verse are in the plural, attributed to Muslims, and the general implication of the verse means take from the wealth of each one of them. Women's jewels, precious stones, and metals are items of wealth included in this general meaning.[87] The majority of scholars argue that even if we accept the generality of the verse, we must recognize that Sunnah restricts the meaning of the verse to only growing wealth or wealth with growth potential. Thus, actual or potential growth is the reason for *zakatability* and not the precious nature of the item.[88] These jewels are usually obtained for personal ornamentation and not for growth or investment, as long as they are not kept for the purpose of hoarding wealth.

Difference on women's gold and silver ornaments

In the letter on *sadaqat* sent by the Prophet (p) there is no reference to women's gold and silver jewelry, nor do we have any authentic, explicit texts which obligate *zakah* or exempt it on this jewelry. All we have is a few sayings whose authenticity and indications are controversial.[89] The reason for the differences in opinion is that some scholars take into consideration the metal of which jewelry is made. Gold and silver are both *zakatable* as money, so these scholars consider gold and silver jewelry also *zakatable*. Other scholars consider the labor involved and the industrial process required to make jewelry and transform the metal from its monetary nature into a commodity ready for personal use that satisfies a natural need of women. Thus jewelry is similar to cloths furniture, and other personal objects that are unanimously exempt from *zakah*. According to these scholars, women's jewelry is not *zakatable*. These rulings apply only to lawful jewelry. Forbidden jewelry is unanimously *zakatable*. Accordingly, there are two groups of scholars, those who consider jewelry *zakatable* exactly like money, and those who consider them non-*zakatable* or *zakatable* within certain restrictions.

Scholars who consider jewelry *zakatable*

Al Baihaqi and others report from 'Alqamah the wife of Ibn Mas'ud asked him about her jewels. He replied, "If they reach 200 *dirhams*, they are *zakatable*." She said, "May I spend their *zakah* on my [orphaned] nephew whose guardian I am?" "Yes," he answered. Al Baihaqi comments, "This is also narrated and linked up to the Prophet (p), but it is unsupported."[90] He also reports from Shu'aib bin Yasar that 'Umar wrote Abu

Musa to[90] "Instruct Muslim women in your area to pay *zakah* on their ornaments." But this is not authentically reported from 'Umar.[91] Ibn Abi Shaibah quotes al Hasan as saying, "I know that none of the [four] Successors said that ornaments are *zakatable*."[92] Al Baihaqi reports from 'A'ishah, "It is all right to wear jewelry if its *zakah* is paid,"[93] But we have on hand a correct report from 'A'ishah contradicting this, as will be seen later. It is reported that 'Abd Allah bin 'Amr used to write his treasurer Salim instructions to pay *zakah* on the ornaments of his daughters every year.[94] Abu 'Ubaid reports from him that he gave his three daughters ornaments worth six thousand dinars. He used to send his slave Jalid every year to pay their *zakah*.[95]

The chains of all the above reports are controversial. Abu 'Ubaid comments, "We have nothing authentic about *zakah* on ornaments from any of the Companions except from Ibn Mas'ud.[96] Ibn Hazm says "The report of Ibn Mas'ud is topmost in its authenticity."[97] Among those who believe that ornaments are *zakatable* are Sa'id bin Musayyib, Sa'ad bin Jubair, 'Ata, Mujahid, 'Abd Allah bin Shaddad, Jabir bin Zaid, Ibn Shabrumah, Maimun bin Mahran, al Zuhri, al Thawri, Abu Hanifah, and his disciples, al Awza'i and al Hasan bin Hay.[98]

Evidence supporting this opinion

1. The general implication of the verse, "and there are those who hoard gold and silver and spend it not in the way of God. Announce unto them a most grevious penalty." Gold and silver mentioned in this verse include that which is used in women's ornaments as much as it includes money and bullion. Consequently, unless *zakah* is paid, the owner will be branded with its heat on the Day of Resurrection.

2. The general meaning of the sayings of the Prophet (p), "On silver, one-fourth of one-tenth is obligated; no *sadaqah* is required on what is less than five *uqiyyah*." This implies that silver is *zakatable* once it reaches five *uqiyyah*, as do the general texts of *zakah* on gold, such as "There is no owner of gold that does not pay its *zakah* . . . etc.

3. There are a few sayings about *zakah* on ornaments in particular that are considered correct by some leading scholars. Among these sayings are the following:
    (a)   Abu Daud reports from 'Amr bin Shu'aib from his father from his grandfather, that a women[99] with her daughter came to the Prophet (p). On the wrist of her daughter were two thick bracelets of gold. the Prophet asked, "Do you give *zakah* on this? She replied "No." "Does it please you for God to embrace you with two bracelets of fire on the Day of Resurrection?" he warned. The narrator says, "She took them off and tossed them to the Prophet (p), saying, They belong to God and His Messenger."[100]

    (b) Abu Daud, al Daraqutni, al Hakim, and al Baihaqi report from 'A'ishah that "The Messenger of God (p) entered my room and found in my hand a few rings of silver. He said, A'ishah, what is this?' I said, 'I made them in order to use them as ornament [to please you] O Messenger of God.' He said, Do you pay their *zakah*?' I answered 'No,' or negatively. He said, 'That would be enough for you of the fire,'[101]

(c)   Abu Daud and others report from Umm Salamah, "I used to wear some ornaments of gold, and I asked, O Messenger of God, is this hoarding? He said, "That which reaches [*nisab*], if *zakated*, is not hoarding." Al Mundhiri comments, "In its chain there is 'Attab bin Bashir (Abu al Hassan al Harrani); al Bukhari reports from him, but others cricize him."[102]

Those who exempt ornaments from *zakah*[103]

Ibn Hazm in *al Muhalla* writes, "Jabir bin 'Abd Allah and Ibn 'Umar said, "There is no *zakah* on ornaments " This is also the view of Asma' bint Abu Bakr, and similar view is correctly reported from 'A'ishah. This is also the opinion of al Sha'bi, 'Amrah bint 'Abd al Rahman, Abu Ja'far, and Muhammad 'Ali. It is reported from Taus, al Hasan, and Sa'id bin al Musayyib, There are two differing reports from Sufian al Thawri, one that women's jewelry is *zakatable* and one that it is not.[104] Al Qasim bin Muhammad ('A'ishah's nephew), Malik bin Anas, Ahmad bin Hanbal, and Ishaq bin Rahwayh say that women's jewelry is not *zakatable*. This is the most famous opinion of al Shafi'i, according to al Khattabi,[105] and it is the opinion of Abu 'Ubaid as well.

Evidence supporting this view

In principle, people are not obligated to pay *zakah* without a text from *Shari'ah*, and there is neither an authentic text about *zakah* on women's jewelry nor a correct analogy to a ruling based on an authentic text. Moreover, *zakah* is obligated on actually or potentially growing wealth, and jewelry is neither. Jewelry is for wearing and do for investment. The analogy to animals for personal use is obvious. Those animals are not *zakatable* because they are not used for growth.

There are also authentic reports from some Companions to the effect that *zakah* is not obligated on ornaments: Malik in *al Muwatta'* reports from al Qasim bin Muhammad[106] that 'A'ishah, the wife of the Prophet (p) was the guardian of her orphaned nieces. They used to wear ornaments, and she did not give *zakah* on their ornaments.[107] He also reports from Nafi that 'Abd Allah bin 'Umar's daughters and female slaves wore gold ornaments, and he did not pay *zakah* on their ornaments.[107] Ibn Abi Shaibah reports from al Qasim that "Our assets were kept with 'A'ishah. She used to pay *zakah* on them, except for the ornaments," and from 'Amrah that "We were orphans under the guardianship of 'A'ishah. We had ornaments and she did not pay *zakah* on them." Ibn Abi Shaibah and Abu 'Ubaid and others report similar things from Jabir bin 'Abd Allah and Asma bint Abu Bakr in addition to 'A'ishah and Ibn 'Umar.[108] Ibn al Zubair narrates from Jabir, "There is no *zakah* on ornaments. I said, 'It may be as much as a thousand dinars.' He answered, 'It is for wearing or lending.'" In another version he says, "Verily, that is too much." It is reported from Asma' that she did not use to pay *zakah* on ornaments, and al Shafi'i adds, "It is also reported from Ibn 'Abbas and Anas bin Malik, but I do not know whether it is authentic from them. The meaning of those reports is that there is no *zakah* on ornaments."[109]

Al Qadi Abu al Walid al Baji, in his commentary on *al Muwatta'*, writes, "This is a known opinion among the Companions. 'A'ishah (m) is perhaps the most knowledgeable, since she is the wife of the Prophet (p) and not a person who may have missed his ordinances on such a matter. Also, 'Abd Allah bin 'Umar is the brother of Hafsah, the wife of the Prophet (p) and she would have been aware of any requirement on them."[110] One can use as supporting evidence what is said by Yahya bin Sa'id, "I asked 'Amrah about *zakah* on ornaments. She said, 'I have never seen a person that pays *zakah* on them.' Al Hasan is reported to have said, "I know of none of the Successors who said there is *zakah* on ornaments."[111]

Ibn al Jawzi in *al Tahqiq* reports, with his own chain, from 'Afiah bin Ayub from al Laith bin Sa'd from Abu Zubair from Jabir from the Prophet, (p), that "There is no [obligated] *zakah* on ornaments."[112] Al Baihaqi notes that 'Afiyah is unknown. "We know of no criticism of him," Ibn al Jawzi counters. Ibn Daqiq al 'Id adds, "I have read it handwritten by our teacher, al Mundhiri, that 'nothing reached me that makes 'Afiyah bin Ayub weak.'"[113] The Prophet said, "O womenfolk, give for charity even out of your ornaments."[114] This is reported by al Bukhari, al Tirmidhi, and others, Ibn al 'Arabi comments, "The obvious literal implication of this saying is that there is no obligated *zakah* on ornaments." His telling women to "give charity even out of your ornaments" means *zakah* is not obligated on them, and they are urged to give voluntary contributions.[115] It is not linguistically correct or usual to ask someone to give voluntarily something he or she is obligated to give anyway as *zakah*. It makes more sense to encourage someone to give voluntarily what is spared from *zakah*.

Analysis of different views

After presenting the differing views of jurists, I may say that what seems to carry most weight is that *zakah* is not obligatory on jewelry, within certain limits. This opinion is consistent with the general conditions of *zakatability*. That is, *zakah* is compulsory on actually or potentially growing assets, such as money and business inventory. Women's jewelry is worn not for growth but for personal use and lawful ornamentation. It satisfies personal needs of women, natural desires which are taken into consideration in Islam. Gold and silver jewelry is lawful for women, while it is not for men. Hence jewelry for women is something like expensive clothes, furniture, and other sorts of personal ornaments that are lawful for her. It carries great similarities to jewelry made of pearls, diamonds, and other precious stones, which are made lawful for woman by the texts of Qur'an.[116] These pearls, precious stones, and valuable clothes are exempt from *zakah* by the unanimous opinion of leading scholars, in spite of their high value. We realize from the Prophet's tradition that *zakah* is not required on all kinds of wealth, but only on growing items. Homes inhabited by their owners, means of personal transportation, and tools are indisputably exempt from *zakah*. Even the Hanfite jurists, who consider *zakah* obligatory on jewelry, have decided that the reason for *zakatability* is the position of an asset in excess of personal needs, that is designed for profit.[117] Does this reason apply in the case of lawful jewelry for women, which is neither designated for growth nor in excess of personal needs?

Hanafites also exempt from *zakah* working animals used in watering and cultivating, in spite of the fact that the same animals, were they naturally pastured and not used in work., would be *zakated*. Being working animals makes them similar to tools and things designated for personal use. How can the same Hanafites obligate *zakah* on jewelry, which is also for personal use? I firmly believe that *Shari'ah* treats similarly things that are similar, and whenever similar things are not treated similarly, it is an error of judgement on the part of the jurists. This is perhaps the reason for which Abu 'Ubaid criticizes those who obligate *zakah* on jewelry while exempting working animals. It is extremely unlikely that *Shari'ah* would exempt jewelry made of pearls, diamonds, and other precious stones that are very often more expensive than gold and silver, and obligate *zakah* on jewelry of gold and silver only. The first kind of jewelry is usually used by rich women, while the second is used by middle class and sometimes poor women. Does it make sense for *Shari'ah* to make middle class and poor women pay *zakah* on their jewelry and exempt the higher class women from similar payment? Exempting them all from *zakah* is just and reasonable according to the whole spirit of *zakah* rulings.

The leading Zaidi scholar al Hadi is consistent with himself when he declares that *zakah* is required from all jewelry, whether made of gold and silver or of pearls and precious stones. On the other hand, exempting one and obligating the other does not seem rational to those who look for the reason behind the rulings of *Shari'ah*, who constitute the majority of Muslim scholars. The opinion I select is supported by the rule of *zakah* collection which states that *zakah* is paid out of the same *zakatable* asset and its increment. This rule is not broken except in necessity, as in the case of owning less than 25 animals, where *zakah* is paid in sheep and not camels, for reasons described earlier in this part. How can a woman pay *zakah* (2.5%) out of her jewelry, except by being unnecessarily forced to sell some or all of it? In all other applications of *zakah* there is no such requirement. 'Why should an exception be made here? The theory of "growing assets" assumes that *zakah* is collected out of the increments of the asset without reducing the asset itself, in order to preserve it as a source of income for the owner. The result of obligating *zakah* on jewelry, which does not grow, is to consume the asset itself as the years go by. Maimun bin Mahran points out that "We have a necklace whose *zakah* that I paid throughout the years reached about its value."[118] I think that the spirit of *Shari'ah* in regard to *zakah* does not approve of this.

Ibn al 'Arabi in *Ahkam al Qur'an* argues that "the intent of growth would obligate *zakah* on things that since they do not grow on their own are not otherwise *zakatable*, such as all commodities that comprise business inventory. By the same token, the intent of abstention from growth in gold and silver by making them into jewelry for person use must waive *zakah*. If a condition whose existence makes *zakah* required on an asset that is not otherwise *zakatable*, its absence must exempt from *zakah* an asset that would otherwise be *zakatable*."[119]

Additionally, the texts that talk about the *zakatability* of gold and silver consider their use as measures of prices; that is, as money. Even the verse "and those who hoard gold and silver and spend it not in way of Cod. . . " indicates by using the words "hoard" and "spend" that gold and silver are meant here as money, because money is what is usually hoarded and not spent, while common jewelry is not considered a treasure and is not readied for spending.

The view that I select here is the same as that of the great scholar Abu 'Ubaid, who says in his book *al Amwal*:

"The Prophet (p) said , "If sliver money reaches five *uqiyyah*, there is one-fourth of a tenth due on it." Here the Messenger of God (p) restricts *zakah* to silver money. He does not include all forms of silver, but minted silver only, by using a word that is only used for silver coins that have been minted and are used as money.[120] By the same token, the word "*uqiyyah*" only has the meaning of *dirhams*. Each *uqiyyah* is worth is worth 40 *dirhams*, and *zakah* is obligated on *dirhams*. Muslims unanimously consider *dinars* also *zakatable*, for *dinars* are also mentioned in some sayings linked up to the Prophet (p).[121] Muslims have no difference in regard to the *dirham* and the *dinar*, while they differ on jewelry because the latter is for personal use, while the only use for gold and silver money is in circulation. The *zakatability* of money must then be different from that of jewelry, which is more similar to furniture and clothes, and this is the reason many scholars consider jewelry non-*zakatable*.

On similar grounds, Hanafites, who obligate *zakah* on jewelry, say that working camels and cows are not *zakatable* because of their similarity to things designed for personal use. Jurists of Hijaz obligate *zakah* on working camels and cows and exempt jewelry. Both these scholars are not being consistent. Since these items are similar with regard to being commodities designated for personal use, they should all be either exempt from *zakah* or not.

In my view, both are not *zakatable* on the grounds mentioned above. As for the saying in which the Prophet asked the Yemeni woman who had two gold bracelets, "Do you pay their *zakah*?" it is only known through one chain, which is criticized by many scholars in the past and the present.[122] If this saying is correct, the Prophet may have meant by "*zakah*" lending those bracelets to others free of charge, as explained by some scholars, including Sa'id bin al Musayyib, al Sha'bi, al Hasan, and Qataiah, who says, "Its *zakah* is lending it to other women free of charge."[123] If *zakah* on jewelry were obligated the same way it is obligated on silver money, the Prophet (p) would not have limited himself to giving that advice to a particular women when he saw her bracelets. That issue would have been treated like *zakah* on other items that are repeatedly mentioned in many of his letters, instructions, and traditions. It would have been practiced by the Successors after him. In none of their instructions do we find anything about *zakah* on women's jewelry. As for the saying from 'A'ishah, "It is all right to wear jewelry if you pay its *zakah*," I find that its *zakah* is lending it freely to others, especially since her nephew al Qasim bin Muhammad denied that she instructed any woman in her family, including he nieces, to pay *zakah* on their jewelry. Nothing is authentic about the *zakatability* of jewelry from a Companion except from Ibn Mas'ud. The saying of Abd Allah bin 'Amr that he used to pay *zakah* on the jewelry of his daughters has problems in its chain similar to those in the saying linked to the Prophet that is mentioned above. The other opinion [that jewelry is not *zakatable*] is reported from 'A'ishah, Ibn 'Umar, Jabir bin 'Abd Allah, and Anas bin Malik [Companions] and many Followers after them. This is also supported by our explanation of the tradition of the Prophet (p)."[124]

After this lengthy but brilliant quotation from Abu 'Ubaid, I would like to mention the following remarks on the arguments presented by these who obligate *zakah* on jewelry.

Disproving the arguments for obligating *zakah* on jewelry

1. The use of the verse "who hoard gold and silver and spend it not in the way of God . . . ." along with the interpretation that hoarding includes women's jewelry is not acceptable.[125] The verse refers to gold and silver that are designated as jewelry for the personal use and enjoyment of women. No one requires that jewelry be circulated and spent in the way of God, except in emergencies.

2. The sayings used by those who obligate *zakah* on jewelry are also disputed by others from the point of view of their authenticity as well as from the point of view of their indications.

(a) The first saying, "and there is one-fourth of a tenth due on silver," is agreed upon as correct, but the Arabic word used for silver in this saying is "*al riqqah*" which literally means silver that has been minted in the form of coins. The word is not used in Arabic for manufactured jewelry.

(b) Some of the other sayings are not proven authentic, to the extent that al Tirmidhi could say, "No saying is correct on this question."[126] Ibn Hazm, who obligates *zakah* on jewelry, does not depend on those sayings. He, in fact, disagrees with the very use of those sayings as arguments for obligating *zakah* on jewelry. He argues, "Those who see that *zakah* is required on jewelry use fumbling sayings and reports which we need not be occupied with."[127] In his argument, Ibn Hazm depends only on the comprehensive implications of the basic texts of *zakah* on gold and silver. However, let me take time to review the chains of those sayings anyway.

The saying from 'Amr bin Shu'aib is reported by al Nasa'i as mursal. Al Mundhiri marks it in *al Targhib wa al Tarhib* as weak. We have discussed it earlier and quoted the opinion of Abu 'Ubaid on it. The saying reported from 'A'ishah about the bracelets has Yahya bin Ayub al Ghafiqi in its chain. Yahya is acceptable to al Bukhari and Muslim and others; he was trusted, but al Dhahabi quotes differing opinions about him from several critics. He quotes Ibn Ma'in as saying, "His sayings' reports are fair," and Ahmad as saying, "He had a bad memory" Ibn al Qattan and Abu Hatim are quoted as saying, "His reports must not be accepted," and al Nasa'i saying he was not a strong link, and al Daraqutni saying "Some of his reported sayings have discrepancies."[128] The latter mentions several of these discrepancies of Yahya, which are rejected. The report of a person who is extremely controversial should not be used on issues that are not agreed upon, especially when we have on hand correct reports that 'A'ishah's practices are in opposition to his saying.

The saying from Umm Salamah is commented on by al Mundhiri, who says, "'Attab bin Bashir is in its chain. Al Bukhari uses his reports, but more than one scholar criticizes him." In *al Mizan*, al Dhahabi says about 'Attab, "Ahmad said, 'I hope he is all right, he reports from Khasif some unacceptable reports which I think are the mistake of Khasif.'" Al Nasa'i says, "He is not that [good] in [reporting] sayings." Ibn al Madini notes, "Our colleagues consider him weak." Ibn Ma'in once remarked, "He is trustworthy" and another time "He is weak." "We leave his reports aside" 'Ali indicates.

Lastly, Ibn 'Adi says, "I hope he is all right."[129] All this means that none of the leading critics are firm about Yahya bin Ayub's trustworthiness, and some of them grade him weak. The fact that al Bukhari reports from him should not be over-estimated by the reader. Ibn Hajar notes that, "Al Bukhari reports from him only two sayings. In one of them there is another supporting it, while in the other his name is associated with other names."[130]

Al Zaila'i in *Nasb al Rayah* says, "The authors of the two correct books [al Bukhari and Muslim] may report from a person who is controversial, but when they do so, they select from his reports those sayings that are either supported by other chains or that are obviously witnessed and known from other sources. They do not report from the controversial person saying in whose chain he is singled out, especially in cases where trustworthy reporters contradict his reports."[131] Moreover, in the chain of this saying, Thabit bin 'Ajlan is the only one who reports from 'Attab bin Bashir, as stated by al Baihaqi.[132]

Thabit, whose reports are used by al Bukhari, is also controversial. Ibn Ma'in views him as trustworthy. Ahmad says, "I abstain from giving an opinion on him." Abu Hatim says, "He is fair, "and Ibn 'Adi gives three strange examples reported by him. Al Aqili comments on him in *The Weak*, "He is not usually followed by others in his reports." Al Baihaqi adds, "And among his reports that are negated is the saying reported from 'Attab bin Bashir from 'Ata from Umm Salamah," and he cites the saying we have on hand. Al Hafiz 'Abd al Haqq says, "It is authentic but must not be used in argument." This is rejected by Abu al Hasan bin al Qattan, who continues, "al 'Aqili is also biased against him. Those who are not known at all as trustworthy may be described as such, but if a person who is known as trustworthy is singled out in the chain, this does not bring harm to the chain, unless singling out occurs very often." Al Dhahabi argues with Ibn al Qattan, "This is true if the person is known as trustworthy, but a person about whom a leading critic like Ahmad abstains from giving an opinion, while some others consider him trustworthy and Abu Hatim calls him 'fair',[133] must not easily be upgraded to the degree of trustworthiness. If such a person is singled out in the chain, then it must be negated." Thus al Dhahabi gives weight to the opinion expressed by 'Aqili and 'Abd al Haqq.[134]

Moreover, al Bukhari only reports one saying from Thabit in the chapter on slaughtering. This saying is supported by other sayings in the chapter on cleansing, according to al Hafiz.[135] As we know from the methods of al Bukhari and Muslim, the inclusion of this saying must not be taken as grading of Thabit trustworthy. Both Muslim and al Bukhari do not mention the saying under discussion, or any other on the subject of *zakah* on jewelry. The saying reported from Umm Salamah through Thabit and 'Attab, in view of this controversy about them, must not be accepted as proof in such a controversial question.

Ibn Hajar, in the introduction to *Tahdhib al Tahdhib*, says, "The benefit of bringing out all that is said about a reporter, whether good or bad, becomes obvious in controversial matters."[136]

Furthermore, I should mention that I see these reported sayings as even more dubious because they were not commonly known to Companions, in spite of the fact that the Companions had different opinions on the *zakatability* of jewelry. If such sayings were known to the Companions, they would not have been so varied in their opinions and practices. This may mean that those reported sayings are either overridden by later sayings or are not authentic, since it is extremely unlikely that the Companions would differ on an issue and not use what they heard from the Messenger of God to support their views. We know, however, that 'Aishah's practice to the opposite of these sayings is authentically reported.[137]

Lastly, al Baihaqi, supported on this point by al Nawawi and al Mundhiri,[138] says "The report of al Qasim and Ibn Abi Mulaikah from 'A'ishah that she was not paying *zakah* on the jewels of her nieces, in spite of the fact that she is correctly reported to have believed in paying *zakah* or, orphan's wealth, brings some doubt to the report raised to the Prophet [that there is *zakah* on jewelry] for how could she not practice something that she herself reports from the Prophet (p), unless she knew it was annulled?"[139]

(c)   Some scholars attempt to find a consistent interpretation of these sayings, assuming they are acceptable, in that *zakah* on jewelry was obligatory in the early stage in Madinah, when the use of gold as jewelry by women was itself forbidden, but the moment the use of gold jewelry became permissible for women, *zakah* on that jewelry was waived, the same way *zakah* was waived on working livestock. Al Baihaqi says, "This is the view of many of our colleagues." He gives a report of sayings which indicate the prohibition of golden jewelry and an account of sayings that allowed it later for women. He comments that these sayings indicate that the use of golden jewelry by women is permissible, which means that those reports on its prohibition are superseded by the newer sayings that allow it.[140] This interpretation has no bearing on the report from A'ishah that bracelets of silver were *zakatable*, since not a single scholar claims that silver jewelry was also prohibited for women.[141]

(d)   Another interpretation may come to mind with regard to the two sayings from 'A'ishah and from Umm Salamah, assuming they were authentic. The Prophet (p) may have had a special and stricter approach in dealing with his own family, taking them further away from the desire for luxury and ornaments, since they are supposed to set an example for all other women, as indicated by the verse, "O consorts of the Prophet, if any of you were guilty of evident unseemly conduct, the punishment would be double for you."[143] So it may be a special ruling restricted to the wives of the Prophet, not given as a religious opinion applicable to other Muslim women. On these ground 'A'ishah's not paying *zakah* on the jewelry of her nieces be may understood.

(e)   Some other scholars have yet a third interpretation of these sayings, again just assuming they are authentic; that is, the Prophet (p) noticed extravagance and excess above that which is customary[144] in those specific cases mentioned in the sayings, so he obligated *zakah* on those grounds. This interpretation is supported by the word in one of the sayings, describing the bracelets as big or huge or describing the rings as big. Those sayings may be used to mean that *zakah* is obligated if the amount of jewelry is more than what is usual and customary.[145]

(f)   Some Companions who obligate *zakah* on jewelry consider jewelry *zakatable* only once in the lifetime rather than repeatedly every year. This is reported from Anas bin Malik.[146]

(g)   Some other Companions and Followers have another interpretation of *zakah* on jewelry. It is that *zakah* fulfilled by lending the jewelry free of charge to other women to use on festive occassions. This is reported by Al Baihaqi from Ibn 'Umar and Ibn al Musayyib,[147] and it is also reported by Abu 'Ubaid and Ibn Abi Shaibah from Ibn al Musayyib, al Hasan al Basri Qatadah, and al Sha'bi.[148]

All these different interpretations make it impossible to use these sayings as evidence supporting *zakatability* of jewelry, in accordance with the well-known rule of jurisprudence: If the evidence has different possible interpretations, it cannot be used to support one of them against the others. This is certainly on the assumption that the sayings are acceptable from the point of view of their authenticity, though in fact, each of them is also disputable on that ground.

Surprisingly enough, the jurists who belong to the school of rationalization use sayings and reports as evidence in this debate, while jurists belonging to the school of sayings use rationalization as their evidence.[148]   As for the reports from some Companions like Ibn Mas'ud, (authentically reported) and Ibn "Amr (disputed in its authenticity), it should be noted that they do not give their opinions as applicable to all people. All that is indicated by these reports is that these Companions used to pay *zakah* on the jewelry of their own wives and daughters, which may be an indication of their piety and preference for removing all doubt on their part in a matter on which they do not have a ruling from the Messenger. The only report that falls beyond this interpretation is the one attributed to 'Umar when he wrote to Abu Musa to order Muslim women to pay *zakah* on their jewelry. This report is not proven correct, and al Hasan denies that any of the Successors obligated *zakah* on jewelry.

Jewelry used as hoarded treasure is *zakatable*

The opinion expressed earlier that jewelry is not *zakatable* applies only to jewelry that is used as women's ornaments. As for women's gold and silver jewelry that is used as a storage of value for the purpose of hoarding, and is looked upon as an accumulation of wealth, this is *zakatable*, just like money. It is reported from Sa'id bin al Musayyib that "If jewelry is worn and used, it is not *zakatable*, but if it is not worn or used, it is *zakatable*."[150] Malik says, "Those who own gold and jewelry made of gold or silver which is not used for ornamental wearing, must pay *zakah* on it every year. Jewelry should be weighed and *zakah* paid at the rate of one-fourth of one-tenth, unless the total weight is less than the equivalent of 40 *dinars* or 200 *dirhams*. Then they are not *zakatable*. As for jewelry that is broken and in need of repair in order to be worn, it is still considered used jewelry, and is not *zakatable*."[151]

Al Nawawi says, "Our colleagues say that if jewelry is not held for the purpose of customary use (lawful, desired, or prohibited) but rather for the purpose of hoarding and accumulation, then it is *zakatable*, as correctly confirmed by the majority."[152] Similarly, al Laith bin Sa'd says, "Jewelry used for wearing and lending to others is not *zakatable*, but that used as hoarded treasure is *zakatable*."[153] This means that when Jewelry is not intended for customary use, it is treated like an attempt to escape *zakah*, Ibn Hazm argues with al Laith, "If this is so, then a person who buys house or orchard in order to avoid *zakah* should also be *zakatable*."[154] I believe that the spirit of *Shari'ah* tries to annul all mischief and to treat cheaters in such a way that gives them the opposite of their intent. Hanbalites have established the opinion that any person who holds jewelry as a means to avoid *zakah* is *zakatable*.[155] We will discuss further the mischief in *zakah* in the chapter dealing with zakah payment, God willing. Jewelry owned by men and used as ornamentation by their female family members or other females is treated like jewelry owned and used by women, i.e., it is not *zakatable*, since it is designated for lawful customary use and not for growth.[155]

Jewelry above a customary limit is *zakatable*

If the quantity of jewelry exceeds the customary amount and reaches extravagance, the extra is *zakatable*. This is on the grounds that *zakah* is waived from jewelry because it is used by women just like clothes and household goods. What is above the customary and moderate use is either prohibited or at least discouraged; it is in all cases not approved by *Shari'ah*. Al Nawawi says "our Shafi'ite colleagues argue that jewelry is made lawful only within the limits of non-apparent extravagance, but once it reaches the extravagant limit, then it becomes prohibited according to most jurists from Iraq."[156] Ibn Hamid, a Hunbalite, says that "if jewelry is below one thousand *mithqal* it is lawful. Once it reaches that such, it becomes unlawful and consequently *zakatable*, in accordance with what is reported by Abu 'Ubaid and al Athram from "Amr bin Dinar: Jabir was asked if jewelry was *zakatable* and he answered that it was not. Then he was told, 'Even if it amounts to one thousand *dinars*?' He answered, 'That is indeed too much.'"[157] Jewelry exceeding customary limits is surely extravagance and no longer needed as normal ornamentation for women.[158]

On the other hand, the author of *al Mughni* argues that *Shari'ah* makes the use of jewelry lawful without limit, thus it is not acceptable to limit that use by personal opinions.[159] It seems that he forgets that the use of lawful things in *Shari'ah* is restricted by two principles: avoidance of extravagance and avoidance of prideful showing off. The Prophet (p) is reported to have said, "Eat and drink and dress without extravagance or pride."[160] The saying about the Yemeni woman who entered the presence of the Messenger with her daughter, who had two huge golden bracelets on the (daughter's) arm and was told by the Prophet (p) about their *zakatability*, may be considered a case for this argument. That is, the Prophet (p) found that the amount of jewelry was way beyond the limit of customary and usual use and was extravagant for that young woman. Some scholars take this saying to mean exactly that. That is, that *zakah* is obligated on what exceeds the customary amounts.[161] This may be the reason why 'Abd Allah bin 'Amr used to pay *zakah* on the jewelry of his daughters. He was reported to have bought his three daughters jewelry worth 6000*dinars*. This is definitely above the customary amount.

Does *zakah* then become obligatory on all the jewelry owned by the person or on that part which is above the customary limit? It seems from the above-cited sayings that all the jewelry becomes *zakatable* as a means of cleansing the whole amount, because of its exaggeration in exceeding the lawful limit. The opinion that claims that all jewelry in any amount is not *zakatable* ends up putting a large portion of the wealth of the Muslim community in the idleness of extravagant amounts of jewelry and ornaments that are only rarely used by women and that are usually stored in private boxes in banks.

What is the limit of extravagance? It seems to be difficult to put an objective definition of extravagance, since its boundaries differ from one community to another and from one neighborhood to another. An amount that is extravagant is a poor country for a poor family may be very customary or less than normal for a rich family in a rich country. The real determinant of the limit of extravagance are the customs of the area.[163]

I should mention that pearls, diamonds, and other precious stones must be treated the same way as gold and silver jewelry. It they are within the limit of customary use they are not *zakatable*, but if they exceed that limit and become a means of prohibited extravagance, they must not be exempt from *zakah*. If they are held as a store of treasure and an accumulation of wealth or in order to escape *zakah* payment, they must be *zakatable*.

Summary

The preceding rulings and opinions can be summarized in the following points:

A. Jewelry made of gold and silver that is held as a treasure and an accumulation of wealth is *zakatable*, the same as if it were being held as bullion or coins.

B. If the jewelry is obtained for personal use as ornament, then we should distinguish between lawful and unlawful use. Jewelry and ornaments designated for house decoration, utensils, or use by men are prohibite. This jewelry and ornamentation is *zakatable*.

C. Jewelry that is extravagant even though it is used by women is *zakatable*. Extravagance is the excess above customary use by women within their community.

D. Jewelry held for lawful use as women's ornamentation without extravagance, or for lawful use by men, such a silver rings, is not *zakatable*, because it is not designated for profit and is in fact part of the materials used personally, like clothes and furniture, designated for lawful use.

E. There is no difference in these rulings whether the legal ownership of the jewelry is in the hands of men or women.

F. Once *zakah* becomes obligatory, then the rate is that of money, two-and-a-half percent every year.

G. Definitely the minimum exempt, *al nisab*, should be observed at 85 grams for gold. It should be noted, however, that the value of the jewelry and ornaments is the criteria and not their weight only, because the craftsmanship adds value to jewelry.

Footnotes

1. 'Ali 'Abd al Wahid Wafi, *Political Economics*, fifth printing, pp. 140-144, and 'Abd al Aziz Mar'i, *Monetary and Banking Systems*, pp. 11-15.

2. This includes the stability of the metal, its characteristic of not rusting, and non-deterioration, the stability of its relative value, its divisibility, and the divisibility of its value, the difficulty of cheating, and the easiness of inspecting its purity, the low but stable production of the metal throughout centuries, etc. See *Monetary and Banking Systems*, pp. 15-17.

3. See the booklet on currencies by al Maqrizi, printed as a section of *Arabian Currencies*, published by Father Anstas al Karmali, p. 25 and on.

4. *Ibid*, p. 30, with regard to the saying his *al Talkhis*, p. 183, al Hafiz says, "Reported by al Bazzar, who grades it peculiar, and by Abu Daud and al Nasa'i, from Taus from Ibn 'Umar, graded correct by Ibn Habban, al Daraqutni, al Nawawi, and al Qashiri. Al Albani adds, "and Ibn Daqiq al 'Id and al 'Ala'i as in *Silsilat al Ahadith al Sahihah*, part two, saying number 164." The rest of the saying reads, "and size measurements are those of the Madinans."

5. *Sura al Tawbah*, 9:34-35.

6. Reported by Muslim in the chapter on *zakah*; also reported by al Bukhari, Abu Daud, Ibn al Mundhir, Ibn Abi Hatim, and Ibn Mardawayh. See *Subul al Salam*, part two, p. 129, al Halabi Print.

7. Al Hafiz Ibn Hajar quotes al Shafi'i as saying, "The Messenger of God (p) imposed *zakah* on silver. Muslims after him collected *zakah* from gold too, either on the basis of a saying that did not reach us, or by analogy." Ibn 'Abd al Barr adds, "Nothing is authentically reported from the Prophet (p) on gold." See *Subul al Salam, Ibid*. In my opinion, the verse about hoarding is sufficient evidence for the *zakatability* of gold. It is supported and explained by the correct saying mentioned above. The statements of al Shafi'i Ibn 'Abd al Barr refer to *nisab* and rate, since there is no saying that is correctly reported about *nisab* and rates of *zakah* on gold. However, these are unanimously agreed upon, as will be shown later.

8. Bahrain, as in *al Fath*, Vol. 4, pp. 59-60, is the name of a well-known land east of the Arabian peninsula. Its center is the town of Hajar (today al Hasa'). See also the word Bahrain in *Mu'jam al Buldan*, Vol. 1, p. 346.

9. *Monetary and Banking Systems, op.cit.*, p. 31.

10. Mahmud Abu al Sa'ud, *Outlines of Islamic Economics*, p. 40 and on. There you will finds the details of the mentioned experiment, which was carried out in Vorgel, Austria. It had succeeded in reducing unemployment, interest rates, and hoarding, and was repeated in some other countries, where it was strongly opposed by central banks.

11. See the section on the *zakatability* of children and insane persons in the preceeding part.

12. *Al Mughni*, Vol. 3, p. 7.

13. Such as Dr. Fadl al Rahman, who assumed the chairmanship of the Committee on Islamic Research in Pakistan at the time of Ayub Khan. He called for an increase in the rate of *zakah* at this time and for determining *nisab* at 2939 Pakistani rupees because economists today exempt from taxes income below that level. This opinion raised a wave of rejection and responses from Pakistani scholars. See the magazine *Islamic Resurgence*, Vol. 12, no. 2, the article by Shaikh al Bannuri. It is reported that Fadl al Rahman was fired from the committee after he made a few statements that were considered ill-intended and non-Islamic.

14. *Sura al Nur*, 24:63.

15. Reported by Ahmad and Muslim from Jabir. It is also reported by Ahmad and al Bukhari from Abu Sa'id.

16. *Commentary on Muslim*, Vol. 7, p. 48, at the beginning of the chapter on *zakah*, and *al Majmu'* Vol. 6, p. 5.

17. That is why 'Ata said they had silver and gold currency. See *Musannaf Ibn Abi Shaibah*, Vol. 3, p. 222, Hydarabad Print.

18. *Al Mughni*, Vol. p. 1.

19. *Nail al Awtar*, Vol. 4, p. 139.

20. *Al Mughni*, Vol. 3, p. 4.

21. In its chain there is Ibrahim bin Isma'il bin Majma', described by Ibn Ma'in as "he is nothing," by Abu Hatim as "He writes his narrations, but cannot be relied on since he has illusions." Ibn Hazm in *al Muhalla*, Vol. 6, p . 69, mentions the saying and grades it weak on p. 72, because of 'Abd Allah bin Waqid , whom he calls unknown. The late Ahmad Shakir asks, "How could he be unknown, when he is 'Abd Allah in Waqid bin 'Abd Allah bin 'Umar?" He is trustworthy; he narrates from his grandfather and died in the year 119 H. Ibn Hazm was wrong in making his narration from Ibn 'Umar from 'A'ishah, since it is reported by Ibn Majah and al Daraqutni from both Ibn 'Umar and 'A'ishah.

22. Also mentioned by Abu 'Ubaid in *al Amwal*, p. 409, and Ibn Hazm in *al Muhalla*, Vol. 6, p. 69. The latter grades it weak on p. 71, because it is *mursal* and it has Ibn Abi Laila, who is weak in memory, in its chain. Al Hafiz, in *al Talkhis*, p. 182, writes "Its chain is weak." It is also reported by Ibn Zanjawaih in *al Amwal* from al 'Arzami, whose narration is disregarded. See *Nasb al Rayah*, Vol. 2, p. 369, *al Dirayah*, p. 161, and *al Mir'at*, on *al Mishkat*, Vol. 3, p. 43.

23. Mentioned by Ibn Hazm in *al Muhalla*, Vol. 6, p. 69. On p. 72 he says "it is *mursal* and has an unknown link in its chain." On p. 31 he says "Muhammad bin 'Abd al Rahman is unknown." Ahmad Shakir disagrees with this, claiming "But he is known. He is Muhammad bin 'Abd al Rahman al Ansari, a trustworthy Follower".

24. The saying is graded weak by Ibn Hazm in *al Muhalla*, Vol. 6, under the title "*zakah* on Gold". Later on, he revised his view and graded the *hadith* correct. It is graded good by al Hafiz in *Bulugh al Maram*, though the author of *al Talkhis* finds in it a reason for rejection. See p. 182. Al Daraqutni says, "It is correct as a statement of 'Ali". This seems to be correct. The question will be discussed in more detail in the chapter on *zakah* on income. See *Nail al Awtar*, Vol. 4, pp. 137-138.

25. Al Sarakhsi in his *Usul* says, "There is no disagreement among our scholars, whether ancient or late, what a Companion says is accepted as evidence in the questions that cannot be derived by analogy. The quantities are of that nature." He mentions several examples that are accepted by Hanafites, p. 110.

26. *Al Amwal*, p. 419, see also *Sunan Abu Daud*, chapter on the amount of ransoms. There is a saying there from 'Amr bin Shu'aib from his father from his grandfather, that "Ransom at the time of the Messenger of God (p) was 800 *dinars* or 8000 *dirhams*."

27. *Al Muhalla*, Vol. 6, p. 69.

28. *Ibid.*

29. *Ibid*, p. 69-70.

30. *Ibid.* p. 66.

31. *Al Muwatta'*, chapter on *zakah*, section on *zakah* on gold and silver, Vol. 1, p. 246, al Halabi Print.

32. *Al Umm*, Vol. 2, p. 34.

33. *Al Amwal*, p. 409.

34. *Al Mir'at*, Vol. 3, p. 43.

35. See *al Ajwibah al Fasilah*, by the late scholar al Laknawi, pp, 51-52, and the work of Shaikh Husain al Ansari on the acceptance of weak sayings when received with approval by people, p, 228, and the commentaries of my colleague, Shaikh 'Abd al Fattah Abu Ghuddah.

36. The saying is reported by Ibn Habban in his correct collection and al Hakim in *al Mustadrak*, Vol. 1, p. 395. The latter grades it correct and this is approved by al Dhahabi. It is also reported by al Baihaqi, Vol. 4, pp. 89-90. He quotes a group of critics because they grade this saying good as raised to the Prophet. Al Haitami mentions it in *Majma' al Zawa'id*, Vol. 3, p. 72, and says it is reported by al Tabarani in *al Kabir* with Sulaiman bin Daud in its chain, who is considered trustworthy by Ahmad but is criticized by Ibn Ma'in. Ahmad says the saying is correct. Al Haitami says "the rest of the chain's links are trustworthy. The late Ahmad Shakir supports it as correct in his commentary on *al Muhalla* as mentioned in Vol. 6, p. 13, and p. 34.

37. *Ibid*, p. 524-525.

38. Published by Father Anstas al Karmali, member of the Arabic Language Institute in Cairo, in *Arabian Currencies*, pp. 9-18.

39. At the beginning of the chapter on sale contracts, al Nawawi quotes it in *al Majum'*, Vol. 6, pp. 1-16.

40. *Ibid.*

41. *Ibid*, Vol. 6, pp. 14-16.

42. Published by al Karmali, pp. 21-73.

43. *Ibid*, pp. 103-109.

44. Dr. 'Abd al Rahman Fahmy, *Coin Minting in Early Islam.*

45. *Rad al Muhtar*, Vol. 2, p. 40.

46. Booklet on the verification of the *dirham* and the *mithqal*, in the book of Father al Karmali, p. 78.

47. See *al Khutat al Tawfiqiyyah*, Vol. 20, p. 33, and *Encyclopedia of Islam*, Vol. 9, p. 228. Zembaro says, "Al *dirham* is also the name for a weight measure." A *dirham* equals 3.184 grams. It is completely different from the coin that carries the same name. This weight measure remained in use until our days, and it is used by pharmacists and goldsmiths.

48. See *Verification of the Weight of Mithqal, dinar, and dirham*, p. 28, and on. Also see *Diya'al Din al Payyis, al Kharaj in the Islamic State*, p. 337, and on.

49. *Al Kharaj in the Islamic State*, pp. 337-338.

50. It is noted that this result is very close to the conclusions of the late Malikite scholar al Dardir in his *al Sharh al Saghir*, that *nisab* of silver *dirhams* is 185 and five-eights, which equals 579.15 grams. Thus a *dirham* is equal to 2.896 grams, although we do not know the basis for his conclusions. See *al Sharh al Saghir*, commentary on Bulghat al Salik, Vol. 1, p. 217.

51. See Dr. 'Abd al Rahman Fahmy, op. cit.

52. Estimated by the scholar al Fazin Turi at 60 rupees and by the scholar al Laknawi in his *Arkan al Arba'ah*, p. 178 at 55 rupees. See *Mir'at al Mafatih*, Vol. 3, p. 41. It is also estimated at 50 Riyals in Saudi Arabia.

53. This is indicated by historians' reports that the *dinar* equalled ten *dirhams* during the first era of Islam. In the Umayyad era it became equal to 12 *dirhams*, and during the 'Abbasite era it became equal to 15 *dirhams* or more. See *al Kharaj in the Islamic State*, p. 347. 'Ali Mubarak quotes al Maqrizi, "At the , time of al Hakim, a Fatimite, the number of *dirhams* increased to the extant that a *dinar* was exchanged for 34 *dirhams*. See *al Khutat al Tawfiqiyyah* Vol.2, p. 43. 'Abd al Rahman Fahmy discusses the same in his book, using a table that shows the rate of exchange between *dinar* and *dirham* in the different Islamic eras. "One *dinar* reached sometimes 35 *dirhams*," he notes, p. 35.

54. *Halqat al Dirasat al Ijtima'iyah*, p. 238.

55. *Hujjat Allah al Balighah*, Vol. 2, p. 505.

56. This may be supported by s report from Abu Daud, "Ransom used to be 800*dinars* or 8000 *dirhams*, at the time of the Prophet." 'Umar during his caliphate declared that camels had become expensive, and determined ransom at 1,000 gold *dinars* or 12,000 silver *dirhams*.

57. *Sura Yasin*, 36:35.

58. *Al Mabsut*, Vol. 2, p. 150.

59. *Fath al Qadir*, Vol. 1, p. 495, and *al Bahr*, Vol. 2, p. 230.

60. *Monetary and Banking Systems*, pp. 20-22.

61. *Ibid*, pp. 65-67.

62. The booklet *al Tibyan fi Zakat al Athman*, by Shaikh Muhammad Hasanain Makhluf al 'Adawi, p. 33.

63. *Al Fiqh 'Aala al Madhabib al Arba'ah*, p. 486.

64. *Ibid*.

65. Such as the controversy that came about when coffee started to be used over whether it is lawful or not. Several booklets were written until the issue settled on lawfulness. See *al Fawakeh al 'Adidah*, by al Manqur, Vol. 1, pp. 410-413. There, the author quotes the opinions of Ibn Hajar al Haithami al Shafi'i, Zarruq and al Hattab, both Malikites, and others.

66. *Monetary and Banking Systems*, p. 29.

67. *Bidayat al Mujtahid*, by Ibn Rusud, Vol. 1, p. 250.

68. This indeed supports the view I expressed earlier about animals put together in grazing, which was that the *zakah* administrators may treat corporations as one single entity, if this is found administratively better. I follow the Shafi'i school on this matter.

69. *Al Durr al Mukhtar* and its commentary, *Radd al Muhtar*, Vol. 2, p. 45.

70. It was mentioned earlier that the saying is weak, and we shall refer to it with more details in chapter nine.

71. *Al Mughni* with commentary, Vol. 2, p. 499.

72. *Ibid*, p. 497.

73. Ibn 'Abidin, a Hanafite, quotes from *al Bada'i*, "The person who claims it here is the governor, because he is the one who has the responsibility of collecting *zakah* on livestock. When wealth increased tremendously at the time of 'Umar (m), 'Uthman realized that investigating all the wealth creates great inconvenience for the owners, and preferred to leave the calculating of *zakah* to the owners themselves. This was unanimously approved by the Companions. Owners of wealth became like agents of the government in calculating *zakah*, without affecting the right of the government to collect it if it so decided. It is for this reason that jurists of our school say that if it were known that owners of wealth in certain towns did not pay *zakah* on non-apparent wealth the governor must collect it." *Raddal Muhtar*, Vol. 2, p. 6.

74. *Ibid*, pp. 6-7.

75. *Ibid*.

76. *Al Rawdah*, Vol. 2, p. 199.

77. See the section on basic needs in chapter one of the book.

78. Some Hanafites argue with Ibn Malik on the basis that *zakah* is obligatory on money even if it is designated for these expenses. But it seems that Ibn Malik's opinion is more consistent with the obvious meaning of the texts on gold. That is why some scholars of the Hanafite school opt for it. It is described as the correct view in *Radd al Muhtar*, Vol. 2, p. 8. It is also the strongest in my opinion, because of its consistency with the principle of "being surplus above basic needs," mentioned in chapter one.

79. What is meant by clothing is what satisfies essential needs, and not luxurious clothes, described by Ibn Malik as clothes needed to protect the body against heat and cold.

80. About the prohibition of silver and gold utensils, see my book, *al Halal wa al Haram fi al Islam*, chapter on household goods.

81 *Ibid*.

82. *Al Mughni*, Vol. 3, pp. 15-15.

83. *Ibid*.

84. *Al Halal wa al Haram fi al Islam*, chapter on clothing and ornament.

85. Ibn Qudamah says "for men, a silver ring is allowed, because the Prophet wore a ring of silver" and this is agreed upon. Also lawful is the decoration of the sword by making its handle out of silver or by decorating it with silver. Anas reports that "the handle of the sword of the Messenger of God (p) was made of silver," and Hisham bin 'Urwah says that "the sword of al Zubair was decorated with silver." Both are reported by al Athram with his own chain. See *al Mughni*, Vol. 3, pp. 14-15.

86. *Sura al Nahl*, 16:14. The meaning, however, is mentioned in several other *suras*.

87. *Al Rawd al Nadir*, Vol. 2, pp. 409-410.

88. *Ibid*.

89. I will mention shortly the most important of those sayings.

90. *Al Sunan al Kubra*, Vol. 4, p. 134, title: Those who obligate *zakah* on jewelry.

91. Al Baihaqi says, "This is *mursal* because Shu'aib bin Yasar did not see 'Umar."

92. *Al Musannaf*, Vol. 4, p. 28.

93. *Al Sunan al Kubra*, op. cit. See also *al Amwal*, p. 440.

94. *Ibid.*

95. *Al Amwal*, p. 446.

96. *Ibid*, p. 446.

97. *Al Muhalla*, Vol. 6, p. 75.

98. *Musannaf Ibn Abi Shaibah*, Vol. 4, p. 27, *al Amwal*, pp. 441-442, *al Muhalla*, Vol. 6, p. 76, and *al Mughni*, Vol. 3, p. 100. It should be noted that it is reported from Ibn al Musayyib that "*zakah* on jewelry is lending it," as will be shown shortly.

99. In Ibn Abi Shaibah's and Abu 'Ubaid's, it was a woman from Yemen.

100. Abu Daud does not comment on this saying. Al Mundhiri in his *Mukhtasar al Sunnan* says that "al Tirmidhi reports it similarly and comments, 'Nothing is authentic on this question from the Prophet (p)'." Al Nasa'i also reports it connected and *mursal*, indicating that the *mursal* version is more correct. See *Mukhtasar al Sunan* of al Mundhiri, Vol. 2, p. 175. Al Mundhiri also mentions this saying in the chapter on *zakah* of his *al Targhib*; he marks it weak and does not make any further comment. Al Hafiz in *al Talkhis*, p. 183, says "Reported by Abu Daud from Husain al Mu'allim, who is trustworthy, from 'Amr." This disproves the claim of al Tirmidhi, who affirms that it is only reported from Ibn Lahiy ah and al Muthanna bin al Saban from 'Amr.

101. Al Hafiz in *al Talkhis*, p. 184, says "Its chain satisfies conditions for the correct, But this saying contradicts what is authentically reported from 'Aiahah that she did not pay *zakah* on the jewelry of her nieces, although it is authentically reported that she used to pay *zakah* on the orphans, other wealth.

102. *Mukhtasar al Sunan*, Vol. 2, p. 175.

103. Under this title one can also include those who say that jewelry is *zakatable* only once in a lifetime, as reported from Anas and those who say that *zakah* on jewelry is satisfied by lending it free of charge, as reported from some Companions and Followers.

104. *Al Muhalla*, Vol. 6, p. 176.

105. *Ma'alim al Sunan*, Vol. 3 p. 176. This is the reported view of Shafi'ites, as reported in *al Majmu'*, Vol. 6, p. 136.

106. He is al Qasim bin Muhammad bin Abu Bakr, nephew of 'A'ishah and one of the most famous seven jurists of Madinah.

107. *Al Muwatta'*, Vol. 1, p. 250.

108. *Ibn Abi Shaibah*, Vol. 4, p. 28, and *al Amwal*, p. 443.

109. *Al Umm*, Vol. 2, p. 41. Printed by al Matba'ah al Fanniyah al Muttahidah. Non-*zakatability* is reported from Anas by Abu 'Ubaid, p. 442, and al Baihaqi, Vol. 4, p. 138.

110. *Al Muntaqa*, commentary on *al Muwatta'* by Abu al Walid al Baji, Vol. 2, p. 107.

111. *Ibn Abi Shaibah*, Vol. 4, p. 28, and *al Amwal*, p. 442.

112. Reported by al Baihaqi in *al Ma'rifah* from 'Afiah bin Ayub from al Laith from Abu al Zubair, from Jabir. He notes that "it is sourceless." It is reported as a statement of Jabir himself. 'Afiah is described as weak. Ibn al Jawzi says, "I know no criticism of him." Al Baihaqi says he is unknown, and Ibn Abi Hatim quotes a citation of him as trustworthy from Abu Zar'ah. See al Talkhis, p. 183.

113. *Nasb al Rayah*, Vol. 2, pp. 374-375, and *al Mirqat*, Vol. 3, p. 82.

114. Reported by al Bukhari in a section on "Salat al 'Idain," as part of a long saying. He also mentions it in the chapter on *zakah*, under the title of "Paying *zakah* to husbands and to orphans under one's guardianship." See *Fath al Bari*, Vol. 3, pp. 210-211, also reported by al Tirmidhi in the chapter on *zakah* under the title of "*zakah* on jewelry." See *al Tirmidhi*, with commentary by Ibn al 'Arabi, Vol. 3, p. 129.

115. *Commentary on al Tirmidhi*, Vol. 3, pp. 130-131.

116. Such as verse 14 of *sura al Nahl*, "and from it you extract jewels that you wear."

117. *Al Bahr al Ra'iq,* Vol. 2, p. 218.

118. *Al Amwal*, p. 442.

119. *Ahkam al Qur'an*, Vol. 2, p. 919, and *Sharh al Tirmidhi*, Vol. 3, p. 131. Both by Ibn al 'Arabi.

120. We must remember that Abu 'Ubaid was a leading scholar in the Arabic language as well as jurisprudence and sayings. He has a book on non-familiar words in the sayings, which was printed in Hyderabad, India, 1964.

121. We mentioned most of them under *nisab* on money.

122. This saying is from 'Amr bin Shu'aib from his father from his grandfather. His grandfather was Muhammad bin 'Abd Allah bin 'Amr bin al 'As. 'Amr bin Shu'aib was a scholar of his time, and died 118 H. He was controversial as far as his trustworthiness as a reporter of sayings is concerned. Ibn Ma'in, Ibn Rahawayh, al Awza'i, and Saleh Jazrah grade him trustworthy. Al Bukhari in his history mentions his trustworthiness, although he does not report from him in his collection of correct sayings. Ahmad Ibn Hanbal says, "'Amr bin Shu'aib has sayings that are rejected. I write his reports just for consideration, but he is not acceptable." Ibn Hanbal further says "I may sometimes accept his reports, but I have some doubts about him." Abu Zar'ah says, "He is criticized because of the numerous sayings he reports from his father from his grandfather. It is said that he only heard a few sayings, and that he inherited a written pamphlet which he quoted. He is also criticized for telling everything he heard," Ibn al Madini answered when asked about him, "All that is reported from him by Ayub and Ibn Jurais is correct, but what he reports from his father from his grandfather is weak." Yahya bin Ma'in has a similar opinion about him. Ibn Habban says that when he reports from trustworthy narrators other than his father,

it is acceptable, but in what he reports from his father from his grandfather there are many rejectable sayings. Consequently, he must not be accepted. Al Dhahabi in *al Mizan* concludes that his narrations are good. See *al Mizan*, Vol. 3, pp, 263-268. Al Hafiz in *al Fath* says the biography of 'Amr seems to be strong, but only when his narrations are not opposed by others." With respect to the question on hand, his narration is opposed by correct reports from 'A' ishah, Ibn 'Umar, Jabir, and other Companions that they used to pay *zakah* on jewelry. 'Abd Allah bin 'Amr, his grandfather, was a contemporary of those Companions, and does not oblige them with the sayings he heard from the Messenger of God (p) about that woman and her daughter. Had he done so they would have accepted it and it would have been frequently reported to us.

123. Ancient Arabs used to lend jewelry and wedding clothes to the bride for her wedding celebration. Prominent families do that today for expensive fees, both in the West and in Arab countries. I wish the same could be done by charitable organizations. This may be a form of *zakah* on jewelry and wedding clothes.

124. *Al Amwal*, p. 446.

125. As stated by al Dahlawi in his *Hujjat Allah al Balighah*, Vol. 2, p. 509.

126. *Commentary of Ibn al 'Arabi on al Tirmidhi*, Vol. 3, p. 131.

127. *Al Muhalla*, Vol. 6, p. 78.

128. *Al Mizan*, Vol. 3, p. 282, biography no. 2438, Sa'adah Print 1325 H.

129. *Ibid*, p. 27.

130. *Hadiy al Sari*, the introduction of *al Fath*, Vol. 2, pp, 189-190.

131. *Nasb al Rayah*, Vol. 1, p. 342.

132. *Ibid*, Vol. 2, p. 372.

133. The description "has a good narration" is one of the low grades of acceptability, the fourth or sixth, according to different classifications, See *al Sakhawi* in commentary on *al Alfiyah*, and *al Sundus*, commentary on *al Nukhbah*. See also *al Raf'wa al Takmil*, pp. 109, 116, 124.

134. *Al Mizan*, Vol.1, pp. 364-365.

135. *Hadiy al Sari*, Vol. 2, pp. 155-206.

136. Ibn Hajar, *Tahdhib al Tahdhib*, Vol. 1, p, 5.

137. Al Hafiz in *al Talkhis* says "One may reconcile her action and her narration if he assume that she used to believe in the obligation of *zakah* on jewelry and not on orphans' assets, but it seems that this reconciliation is difficult to accept and is not obvious from the wording of the saying itself."

138. *Al Majmu'*, Vol. 5, p, 35, and *Mukhtasar al Sunan*, Vol. 2, p. 176.

139. Al Kamal bin Humam in *Fath al Qadir*, Vol. 1, p. 526, comments on this saying, "it is opposed by a report in *al Muwatta'* from 'Abd al Rahman bin al Qasim from his father that 'A'ishah was the guardian of her orphaned nieces, and did not pay *zakah* on their jewelry." 'A'ishah is the Companion who narrates the saying about the big rings. The action of a narrator in contradiction to his or her report means to us that the report is annulled. This annulment is disputed on the basis of a report that 'Umar wrote to al Asha'ari about *zakah* on jewelry, which implies that this is accepted as a ruling. If the annulment is disputed and the rule is verified. a ruling of annulment cannot be accepted.

It is known, however, that the report about 'Umar writing to al Ash'ari is not correct, and al Hasan denies that any of the four *Khulafa'* ordained *zakah* on jewelry. Abu 'Ubaid says that *zakah* on jewelry is not authentically reported from any Companion except Ibn Mas'ud. The doubt thrown by al Baihaqi and others on the report about the big rings is very well-supported.

140. This unanimity is quoted by al Baihaqi in his *al Sunan*, Vol. 4, p. 142, and by Ibn Hajar in *al Fath*, Vol. 10, p. 260. It is an established practice throughout centuries in all Muslim countries, which opposes the claim of Shaikh Nasir al Din al Albani in his booklet on the wedding practices on p. 26 that wearing gold is prohibited for women the same way it is for men, except when it cut cut into pieces, like gold buttons, for instance. This unanimity is supported by two things:

(1)   the difference of opinion among leading jurists on the *zakatability* of women's jewelry implies that they agree on the lawfulness of jewelry for women, since if jewelry were prohibited for women, it would be *zakatable* without any dispute, and

(2)   the lawfulness of women's jewelry is well-established, throughout time in Muslim lands, since the era of the Companions. No Muslim scholar objected to it, and the whole Muslim community cannot agree to a thing that is prohibited and preserve that agreement in theory and practice for centuries. This means that the sayings that imply the lawfulness of gold and silk to women are the latest. They supercede any other reports, because it is inconceivable that sayings prohibiting gold for woman came later and yet all the Companions agreed otherwise. I fully agree with al Albani's view that anything that reaches the level of extravagance is prohibited, such as big and expensive rings. One may argue that those sayings that mention the prohibition refer only to extravagance and excess.

141. *Al Sunan al Kubra*, Vol. 4, pp. 140-14".

142. *Sura al Ahzab*, 33:32.

143. *Ibid*, 33:30.

144. *Nihayat al Muhtaj*, Vol. 2, p. 88.

145. *Ibid*.

146. *Al Muhalla*, Vol. 6, p. 78, and *al Sunan al Kubra*, Vol. 4, p. 138.

147. *Al sunan al Kubra*, Vol. 4, p. 140.

148. *Al Amwal*, p. 443, and *al Musannaf*, Vol. 4, p. 28.

149. This may indicate that the classification of the leading scholars into the people of opinion and the people of sayings is very exaggerated and unrealistic, since the people of opinion do not refuse saying and the people of sayings do not refuse the application of human reasoning. The great scholar Shaikh Muhammad Abu Zahrah shows in his book *Malik* that he was one of the people of opinion as much as he was one of the people of sayings.

150. *Al Amwal*, p. 443.

151. *Al Muwatta'* with its commentary, *al Muntaqa*, Vol. 2, p. 107. This is indicated by Malik's statement that if jewelry is broken and becomes irreparable, or if the owner does not want to repair it, it then becomes *zakatable*, See *Bulghat al Salik*, Vol.1, p. 19, and *al Rawdah*, by al Nawawi, Vol. 2, p. 261.

152. *Al Majmu'*, Vol. 6, p. 36, and *al Rawdah*, Vol. 2, p. 260.

153. *Al Muhalla*, Vol. 6, p. 76.

154. *Ibid*.

155. *Al Mughni*, Vol. 3, p. 11.

156. *Al Majmu'*, Vol. 6, p. 40.

157. *al Mughni*, Vol. 3, p. 11. See narration no. 1275 in *al Amwal*, p. 442. It is also reported by al Shafi'i and al Baihaqi. See *al Sunan al Kubra*, Vol. 4, p. 138.

158. *Al Mughni*, Vol. 3, p. 11.

159. *Ibid*.

160. Reported by al Bukhari as suspended. See *Ibn Kathir*, Vol. 2, p. 182. Also reported by al Nasa'i in his *Sunan*, chapter on *zakah*, titled "Cheating in *zakah* payment," Vol. 5, p. 79, al Matba'ah al Masriyah Print.

161. *Nasb al Rayah*, Vol. 2, p. 375, and *al Mirqat*, Vol. 4.

162. *Al Amwal*, p. 440.

163. Al Ramli in *Nihayat al Muhtaj* says about men's rings and their weights, "What is acceptable is to leave this matter to the usual customary practices of the time. What is above this custom may be considered extravagant."

CHAPTER FOUR

ZAKAH ON BUSINESS INVENTORY

God makes it lawful for Muslims to engage in business and to make profit, provided they do not indulge in trading commodities that are prohibited in Islam, and that they observe ethical values is their transaction, such as honesty, truthfulness, and kindness. Also, business engagements must not be a hindrance to the remembrance of God, or the fulfillment of spiritual and material obligations prescribed by Him.[1]

Since practicing trade is lawful, several sayings ordain the guardians of orphans to invest orphans, wealth in trade so that it is not exhausted by the repetitive payment of *zakah*. It is normal that a part of the wealth of any nation is used in trade and business exchange, and it is no wonder that Islam prescribes *zakah* on assets invested in business and commerce as well as on the income derived therefrom. Like *zakah* on money, *zakah* on business is an expression of thankfulness to God for His bounties by caring about those of His servants who are in need.

Islamic jurisprudence addresses itself to the details of this kind of *zakah*. Business inventory is called by jurists *'urud al tijarah*,[2] which means any commodities obtained for the purpose of resale for profit, except liquid monetary assets. This definition includes machinery, furniture, clothing, foodstuffs, ornaments, jewelry, livestock, plants, land, buildings, etc. Some jurists define *'urud al tijarah* as anything that one buys in order to sell for profit.[3] A Muslim who owns business inventory equal to *nisab* of money or more at the end of a *zakah* year must pay its due *zakah* at the rate of two-and-a-half percent. This *zakah* is levied on the principal and increments accruing above the principal.

This chapter has four sections, The first deals with the obligation of *zakah* on business inventory, the second disproves the arguments of those who do not obligate *zakah* on business, the third section describes the conditions for this kind of *zakah*, and section four deals with the methods of paying *zakah* on business inventories.

SECTION ONE

THE OBLIGATION OF *ZAKAH* ON TRADE

Evidence of this obligation is taken from the four sources of *Shari'ah* in Islam: Qur'an, Sunnah, *ijma* and analogy.

The Qur'an

God says, "O ye who believe, give of the good things which ye have honorably earned, and of the fruits of the earth which we have produced for you."[4] Imam Bukhari indicates in his chapter on *zakah* in his correct collection[5] under the section on *sadaqah* on crafts and business that this *sadaqah* is taken in accordance with the verse, "O ye who believe, spend out of the good things which ye have earned," Imam al Tabari comments, "Pay *zakah* out of the good things you earn in your economic activity, such as business, industry, or gold and silver," He also reports through several chains, from Mujahid, that the words "good things you have earned" means by making trade.[6] Imam al Jassas, in his *Ahkam al Qur'an*, says "It is reported that a group of our predecessors explain God's words 'good things you have earned' as through trade. These include al Hasan and Mujahid. However, the general implication of the words covers also all assets earned by other economic activities,"[7] Imam Abu Bakr bin al 'Arabi says that "Our scholars interpret the words of God 'that you have earned' as things earned by means of trade, and the words 'that we have produced from the earth for you' as things earned by means of agriculture."

It should be noted that earnings may come either from the earth or from human effort in trade, industry, hunting and booty obtained in war. As God ordains the rich to give the poor out of all these earnings, trade is no exception and its earnings are also *zakatable*.[8] Imam al Razi points out that the obvious meaning of the verse is that *zakah* is obligated on every asset human beings earn, including trade assets, gold and silver, and livestock, since all these are earned.[9] This is supported by the verse that reads "No profit to him from all his wealth and earnings."[10] "His earnings" are his accumulations from trade.

In addition to that, we must remember that other verses about *zakah* are general and therefore include business assets, such as the verse "and on their wealth and possessions there is the right for he who asked and he who is deprived,"[11] "and on those in whose wealth is a recognized right for he who asks and he who is deprived,"[12] and "Out of their goods take *sadaqah* so by it thou might purify and sanctify them."[13] There is not a single statement in the Qur'an or Sunnah that exempts the assets of Muslim merchants from this recognized right by which Muslims are purified and sanctified.

Ibn al 'Arabi indicates that the verse "Out of their wealth take *sadaqah*" is general and covers all assets, no matter how they are classified or named, and no matter what purpose they are assigned to. Thus anyone who desires to restrict the meaning of this verse is asked to produce supporting evidence.[14]

Remarkably enough, some Arabic tribes meant by "*mal*" [the word used in the verse to mean "wealth] only clothes, furniture, and business assets. It is reported by Malik from Abu Hurairah that "We went with the Messenger of God (p) to the battle of Khaibar, where we did not earn gold or silver but only mal." i.e. clothes and other assets.[15]

The Sunnah

Abu Daud reports from Samurah bin Jundub that " the Prophet (p) used to order us to pay al *sadaqah* out of what we have for sale."[16] To "order" implies to "obligate" and it is clear that *sadaqah* means *zakah*, especially when it is preceeded by the definite article "al". Al Daraqutini reports Abu Dharr "I heard the Messenger of God (p) saying 'Camels are *zakated*, lambs are *zakated*, and clothes and housewares are *zakated*.'"[17] There is no disagreement that clothes and other housewares for personal or household use are exempt, which means that housewares and clothes mentioned in this saying refer to business inventory for resale. This is in addition to the general sayings that obligate *zakah* on all kinds of wealth without discrimination, such as "give *zakah* on your wealth."[18] It is noted that trade inventory is the first kind of wealth that comes under the word "mal" used in sayings, because trade inventory is general and may include anything purchased for sale.[19]

The *ijma'* of Companions, Followers, and our Predecessors

Abu 'Ubaid reports from 'Abd al Qari, "I was appointed as treasurer at the time of 'Umar bin al Khattab. When the time of collection came, he used to calculate the assets of merchants, both present and absent assets, and then take *zakah* on them all, out of the assets that were present."[20] Reported also by Ibn Hazm in *al Muhalla*, where he adds that its chain is correct. There is a report from Abi 'Amr bin Hammas, from his father, who said "'Umar passed by me and said, 'Oh Hammas, pay the *zakah* due on your wealth.' I answered, I have no wealth except hides and bags.' 'Umar replied, 'Evaluate them and pay the *zakah* due on them.'"[22] The author of *al Mughni* comments that "the likes of such a story are common, and none of the Companions negate this ruling, which implies a sort of *ijma'* on this matter."[23]

Abu 'Ubaid reports from Ibn 'Umar that "Slaves and clothe intended for trade are *zakatable*."[24] Al Baihaqi and Ibn Hazm report from Ibn 'Umar that "There is no *zakah* on housewares and cloths, except when they are used for trade." Ibn Hazm adds that this is a correct narration.[25] Moreover, Abu 'Ubaid also reports the obligation of *zakah* on trade from Ibn 'Abbas.[26]

There is no report whatsoever that any Companion disagreed with the opinion of 'Umar, his son, and Ibn 'Abbas. The collection of *zakah* on trade assets continued during the time of the Companions and the era of the Followers. In the preceding chapter, I mentioned that "'Umar bin 'Abd al 'Aziz is correctly reported to have written to one of his deputies to "look for Muslims who pass by your area and take *zakah* out of their merchandize at the rate of one *dinar* for every 40 *dinars*, and apply the same percentage on what is less than that up to a minimum of 20 *dinars*."

Jurists of the Followers era and the generations after them agreed that *zakah* is obligatory on trade assets. This *ijma'* is reported by Ibn al Mundhir and Abu 'Ubaid. Ibn al Mundhir writes that "people of knowledge unanimously agreed that items intended for trade are *zakatable* once a full fiscal year passes. This is reported from 'Umar, his son, Ibn 'Abbas, the seven renowned jurists, al Hasan, Jabir bin Zaid, Maimun bin Mahran, Taus, al Nakha'i, al Thawri, al Awza'i, al Shafi'i, Abu 'Ubaid, Ishaq, Abu Hanifah, and his disciples."[27] It is also the stand of Ahmad and the Maliki school. Abu 'Ubaid says, "all Muslims unanimously agree that trade assets are *zakatable*, and no other opinion is attributed to any of the knowledgeable people."[28]

The judge Ibn al 'Arabi says *zakah* is obligatory on trade assets because of four reasons: One, God says "take *sadaqah* out of their wealth," which means all sorts of wealth; two, 'Umar bin Abd al Aziz ordered *zakah* taken from trade assets on the advice of many scholars in the era of the Followers and no one raised objections to his action; three, 'Umar bin al Khattab collected *zakah* on trade assets long before 'Umar bin 'Abd al 'Aziz, as correctly reported from Anas; and four, the report of Abu 'Daud from Samurah bin Jundub that "The Prophet (p) used to order us to pay *zakah* on what we have for sale." There is no authentic report to the contrary from any our predecessors.[29] Al Khattabi writes that some later people claimed there was no *zakah* on trade assets, but they are preceded by the *ijma'*.[30]

Analogy and Reasoning

Ibn Rushd mentions that trade assets are wealth intended for growth, like the other three forms of wealth that are unanimously considered *zakatable*: agricultural products, livestock, and gold and silver. Thus the analogy is clear and fitting.[31] As for the reasoning that supports this premise, trade assets are like monetary assets. They are exchangeable, valued, and readied for investment and growth. if *zakah* were not to be imposed on trade assets, rich people would always keep their wealth in the form of merchandise and inventory and avoid keeping cash, to escape the payment of *zakah*.[32] It is natural that businessmen keep little cash, since most business transaction take place through credit or through bank transfers, checks, and drafts.

According to the late Rashid Rida, the rationale for this matter is that God imposed *zakah* on the wealth of the rich in order to relieve the poor and needy and to pay for some public interests of Muslims and Islam. *Zakah* also aims at reducing capital concentration in the hands of a few individuals, in accordance with the principle laid down by the verse, "in order that it may not merely make a circuit between the wealthy among you." Moreover, it gives the rich the benefit of purification and sanctification and trains them to be helpful and merciful. With all that in mind, is it reasonable that merchants and businessmen, who may own the bulk of the wealth of a nation, be exempted?[33]

One could also say that merchants need purification more than anyone else, because the ways they earn their wealth may not always be completely clean. The Prophet (p) indicates that "Merchants are resurrected wicked on the Day of Judgement, except for those who fear God, speak the truth, and are righteous."[34] He once said "Merchants are the wicked," and are asked, "O Messenger of God, did not God make business lawful?" He answered, "Yes, indeed, but merchants often swear, commit sins, and lie in their speech.[35] Abu Daud reports from Qais bin Abi Gharazah that "The Messenger of God (p) passed by us and said, 'O merchants, sales are associated with vain talk and swearing, so let it be mixed with *sadaqah*." This *sadaqah* is not a reference to *zakah*, but the saying stresses the point that traders need purification because of errors and impurities that intermingle with their transactions. If merchants need a voluntary charity for their own purification, they certainly are in need of paying *zakah* the prescription for purification and sanctification for all Muslims.

SECTION TWO

ARGUMENTS OF THE OPPONENTS OF *ZAKAH* ON TRADE ASSETS

A. The Zahiri school

According to al Khattabi, Sunnites are generally of the opinion that *zakah* is obligatory on trade assets,[36] except for a few late jurists of the Zahiri school. Ibn Hazm in his *al Muhalla* adopts this view.[37] Some scholars known for their inclination to restrict *zakah*, such as al Shawkani and Siddiq Hasan Khan support this view too. Their arguments can be summarized in the following points:

Firstly, they draw on the *hadiths*, "No *zakah* is obligated on Muslims on their slaves and horses," and I have exempted you from *sadaqah* on horses and slaves."[38] The literal meaning of these sayings is that *zakah* is waived for these two items, whether or not they are trade inventory. The reply of scholars in the majority camp is that studying these two sayings indicates that they waive *zakah* on slaves in household service and horses used for personal transportation. Both serve needs that are unanimously exempt from *zakah*.

Secondly, they argue that in principle it is forbidden to take any part of a Muslim's wealth without clear evidence from God through Qur'an or Sunnah. Trade was practiced in the time the Prophet (p) and there is no correct report obligating *zakah* on trade. As for the saying from Samurah and Abu Dharr, the argument is that they are weak and must not be used as evidence for obligating *zakah*.[39]

The answer to this claim is that there are several verses and sayings that obligate, by virtue of their generality, *zakah* on all assets. The rule is that a general text must not be restricted except by another text, and there is no such restricting text. Furthermore, we have specific evidence to the effect that *zakah* is obligated on trade assets from the Qur'an, Sunnah, Companions' sayings, and *ijma'* of recognized people of knowledge. The saying of Samurah is not criticized by Abu Daud and al Mundhiri. It is graded good by Ibn 'Abd al Barr, and the late Ahmad Shakir says of it, "Its narrators are known and classified as trustworthy by Ibn Hayyan." The saying of Abu Dharr is marked correct by al Hakim; al Hafiz mentions several chains for it and marks one of them as all right. These sayings are supported by the generalities of the main texts, the actions of the Companions, and the *ijma'* in addition to analogy and reasoning.

Thirdly, Abu 'Ubaid mentions that some jurist claim *zakah* is not obligated on trade inventory on the grounds that *zakah* must always be paid out of the asset itself, and in the case of trade merchandise, all scholars accept payment on the basis of value. Abu 'Ubaid continues, "This is an error in judgement, because we know in the tradition of the Messenger of God (p) that *zakah* obligated on one kind of asset may be paid in the form of another kind. For example, in the Prophet's letter to Mu'adh about *jiziah* is written "one each person who is past puberty, there is a due of one *dinar*, on its value is clothes."[40] Also, part of the Prophet's treaty with the people of Najran reads "they are obliged to give two thousand pieces of clothes every year, or their equivalent in silver." 'Umar accepted camels as *jiziah* payment, while its levy was in gold and silver, and 'Ali accepted ropes and needless in payment of *jiziah*. It is also reported from Mu'adh that he took merchandise in the place of *zakah*. He said, "Bring me clothes and men's wear; I accept it in payment of *sadaqah*, since it might be easier for you and more beneficial to the migrants in Madinah." Ibn Mas'ud's wife, it is reported, said to him, "I have a necklace that weighs twenty *mithqal*." He replied, "Pay five *dirhams* on it." (One *mithqal* is worth ten *dirhams*.) Abu 'Ubaid notes that in all these examples, dues are levied on certain items and collected in the form of another. This negates the statement that *zakah* must be waived if it cannot be paid is the form of the same *zakated* item. As for trade merchandise, *zakah* may be collected in kind unless such collection harms the asset by forcing the division of the indivisible, in which case the value should be designated and *zakah* is then paid in value. Muslims agree on the *zakatability* of trade merchandise, and its opponents are not known as people of knowledge. *zakah*, however, is not obligated on these items when they cease to be trade inventory on are assigned for personal or household use, similar to the waiver of *zakah* on camels and cows used for family transportation. Trade assets, like livestock, are designated for growth, exchange, and profit, and as such are *zakatable*. The ratio or *zakah* on livestock is given, while *zakah* on trade is estimated in value.[41]

The *Imami* school

Imami jurists are of the opinion that *zakah* is recommended rather than obligated on trade assets.[42] They have, however, another prescription for trade earnings (excluding capital), saying that one-fifth is due on those profits. They argue that the verse "and know that out of all the booty that ye may acquire, a fifth share is assigned to God, and to the Apostle, and to near relatives, orphans, the needy, and the wayfarer," covers all earnings from business, buried treasures, and other gains. This obligation of one-fifth on business profits comes after deducting the personal and household expenses of the trader. The author of *Jawahir al Kalam* writes that "one-fifth is levied on the residual of profits from trade, industry, and agriculture after the deduction of living expenses for the whole year." He adds, "This is not disputed."[43] Using contemporary terms, this means a levy of twenty percent on net income.

Sunnites argue that this verse refers only to booty acquired in war, as explained by the Messenger of God (p). This interpretation is supported by the context of the verse in *sura al Anfal* itself. If acquired booty [ghanimah] is left general and not restricted to the case of war, then twenty percent on bequests would be due. This obviously contradicts the *ijma'*. Acquired booty cannot consequently mean all earned profits.[44]

SECTION THREE

CONDITIONS OF *ZAKAH* ON BUSINESS ASSETS

Trade is exchange with the intention of making profit.[45] Trade assets are commodities obtained for the purpose of selling for profit.[46] Thus two elements are involved in trade---the action of buying or selling, and the intention of making profit.[47] Buying for the intention of using the asset is not trade. items bought for personal and household use are not trade assets. These two elements must always co-exist in trade.[48] Changing the intention from selling for profit to personal use of an item must remove its *zakatability*.[49]

These are the two main conditions for the definition of trade assets. A few scholars add another condition,[50] that there should be no duplication in *zakah* on any item in one single *zakah* year,[51] since the Prophet (p) said "There should be no duplication in *sadaqah*."[52] Duplication may take place in the case when a commodity, e.g. agricultural land, is purchased for resale with profit, but is cultivated and harvested while in the possession of the merchant. Many scholars suggest that *zakah* on agriculture (ten percent] is applicable on the produce, while others consider *zakah* on trade assets alone is applicable. Although a few suggest that the two *zakah* must apply in this case,[53] the majority are of the opinion that the two forms of *zakah* must not apply together, because that would be duplication in *zakah*.

The above are the conditions of *zakatability* with respect to trade assets. However, we should remember that there are also the general conditions of *zakatability*, which are the same as those of *zakatability* of money, i.e. *nisab*, the passage of one full lunar year, the absence of debts and similar liabilities, and being in excess of essential needs.

Nisab is the equivalent of the value of 85 grams of gold. As for the time if the *zakah* year at which the *nisab* condition should be fulfilled, there are three opinions among jurists. The first is that it is sufficient that *nisab* exist at the end of the *zakah* year. This is reported from Milik and the text of al Shafi'i in his *al Umm*.[54] Secondly, there is the opinion that *nisab* must be fulfilled throughout the whole *zakah* year, and any moment this condition becomes unsatisfied interrupts *zakatability*, and a new *zakah* year begins, until *nisab* remains held for a full *zakah* year. This is the opinion of al Thawri, Ahmad, Ishaq, Abu 'Ubaid, Abu Thawr, and Ibn Mundhir.[55] Third is the opinion that it is sufficient that *nisab* be satisfied at the beginning and the end of the *zakah* year, even if it is broken during the year. This is the opinion of Abu Hanifah and disciples. It aims at removing the apparent inconvenience of requiring continuous evaluation of the trade assets in order to verify the fulfillment of *nisab* throughout the year.

In my opinion, there is no correct text to support requiring *nisab* at the beginning of the year or during it. At the end of the *zakah* year, if the condition of *nisab* is fulfilled, we have on hand a *zakatable* asset. Consequently, I think the opinion of Malik and al Shafi'i is most acceptable. The state can determine the date of *zakah* year ends (i.e. when *zakah* is due.) Any merchant who owns *nisab* at that date is *zakatable*. This approach was practiced at the time of the Prophet (p) and his Wise Successors with respect to *zakah* on livestock. Collectors were sent on a certain date to collect *zakah* on all livestock that were at *nisab* and above, without questioning the owners whether *nisab* was fulfilled throughout the whole year.

SECTION FOUR

HOW *ZAKAH* ON TRADES IS PAID

Trade assets may take one of the following three forms:

1. It could be merchandise and inventory for sale,

2. Cash on hand or in the bank,

3. Or debts and credits extended to agents and others.

Also traders may have liabilities in the form of debts due to other people.

Abu Ubaid reports the ways of calculating *zakah* as perceived by some of the great Followers.[57] He quotes Maimun bin Mahran as saying, "When *zakah* is due, calculate the amount of money, add to it the value of inventory and the amount of debts on customers that you expect to be paid, sum the total, deduct whatever debts you owe to others and pay *zakah* on the net." Al Hasan al Basri says, "When *zakah* is due, one must add the amount of money, plus the value of inventory, plus the amount of debts, except the amount of hopeless debts, and pay *zakah* on the total." Ibrahim al Nakha'i indicates that one must evaluate one's trade assets and pay their *zakah* along with *zakah* due on one's other holdings."[58]

It is clear from these quotations that a Muslim merchant, in calculating *zakatable* assets, must add together what he owns, be that capital, profit, savings, and hopeful debts. He or she is required to take inventory and evaluate it in addition to money and debts, and then pay 2.5% of the total. As for hopeless debts, they are not *zakatable* unless they happen to be paid back. Then they must be *zakated* once only,[59] on the basis of similarity with earned wealth that is *zakated* at the time it is acquired. It is obvious that liabilities are deducted from assets and only the net is *zakatable*.

Malik distinguishes between monopolistic and non-monopolistic merchants

According to Malik, a monopolistic merchant is one who buys commodities and waits until prices go up to sell, while a non-monopolistic merchant is one who buys to sell on regular basis without giving much attention to storage or to waiting for a price change.[60] Ibn Rushd writes "Malik says a monopolistic merchant must pay *zakah* on his inventory when he sells them, once only, even if his stock was kept for several years, while the other merchant is required to pay *zakah* on the inventory each year.

The majority, including al Shafi'i, Abu Hanifah, Ahmad, al Thawri, al Awza'i, and others, do not make any distinction between these two merchants."[61] Ibn Rushd comments on Malik's view, "This seems to be an intrusion into *Shari'ah*, rather than a deduction from its principles. Things like this are usually called loose analogy (*al qiyas al mursal*), which do not rely on a principle mentioned in *Shari'ah* but only on pure rationalization of *Shari'ah*'s interests. Malik accepts such an approach." Furthermore, Malikites have different opinions about the case in which the merchandise of a non-monopolistic merchant remains in stock for several years. Is he required to pay *zakah* every year, or should he be treated like the monopolistic merchant who at the time of purchase anticipates a long waiting period ? Sahnun says that stagnant inventory may be treated like the merchandise of monopolistic merchant, while Ibn al Qasim does not agree.[62]

It is obvious that the majority's view is stronger than that of Malik, because *zakah* is levied on the grounds that trade assets are potentially growing assets, like money, and there is nothing to substantiate Malik's distinction. It may be mentioned, however, that at times of general economic recession, the opinion of Malik may have a certain applicability in order to reduce the burden of merchants by collecting *zakah* on actual sales instead of on inventories.

Fixed assets are not subject to *zakah*

Business assets referred to with respect to *zakatability* are only those assets that are liquid or circulating, or what is usually called the circulating capital. Buildings, furniture and fixtures of stores that are not acquired for sale are not included in *zakatable* assets. Jurists define *zakatable* assets of trades as those materials that are purchased for resale with profit.[63] The saying narrated by Samurah states that "the Prophet (p) used to ordain us to pay the *sadaqah* on what we designate for sale." Consequently, it is said that containers, cages, scales, machinery and tools are not included in *zakatability*.[64] Some jurists go on to distinguish between containers and packages sold with the merchandise and those that are not sold, the former being *zakatable* while the latter are not.[65]

Pricing of inventory for *zakah* purposes

The majority's view is to use current prices on the due dates of *zakah*. This is also reported from the Follower Jabir bin Zaid: Evaluation is done at the prices of the day *zakah* becomes due. Ibn Abbas is reported to have said that "It is allright to wait untill the merchandise is sold, and then the due *zakah* is paid according to the actual proceeds."[66] Yet a third view is reported by Ibn Rushd without attribution to any specific jurist, which is to appraise the inventory at its purchase price.[67] Since prices may go up or down, it is not fair for the payer or the recipient of *zakah* to consider anything but prices that are current on the day of payment, especially since *zakah* is, in fact, due on principal and accrued profit. The majority's view is obviously most reasonable here. But it should be noted that wholesale prices, and not retail prices must be used if any liquidation of inventory is to be done it will be at current wholesale prices.

Payment of *zakah* in kind or in value

Naturally, there are several opinions. Abu Hanifah and report from al Shafai'i leave it to the merchant to make the choice especially when inventory takes the form of consumer goods.[68] Another report from al Shafai'i makes payment obligatory in kind and not permissible in value.[69] Al Muzani says that "Merchandise *zakah* is paid in kind and not in value."[70] Yet another view is that of Ahmad and a third report from Al Shafi'i that *zakah* must only be paid in value because *nisab* in trade's assets is only a matter of valuation.[71] The author of *al Mughni* writes "we do not think that *zakah* is levied on the kind of the asset but only on its value."[72] This last opinion seems to me the most rational, because it is most beneficial to the poor, leaving him with the choice of commodities he needs most. This method is also easier for the state to collect. Paying *zakah* in kind may also be practiced when the payer knows that the poor need that commodity and the merchant pays it directly to the poor. Ibn Taimiyah was asked whether a merchant could pay *zakah* in kind or not, and he answered, "That depends. Some people say it is paid in kind always, others say it should always be in value, while the third opinion says it depends which is most beneficial and convenient method of payment for the payer, the receiver, and the collector in each particular case." "The last view, he continues, seems to be the most fair, i.e., *zakah* be paid in kind when it benefits the poor most or paid in value when this is better for him."[73]

Footnotes

1. See al Qardawi, *al Halal Wa al Haram*, chapter on crafts and earnings.

2. Jurists use for "Trade wealth" the Arabic word *"Urud al Tijarah" "Tijarah"* means "trade" and *"Urud"* is the plural of *"'ard"* which means commodities and wares other than gold and silver according to the dictionary *al Taj*. Al Nawawi says that the *mal* of trade is anything that, when obtained, is intended for trade.

3. *Matalib Uli al Nuha*, Vol. 2, p. 96.

4. Volume 11, p. 143, Al Sha'b print.

6. *The commentary Al Tabari*, Vol. 3 pp. 555-556, edited by Ahmad and Mahmud Shakir.

7. Al Jasaas, *Ahkam Al Qur'an*, Vol. 1, p. 543.

8. *Ibid*, Vol. 1, p.235.

9. Al Razi, *Al Tafsir Al Kabir*, Vol. 2 , p.65.

10. *Surah al Mesad*, 111:2.

11. Surah al Dhariyat, 51:19.

12. Surah al Ma'arij, 70:24-25.

13. *Surah al Tawbah*, 9:103.

14. *Sharh al Tirmidhi,* Vol. 3, p.104.

15. *Commentary al Qurtubi*, Vol. 8, p.245.

16. Reported by al Daraquani, p.214, and Abu Daud via Ja'far bin Sa'd from Khubaib bin Sulaiman bin Samurah from Samurah, Abu Daud made no comment, nor did Al Mundhiri. See *Mukhtasar Al Sunan*, Vol. 2, p.175. Ibn al Humam says this means they approve the saying, as in *Al Mirqat*, Vol. 4, p.158, Multan Print. Ibn 'Abd al Barr grades it good. See *Nasb al Rayah*, Vol. 2, p. 376. Al Hafiz says in *Bulugh Al Maram*, p.124 that "its chain is soft." Ibn Hazm claims that Ja'far, Khubaib and Sulaiman are unknown. Ahmad Shakir writes in his footnote on p. 234, Vol. 5 of *al Muhalla* that "They are known, they are mentioned by Ibn Habban as among the trustworthy". Al Dhahabi quotes Ibn Al Qattan" The trustworthiness of either of them is not determined, in spite of efforts made by critics of hadith. This chain has a few other similarities in its vagueness. Abd al Haqq al Azdi says Khubaib is weak and Ja'far is not dependable. Anyhow this chain is dark and does not stand. See *Al Mizan*, Vol. 1, p.150.

17. *Al Muhalla*, Vol. 5, pp. 234-235.

18. Al Tirmidhi reports it and comments, "good correct" Vol. 3, p. 91, print of Al Asriyah.

19. *Matalib Uli Al Nuha*, Vol. 2, p. 96.

20. The story is reported by Ibn Abi Shaibah, too. See *Al Muhalla*, Vol. 6, p.34, where Ibn Hazm comments that its chain is correct. But he claims that the word "assets of merchants" means gold and silver and not merchandise. This interpretation seems to be far from the obvious words of the text.

21. The author of *Usd al Ghabah* says Hammas Al Iaithi, is mentioned by al Waqidi among those born at the time of the Prophet (p) he usually reports from 'Umar.

22. In *al Talkhs*, p.185. Al Hafiz says this is reported by Al Shafi'i, Ahmad, Ibn Abi Shaibah, 'Abd al Razzaq, Sa'id bin Mansur and Al Daraqutni. See also *al Umm* of al Shafi'i, Vol. 2, p. 38, *Sunan al Baihaqi*, Vol. 4, p.147. Ibn Hazm grades the story weak claiming that Hammas and his some are unknown, while Ahmad Shakir writes in his footnote on *Al Muhalla*, Vol. 5, p.235 that they are known and trustworthy.

23. *Al Mughni*, Vol. 3. p. 35.

24. *Al Amwal*, p. 425.

25. *Al Muhalla*, Vol. 5, p. 234, and *al Sunan al Kubra*, Vol. 4, p. 147.

26. *Al Amwal*, p. 426. Ibn Hazm grades the story good, but makes a twisted interpretation. See *Al Muhalla*, Vol. 5, pp. 234-235.

27. *Al Mughni*, Vol. 3, p.30.

28. *Al Amwal*, p. 429.

29. *Sharh Al Tirmidhi*, Vol. 3, p. 104.

30. *Ma'alim al Sunan.* Vol. 2, p.223.

31. *Bidayat al Mujtahid*, Vol. 1, p.217, Al Halabi Print.

32. *Commentary al Manar*, Vol. 10, p.591, second edition.

33. *Ibid.*

34. Reported by al Tirmidhi (who calls it good correct) Ibn Majah, Ibn Habban (in his correct collection) and al Hakim. The latter grades it correct.

35. Reported by Ahmad (via a good chain) and Al Hakim. The latter indicates that the chain is correct.

36. An old opinion that no *zakah* is obligated on trade is attributed to al Shafi'i, but many of his disciples challenge that. See *al Rawadah* of Al Nawawi, Vol. 2, p.16.

37. *Al Muhalla*, Vol. 6, pp. 233-240.

38. Their grading is discussed in previous chapters.

39. *Al Rawdah al Nadiyah*, Vol. 1, p. 192-193.

40. Reported by Ahmad, Abu Daud, al Nasai, al Tirmidhi, al Daraqutni, Ibn Habban, al Hakim, and al Baihaqi from Masruq from Mu'adh. Al Tirmidhi grades it good.

41. *Al Amwal*, p.427.

42. *Al Mukhtasar al Nafi'*. See *Fiqh al Imamiyah*, p.54.

43. *Jawahir al Kalam*, Vol. 2, p.126.

44. *Al Rawdah al Nadiyah*, Vol. 1, p.219.

45. *Radd al Muhtar*, Vol. 2, p.18.

46. *Matalib Uli al Nuha*, Vol. 2.

47. *Radd al Muhtar*, Vol. 2, p. 18-19. See also its commentary, and *Bulghat al Salik*, Vol. 1, p. 224, and its commentary.

48. This is the majority's view. The Hanbalites, Ibn 'Aqil and Abu Bakr consider the change of intention from personal use to trade for any item sufficient to include that item in *zakatability*.

49. *Radd al Muhtar*, Vol. 2, p. 19.

50. *Ibid*, p. 18.

51. *Al Mughni*, Vol. 2, p. 629.

52. *Al Amwal*, p. 375.

53. *Radd al Muhtar*, Vol. 2, p. 19, *al Mughni*, vol 2, p. 630.

54. *Al Majmu'*, Vol. 1, p. 55.

55. *Al Mughni*, Vol. 3, p. 32.

56. *Al Rawdah*, Vol. 2, p. 267.

57. *Al Amwal*, p. 426.

58. *Ibid*.

59. This is the view of Malik regarding all debts.

60. *Bulghat al Salik*, Vol. 1, p. 224. Al Sawi in his commentary quotes Ibn 'Ashir: it seems that craftsmen are among the non-monopolistic; merchants are also non-monopolistic.

61. *Bidayat al Mujtahid*, Vol. 1, pp. 260-261.

62. *Sharh al Risalah*, by Zarruq, Vol. 1, p. 325.

63. *Matalib uli al Nuha*, Vol. 2, p. 96.

64. *Ibid, Fath al Qadir*, Vol. 1, p. 527, *Bulghat al Salik*, Vol. 1, 235, and *Sharh al Azhar*, Vol. 1, pp. 479-480.

65. *Matalib Uli al Nuha*, Vol. 2, p. 96.

66. *Al Amwal*, p. 426.

67. *Bidayad al Mujtahid*, Vol. 1, p.260.

68. *Al Mughni*, Vol. 3, p.31.

69. *Al Rawdah* , Vol., p. 273.

70. *Bidayat al Mujtahid*, Vol. 1, p.260.

71. *Al Mugani* and *al Rawdah*.

72. *Al Mughni, ibid.*

73. *Fatawa Ibn Taimiyah*, Vol. 1, p.299.

CHAPTER FIVE

ZAKAH ON AGRICULTURE

Land is one of the greatest bounties of God. He subjects this earth to mankind and makes it cultivable, to produce plants and fruits. He created the laws of nature and made them benefit human beings in their living and subsistence. The importance of land as an origin of agricultural and other resources has always been recognized, to the extent that physiocrats in Western economics called for one single tax on land. God says "We indeed have placed you with authority on earth and provided you therein with means for the fulfillment of your lives: small are the thanks that ye give."[1] Who created land and submitted it to our authority? Who made land arable or nonarable ? Who created the seeds that, put inside the soil, grow into bushes and trees? Who nourishes seeds and waters them from clouds or springs? Who makes plants breathe the carbon gas that human beings discharge, and discharge the oxygen that human beings need in a fantastic exchange of benefit? Who created the sun that provides plants and trees with light and heat indispensable for their growth? All these are only a few of the bounties God created for us human beings. Should we not be thankful?[2] God says "See ye the seed that ye sow in the ground? Is it ye that cause it to grow or are we the cause ? Were it our will, we could crumble it to dry powder and ye would be left in wonderment, saying 'We are indeed left with debts, indeed are we shut out of the fruits of our labor'"[3] "And the earth we have spread out, set thereon mountains firm and immovable, and produced therein all kinds of things in due balance. And we have provided therein means of subsistence for you and for those for whose subsistence ye are not responsible. And there is not a thing but its treasures are with us, but we only send down thereof in due and ascertainable measures. And We send the fecundating winds, then cause the rain to descend from the sky therewith providing you with water, though ye are not the guardian of its stores."[4] Then let man look at his food. For that We pour forth water in abundance. And We split the earth in fragments. And produce therein corn. And grapes and nutritious plants. and olives and dates. And enclosed gardens dense with lofty trees. And fruits and fodder. For use and convenience to you and your cattle."[5] A sign for them is the earth that is dead, We do give it life and produce grain therefrom of which ye do eat. And we produce therein orchards with dates palms and vines and We cause springs to gush forth therein, that they may enjoy the fruits of this. It was not their hands that made this; will they not then give thanks."[6]

Indeed, all that the ground produces is but a part of the bounties of God. It is therefore natural that we are required to give thanks to God for these bounties that we use. The first expression of thankfulness is to give due *zakah* on it, showing gratitude to God and helping His needy servants. This *zakah* on grain, lands and fruits is known, in *Shari'ah* as "'*ushr*" (the 10%). Unlike other forms of *zakah*, *zakah* on agriculture does not require the passage of one full year. It is payable at the time of harvest because at the moment they are harvested, produce and crops represent the realized growth from land, and we have seen in chapter one of this part that growth is the reason for *zakatability*.

This chapter will have nine sections as follows:

Section 1: The obligation of *zakah* on agriculture.
Section 2: Products that are subject to *zakah*.
Section 3: *nisab*.
Section 4: Rates of *zakah*.
Section 5: Estimation of the harvest.
Section 6: Parts of the harvest that may not be counted for *zakatability*.
Section 7: Deduction of debt and expenditure.
Section 8: *zakah* on rented land.
Section 9: The combination of '*ushr* and *kharaj*.

SECTION ONE

OBLIGATION OF *ZAKAH* ON AGRICULTURE

In the Qur'an

A. God says, "O ye who believe, give of the good things which ye have earned and of the fruits of the earth which We have produced for you, and do not even aim at getting anything which is bad in order that out of it ye may give away something, when ye yourselves would not receive it except with closed eyes."[8] The obligation of *zakah* is inherent in this command to spend. Very often Qur'an uses the word "spending" for *zakah*. Al Jassas comments on this verse, "What is meant is *zakah*, especially since the following sentence forbids selecting bad goods as payment. Earlier and later generations agree that *zakah* is what is meant in this verse."[9]

B. God says, "It is He who produceth gardens, with trellises and without, and dates and tilth with produce of all kinds, and olives and pomegranates, similar (in kind) and different (in variety). Eat of their fruit in their season but render the dues that are proper on the day that the harvest is gathered."[10]

Many of the predecessors interpret "dues" in this verse to be due *zakah*. Al Tabari reports that Anas interprets this verse to mean the obligatory *zakah*. He also reports from Ibn 'Abbas, through several chains, "it is the one-tenth and the half-tenth dues." Another version from Ibn 'Abbas say, "Dues means the prescribed *zakah* on the day when the quantity of the harvest is measured and known." It is also reported that Jabir bin Zaid, al Hasan, Sa'id, Muhammad bin al Hanafiyah, Taus, Qatadah and al Dahhak interpret the verse as the obligatory *zakah* i.e. the one-tenth or half-tenth dues."[11] Al Qurtubi says that Ibn Wahb and Ibn al Qasim report the same from Malik. It is also the opinion of some of the disciples of al Shafi'i,[12] and of Abu Hanifah and his disciples as well.[13]

Others claim that this order came before the specific *zakah* was prescribed. It was substituted by it when the one-tenth and the half-tenth dues were prescribed. Al Tabari reports from Ibn 'Abbas and from Ibrahim al Nakha'i "surah six is Makkan, and the order was later substituted by the one-tenth and the half- tenth dues. There is also a narration from Muhammad bin al Hanafiyah to the same effect. Sa'id bin Jubair and al Hasan are also reported to share this view. Al Suddi says, "They were taught to give to whoever comes to them on the day of harvest, then *zakah* was ordained in substitution of that, and God prescribed on what comes forth from the earth dues of one-tenth and one half-tenth. "A similar report is also narrated from Atiyah al 'Awfi.[14]

Al Tabari, after giving all these reports, concludes that the verse was superceded later by *zakah*. He adds that *zakah* cannot be paid on the day of harvest because drying or cleaning the grain or fruit is necessary.[15] This is surprising from al Tabari since he is usually very cautious about the superceding of one verse by another. Throughout his commentary he denies many claimed supercedings and annulments. As a matter of principle, annulment of one text by another can only be resorted to when there is complete contradiction between their rulings, to the extent that both texts cannot be worked out together. The relation between the verse "and give its dues on the day of harvest" and the correct hadith that imposes the one-tenth and the half-tenth dues is not that of total contradiction but rather the relation of the general to the specific.

It seems that the confusion is a matter of terminology, because the word 'annulment' in Arabic "*naskh*" is commonly used by predecessors, including many Companions, in a general meaning that covers not only strict elimination of the ruling of the text as defined by the scholars of jurisprudence, but also any restriction of a general text, limitation of an absolute, or details of global rule. In his *al Muwafaqat*, al Shatibi writes, "It seems that earlier scholars used the term "*naskh*" in more general meaning than the scholars of *usul*; limiting an absolute text, restricting a general text, providing details of a global one or removing some of the implications of an earlier text by a later one. All this used to be called annulment or *naskh*, since they all have some common element in their meaning."[16] Ibn al Qayim adds, "Early scholars use the term 'annulment' sometimes in the meaning of eliminating the ruling completely, which is the only use of the term by later generations of scholars. But the former also used the same term to mean restricting or limiting a general or an absolute text."[17]

In commenting on the reports of substitution of the dues mentioned in the above verse by the later preseciption of *zakah*. Ibn Kathir says, "Calling this substitution an annulment is not granted, because we have something that was first made obligatory, then its details were provided, and the ratios and quantities were given later on. It is said these details were given in the second year of Hijrah."[18]

One can conclude that the "proper dues" in the verse are those whose details and descriptions were later given as one-tenth and half-tenth. As for the objection that the right due could not possibly be paid on the day of harvest because of the necessary operations of cleaning or drying, the reply is that the four kinds of produce mentioned in the verse- grain, dates, olives, and pomegranate - do not necessarily need drying and can be dispensed on the day of harvest. Additionally, a few scholars interpret the words "render the dues" as "be ready to pay it."[19]

In Sunnah

A. Ibn 'Umar narrates that the Prophet (p) said, " On that which is watered by the sky or by springs, one-tenth is obligatory, and on that which is irrigated by carried water a half-tenth is obligatory."[20]

B. Jabir narrates from the Prophet (p), "One tenth is obligatory on that which is watered by rivers or clouds, and half-tenth is obligatory on that which is watered through means of transported water."[21]

C. There are also several saying that determine *nisab* of grains and fruits and sayings that about sending collectors for *zakah* on agriculture.
In *ijma'*

Muslims scholars have unanimously agreed on the obligation of the one-tenth or the half-tenth dues, although they may have differences about details.[22]

SECTION TWO

ZAKATABLE AGRICULTURAL PRODUCTS

In this section I will review the different scholarly opinions and then conclude with a comparison and reflection to select the best among them.

1. The view that *zakah* is obligated only on four food items

'Abd Allah bin 'Umar and a few Followers consider *zakah* obligatory only on wheat, barley, date, and raisin . This is also reported from Musa bin Talhah, al Hasan, Ibn Sirin, al Hasan bin Salih, Ibn Abi Laila, Ibn al Mubarak, Abu 'Ubaid, and a report from Ahmad.[23] Ibrahim adds a fifth item, corn.[24] They provide the following documents in support of their view:

A. Ibn Majah and al Daraqutni report from Amr bin Shu'aib from his father from his grandfather that "The Messenger of God (p) only enacted *zakah* on wheat, barley, date, and raisin." Ibn Majah's version adds "corn."[25]

B. A report narrated by Abu Burdah from Abu Musa and Mu'adh that the Messenger (p) sent them to Yemen to teach people and ordered them not to take *sadaqah* except from these four foods - wheat, barley, date, and raisin.[26]

Moreover, there is no text or known *ijma* that imposes *zakah* on other than these four products. Other crops are not as common as these four and must not be considered similar to them.

2. The view that imposes *zakah* on edible preservable items

Malik and al Shafi'i consider edibility and preservability as the necessary conditions for *zakatability* of agricultural products. Consequently, wheat, barley, corn, grain, and rice are all *zakatable*. By "edibility" they mean that the item should be a major foodstuff and not a secondary one, an item that people normally eat for subsistence. Consequently, almond, walnut, and pistachio are not *zakatable* although they can be stored, while apples pomegranates, pears, peaches, and plums are also not *zakatable* because they cannot be dried and stored. Malikites differ on the *zakatability* of figs. Malik himself is reported to have excluded figs, plums, pomegranates and all fruits from *zakah*,[27] while some of his disciples consider figs *zakatable* because the two conditions of edibility and storability are fulfilled.[28] Al Khurashi counts twenty *zakatable* food items which include garbanzo beans, lentil, wheat, barley, rice, dates, olives, raisin, sesame, and others.[29]

Al Qurtubi says that al Shafi'i believes in no obligatory *zakah* on fruits except dates and grapes, because the Prophet (p) took *zakah* on these two products, as primary preservable foods in Hijaz . On the other hand, walnuts and almonds are not *zakatable* although they are non-perishable, because they were not primary foodstuff in Hijaz, but were used only as fruits. Al Shafi'i continues, "olives are also not *zakatable* because they are associated with pomegranates in a verse, "and olive and pomegranate"[30] and since the pomegranate is not *zakatable*, neither must the olive be."

There is, however another report from al Shafi'i that olives are *zakatable*.[31] Which is the opinion of Malik too.[32] Al Qurtubi continues, "They both agree that pomegranates are not *zakatable*, while according to the verse quoted at the beginning of this chapter, pomegranates must be *zakatable*."[33]

Their argument is based on two points. The first is a saying narrated by Mu'adh which reads, "Cucumbers, watermelons, pomegranates, sugarcane , and vegetables are exempt : the Messenger of God (p) exempted them", reported by al Baihaqi in *al Sunnan Al Kubra*. He also reports a few other sayings and comments, "All these sayings are *mursal* but there are several narrations of them which must strengthen each other." This is further supported by statements of some Companions such as 'Ali, 'Umar, and 'A'ishah. And the second is that foodstuffs are highly useful, like livestock, so they must likewise be *zakatable*.[34]

Both of these two points do not stand up against the sweeping generalization of the text in Qur'an and Sunnah which indicate that the obligation of *zakah* is on all that comes from the earth or is watered by the sky.[35]

3. The view that non-perishable crops that can be dried and measured are *zakatable*

Ahmad is reported in *al Mughni* to have said that these three conditions must be met for *zakatability*, whether the crop is a food item or otherwise.[36] Thus grain, cotton, sesame, some vegetables and many fruits are included. However, some fruits like apple, pear, peach, and apricot and some vegetables like cucumber, eggplant, and carrot are all not *zakatable*.

This view is based on the generality of the saying: "There is one tenth obligatory on that which is watered by the sky " and the Prophet's order to Mu'adh: "Take grain out of grain,"[37] and the saying: "There is no *zakah* on grain or date that are less than five *wasq*"[38] reported by Muslim and al Nasa'i. This last saying means that for *zakatability* the measurability is a required condition.[39]

4. The view that anything that stems from the soil is *zakatable*

According to Abu Hanifah anything that is planted and harvested with the intention of making a profit, is *zakatable*. Natural forests, bushes and plants that grow on their own are not *zakatable* except when the owners intend to use the land for lumber or fodder plantation. In this case those products become *zakatable*.[40] Abu Hanifah does not consider any of the conditions of edibility, driability, non-perishability, or measurability. Daud and his zahiri disciples go along with Abu Hanifah on this issue. This is also reported to be the view of 'Umar bin Abd al Aziz, Mujahid, Hammad and a report from al Nakha'i.[41] Abu Yusuf and Muhammad do not agree with their teacher Abu Hanifah on the *zakatability* of vegetables.

According to Abu Hanifah and his two disciples, sugarcane, safran, cotton, and other fibers, all fruits, and spices are *zakatable*. So are vegetables, in his view only. Abu Hanifah uses the following in support of his opinion. Firstly, he says the general terms of the verse in surah *al Baqara* "and from what We have produced for you from the earth" make no exception of any agricultural products.[42] Secondly, the verse "and render its right dues on the day of its harvest" comes after the mention of several kinds of trees and fruits.

If *zakah* should cover fruits it must also cover vegetables because the latter are easier to produce and to transfer to the poor and needy, even more so than grains.[43] Thirdly, the saying "A due of one-tenth is obligatory on that which is watered by the sky and half-tenth is required on that which is watered by carried water" does not distinguish between edible or non-edible, perishable or non-perishable, measurable or non-measurable crops.

Discussion and analysis

The view of Abu Hanifah seems to be the strongest. It suits the general objectives of *zakah* and the justice of its implementation as expressed in the texts of Qur'an and Sunnah. We must also remember that this is the opinion of several great scholars such as 'Umar bin Abd al Aziz, Mujahid, Hammad, Daud, and al Nakha'i.[44] The few sayings that talk about four food items are either *munqati'* (interrupted) or weak.[45] Even if one were to accept the sayings, the restriction to the four items can be interpreted as a mere reference to items present at the time of the Prophet.[46] It is remarkable that none of the four schools of thoughts took such limitation for granted.

Amazingly enough, the late Rashid Rida supports this narrow view, after he adds corn to the four other crops, saying 'If anything must be added by analogy it is rice especially in areas where rice is the main subsistence'.[47] This is amazing because Rida himself uses the argument of generality with respect to trade assets. The generality argument is in fact more applicable to the produce of earth that is referred to in the verses than to any thing else.

On the other hand, a Malikite like Ibn al 'Arabi supports the position of Abu Hanifah in his *Ahkam al Qur'an*.[48] He also writes in the commentary on Al Tirmidhi, "The strongest view is that of Abu Hanifah, because it is more advantageous to the needy, most supported by the general terms of the texts and more appropriate as an expression of gratitude for Gods' grace."[49]

In his explanation of the verse "and give its right dues . . . ", Ibn al Arabi says " Abu Hanifah hits truth in obligating *zakah* on foodstuff and other crop, as implied by the general terms of the Prophet's saying, 'and one-tenth is obliged on what the sky waters'. Ahmads' opinion depends on a weak argument in mistakenly interpreting the saying 'there is no *zakah* on what is less than five *wasq*' to mean there is a condition of measurability, instead of a minimum for *zakatability* that applies to all crops, measurable or not. The edibility condition of the shafi'ites is baseless. God reminds of His grace in providing food and fruits and obligates dues on both, in spite of differences in kinds of crops or in the way a given crop is used, such as using oil extracted from a crop for light to enjoy the grace of vision and the removal of darkness. How could anyone claim that *zakah* is not obligated on vegetables because they usually are distributed fresh and not dried knowing that fresh date and fresh grape are both *zakatable* without any need for drying. Fresh fruits are an essential part of the bounties God bestows on us. He even mentions them as some of the enjoyments offered in Heaven as in the verse 'in them will be fruits and dates and pomegranates,'[50] and also the verse, 'for that We pour forth water in abundance, and we split the earth in fragments, and produce therein grain, and grapes and nutritious plants, and olives and dates, and enclose gardens dense with lofty trees, and fruits and fodder'.[51] Ibn al Arabi continues, 'One may argue that we have no report that the Prophet (p) collected *zakah* from the vegetables in Madinah and Khaibar. My answer to this is that lack of evidence that he collected *zakah* is not evidence that *zakah* is not required, especially since we have sufficient proof in the Qur'an itself.'

The saying that reads "No *zakah* is obligated on vegetables" has a weak chain and does not help as evidence.[52] Al Tirmidhi indicates the chain of this saying is incorrect: nothing authentic is reported from the Prophet (P) on this issue.[53] Some Hanafi jurists tend to understand this saying as a reference to the perishability of vegetables and an advice to *zakah* collector not to collect vegetables because they cannot be preserved.[54] Those jurists require that producers of vegetables distribute their *zakah* directly although some suggest that *zakah* be assessed and collected in value instead of in kind. It is reported by Yahya bin Adam from al Zuhri that "anything other than wheat, barley, date, grape and olive should be *zakated* in value ."[55]

'Ata says, "Vegetables, walnuts, almonds and fruits are not subject to the one-tenth due. But whatever is sold of them is subject to *zakah* if the value is two hundred *dirhams* or more."[56] Similar opinion is reported from al Sha'bi.[56] Abu 'Ubaid attributes similar views to Maimun bin Mahran, al Zuhri and perhaps al Awza'i.[56] Al Zuhri and Maimun apply here the *nisab* and rate applicable to silver.[56] Abu 'Ubaid further reports that Malik applies the same to fresh date, grape and olive. The latter adds, however, another condition, that the crop must be five *wasq* or more.[57]

The idea of calculating *zakah* of perishable vegetables and fruits on the basis of value is very practical but I tend to differ with the above scholars on the *nisab* and ratio, since changing the mode of payment from in kind to value does not necessitate a change in the rate and *nisab* of *zakah*. I believe that the rates and *nisab* of agriculture must still be applicable. We have on hand a report from Al Sha'bi that the value of grapes is *zakated* at the rate of one-tenth or one half-tenth.[58] Ibn Abi Zaid in *al Risalah* mentions that "Olives are subject to *zakah* if the crop is five *wasq* or more, and *zakah* can be paid out of the olive oil or the proceeds of sale." And in his comments *al Risalah*, Ibn Naji adds "this is also reported from Malik. The generally accepted opinion in the Maliki school is that *zakah* on olive oil is paid in oil, while *zakah* on olives sold unsqueezed is paid in value."[59]

SECTION THREE

NISAB OF AGRICULTURE

Survey of Views on *Nisab*

The majority of Muslim scholars since the eras of the Companions and Followers believe that crops must be at least five *wasq* to be *zakatable*,[60] based on the Prophet's saying, "No *sadaqah* is obligatory on anything less than five *wasq*," a correct and agreed upon saying.[61] Abu Hanifah says *zakah* is obligatory on agriculture regardless of the amount of crop, since the saying of the Prophet,"A one-tenth due is obligatory on that which the sky waters," is general. This is also correct and reported by al Bukhari and others.[62] According to Abu Hanifah the condition of *nisab* is not applicable because the condition of the passage of one year is not required. Yahya bin Adam reports a similar opinion from Ibrahim al Nakha'i.[63] 'Ata is said to be of the same view.[64] Abu Raja'al 'Utaridi says Ibn 'Abbas used to collect *zakah* in Basrah even from bunches of fresh onions.[65] Furthermore, Ibn Hazm indicates that Mujahid, Hammad, 'Umar bin 'Abd al Aziz, and al Nakha'i all obligated *zakah* on all the land produce, whether big or small in quantity. Reports from the last three are extremely correct.[66] Umar bin 'Abd al 'Aziz says that of each bunch of spinach and the like, one bunch must be paid as *zakah*.[67] Daud al Zahiri holds that for items that are measurable, the condition of five *wasq* is necessary, while this condition does not apply to crops that are not measurable.[68] This seems to be a reconciliation of the above two sayings.[69] The author of *al Bahr* reports yet another opinion from al Baqir and al Nadir, that *nisab* is a necessary condition only on date, raisin, wheat, and barley, since these were the most common foodstuff at the time of the Prophet (p).[70] Al Shawkani comments, "This looks like restricting a general text without any supportive evidence."[71]

Discussion and analysis

Abu Hanifah's opinion in obligating *zakah* on any quantity, with no consideration of *nisab*, contradicts the correct saying mentioned at the beginning of this section. It also appears to be in direct conflict with the general principle that *zakah* is levied on the rich alone, and *nisab* is the criterion for richness. The seeming opposition of the two sayings is not an argument, because both of them can be interpreted in such a way that remove contradiction. According to Ibn al Qayyim, "the saying 'A one-tenth due is obligated on which the sky waters' is said in the context of distinguishing between cases that require a rate of one-tenth and cases where a rate of only a half-tenth is required. This saying does not touch the matter of *nisab*. On the other hand, the saying of the five *wusq* is a clear text on the issue of *nisab*. This cannot be challenged by the general text of the former saying."[72]

Ibn Qudamah says, "Since the saying 'There is no *sadaqah* obligatory on that which is less then five *wasq* is specific, it has priority in determining *nisab*. This is like the case of other *zakatable* items, such as camels and silver. In both cases there are general sayings whose purpose is to indicate the *zakatability* of the item, while there are texts whose purpose is to set *nisab*, like 'There is no *sadaqah* obligatory on that which is less than five camels.' and 'There is no *sadaqah* obligatory on that which is less than five *uqiyyah*." Ibn Qudamah goes on "The passage of a year is disregarded in agriculture because the time of harvesting represents the complete cycle of growth for the land. So there should be no association between *nisab* and the passage of a year. Finally, *nisab* is the determinant of richness in matters of *zakah*, and *zakah* is only obligated on the rich."[73]

Required *nisab* on grain and fruits

Correct sayings determine *nisab* at five *wasq*. A *wasq* unanimously equals sixty *sa'*. This is even mentioned in a saying, although it is a weak one.[74] A *nisab* is thus three hundred *sa'*. Unanimity on this estimation is mentioned by Ibn al Mundhir.[75]

The *Sa'*

Sa' as in *Lisan al 'Arab* is a measure of volume or capacity used in Madinah. It equals four *mudd*. It is mentioned in several sayings with regard to the *zakah* of breaking the fast.[76] It is said that Prophet (p) used one *sa'* (of water) for his washing (*ghusl*) and one *mudd* for his ablution (*wudu'*)[77], so the *sa'* of the Prophet is four *mudd*. One *mudd* equal what fills the two hands put by each other with fingers stretched. The Prophet (p) standardized measures of capacity, stating, as narrated by Ibn 'Umar, "The (standard) measures are the measures of Madinah, and the (standard) weight are the weights of Makkah."[78] People of Madinah were farmers and their measures of capacity are more widely known and more accurate, while people of Makkah were men of trade, and their weights were more common and more accurate.

Differences on the weight equivalent of *sa'* among jurists of Hijaz and Iraq

Abu Hanifah and his disciples --- Iraqis -- estimate the weight of one *sa'* at eight Baghdadi *ratl*, while Malik , Shafi'i, Ahmad and others -- Hijaziz -- estimate it at five and one third *ratl*.

Iraqi jurists argue that the *sa'* at 'Umar's time weighted eight *ratl*.[79] They also depend on the claim that the Prophet used eight *ratl* for his washing, two *ratl* for his ablution, or one *sa'* for his washing and one *mudd* for his ablution.[80] They conclude that one *sa'* must equal eight *ratl*, while one *mudd* equals two *ratl*.

As for the Hijazis, their evidence is the predominant practice of the residents of Madinah generation after generation from the time of the Prophet. Ibn Hazm says "This is overwhelmingly known in Madinah, and it is obvious to everybody, young or old, righteous or wicked, knowledgeable or ignorant. Rejecting such a fact is like rejecting the fact that the Grand Mosque is in Makkah or rejecting the known site in Madinah of the dome over the Mosque of the Prophet--- it is absurdly unreasonable," He continues, "Even Abu Yusuf, upon visiting Madinah changed his view to that of Hijazi Jurists."[81] He is referring to the story reported by al Baihaqi from al Husain bin al Walid, "We went to visit Abu Yusuf upon his return from pilgrimage. He told us, 'I want to inform you of a matter that worried me for some time until I went to Madinah. There, I asked about the *sa'* and they answered that the *sa'* they have today is the same *sa'* used by the Messenger of God (p). I asked if they could provide proof for this statement. They said they would bring me their proof tomorrow. The next day, about fifty elderly sons if *Ansar* and *Muhajirin* appeared before me, each of them carrying a measure of one *sa'*. Each narrated from his father and his and ancestors that this was the measure used at the time of Prophet (p). I looked at these measures and found them all equal. I compared the weight of the *sa'*'s contents and found it is little less than five-and a-third *ratl*. To me, this was overwhelming evidence, and I changed my view from that of Abu Hanifah to that of the residents of Madinah."[82] Al Husain continues, "I went for pilgrimage the next year and met Malik, and asked him about the *sa'*. He said that the *sa'* we have today is the same *sa'* of the time of the Prophet (p). I asked how much it weighed, and he answered, 'This is a measure of capacity. It cannot be converted into weight.'"[83]

In the third century of Hijrah, Ahmad said, "I weighed the contents of one *sa'* of wheat and found it five *ratl* and one-third." Hanbal quotes his father, Ahmad, "I took that *sa'* from Abu al Nadr, who told me he took it from Abu Dhu'aib, who told me this is the *sa'* that was known in Madinah at the time of the Prophet." Ahmad says, "I weighed the contents of a *sa'* full of lentil and found it equal to five and one-third *ratl*."[84]

Reconciliation of these two estimations

Three propositions are suggested to reconcile the two views on the weight of the contents of the *sa'*.

A.   Some Hanafites suggest that the *ratl* of Madinah is two thirds of the *ratl* of Baghdad. Ibn al Humam supports this proposition. It means that the *sa'* as a capacity measure is agreed upon, but the weight of the *ratl* is different between Baghdad and Hijaz.[85]

B.   Ibn Taimiyah suggests that there used to be two measures of capacity; the Hijazi measure called *sa'* is used only for grain and foodstuff. A *sa'* of grain equals in wight five and one-third *ratl*. Another measure was used only for liquid, also called *sa'*, and equaling eight *ratl* sin weight.[86] According to this reconciliation, the *ratl* is the same in Iraq and Hijaz, while there are two different volume measures, depending on the material measured.

C.   For our modern age, 'Ali Mubarak suggests a third way of reconciliation. He claims there is no real difference the volume of *sa'* in Iraq and Hijaz, nor is there a difference between their *ratl* as a measure of weight.[87] If you weigh the one *sa'* full of grain, it is five and one-third *ratl*, and if you weigh one *sa'* full of water it is eight *ratl*s.

It should be noted that the eight *ratls* is only an approximation, because the exact weight of the water is a little bit less than eight *ratls*. Thus, according to Mubarak, the Iraqis considered the weight of water, while the Hijaziz considered the weight of grain.[88]

With all this, it becomes apparent that the weight of one *sa'* of grain is five and one-third *ratl*. The late al Rayes says, "There should be absolutely no doubt about this. It is supported by the strong experience of the residents of Madinah. Malik himself studied the measure of *sa'* and the weight of one *sa'* full of grain in the presence of Harun al Rashid (an Abbasite *Khalifah*) and convinced Abu Yusuf of it." Al Rayes continues, "Who knows the traditions of Madinah better than Malik?! And whose testimony is more valuable than that of Abu Yusuf?! This determination of the weight of one *sa'* suits best the proportions of *nisab* on grain as compared with other *nisabs*. It is known that one *sa'* is four *mudd* and one *mudd* is the fill of the two hands together. Who can imagine that the fill of two hands of an average -size man can be more than one and one-third!"[89]

Determination of *nisab* in contemporary measures

After we studied the determination of *nisab* as five *wasq*, each *wasq* being sixty *sa'*, we can easily transfer these to contemporary capacity measures.[90] In order to give the amount of *nisab* in weight we must remember the experiment of Ahmad. He weighed a *sa'* full or wheat; the weight was five and one-third *ratl*.[91] It is known some agricultural crops are lighter than wheat, such as barley or corn. There is no disagreement among *ahl al hadith* that the weight of a *sa'* is five and one-third *ratl* of average wheat. We must not forget that the quantity of *nisab* is determined in capacity measures and not in weight. If the volume of *nisab* of another crop happens to weigh less than the same volume of wheat, that volume of the other grain is *zakatable* in spite of its lighter weight.[91]

'Ali Mubarak studied the Baghdadi *ratl* and concludes that one *ratl* equals four hundred and eight grams.[92] He also estimates that one *sa'* of water is 2.75 liters. Consequently, the weight of one *sa'* of grains is 2.176 kilograms, By simple arithmetic we find that one *wasq* is 130.56 kilogram of wheat, or 165 liters. This means that the *nisab* is 825 liters or 652.8 kilograms."[93]

Nisab for crops that are not measured by capacity

A few crops cannot be measured by capacity measures because they are usually administered without being condensed or pressurized, such as safron and cotton. Abu Yusuf suggests that the value of such products should be the criteria in *zakatability*. He proposes to consider the value of a *nisab* of the cheapest grain, barley, for example, and apply that value on these crops.[94]

Muhammad suggests to use the largest unit used actually in trade, such as ton, for example, saying that the *wasq* was the highest unit of capacity measure at the time of the Prophet. Thus, for those new crops, we should take five of their highest units of measurement as a *nisab*.[94] This definitely means *nisab* will differ from one country to another. Some countries will use the metric ton, others the English ton, and yet others may use a different unit.

Some jurists suggest that in all crops which are not measured by capacity, *nisab* must be determined as the quantity whose value is two hundred dirhams, applying the *nisab* of money the same way it is applied on trade assets.[95] Lastly, Ahmad suggests we use the weight equivalent of the *nisab* of grain.[96] This means that for crops that are not usually measured by capacity measures, the weight of 653 kilograms must be applied in our times, Ibn Qudamah accuses all these views of being void of any support from a text, a valid analogy, or a sound rationale. He argues that *zakah* cannot be due on all assets regardless of any minimum, nor can the estimation of *nisab* on certain crops be done on the basis or another crop, nor can the value be considered, because in agriculture it is essential that *zakah* be paid in kind.[97]

In my opinion, other crops that are not measurable by capacity must have a *nisab*. Their *nisab* should be estimated on the basis of the value as Abu Yusuf says, but I think the estimation at the cheapest measurable crop is unfair from the point of view of *zakah* payers, although it benefits the poor. An estimation of *nisab* must be fair with both parties, so I suggest averaging the value of *nisab* of different crops. Since this may differ from time to time and place to place, I suggest to determine *nisab* in each case according to the socio-economic variables on the basis of the average value of five *wasq* of different measurable crops. Such an estimation must be done by people of knowledge whenever necessary.

Time and method of determination of *nisab*

The estimation of *nisab* should be done on the dry product after it takes its final form for sale (after cleaning, filtering, skinning, etc.). Al Ghazali in his *al Wajiz* writes that the five *wasq* must be considered in the dried form of raisin, and in grain after cleaning and removal of its bran, except for crops that are sold fresh or with their bran. In this case *nisab* is estimated on them as they are.[98]

SECTION FOUR

RATIOS OF *ZAKAH*

The one-tenth and half-tenth rates

Al Bukhari reports from Ibn 'Umar that the Prophet (p) said, "A one-tenth due is obligatory on that which is watered by the sky or springs or that which is not watered at all, and a half-tenth is obligatory on that which is watered by carried water."[99] Muslim reports from Jabir that the Prophet (p) said, "On that which rivers or clouds water, there is one-tenth due, and in that which is watered by water carried by camels, there is one half-tenth."[100] Yahya bin Adam reports from Anas, "The Messenger of God imposed a one-tenth due on that which the sky waters, and a half-tenth due on that which is watered by animals or men carrying water in containers."[101] Ibn Majah reports from Mu'adh, "The Messenger of God (p) sent me to Yemen and commanded me to collect one-tenth from that which the sky waters, or draws (underground) water through its roots, and half a tenth from that which is watered by pails."[102] Consequently, Abu 'Ubaid concludes that anything irrigated without the use of machine and the payment of labor, whether by rain from the sky or by rivers or springs or what sucks in (underground) water through its roots, the charge on it is one-tenth.[103] The author of *al Mughni* writes, "In all, whenever cost and effort from people or their animals or machines are involved, the ratio is half a tenth. On the other hand, things watered without such cost and effort are charged one-tenth. This is so because cost affects growth and must affect the amount paid as *zakah*, so the rate is reduced."[104] When water is purchased and paid for, the rate is also reduced, according to al Nawawi and others.[105]

Crops watered sometimes at cost and sometimes without cost

A. If plants are watered by carried water half of the year and the other half are left to rain, the percentage of *zakah* becomes seven and a half percent. Ibn Qudamah says "This is not disputed, to my knowledge, since if watering takes place for the whole year the ratio is five percent, so the ratio is proportional to watering."[106]

B. If plants are watered most of the year, the ratio becomes five percent and the small portion of total season is disregarded. By the same token, the ratio must be ten percent if they are not watered most of the season. This is according to 'Ata, al Thawri, Abu Hanifah, one of two reports from al Shafi'i, and the official position of the Hanbalites.[107]

C. If the ratio of watering to the total season is not known the percentage applicable must be one-tenth, to be on the safe side.[108]

Consideration of effort and cost in other than watering

The question arises of whether costs spent on other than watering is considered in the reduction of the *zakah* percentage. This might include digging trenches and canals for irrigation, establishing a sprinkling system, and the like. Ibn Qudamah suggests that the cost of canals and trenches be of no effect on *zakah* because such cost is implied in the reclamation of land and its preparation for agricultural use.[109] Al Rafi'i expresses a similar view,[110] while al Khattabi distinguishes between the initial cost of irrigation canals and the cost of maintaining them, and concludes that if a substantial amount is assumed yearly for the operation and maintenance of such canals and wells, the rate must be reduced to five percent.[111] Al Rafi'i reports that some Shafi'ites share the same view with al Khattabi.[112]

SECTION FIVE

PRE-ESTIMATION OF CROPS

The Messenger (p) started a tradition of estimating the amount of dates and grapes before the harvest, while the fruits are still on the trees, with no need of actual measuring or weighing. The purpose of this pre-harvest estimation, made by experts, is to determine the amount of due *zakah* and to leave the farmer the freedom of disposing of the crop any time, without having to wait for the *zakah* collector.[113] Al Khattabi says "this pre-harvest estimation allows farmers to take the best opportunities for collecting their fruits and selling them without having to wait for the *zakah* officers on the day of harvest, provided that when pre-estimation is done and the due amount of *zakah* is determined the farmer guarantees the delivery of *zakah* due to its collector.[114] 'Umar bin al Khattab and Sahl bin Abi Hathamah, Marwan, al Qasim bin Muhammad, al Hasan, 'Ata, al Zuhri, 'Amr bin Dinar, Malik, al Shafi'i, Ahmad, Abu 'Ubaid, Abu Thawr, and the majority of scholars approve of the pre-harvest estimation. On the other hand, Abu Hanifah does not accept it on the grounds that it is mere speculation.[115]

The majority provides the following supporting evidence:

1. Sa'id bin al Musayid reports from 'Attab bin Usaid "The Prophet (p) used to send officers to estimate--before the harvest--grapes and fruits."[116]

2. From Sa'id bin al Musayib, "The Messenger of God (p) commanded that grapes be estimated before the harvest the way dates are estimated, and their due *zakah* be collected in the form of raisins, the same way due *zakah* on dates is collected (after drying)."[117]

3. The Prophet (p) practiced pre-harvest estimation. He estimated the crop of an orchard that belonged to a woman in Wadi al Qura at ten *wasq*, and told the woman to measure the actual crop. She did, and it came to exactly what the Prophet (p) estimated.[118]

4. Abu Daud reports from 'A'ishah about Khaibar, "The Prophet (p) used to send "Abd Allah bin Rawahah to the Jews to estimate the date crop before it was ripe and edible."[119]

5. From Sahl bin Abi Hathamah, "The Messenger of God (p) said, "When you estimate before the harvest, do not count one-third of the fruits, or at least one-fourth (to be more fair in estimation)."[120]

In *Ma'alim al Sunan*, al Khattabi says, "This saying confirms the practice of pre-harvest estimation which is the view of the majority, except for a report from al Sha'bi that estimation is a fabrication. Scholars of the school of opinion deny estimation, claiming that estimation was used only to put pressure on farmers not to cheat rather than to determine the due amount of *zakah*, and such estimation is only speculation, i.e. a sort of gambling that may have been permissible only before gambling was prohibited." Al Khattabi continues, "but pre-harvest estimation was practiced a long time after the prohibition of gambling during the era of the Messenger, Abu Bakr, and 'Umar. The masses of Companions permitted it, since none of them is reported to have opposed such a practice. Moreover, claiming that estimation is merely speculative is not valid, because estimation is the result of the exertion of best efforts by experienced experts. It is therefore like *ijtihad*, and *ijtihad* is always practiced when a fixed rule is not available. It is similar to estimation of the value of destroyed property in order to impose the compensation on the person who destroyed it."[121]

Time and procedure of pre-harvest estimation

Pre-harvest estimation must be done when fruits start to ripen and before the time of harvest, because the need for this estimation becomes important at that time. This is in accordance with the saying from 'A'ishah mentioned above.[122] If estimation is found to be far from actual reality, the due amount of *zakah* remains as estimated and need not be adjusted. Al Qasim bin Muhammad answered such a question with "You must pay according to the estimation. It is the error of the person who made it."[123] This is also the opinion of Malik, provided that the estimator is honest and experience, because according to him the estimation is final as far as the due amount of *zakah* is concerned. Abu 'Ubaid comments, "This is agreeable if the variance is withing reasonable limits which are usually forgiven in normal transactions, but if the difference is big, a correction becomes due like in other transactions."[123]

Ibn Hazm argues that the mistake of the estimator or his dishonesty must be corrected because God says "Be establishers of justice and balance." Whether the estimation is more or less than actuality, it is unjust to either the payer or the recipient of *zakah*. A claim that the estimator made an error or was dishonest must be proven by factual evidence.[124] However, I believe that the opinion of Abu 'Ubaid is more reasonable and practical.

Estimation of other crops

The majority of scholars believes that only dates and grapes can be estimated before the harvest, and this estimation must not be applied to other fruits. This is also the view of Malik and Ahmad.[125] Al Zuhri, al Awza'i, and al Laith extend pre-harvest estimation to other fruits such as olives, because the need for such an estimation exists with respect to other fruits the same way it exists for dates and grapes.[126]

I conclude that pre-harvest estimation must be practiced only according to need, whatever the fruit. This is a matter that depends on the practical experience of people and the opinions of experts as well as on the technology of the times. If pre-harvest estimation is needed for any fruit for the benefit of *zakah* administrators or farmers, it can be applied in analogy to estimation of dates and grapes.

SECTION SIX

EASINESS IN ESTIMATION

There are several indications that the estimation of the amount of *zakatable* crops should be easy on the payer. These include the following:

1. Sahl bin Abi Hathamah narrates from the Prophet (p) "When you estimate, leave one-third, and if not leave one-fourth (uncounted)".

2. Ibn 'Abd al Barr reports from Jabir from the Prophet (p) take it easy in estimation . . ."[127]

3. Abu 'Ubaid reports from Makhul "When the Messenger of God (p) sends estimators he tells them, "Make it easy, because orchards usually include trees left for charity and trees left for passers-by to eat from."[128]

4. Al Awza'i is reported to have said, "It reached us that 'Umar bin al Khataab said to make it easy for people when you estimate, since trees usually include those designated for charity, passers-by, and family to eat from."[129]

5. From Bashir bin Yasar, "'Umar bin al Khattbb sent Abu Hathamah from *al Ansar* to make the estimation of fruits of Muslim, and told him, 'If you find them among their trees eating, don't count the trees they are eating from.'"[130]

6. Sahl bin Abi Hathamah reports that Marwan appointed him an estimator of dates. He estimated the orchard of Sa'd bin Abi Sa'd seven hundred *wasq* and said, "If it were not for the forty cabins and booths in which people live I found in it, I would have estimated it at nine hundred *wasq*, but I left for them what they were eating."[131]

The first of these sayings is graded correct by a group of leading scholars, and is supported by the saying from Jabir and that of Makhul as well as by the practices of the Companions. Ibn Hazm says, "Here we have the practice of the Companions 'Umar and Abu Hathamah and Sahl, in the presence of all other Companions, without any report to the contrary from any one of them."[131] Several sayings and stories from the Companions imply the urging of easiness and kindness in estimation.

Ibn Qudamah says that "the estimator must not count one-third or one-fourth of the total fruits as a gesture of kindness to the payer, because they usually need that much for their own food, for charity, passers-by, and guests. If one counts everything it becomes harsh on them. Ishaq, al Laith, and Abu 'Ubaid are reported to be of the same view. How much is left is a matter that is decided by the estimator on the basis of his observation and the location of the orchard. But if the estimator does not leave anything uncounted, the owner may eat as much as one-fourth and deduct that from the *zakatable* estimated total. If the government does not send an estimator, the owner may get a non-partisan estimator and may deduct between one-third and one-fourth for the above-mentioned purpose."[132]

If the fruits or crop are not estimated prior to the harvest day, owners may still eat, or give gifts up to a reasonable amount without being charged *zakah* on it. Ahmad was asked about wheat eaten before being dried and answered, "It is all right, because it is customary for growers to eat from this crop, in similarity to fruit growers."[132] Abu Yusuf and Muhammad say that what is eaten by growers, their guests, and families, is always deductible, even if it equals all the crop.

On the other hand, Malik and Abu Hanifah believe that nothing should be left uncounted. Even fruits eaten by growers must be estimated and included in the total count of *zakatable* crops.[133] Ibn al 'Arabi says al Thawri also shares this view.[134] Ibn Hazm claims it is not permissible to charge *zakah* on what is eaten by growers and their families or given for charity, on the grounds that *zakah* is due after the harvest, so things eaten or given away before the harvest are not included in principle. He adds that otherwise we would be imposing hardship on the payers, because what is eaten in that period is difficult to estimate, and God says "On no soul does God place a burden greater than it can bear."[135] Ibn Hazm depends on the saying from Sahl and similar stories in his presentation.[136]

Those who disagree on leaving anything uncounted have their own answer to the saying from Sahl. Some of them claim it was only meant for a specific case, that of Khaibar. Some others say the meaning of "leaving some to them" is not to collect all the due *zakah* from them, although they are charged the whole due amount according to accurate and comprehensive estimation, but to leave one-third or one-fourth of the *zakah* due for growers to distribute privately to their poor neighbors or kin.[137] Others provide yet a different explanation, saying that what is left uncounted is merely for the expense of the growers in cultivating and planting the land.

In my opinion, the saying from Sahl must be applied, especially since it is supported by the practice of 'Umar and Ahmad, Ishaq, al Laith, al Shafi'i--his former view--and Ibn Hazm. This saying, in fact, provides us with an important rule, the consideration of reasonable conveniences of the *zakah* payer and family and of circumstances surrounding the case that might require certain reduction in the estimation of required dues. This complies with the general condition in *zakatable* assets, which is that they must be in excess of essential needs of the owner. This approach of considering special circumstances has only recently been discovered by man-made taxation systems.

SECTION SEVEN

DEDUCTION OF DEBTS AND EXPENSES

Are debts and expenses deductible?

Two kinds of debts may be owed by owners of crops, namely debts accrued for payment of farming expenses for the crops themselves, and debts for personal and other purposes. Abu 'Ubaid reports from Jabir bin Zaid about debts for farming and debts for family use that Ibn 'Abbas said "Debts spent on the land must be paid back first," and Ibn 'Umar said, "Both debts on farming and family must be deducted."[138] Yahya bin Adam quotes Ibn 'Umar, "The farmer should start paying back his debts, then must pay *zakah* on the residual," while Ibn 'Abbas says that "debts spent on farming must be paid back and the residual is *zakatable*."[139] Obviously, Ibn 'Abbas and Ibn 'Umar agree that debts on farming are deductible, but they do not agree on deducting debts for family and personal use.

Abu 'Ubaid reports from Makhul, "*zakah* is only due on the residual after debts are deducted, if it satisfies *zakatability* conditions."[140] Similar views are reported from 'Ata and Taus,[140] as well as a group of Iraqi jurists, including Sufyan al Thawri.[141]

There are two reports from Ahmad, one is agreement with the view of Ibn 'Abbas and the other in agreement with the view of Ibn 'Umar. Ibn Qudamah comments, according to one report, "All debts are deductible; one-tenth is obligated on the residual if it is *nisab* or more, because we are dealing with *zakah*, and the principle is that debts are deductible."[142] Abu 'Ubaid supports the view of Ibn 'Umar, and adds the condition that debts must be valid. "Valid debts that are due on the farmer are deductible from *zakatable* crops, as stated by Ibn 'Umar, 'Ata, and Makhul. It is in accordance with Sunnah, since the Prophet (p) made *zakah* on the rich to be rendered to the poor. Those who are under debt are not rich; they may even deserve *zakah* as recipients," Abu 'Ubaid remarks.

Concerning the deductibility of *kharaj*, a real estate tax on land, Yahya bin Adam reports from Sufyan al Thawri that debts and *kharaj* are deductible, and if the residual reaches five *wasq*, it is *zakatable*.[144] Abu 'Ubaid reports from Ibrahim bin Abi 'Ablah, that 'Umar bin Abd al Aziz wrote to his officer in Palestine, 'Abd Allah bin 'Awf, that *kharaj* should first be collected from *kharajable* land in the hands of Muslims, then *zakah* should be levied on the residual.[145] This is also the view of Ahmad, on the basis that *kharaj* is a cost of the land, which is deductible from *zakatability*, as in *al Mughni*.[146] This is consistent with Ibn 'Abbas and Ibn 'Umar's view that costs of farming are deductible.

The rent of land rented for farming must be treated like *kharaj*, by analogy, since the majority of jurists consider *kharaj* a form of land rent. Yahya bin Adam asked Shuraik about a person who rents a plot to farm for a given amount of grain. We was answered, "He should deduct the amount of rent from its output and pay *zakah* (ten or five percent) on the residual, the same way debts are deductible."[147]

Now we come to considering expenditures spent on farming even when they do not take the form of debts. These may include the cost of seed, fertilizer, pesticide, labor involved in cultivating, irrigation, harvesting, weeding, drying, etc. Are these costs deductible like *kharaj*, debts, and rent? Ibn Hazm argues that these expenses are not deductible, whether their total is high or low. He reports from Jabir bin Zaid that Ibn 'Abbas and Ibn 'Umar disagree on this issue. The first says expenses are deductible, while the other says they are not. 'Ata is reported to reduce the amount of the crops by the amount of expenses. Ibn Hazm continues, "it is not permissible to make any reduction of a due imposed by God without valid textual support from Qur'an or Sunnah". He further states that "Malik, al Shafi'i, Abu Hanifah and the Zahiris are of the same view."[148]

It should be noted that the report he cites about Ibn 'Abbas and Ibn 'Umar agreeing on deducting expenses was mentioned earlier in this section, where the word used was debt caused by farming expenses. We learned there that both Ibn 'Abbas and Ibn 'Umar agree on deducting the amount of a debt that was used toward farming expenses, although Ibn 'Umar allows deducting other debts too. But Ibn Hazm attributes to them approval of the deduction of expenses in the case where there is no borrowing.

The most remarkable and direct statement about expenses comes from 'Ata' and is refered to by Ibn Hazm. Yahya bin Adam reports from Isma'il bin 'Abd al Malik that he asked 'Ata about farming a lot of land, and 'Ata answer, "Deduct your expenditure and pay *zakah* on what is left."[149] "There seems to be no agreement among scholars on deducting the costs of farming," Ibn al 'Arabi says, "and my opinion is that costs of farming must be deducted and *zakah* charged on the residual only. The statement in the saying 'Leave aside one-third or one-fourth' is a reference to the cost of farming." He continues, "I even ran a few experiments and found the cost is about that much."[150] This view of Ibn al 'Arabi implies that the deduction of cost and expenses and the exclusion of one-third or one-fourth in the estimation must not be implemented together, though the deduction of expenditure seems to be accepted by Ibn al 'Arabi even if it were more than one-third, and on all kinds of agricultural output whether estimated before the harvest or not. Ibn al Humam rejected this opinion, saying that the differences in the applicable percentage of *zakah* (i.e. five or ten percent) is meant as a compensation for costs involved. If expenditure is to be deducted, then ten percent must always be applied, but if the ratio is already reduced to five percent, costs must not be deducted.[151]

It seems likely that at the time of the Prophet (p) the major and most visible factor of cost was that of water that had to be carried to the land. Consequently, the rate was reduced in compensation for that cost. Other costs are not mentioned by any text, but it seems that the spirit of *Shari'ah* must accept the deduction of expenditure from *zakatable* crops on the following two grounds:

Firstly, cost and expenditure are usually considered in *Shari'ah*. The obvious example is the reduction of rate from ten to five percent because of the cost of irrigation. Sometimes the cost may be high enough to remove the *zakatability* of the asset, as in the case of livestock fed by purchased fodder most of the year.

Secondly, growth in fact is the surplus and surplus can only exist after considering the cost involved. This is perhaps why some scholars say production expenditure is like cost price for the output. We must remember that if cost is to be deducted, the expenses of irrigation must not be include, because such expenses are taken care of in the reduction of the ratio of *zakah* to five percent. As an example, if the product is ten tons of cotton and the cost, including real estate tax and not including irrigation is the value of three tons, only seven tons are *zakatable*. The rate depends on whether the land was watered by rivers or rain (ten percent) or by direct carrying of water (five percent).

SECTION EIGHT

ZAKAH ON RENTED FARMLAND

Zakah is obligated on the owner when he farms the land

When agricultural land is farmed by the owner, its *zakah* is due from the owner himself, but when the owner lends his land, free of charge, for someone else to farm, *zakah* is then due on the farmer.[153]

The owner as a partner in farming

When farming is done in certain forms of partnership, such as sharecropping , within the conditions required in *Shari'ah*, each partner becomes responsible for *zakah* on his or her own share, if the partner's share reaches *nisab*, either alone or when combined with output accruing to the partner from other sources. If the share of a partner does not fulfill the condition of *nisab*, he is not *zakatable*, although the other partner or partners may be zakated. Al Shafi'i differes on this issue, suggesting that if the total output of the partnership reaches *nisab*, it becomes *zakatable* and the partners are obliged to pay *zakah*, each in proportion to his or her share in the output.[154]

Rented land

When land is rented to the farmer for a given amount of money or any commodity, *zakah* (the ten or five percent) becomes due on the owner, according to Abu Hanifah. He argues that *zakah*, though usually collected from the output, is in fact a levy on the land. In renting, the land remains owned by the owner and not by the user, and since *zakah* is a charge on the land, similar to *kharaj*, it is his responsibility to pay it.[155] Renting is like farming, a sort of growth of the land, and out of this increase *zakah* is paid.[156] A similar view is reported by al Nakha'i.[157]

On the other hand, the majority is of the opinion that *zakah* is charged to the renter, on the grounds that *zakah* is a levy on the output and not on the land. Consequently, the owner of the output is responsible for *zakah*. It becomes obvious to us, along with Ibn Rushd, that there is a difference in the philosophy of *zakah*. Is it on the land or on the output, or maybe on both together? There seems to be no one who mentions that *zakah* could be on both land and output together, although this looks to be the truth of the matter. When the owner is the same as the farmer, the problem does not exist, but when the owner and the farmer are different persons, the majority argues that since *zakah* is paid out of the output it is responsibility of the person who owns the output, while Abu Hanifah refers to the basis of *zakah*, which is the growth of the land itself.[158]

Analysis and discussion

Ibn Qudamah prefers the majority's view. He challenges the position of Abu Hanifah, saying that if *zakah* is a charge on the land, it must be levied even when the land is not farmed, especially since *kharaj*, considered by Abu Hanifah similar to *zakah*, is imposed regardless of farming and output. Furthermore, if *zakah* is on the land, it must be determined according to the amount of land and not the amount of output. As for its dispersement, it must be similar to those of fai'.[159] Everybody knows *zakah* is a percentage of the output and must be dispersed like other forms of *zakah* and not like fai'.

Al Rafi'i says the renter is required to pay *zakah* regardless of the rent, like a businessman who is required to pay *zakah* in addition to the rent he might be paying for his store.[160] But one may differ with al Rafi'i on this analogy, because the merchant pays *zakah* at the end of the year after deduction of rent and other costs. *zakah* on agriculture has no yearly condition. It is due on the harvest, and if rent is not deducted from the harvest where would it be deducted from otherwise? It seems unfair that the renter be asked to pay both *zakah* and rent while the owner is charged nothing, Justice requires that both parties share in the payment of *zakah*. Neither should be allowed to escape it while the whole burden is unjustly thrown on the other. Ibn Rushd is intelligent enough to realize that *zakah* is in fact on the land and its output together.

In my opinion, the farmer who pays rent should be allowed to deduct the rent along with other expenses and debt from the output and pay *zakah* on the residual, if it reaches *nisab*, while the owner must be required to pay *zakah* on his share of the growth of the land, which in this case is the total rent he or she receives, if it reaches *nisab*. Payment is calculated according to the rate that applies on the output itself, i.e. ten percent or five percent. The owner is certainly allowed to deduct from the rent costs that might be involved, such as real estate taxes, along with expenditures and debts.

This approach of sharing in the payment of *zakah* prevents duplication in *zakatability,* because the rent that is deducted from zakatable output, as far as the farmer is concerned, is included in the *zakatable* output of the land owner. Each is charged with what belongs to him or her from the profit on the land, and on the basis of the income that accrues to him or her from it. I suggested this reconciliation in 1963, and it was rejected then by many of the scholars of al Azhar, but recently I read in *The Way Islam Organizes Society*, by the late Shaikh Abu Zahrah, p. 159, his statement, "Some contemporary scholars suggest in a proposal for a *zakah* act that *zakah* be shared by the owner and renter, where each of them is charged according to the profit he or she gets after payment of taxes, as far as the farmer is concerned." This is, praise be to God, the opinion I feel most comfortable with and I share and support.

SECTION NINE

THE CASE OF *'USHR* AND *KHARAJ*

Hanafites have a condition for *zakatability*, which is that land must not be *kharaji* land. If the owner pays *kharaj* for his land, *zakah* must be waived. On the other hand, the majority of scholars believe that Muslims must pay *zakah* on their agriculture, regardless of whether *kharaj* is obligated on the land or not.

'Ushri land

Lands may be classified as either *'ushri*, i.e. lands on whose output *'ushr* (the *zakah* of ten or five percent) is due, or *kharaji*, on which *kharaj* is due.

Abu 'Ubaid lists the following as *'ushri* lands:

First, all lands whose owners accepted Islam, as in Madinah, Yemen, and Bahrain. To this Makkah is added, because although there was brief fighting, the Prophet (p) protected the persons and properties of the Makkans. Second, lands acquired by fighting and distributed among the Muslim conquerors, after one-fifth had been set aside as prescribed by the Qur'an. The distributed four-fifths is considered *'ushri* because ownership has been transferred to Muslims. Third, land not owned by anyone and given by the state to individuals to farm, and fourth, land not in use that is reclaimed by Muslims. These sorts of lands are all mentioned in sayings, and are all *zakatable*, according to the tenets of *zakah* in Qur'an and Sunnah.[161]

Kharaji lands and the origin of their definition

Abu 'Ubaid defines *kharaji* lands as "lands that are either conquered in war, but left in the hands of local farmers instead of being confiscated and distributed among the Muslim conquerors, (like the lands of Iraq, Persia, Syria, Egypt, and North Africa) or land whose owners entered under the authority of the Islamic state as a result of treaties that included a clause to this effect (such as some areas in the southern tip of the Arabian Peninsula, some areas in Persia, and certain Armenian areas). Whatever taxes are imposed on these lands is called *kharaj* and goes to the state budget, to be spent for the general interest of Muslims.[162]

Abu 'Ubaid means by conquered lands, those lends whose people were defeated in war with Muslims. Such lands are treated in accordance with the Qur'an[163] and Sunnah,[164] which require that ownership be transferred to the whole Muslim society, present and future generations, as represented by the Islamic state. This policy was applied en masse at the time of 'Umar, making his era rich in the minute details that arise in application. Jurists use the term "*waqf* for all Muslims" to express the principle that the land becomes a trust for the benefit of all Muslim generations, whereby a tax is levied on it on yearly basis. This tax, called *kharaj*, is like rent of the land paid to the treasury of the state, and is not waived even if ownership of the land is transferred to Muslims or if the users themselves convert to Islam, because of its nature as rent payment.[165]

This policy was applied by 'Umar on the conquered lands in Iraq and Syria, instead of dividing these lands and distributing them among the soldiers as asked by Bilal and a few other Companions. 'Umar provided verses from *surah al Hashr* to support his position: "What God has bestowed on His Apostle (and taken away) from the people of the townships belongs to God, to His Apostle, and to kindred and orphans, the needy and the wayfarer; in order that it may not (merely) make a circuit between the wealthy among you. So take what the Apostle assigns to you, and deny yourselves that which he withholds from you. And fear God, for God is strict in punishment. (Some part is due) to the indigent *Muhajirs*, those who were expelled from their homes and their property while seeking grace from God and (His) good pleasure, and aiding God and His Apostle. Such are indeed the sincere ones."[166] 'Umar argued that according to these verses, God includes all future generations of Muslims in land distribution, and if land is distributed to the present soldiers, nothing will be left for future generations, while if it is kept in trust with the state and a charge imposed on it to benefit the treasury, then even a shepherd in Yemen would receive his share from the state treasury without being undignified.[167] The purpose of this policy is so that wealth "may not merely make a circuit between the wealthy among you." The distribution of the return, called fai' according to these verses, includes the present generation of soldiers, i.e. the migrants and the supporters, as well as all future generations. By this form of distribution, Islam avoids the common capitalist mistake of prefering the interests of the present generation over those of future generations, as well as the mistake of communism of imposing heavy sacrifices on the on present generation for the benefit of development.

It is perhaps for that reason Mu'adh, the great Companion scholars, told 'Umar, "If you distribute the land now, something very undesirable might happen. You will create a class of very rich individuals whose wealth will be inherited by their sons and daughters, and nothing will be left for the future generations who will carry out the responsibility of defending Islam and its society. Please do something that helps present as well as future needs."[168] 'Umar's basic argument, derived from these verses, was that "he must not leave future generations with nothing."[169] Ibn Qudamah says "Khaibar is, to the best of my knowledge, the only conquered land which was distributed among Muslims soldiers. The Messenger of God (p) divided half of its land among Muslims. All that was conquered during the time of 'Umar and his successors, including Syria, Iraq, and Egypt, was not distributed."[170]

Sale of *kharaji* land

The majority of scholars, including Malik, al Shafi'i and Ahmad, believe *kharaji* lands cannot be sold because they are *waqf* (trust). 'Umar questioned 'Utbah bin Farqad because he bought a lot of *kharaji* land, "From whom did you buy it?" "From its owners," 'Utbah answered. When the people in Madinah gathered, including migrants and supporters, 'Umar told 'Utbah, "These are the owners. Did you buy It from them?" He said "No" Then 'Umar replied, "Return it to whomever you bought it from and take back your money."[171]

Some scholars approve of the inheritance and sale of *kharaji* land, provided that the buyers continue paying its *kharaj*. Some others allow purchasing this kind of land only from the original non-Muslim holders. It is reported that Ibn Mas'ud bought a piece of land from a Persian and pledged to pay its *kharaj*.[172]

Ibn Qudamah points out, "Even if purchasing this kind of land is permitted, buyers have to continue the payment of *kharaj* that was imposed on the sellers. This purchase then is actually a transfer of holding the land, without a real transfer of ownership. When Ibn Mas'ud set the condition that the buyer continue paying *kharaj*, he made this contract a form of rent and not a sale."[173]

Kharaj is eternal

It is obvious that *kharaj* lands belong to the whole Muslim nation. A transfer of holding of the land from one person to another cannot be considered a transfer of ownership. *Kharaj* imposed on the land is like a rent paid to the owner, as represented by the Islamic state, which uses this rent to serve public interests, including improving the productivity of *kharaji* lands. If the holders of *kharaji* land became Muslim, or if the holdings transfer to Muslims, *kharaj* remains undisturbed. On this Muslim jurists have no differences, because no one has the authority to waive such a rent that belongs to all Muslim generations.

A question arises about *kharaji* lands which--for any reason--are held by Muslims who are subject to *zakah*. Are these Muslims required to pay *kharaj* and *zakah* simultaneously, or must one of them be waived in order to avoid paying two taxes on the same land? Abu Hanifah and his disciples decide that the output of *kharaji* land is exempt from *zakah*. They set for the *zakatability* of agriculture the condition that the land must not be *kharaji*. Abu 'Ubaid reports from al Laith and Ibn Abi Shaibah from al Shabi and 'Ikrimah that *kharaj* and *'ushr* must not be combined on the same land.[174]

Firstly, Ibn Mas'ud reports from the Prophet (p) " *'Ushr* and *kharaj* must not be due together on a Muslim's land."[175]

Secondly, Abu Hurairah narrates from the Messenger of God, "Iraq will prevent (the payment of dues on) its *dirhams* and measured food, Syria will prevent (the payment of dues on) its measured food and *dinars*, Egypt will prevent (the payment of dues on) its measured food and *dinars*. And you will return to where you started." Abu Hurairah adds, "The Prophet said that three times: my flesh and blood give witness." Reported by Muslim and Abu Daud.[176] This saying, in which the Prophet (p) predicts that in later days people will not pay their dues, indicates that these dues refer to *kharaj* and not *'ushr*, because *'ushr* is only on the output, while *kharaj* can be either money or a given amount of measured food.

Thirdly, Abu 'Ubaid reports from Tariq bin Shihab that 'Umar bin al Khattab wrote regarding a woman who became Muslim in the area of Nahr al Malik,[177] "Give her her land, and she should continue the payment of *kharaj* on it,"[178] indicating that Umar ordered the collection of *kharaj* and not *'ushr* from her.

Fourthly, no political ruler, oppressive or just, is reported to have collected *'ushr* from *kharaj*i lands that are in the hands of Muslims, since 'Umar imposed *kharaj*. This position may be interpreted as a practical *ijma'*.

Fifthly, *kharaj* is imposed on the same principle as *'ushr*, i.e. on arable growing land. If the land is not arable, no *kharaj* or *'ushr* is imposed. Consequently, they may not be imposed concurrently on the some land. This is like owning cattle for the purpose of trading. Even after the passage of a year , *zakah* on livestock and *zakah* on trade assets are not both imposed. This is a unanimous position of Muslims, taken in order to avoid duplication, which is forbidden by the saying, "No duplication in *zakah*."

Sixthly, *kharaj* was originally imposed on conquered land that is left in the hands or pre-Islamic owners, as a form of penalty to the conquered, while *'ushr* is imposed on Muslims as a form of worship and an expression of gratitude to who purifies the person and the property. The two dues are obligated for different reasons and therefore must not be combined.[179]

However, the majority of scholars believe that *'ushr* as a required obligation must not be waived on *kharaji* lands. This opinion is founded on the following evidence:

Firstly, the texts that make *zakah* obligatory on agriculture are general, clear cut, and lack any distinction between the two kinds of land. Examples are the verses, "O ye who believe, spend from the good things ye have acquired and from that which We have produced for you from the earth," and "And give its proper due on the day of its harvest," and the saying (which is agreed upon) "And there is one-tenth obligated on that which the sky waters." *Kharaj* is imposed on the land itself, whether cultivated or not, whether it happens to be in the hands of a Muslim or an unbeliever, while *'ushr* is imposed on the output if it belongs to Muslims.

Secondly, '*ushr* and *kharaj* are two separate dues imposed for different reasons. Nothing precludes their coexistence. The reason for *kharaj* is controlling the land in such a way that offers ability to make use of it, while the reason for '*ushr* is the presence of output. '*Ushr* relates directly to the output of the land, while *kharaj* relates to the liability of the holder. Just like those of *zakah*, the proceeds of '*ushr* are distributed to the eight categories mentioned in the verse "The *sadaqat* are only for the poor . . . ." while the proceeds of *kharaj* are used for salaries of soldiers and civilians and for public interests. With all these differences, there should be no reason why '*ushr* and *kharaj* cannot be levied together on the same land. It is just like paying a rent for a store and *zakah* on inventory. This is similar to the case of a person who, while in the state of *ihram* for pilgrimage, kills an animal that is owned by someone else. This person is required to compensate the owner, in addition to the kaffarah required from him because he or she was in a state of *ihram*.

Thirdly, '*ushr* is obligated by clear texts from Qur'an and Sunnah. It must not be waived because of *kharaj* that came about through *ijtihad*.[180]

Weighing these opinions

The arguments given by the majority of jurists are clear cut and strong, both in their authenticity and their indication. The Hanafites cannot challenge them, and the waiver of *zakah* they suggest is not accepted. Ibn al Mubarak, after looking at this evidence, comments, "Should we leave what God says for what Abu Hanifah says?" The majority of scholars disprove the argument of the Hanafites as follows:

Firstly, the saying "*Ushr* and *kharaj* must not be combined" is according to al Nawawi, false and unanimously graded weak. In its chain, Yahya bin 'Anbasah singly narrates from Abu Hanifah from Hammad from Ibrahim from 'Alqamah from Ibn Mas'ud from the Prophet (p). Al Baihaqi says this saying is narrated by Abu Hanifah from Hammad from Ibrahim as being Ibrahim's own statement. Yahya mistakenly connects it to the Prophet. Yahya is openly known as weak, because he attributes to trustworthy individuals false sayings. Al Suyuti in al La'ali quotes Ibn Habban and Ibn 'Adiy, "This saying is false, narrated by Yahya, who is a liar."[183]

Secondly, al Nawawi says about the saying from Abu Hurairah which begins, "Iraq will prevent . . . .", "There are two famous interpretations of this saying, namely that they will become Muslims and therefore *jizyah* will be eliminated or that there will be so many disasters and so much misery that people will refuse to pay the dues obligated on them. This saying does not mean non-obligation of '*ushr*, because it speaks about *zakah* due on gold and silver. If it implies the elimination of '*ushr*, it must also mean the elimination of all *zakah*.[184]

Thirdly, as for the story or the Persian woman who converted to Islam, *kharaj* was mentioned by 'Umar to make it clear that *kharaj* remains obligated, and is not like *jizyah*, which is eliminated by conversion to Islam. The story does not say anything about '*ushr*. Some scholars also mention that this might be an instruction from 'Umar to the *kharaj* collector, who is usually a different officer from the '*ushr* collector.[185]

Fourthly, the claim that rulers since 'Umar have agreed not to collect *kharaj* and *'ushr* from the same land is defeated by the authentic report that 'Umar bin 'Abd al 'Aziz collected *'ushr* and *kharaj* together. Yahya bin Adam reports that Umar bin Maimun bin Mahran said, "I asked 'Umar bin 'Abd al 'Aziz about a muslim who holds *kharaji* land. 'Umar answered, 'Take *kharaj* from here' as he pointed to the crop with his hand. Shuraik thought 'Umar may not have said exactly that, so he researched until he was informed, then he followed suit."[186] The claim that 'Umar and the Companions did not collect *'ushr* and *kharaj* simultaneously is refuted, because during that time the holders of land in conquered areas were still disbelievers. No one can make the assertion that they did not collect *'ushr* from those who became Muslim.[187]

Fifthly, the claim that *kharaj* and *'ushr* are imposed for the same reason is disproved by the fact that *'ushr* is imposed on crops while *kharaj* is imposed on the land, whether it is cultivated or not. In other words, *kharaj* is imposed for having the ability to use the land, while *'ushr* is imposed for having an output.[188]

Sixthly, the claim that *kharaj* is a punishment for the owner's disbelief is disproved by the similarity between rent and *kharaj*. *Kharaj* is a rent taken for permitting the holder to use the land, like what is called today real estate tax. The *kharaj* payer rents the land in order to cultivate it.[189]

As for the calculation of the payment due as *'ushr* my position is to treat *kharaj* as a debt on the farmer that must be deducted from the output before the calculation of *'ushr*.

What has happened to *kharaji* land today

Let us look at a map of the Muslim world today to see what has happened to *kharaji* lands in Egypt, Syria, Iraq, etc. Are they still kharaji?

Many late Hanafite jurists declare that the lands of Syria and Egypt are no longer *kharaji*, because upon the deaths of their owners those lands were returned to the treasury, and any selling that took place by the state treasury is complete and final, without *kharaj*.[190] Accordingly, if *kharaj* is eliminated, *'ushr* is obligated as the *zakah* on Muslim agriculture. Real estate taxes on agricultural land are the common practice of all modern states, regardless of whether the land is *'ushri* or *kharaji*. Consequently, the only suitable solution is to impose *'ushr* on all land owned by Muslims if the output reaches *nisab*, in addition to the real estate tax levied on all lands.

Contemporary comments on combination of *'ushr* and *kharaj*

Dr. Ahmad Thabit Awaidah says "We are supposed to refer to the distinction Muslims made between agricultural income and real estate income when they separated *kharaj* from *zakah*. This distinction constitutes the base for the contemporary distinction of the source of income in taxation. Many countries today have taxes on real estate income different from the taxes on agricultural income. The majority of jurists consider *kharaj* a tax on the real estate income, while *zakah* on crops is like a tax on the agricultural income. A Muslim who farms land owned by a non-Muslim must pay *zakah* on his output, in addition to *kharaj* paid by the owner. By the same token, a Muslim who owns and farms *kharaj* land must pay *'ushr* as well as *kharaj*."[191]

After disproving the evidence of the Hanafites and supporting the majority's view, the late Shaikh Mahmud Shaltut and Muhammad al Sayes write, "Once we note that *'ushr* is a religious obligation on Muslims and *kharaj* is an obligation by *ijtihad* created to finance the needs of the Muslim community, we can understand the state's right to impose taxes on Muslims and non-Muslims in order to satisfy public needs, in addition to what God imposed on Muslims. The levying of *kharaj* does not mean an exemption from *zakah*, which is obligated by Qur'an and Sunnah."[192]

Footnotes

1. *Sura al A'raf,* 7:10.

2. See *al 'Ilm Yad'u Ila al Iman,* (Knowledge Calls for Faith) translated by Muhammad Salih al Falaki.

3. *Sura al Waqi'ah,* 56:63-67.

4. *Sura al Hijr,* 15:19-22.

5. *Sura 'Abasa,* 80:24-32.

6. *Sura Ya-Sin,* 36:33-35.

7. This is famous among Hanafites. Strangely enough, some Hanafites claim that calling it *zakah* is only allegoric, or in accordance with the view of the two disciples who require in *'ushr* the conditions of *nisab* and storability that apply on *zakah*. This is in opposition to Abu Hanifah. Ibn al Humam says "That does not matter. There is no doubt that *'ushr* is *zakah*, since it is spent the same way. The matter is that certain kinds of *zakah* require certain conditions, which are not necessary for other kinds." See *Fatah al Qadir,* Vol. 2, p. 2.

8. *Sura al Baqarah,* 2:267.

9. *Ahkam al Qur'an,* by al Jassas, Vol. 1, p, 543.

10. *Sura al An'am,* 6:141.

11. *Commentary of al Tabari,* Vol. 12, pp. 158-161.

12. *Commentary of al Qurtubi,* Vol. 7, p. 99.

13. *Bada'i al Sana'i ,* Vol. 2, p. 53.

14 *Al Tabari,* Vol. 12, pp. 168-170.

15.   *Ibid.*, pp. 170-173.

16.   *Al Muwafaqat*, Vol. 3, p. 75.

17.   *I'lam al Muwaqqi'in,* Vol. 1, pp. 28-29, al Muniriyah Print.

18.   *Commentary of Ibn Kathir*, Vol. 2, p. 182.

19.   *Commentary of al Futuhat al Iahiyah*, with *Hashiyat al Jamal* Vol. 2, p. 99, al Halabi Print.

20.   The author of al Muntaqa says it is reported by the group, except for Muslim. See *Nail al Awtar*, Vol. 4, p. 139-140, Uthmaniyah Print.

21.   Reported by Ahmad, Muslim, al Nasa'i and Abu Daud, see *Ibid.*

22.   *Bada'i al Sana'i*, Vol. 2, p, 54.

23.   *Al Muhalla*, Vol. 5, p. 209 plus.

24.   *Al Mughni*, Vol. 2, p. 631.

25.   Al Shawkani says Muhammad bin 'Ubaid Allah al Ruzami is in its chain, and he is disregarded. See *Nail al Awtar*, Vol. 4, p. 143.

26.   Al Hafiz says it is reported by al Tabarani and al Hakim (see *Bulugh al Maram*, p. 122). The author of *al Talkhis* writes that al Baihaqa says, "Its narrators are trustworthy, and the saying is connected to the Prophet," The author of *al Dirayah* writes on page 174, "In the chain there is Yahya bin Talhah, about whom people differ. This saying, however, is the best we have on this subject." The author of *al Mirqat*, Vol. 3, p.39, adds, "it is not agreed upon whether the saying is connected to the Messenger or not." See also *al kharaj*, by Yahya bin Adam, p. 153, *al Sunan al Kubra*, Vol. 4, p. 125, *Nasb al Rayah*, Vol. 2, p. 319, and *Al Muhalla*, Vol. 5, p, 221.

27.   *Al Muwatta*, Vol. 1, p. 276.

28.   Al Qurtubi in his commentary quotes these views, Vol. 7, p. 103.

29.   *Sharh al Kharashi on Khalil* with *Hashiyat al 'Adawi*, Vol. 2, p. 168.

30.   *Sura al An'am*, 6:141.

31.   *Al Qurtubi, op cit.*

32.   *Al Muwatta*, Vol. 1, p. 272. Malik says the one-tenth is taken from olives after they are squeezed, provided that the crop reaches five *wasq*.

33.   *Al Qurtubi, op. cit.*

34.   *Al Muhadhdhab* with *al Majmu*, Vol. 5, p. 493.

35. *Sharh al Risalah*, by Zarruq, Vol. 1, p. 329.

36. Vol. 2, pp. 690-692.

37. This is part of the saying reported by Abu Daud and Ibn Majah as stated in *al Muntaqa*. Al Shawkani says al Hakim grades it correct according to the criteria of al Bukhari and Muslim, but in its chain, 'Ata' narrates from Mu'adh. In fact, he did not hear from Mu'adh.

38. *Nasb al Rayah*. Vol. 2, p. 384.

39. *Al Mughni*, Vol. 2, p. 692.

40. *Al Hidayah* with *al Fath*, Vol. 2, pp. 2-5. The author of *al Fath*, p. 2, says nothing came about medicines or tree sap. But this must be applied only to the case where medicinal plants and products from tree trunks are not produced on a commercial scale. In such cases they would be *zakatable*.

41. *Al Muhalla*, Vol. 5, p. 212-213.

42. Al Razi says in his commentary, Vol. 7, p. 65, "Apparently the verse indicates the obligation of *zakah* on all that is produced by the earth, in accordance with the view of Abu Hanifah. His use of this verse makes his argument very strong. His opponents, however, restrict the general implication of this verse by the saying of the Prophet (p), 'No *zakah* is obligated on vegetables.' But I think this saying is not strong enough to restrict the general implication of a verse. This leaves Abu Hanifah's argument very difficult to challenge."

43. *Bada'i al Sana'i*, Vol. 2, p. 59.

44. I find no substantial difference between the opinion of Abu Hanifah and that of the mentioned scholars, because the exception Abu Hanifah makes for firewood, cane, and grass does not really make him a restrictor of the general concept of *zakah* on what is produced by the earth through agriculture, since it is a very minor exception.

45. *Al Mirqat*, Vol. 3, p. 39.

46. *Ibid*, Vol. 4, p. 153.

47. *Al Mughni* with *al Sharh al Katir*, Vol. 2, p. 551.

48. *Ahkam al Qur'an*, part 2, p. 749-752.

49. *Sharh al Tirmidhi*, Vol. 3, p. 135.

50. *Sura al Rahman*, 55:68.

51. *Sura 'Abbas*, 80:25-31.

52. See the comment of al Hafiz in *al Talkhis*, p. 179, also *Fath al Qadir*, Vol. 2, p. 3,

Mustafa Muhammad print. Al Haithami mentions this saying in *Majma' al Zawa'id* connected to the Prophet from Talhah, and says, "Al Tabarani adds it in *al Awsat* and *al Batra*. The chain has al Harith bin Nabhan, who is disregarded. Ibn 'Adi abstains from giving an opinion about him, Vol. 3, pp. 68-69.

53. Chapter "*Zakah*", section title, "Texts on the subject of *zakah* on vegetables." See the correct collection of al Tirmidhi with *Sharh Ibn 'Arabi*, p. 132-133.

54. *Bada'i al Sana'i*, Vol. 2, p. 59.

55. *Al kharaj* by Yahya bin Adam, p. 1.

56. *Al Amwal*, p. 504.

57. *Ibid*, p. 496.

58. *Al Kharaj*, op. cit, p. 152.

59. *Sharh al Risalah,* by Ibn Naji, Vol. 1, pp. 320-321.

60. *Al Mughni*, Vol. 2, p. 695.

61. The author of *al Muntaqa* says it is reported by the group, from Abu Sa'id.

62. *Al Mughni, ibid.*

63. *Al kharaj*, p. 144.

65. *Ibid*, p. 145; the saying is weak.

66. *Al Muhalla*, Vol. 5, p. 112.

67. *Ibid*, p. 113, and *Fath al Qadir*, Vol. 2, p. 3.

68. *Al Muhalla*, p. 241.

69. *Nail al Awtar*, Vol. 4, p. 151.

70. *Al Bahr al Zakhkhar*, Vol. 2, p. 169.

71. *Nail al Awtar*, op. cit.

72. *I'lam al Muwaqqi'in*, Vol. 3, pp. 229-230.

73. *Al Mughni*, Vol. 2, p. 695-696.

74. Reported by Ibn Majah from Jabir. Its chain is weak. Also reported by Abu Daud, al Nasa'i, and Ibn Majah through Abu al Bakhtari from Abu Sa'id, connected to the Prophet. This is interruptes because Abu al Bakhtari did not hear from Abu *sa'id*, as stated by al Bukhari. He was not even a contemporary of Abu *sa'id*, according to

Abu Hatim. Al Daraqutni reports the saying from 'A'ishah, but it is also weak. Al Hafiz shows the weakness of all chains of this saying in *al Talkhis*, p. 180, India print.

75. *Al Majmu'*, Vol. 5, p. 447.

76. *Sa'* is also needed in determining, *kaffarah* for a broken oath, and the recompense in pilgrimage.

77. Reported by Ahmad, Muslim, al Tirmidhi, and Ibn Majah from Safinah from the Prophet. Al Tirmidhi adds, "There are also reports on the same from 'A'ishah, Jabir, and Anas." See *Sunan al Tirmidhi*, edited by Ahmad Shakir, Vol. 1, p. 84.

78. Al Hafiz says on page 183 of *al Talkhis* that it is reported by al Bazzar, who grades it "strange." Also reported by Abu Daud and al Nasa'i, from Taus from Ibn 'Umar. This saying is graded correct by Ibn Habban, al Daraqutni al Nawawi, and Abu al Fath al Qashiri.

79. *Bada'i al Sana'i*, Vol. 2, p. 73.

80. These sayings are mentioned in *al Amwal*, pp. 514-516. Abu 'Ubaid explains that the Prophet (p) used to bathe sometimes with one *sa'* full of water and sometimes with eight *ratl*. He also used to make ablution sometimes with one *mudd* and other times two *ratl*. These sayings thus talk about different occasions.

81. *Al Muhalla*, Vol. 5, p. 246.

82. *Al Sunan al Kubra*, by al Baihaqi, Vol. 4, p. 171.

83. *Ibid*. It seems that a story similar to that of Abu Yusuf was repeated with some other Madinan. Al Darnqutni reports from Ishaq al Razi, "I asked Malik bin Anas about the size of the *sa'* of the Prophet. He said, 'It is five and one-third Baghdadi *ratls*; I personally verified it.' I mentioned to him that he differs with Abu Hanifah, who says it is eight *ratl*. Malik was very angered and told people sitting around, 'Bring the *sa'* of your grandfather, and you bring the *sa'* of your uncle, and you bring the *sa'* of your grandmother; etc." Ishaq says "Several *sa'*s were brought by the people. Then Malik asked them, 'What do you remember about these?' One said, 'My father told me that his father used this *sa'* in measuring for the Prophet.' Another said, 'My father told me that his mother did the same,' etc. Malik said, 'I verified these measures and found them equal to five and one-third *ratl*,'" Al Daraqutni and al Baihaqi report this story via a good chain, according to al Shawkani's *Nail al Awtar*, Vol. 4, p. 196.

84. *Al Mughni*, Vol. 3, p. 59.

85. *Sharh Fath al Qadir*, Vol. 2, p. 42.

86. *Al Qawa'id al Nuraniyah*, by Ibn Taimiyah, p. 89.

87. *Al kharaj fi al Dawlah al Islamiyah* , by Dia' al Din al Rayes, first printing, p, 301, as

quoted from the article of 'Ali Mubarak titled "Al Mizan fi al Aqisah wa al Awzan," Amiriyah print, pp. 86-88.

88. *Ibid.*

89. *Ibid*, pp. 302-303.

90. *Ibid.*

91. *Al Mughni*, Vol. 2, p. 701.

92. *Al kharaj*, pp. 304-305.

93. *Hashiat al 'Udul ala Sharh al Kharashi,* Vol. 2, p. 168.

94. *Bada'i al Sana'i,* Vol. 2, p. 61.

95. *Al Bahr al Zakhkhar*, Vol. 2, p. 170.

96. *Al Mughni*, Vol. 2, p. 697.

97. *Ibid*, pp. 697-698.

98. *Al Wajiz* and its commentary, printed with *al Majmu'*, Vol. 5, p. 568.

99. Al Hafiz writes on p. 18 of *al Talkhis*, that this is reported by al Bukhari, Ibn Habban, Abu Daud, al Nasa'i, and Ibn al Jarud. Muslim reports the same from Jabir, al Tirmidhi, and Ibn Majah from Abu Hurrirah, and al Nasa'i and Ibn Majah from Mu'adh.

100. Also reported by Ahmad, Abu Daud, and al Nasa'i. See *Nail al Awtar*, Vol.4, p. 139.

101. *Al Talkhis*, p. 181.

102. Reported by Ibn Majah, chapter on *sadaqah* on grain and fruit, from Mu'adh; see *Nasb al Rayah*, Vol. 2, p. 385.

103. Al Nawawi, *al Rawdah,* Vol. 2, p. 244.

104. *Al Mughni*, Vol. 2, p. 578.

105. *Al Rawdah*, Vol. 2, p. 245.

106. *Al Mughni, op. cit.*

107. The other view is to make it proportionate to the number of watering. But the opinion mentioned in the text is more acceptable because of the difficulty involved in keeping records of watering. See *al Mughni*, Vol. 2, p. 700.

108. *Al Mughni, ibid.*

109. *Ibid*, p. 699.

110. *Al Sharh al Kabir* with *al Majmu'*, Vol. 5, p. 578.

111. *Ma'alim al sunan*, Vol. 2, p. 207.

112. *Ibid*, and *al Rawdah*, Vol. 2, p. 244.

113. *Al Muhadhdhab* with *al Majmu'*, Vol. 5, p. 477.

114. *Ma'alim*, Vol. 2, p. 210.

115. *Al Amwal*, pp. 492-493.

116. Reported by Abu Daud, al Tirmidhi, and Ibn Majah. It is interrupted since *sa'id* bin al Musayib did not hear from 'Attab. But it is strengthened by other sayings and by the practice of the Companions and the majority of scholars, according to al Nawawi. See *al Talkhis*, p. 181.

117. Reported by Abu Daud, al Nasa'i, al Tirmidhi, Ibn Habban and al Daraqutni. It is also interrupted. See *ibid*.

118. Agreed upon as narrated by Abu Hamid al Sa'idi. *Ibid*.

119. In its chain is an unknown man. See al Mundhiri, *Mukhtasar al Sunan*, Vol. 2, p. 213.

120. Reported by the five, not including Ibn Majah. Also reported by Ibn Habban, al Hakim in his *al Mustadrak* Vol. 1, p. 402, Abu 'Ubaid in *al Amwal*, p. 485, al Baihaqi in *al Sunan*, Vol. 4, p. 123, and Ibn Hazm in *al Muhalla*, Vol. 5, p. 255. Abu Daud and al Mundhiri are silent about its grade, while Ibn Habban and al Hakim grade it correct. This is agreeably followed by al Dhahabi, Al Tirmidhi adds, "Most scholars agree with its content." See *Mukhtasar al Sunan*, Vol. 2, p. 213.

121. *Ma'alim al Sunan*. Vol. 2, p. 212.

122. *Al Mughni*, Vol. 2, p. 707.

123. *Al Amwal*, pp. 494-495.

124. *Al Muhalla*, Vol. 5, p. 256.

125. *Al Mughni*, Vol. 2, pp. 710-711.

126. *Al Bahr al Zakhkhar*, Vol. 2, p. 172.

127. Mentioned in *Nail al Awtar*, Vol. 2, p. 144. Ibn Lahi'ah is in its chain.

128. *Al Amwal*, p. 487. Also reported by al Tahawi, p. 315, with a good chain, as "Make it

attenuated in charging al *sadaqat*, since there are trees left for charity and for passers-by." See *Faid al Bari,* Vol. 3, p. 47.

129. *Al Amwal,* p. 487.

130. Reported by al Hakim in brief, Vol. 1, pp. 402-403, and Ibn Hazm, *al Muhalla,* Vol. 5, p. 259.

131. *Al Muhalla,* Vol. 5, p. 260.

132. *Al Mughni,* Vol. 2, pp. 709-710.

133. *Bidayat al Mujtahid,* Vol. 1, and *Bada'i al Sana'i,* Vol. 2, p. 64.

134. *Sharh al Tirmidhi,* Vol. 3, p. 143.

135. *Sura al Baqarah,* 2:286.

136. *Al Muhalla,* Vol. 5, p. 259.

137. In *al Rawdah,* Vol. 2, p, 250, al Nawawi says, "This is the old opinion," mentioned also in *al Buaiti* and quoted by al Baihaqi.

138. *Al Amwal,* p. 509.

139. *Al Kharaj,* p. 162. In the commentary, Shaikh Ahmad Shakir writes, "its chain is correct."

140. *Al Amwal,* p. 509

141. *Al Amwal,* p. 163.

142. *Al Mughni,* Vol. 2, p. 727.

143. *Al Amwal,* p. 510.

144. *Al Kharaj,* op. cit.

145. *Al Amwal,* p. 88.

146. *Al Mughni, ibid.*

147. *Al Kharaj,* p. 161.

148. *Al Muhalla,* Vol. 5, p. 258.

149. *Al Kharaj,* p. 161, and also reported by Ibn Abi Shaibah, Vol. 4, p. 23, Multan print.
150. *Sharh al Tirmidhi,* Vol. 3, p. 143.

151. *Fath al Qadir,* Vol. 2, pp. 8-9.

152. Correct sayings come in support of this brotherly practice: "The person who has a piece of land must cultivate it himself or give it free to his brother to do so." Some early scholars consider this obligatory. Ibn 'Abbas sees this saying as encouragement and not obligation. See al Qardawi, *al Halal wa al Haram*, pp. 228-229, fourth printing.

153. *Al Mughni*, Vol. 2, p. 728.

154. *Ibid*.

155. *Ibid*.

156. *Fath al Qadir*, Vol. 2, p. 8.

157. *Al Kharaj*, by Yahya bin Adam, p. 172. The latter reports it from al Hasan bin 'Amarah, who is disregarded.

158. *Bidayat al Mujtahid*, Vol. 1, p. 239.

159. *Al Mughni*, Vol. 2, p. 728.

160. *Sharh al Rafi'i al Kabir*, with al Majmu', Vol. 5, p. 566.

161. *Al Amwal*, pp. 512-513.

162. *Al Amwal*, pp. 513-514 and al *kharaj* by Abu Yusuf, p. 69.

163. *Sura al Hashr*, 59:7-11 speaks about the distribution of *fai'*. 'Umar uses these verses as evidence for requiring holding the land as trust for future Muslim generations.

164. The Prophet distributed half the land of Khaibar among the soldiers and retained the other half as a trust for the public interests of Muslims.

165. *Al Mughni*, Vol. 2, p. 716.

166. *Sura al Hashr*, 59:7-9.

167. *Al Kharaj*, by Abu Yusuf, pp. 23-24.

168. *Al Amwal*, p. 59.

169. *Ibid*, p. 58.

170. *Al Mughni*, Vol. 2, p. 716.

171. *Ibid*, p. 821.

172. *Ibid*, p. 720.

173. *Ibid*, p. 722.

174. *Al Amwal*, p. 91, and *al Musannaf*, Vol. 3, p. 201, Hyderabad print.

175. The author of *Fath al Qadir*, Vol. 2, p. 14, says "it is reported by Abu Hanifah from Hammad from Ibrahim from 'Alqamah from Ibn Mas'ud, connected to the Prophet(p)."

176. Shaikh Ahmad Shakir writes in his commentary on *al Muhalla*, Vol. 5, p. 247, "It is reported by Yahya bin Adam in *al Kharaj*, number 227, Muslim Vol. 3, p. 365, Abu Daud Vol. 3, p. 129, and Ibn Jarud, p. 499."

177. Nahr al Malik is a big orchard near Baghdad.

178. *Al Amwal*, p. 87.

179. *Ahkam al Qur'an*, by al Jassas, Vol. 3, pp. 17-19.

180. *Al Majmu'* Vol. 2, pp, 549-550.

181. *Al Mughni*, Vol. 2, p.. 726.

182. *Al Majmu'*, Vol. 5, pp. 550-553.

183. *Al La'ali' al Masnuah*, by al Suyuti, Vol. 2, p. 70.

184. *Al Majmu'*, Vol. 5, pp. 554-558, and also *al Amwal*, pp. 78-88.

185. *Al Majmu'*, *ibid*.

186. *Al Kharaj* of Ibn Adam, p. 165.

187. *Al Muhalla*, Vol. 2, p. 247.

188. *Al Majmu'*, Vol. 5, pp. 558-559.

189. *Al Mughni*, Vol. 2, p. 726.

190. *Al Bahr al Ra'iq*, Vol. 5, p. 115.

191. From a lecture, "Islam Laid Down the Foundations of Modern Taxation" by Dr. Ahmad 'Awaidah in *al Mawsim al Thaqafi al Awwal li Muhadarat al Azhar*, 1959, p. 302.

192. *Muqaranat al Madhahib* by Muhammad al Sayes and Mahmud Shaltut, p. 54.

CHAPTER SIX

ZAKAH ON HONEY AND ANIMAL PRODUCTS

Section 1: *Zakah* on honey according to those who obligate it and those who do not

Section 2: The obligated rate

Section 3: *Nisab* of honey

Section 4: Animal products such as dairy products, silk, etc.

SECTION ONE

THE OBLIGATORS AND PREVENTORS OF *ZAKAH* ON HONEY

Introduction

Honey is one of the goods bestowed by God on humanity as a food, medicine, and sweet. God mentions it as a sign of His grace to human beings in a *sura* that is named after bees, *sura al Nahl.* God says "And thy Lord taught the bee to build its cells in hills, on trees, and in people's habitation, then to eat of all the produce (of the earth) and find with skill the spacious paths of its Lord: There issues from within their bodies a drink of varying colors, wherein is healing for men; verily in this is a Sign for those who give thought."[1]

Those who believe honey is *zakatable*

Abu Hanifah and his disciples say that *zakah* is obligated on honey, provided that the beehives are not located on *kharaji* land. This is an extension of their principle that *kharaj* and *'ushr* are not concurrent. *Zakah* is also obligated on honey produced on non-arable land, which is by implication non-*zakatable*.[2] This is also the opinion of Ahmad. Al Athram says Ahmad was asked whether he believes that honey is *zakatable*, and answered. "Yes indeed; 'Umar collected *zakah* on honey." Al Athram then asked whether honey growers contribute the amount of *zakah* voluntarily. Ahmad answered, "No, it was imposed on them."[3]

This view is shared by Makhul, al Zuhri, Sulaiman bin Musa, al Awza'i, and Ishaq.[4] The authorof *al Bahr* also attributes it to 'Umar, Ibn 'Abbas, 'Umar bin 'Abd al Aziz, al Hadi, al Mu'ayad bi Allaah, and a narration to al Shafi'i. Al Tirmidhi mentions that most scholars accept this view. This is challenged by Ibn 'Abd al Barr, who asserts the opposite is true.[5]

Evidence for this view

This opinion is supported by two groups of evidence: reports from the Prophet and the Companions, and rationale and analogy. Firstly, the texts:

A. 'Amr bin Shu'aib, from his father from his grandfather, narrates that the Prophet (p) "collected the one-tenth due from honey." Reported by Ibn Majah. Al Daraqutni says "This is narrated from 'Abd al Rahman bin al Harith and Ibn Lahi'ah from 'Amr as linked to the Prophet, and from Yahya bin Sa'id al Ansari from 'Amr as mursal." Al Hafiz notes that this is the problem with this saying, especially since 'Abd al Rahman and Ibn Lahi'ah are not known as accurate. It is noted that 'Amr bin al Harith, who is trustworthy, and Usamah bin Zaid also narrate the same from 'Amr bin Shu'aib, as reported by Ibn Majah and others.[6]

Abu Daud and Al Nasa'i report that Hilal, from Bani Mat'an, used to pay the Prophet (p) the one-tenth due on the beehives be had, and had the Prophet protect a valley known as Salabah for him. When 'Umar became the head of state, Sufian bin Wahb wrote him about this. 'Umar replied, "As long as Hilal gives you that which he was giving the Messenger of God, the one-tenth due on his honey, then keep protecting Salabah for him. If he does not, then what is in that valley is for everybody." Al Hafiz in *al Fath* says the chain of this saying is correct up to 'Amr bin Shu'aib. 'Amr's record is strong, at least when he is not opposed by stronger narrators.[7]

B. It is reported from Sulaiman bin Musa that Abu Sayarah al Muta'i told the Messenger of God "'I have bees.' The Prophet answered, 'Pay the one-tenth due.' I said, O Messenger of God, reserve for me its mountain." The Prophet then protected that mountain for me." Reported by Ahmad and Ibn Majah.[8]

C. Al Baihaqi reports from Sa'd bin Abi Dhubab, "The Prophet (p) employed him (for collecting *zakah*) on his clan. He ordered people to pay the one-tenth due on honey, then brought it to 'Umar, who sold the honey and added its value to the *zakah* funds of Muslims." In the chain of this saying there is Munir bin 'Abd Allah, who is graded weak by al Bukhari and others. In another version, Sa'd tells his clan "There is no good in wealth that is not *zakated*." He continues, "I took out of each ten containers one container and brought it to 'Umar, who put it with the *zakah* funds of Muslims." This version is reported by Sa'id in his *Sunan*.[10] Al Athram reports from him that 'Umar commanded him to collect ten percent from honey.[11]

D. Al Tirmidhi reports from Ibn 'Umar that the Messenger of God (p) said, "On honey, one out of each ten jars is obligated." However, in its chain there is Sadaqah al Samin, who had a weak memory and is disagreed with.

Although all these sayings and stories are not free from critics, they support each other, indicating that there is substance to the ruling on honey. Ibn al Qayyim comments, "Ahmad and his group believe that honey is *zakatable* on the basis that these sayings strengthen each other because they have different sources and chains. Abu Hatim al Razi was asked about the narration of 'Abd Allah, Munir's father, from Sa'd bin Abi Dhubab, and answered that it was correct."[12]

Secondly, the rationale:

The *zakatability* of honey is further supported by reasoning and analogy. Since honey is derived from flowers, is not perishable, can be measured, and its cost is very low, it must be *zakatable* like grains and dates.[13] Abu Hanifah believes that honey on *'ushri* land is *zakatable*, in contrast to honey produced on *kharaji* land. This is based on his opinion that the output of *kharaji* land is not *zakatable*. Ahmad makes no such distinction.[14]

Those who consider honey non-*zakatable*

Malik, al Shafi'i, Ibn Abi Laila, al Hasan bin Abi Salih, and Ibn al Mundhir believe that honey is not *zakatable*, based on the lack of any strong saying or *ijma'* on the matter, and the similarity between honey and milk, which is unanimously not *zakatable*.

The view of Abu 'Ubaid

Abu 'Ubaid seems to have taken a position in the middle. After mentioning the two opinions, he comments, "It seems preferable that producers of honey be encouraged to pay *zakah*, because they may be sinning if they do not pay it. But they should not be obligated to do so, and those who prevent *zakah* on honey must not be fought the way the preventors of other *zakah* can be fought. There is no correct tradition from the Messenger on this subject, nor is honey mentioned in his written ordinances on *zakah*. If *zakah* on honey was like other forms of *zakah*, we would have some text that documents its conditions, minimum exemption, and the date of collection. Accepting its payment, as 'Umar did when *zakah* of honey was brought to him, is another issue. The state must accept this *zakah* when paid by producers."[16]

A defense of the view that honey is *zakatable*

My personal conclusion is that honey, like any other crop, is produced for profit and must therefore be *zakatable*. This is based on the following:

A. The general texts do not make a distinction between one sort of wealth and the other, such as the verses "Out of their wealth take *zakah*," "Spend out of the good things you have earned and out of what We have produced for you from the earth," and "Spend out of what We have given you as subsistence," etc.

B. There is an analogy to grains and fruits that are *zakatable*. The output of farming is like the output of the beehives, and must be treated equally.

C. The sayings and stories that deal with honey in specific, which, although they are criticized, support each other, as stated by Ibn al Qayim. That is perhaps why al Tirmidhi does not negate their authenticity but says, "Nothing of importance is authentically reported from the Prophet on this issue."[17] This statement implies that small things may have been reported. Al Tirmirdhi continues, "But this is the view of most scholars."[18]

Al Shawkani, in *al Dur al Bahiyah*, selects the view that honey is *zakatable*, saying, "A one-tenth due is obligated on honey." In his commentary, Siddiq Hasan Khan supports this view, noting that "the sayings, taken together, do not fall short of substantiating the *zakatability*."[19] The argument that honey, being a liquid produced by animals, is not *zakatable* by analogy to milk, is refuted on the basis that milk is in principle *zakatable* through *zakah* paid on livestock, while bees are not charged anything, so the similarity requires that honey be *zakated*.[20]

SECTION TWO

THE RATIO OF *ZAKAH* ON HONEY

All those who obligate *zakah* on honey agree that the ratio is ten percent, based on the texts reported on the issue and in analogy to fruits and grains.[21] As for consideration of production costs, Abu 'Ubaid reports that 'Umar said honey produced in valleys and plains is *zakatable* at ten percent, while honey produced in mountains is *zakatable* at five percent.[22] This is apparently in consideration of production costs. Al Nasir from Ahl al Bait disagrees, arguing that the rate must be one-fifth, as in the case of *fai'* because honey is not measurable, nor does it come from the earth.[23] He is answered that honey is similar to fruits, because like fruits, 'it came from trees' (the hector). Moreover, one-tenth is indicated by the texts.[24] I think ten percent should be the rate, but it must apply to the net income from honey after deduction of production costs, as with grains and fruits.

SECTION THREE

NISAB OF HONEY

We have no reports about the *nisab* of honey, so people differ on it. Abu Hanifah argues that there is no *nisab*, as with grains and fruits.[25] Abu Yusuf considers *nisab* to be the value of five *wasq* of the cheapest grain, such as barley, in accordance with his view of considering the value of the lowest measurable *nisab* applicable to products that are not measurable. There is also a report from him that *nisab* is ten *ratl*.[25] There are several narrations from Muhammad which set *nisab* at five *faraq*, five *man*, or five *qurbah*, following his rule of using five units usually used for items not mentioned in sayings. One *faraq* is thirty-six *ratl*, one man is two ratl, and one *qurbah* is one hundred *ratl*. There is also a report from Ahmad that *nisab* is ten faraq, attributed to 'Umar. It is reported from Ahmad that one *faraq* is sixteen *ratl*.

My personal opinion is to estimate the value of five *wasq* of an average grain, such as wheat, since it is kind of an average universal food. The Prophet made five *wasq nisab* in grain and fruits, and honey must be treated by analogy. It is by analogy that the rate is determined at one-tenth, so why not determine *nisab* on the same basis of value, especially since considering the value of the lowest grain is not fair to *zakah* payers?

SECTION FOUR

ANIMAL PRODUCTS LIKE SILK AND MILK

Today many industries revolve around animal products like milk, silk, eggs, and meat. Most of these were not large-scale businesses in the time of the Prophet, the Companions, and the great scholars. The result is that we have no reports about these products. One can derive an answer to the question of the *zakatability* of these products from the reasons cited by jurists to establish *zakah* on honey and to exempt the milk of pastured animals from *zakah*. The main reason cited is that the source of milk, livestock, is *zakatable*, while the source of honey is not. This implies that all products whose sources are not *zakatable* are themselves *zakatable*. Therefore, milk and other products of non-*zakatable* fed livestock are *zakatable*, like honey. Each of these is an animal product where the animal is not *zakatable*.

I believe that animal products must be *zakated* at ten percent of the net output unless the animals themselves are considered trade assets. The rule is that anything whose source is not *zakatable* must be *zakated* as an output, like crops with respect to land, honey with respect to bees, dairy products with respect to livestock, eggs with respect to poultry, and silk with respect to the silkworm. This is the opinion of Yahya, a Shi'ite, who obligates *zakah* on silk.[26]

Some jurists treat non-pastured animals used for their products and reproduction like trade assets and obligate a one-fourth of one-tenth due on both the principal and growth. This is reported from some Zaidi jurists such as al Hadi, al Mu'ayad, and others. A person who buys a horse for breeding or a cow for its products is treated as a merchant and *zakated* the *zakah* on trade assets.[27] This is not restricted to producing animals, but to any asset that is used for business, such as houses and buildings owned for the purpose or renting. This issue will be discussed in detail in chapter eight of this part.

Footnotes

1.   *Sura al Nahl,* 16:68-69.

2.   *Al Hidayah* with *Fath al Qadir,* Vol. 2, pp. 5-7 and *Radd al Muhtar,* Vol. 2, pp. 604-605.

3.   *Al Mughni,* Vol. 2, p. 713.

4.   *Ibid,* and *Ma'alim al Sunan,* Vol. 2, p. 209.

5.   *Nail al Awtar,* Vol. 4, p. 146. There are different reports "from 'Umar bin 'Abd al 'Aziz. Al Bukhari, Ibn Abi Shaibah, and 'Abd al Razzaq mention that he says, "*Zakah* is not obligatory on honey." 'Abd al Razzaq also reports that he believes *zakah* is obligated, but via a weak chain, as stated by al Hafiz in *al Fath.*

6.   *Mukhtasar al Sunan*, Vol. 2, p, 209-210.

7.   *Fath al Bari*, Vol. 3, p. 221. Al Hafiz mentions a report by 'Abd al Razzaq from 'Umar bin 'Abd al 'Aziz indicating that Hilal gave that *zakah* voluntarily. Al Hafiz adds that the chain of the first saying is stronger, but it is argued that Hilal's payment was in exchange for protecting property, as indicated by the letter of 'Umar bin al Khattab.

8.   Mentioned in *al Muntaqa* from them both. Al Shawkani says "This is also reported by Abu Daud and al Baihaqi, but is interrupted because Sulaiman did not meet any of the Companions, as stated by al Bukhari. *Nail al Awtar*, Vol. 4, p. 146 and al Talkhis, p. 180.

9.   *Al Talkhis*, p. 180.

10. *Al Mughni*, Vol. 2, p. 715.

11. *Ibid*, p. 714.

12. *Zad al Ma'ad*, Vol. 1, p. 312. The saying is from Munir bin "Abd Allah from his father from Sa'd bin Abi Dhubab.

13. *Ibid*, p. 314.

14. *Ibid*.

15. *Al Mughni*, Vol. 2, p. 713.

16. *Al Amwal*, p. 506-507.

17. *Sharh Sahih al Tirmidhi* by Ibn al 'Arabi, Vol. 2, p. 123.

18. *Ibid*.

19. *Al Rawdah al Nadiyah*, Vol. 1, p. 200.

20. *Al Mughni*, Vol. 2, p. 714.

21. *Ibid*, p. 713.

22. *Al Amwal*, p. 498.

23. *Al Bahr al Zakhkhar*, Vol. 1, p. 174.

24. *Ibid*.

25. *Bada'i al Sana'i*, Vol. 1, p. 61.

26. *Al Bahr al Zakhkhar*, Vol. 1, p. 173.

27. *Sharh al Azhar*, Vol. 1, p. 475.

CHAPTER SEVEN

ZAKAH ON MINERALS AND SEA PRODUCTS

Prologue

PROLOGUE

MINERALS, BURIED TREASURES, AND *RIKAZ*

Ibn al Athir writes in *al Nihayah* "minerals are the jewels extracted from the earth, like gold, silver, copper, and others."[1] Ibn al Humam says "The root of the word *ma'dan* (Arabic for mineral) means to stay or reside." *Ma'adin* (minerals) are called so because they stand still in the earth. Buried treasures are the wealth put in the earth by human beings. *Rikaz* means both minerals and buried treasures. The root of the word *rikaz* means "to stay still".[2] Ibn Qudamah defines minerals as anything put by God in the earth of a nature different from the earth itself and extracted therefrom, which has value. This definition excludes things extracted from the sea, put in the earth by human action, things that are of the nature of the earth such as soil and things that carry no value. Example of minerals are gold, silver, lead, iron, diamond, oil, sulphur, etc.[3]

SECTION ONE

BURIED TREASURE

Buried treasure includes all things of value left in or on the earth by people in the past, such as gold, silver, used metals, and the like. Jurists obligate a charge of one-fifth on the person who finds such wealth, in accordance with the narration of Abu Hurairah that the Prophet (p) said, "One-fifth is obligated on *rikaz*." It is reported by the group.[4] Things buried in the earth are defined unanimously as *rikaz*. Al Nasa'i reports from 'Umar bin Shu'aib from his father from his grandfather, "The messenger of God (p) was asked about lost and found things, and said, 'When you find things on roads used by people or in inhabited areas, you must announce it for one year. If the owner appears, give him what belongs to him, and if not, it is yours. But things found in deserted roads or villages are charged, as in the case of *rikaz*, one-fifth."[5]

These two sayings indicate the following:

A. One-fifth is due on things found where no owner exists, regardless of whether they are on the surface of the earth or inside it. Things found in inhabited areas must be given to owners.

B. The majority of scholars believes that *rikaz* includes anything that exists on the surface of the earth or under it. Al Shafi'i is an exception, because he restricts the meaning of *rikaz* to gold and silver only.[6] The view of the majority is consistent with the general texts.

C. The two sayings apparently indicate that the fifth is obligated on the finder, Muslim or not, minor or adult. This is the view of the majority, Al Shafi'i says non-Muslims are not obligated to pay a fifth, because this payment is a form of *zakah*. It is claimed that he says children and women are not allowed to own found *rikaz*. Ibn Qudamah contends, "We rely on the generality of the saying 'One-fifth is obligated on *rikaz*, and the remainder belongs to the finder."[7] Ibn Daqiq al 'Id notes that the closest view to the text of the sayings is that one-fifth is obligated on all or at least most forms of *rikaz*.[8]

D. Apparently, the saying does not refer to any *nisab*. The fifth is obligated on any quantity of found treasures, according to Malik, Abu Hanifah and his disciples, Ahmad, Ishaq, and al Shafi'i in the old version. This wealth, on which one-fifth is flatly obligated as on *ghanimah*, needs no *nisab*. Finding treasures does not involve great expenditure which needs to be deducted to attenuate the burden of the payer. In this respect they are unlike minerals and grain.[9] The later view of al Shafi'i is to consider *nisab* on found treasures, because the charge is a due on wealth taken from the earth, and must be treated like minerals and grains, which have *nisab*.[9]

E. It is agreed upon to abolish the condition of one year's passage. Dues are obligated immediately, In *al Fath*, al Hafiz writes, "Strangely enough, Ibn al 'Arabi mentions that al Shafi'i retains this conditions, but this is not found in any of al Shafi'i's writings or in the writing or his disciples."[10]

F. The saying does not refer to the disbursement of this fifth due on *rikaz*. Al Shafi'i and a narration from Ahmad show that it must be disbursed like *zakah*, because of a report made by Ahmad that "'Ali bin Abi Talib ordered it given to the needy, and because it is a wealth earned from the earth, which makes it similar to grain and fruit.

Abu Hanifah, Malik, Ahmad in another narration, and the bulk of jurists believe that this fifth is expended the same way the fai' is i.e. as a part of the general budget of the state. Abu 'Ubaid reports from al Sha'bi that a man found one thousand *dinars* buried at the outskirts of Madinah and brought it to 'Umar, who took one-fifth (two hundred *dinars* and returned the remainder to the man. Then 'Umar divided the two hundred among those Muslims who were present, until a few *dinars* remained. 'Umar called the finder and gave him these few *dinars*. The author of *al Mughni* comments, "if it were *zakah*, 'Umar would have restricted its distribution to the deserving recipients instead of all Muslims present then, and definitely would not have given the finder any part of the one-fifth, "Moreover, it is argued that since the fifth is also obligated on non-Muslim finders, and non-Muslims cannot be obligated to pay *zakah*, so it must not be treated like *zakah*. Additionally, it is similar to war booty taken, in fact, from past generations of disbelievers.[12]

Finding treasures is always rare, and more important is the following section on minerals, which usually represent a substantial sector of the economy.

SECTION TWO

MINERALS AND DUES OBLIGATED ON THEM

The required dues on minerals

The importance of minerals, solid and liquid, in human life is unquestionable. If grains and fruits are *zakatable*, should not minerals be *zakatable* too, since all come from the earth? Jurists, in total, do not dispute that there are dues obligated on minerals, although they differ on the details. Dues on minerals are obligated in accordance with the general principle established by the verse, "O ye who believe, spend out of the good things ye have earned and that which We produce for ye from the earth."[13] No doubt minerals are among the things produced for us by God from the earth.

Minerals included in this obligation

Jurists differ on whether this obligation covers all mining activities or only selected metals. It is known that al Shafi'i restricts it to gold and silver only, leaving all other minerals and precious stones un*zakatable*. Abu Hanifah and his disciples include metals extracted from the earth that are usually treated with heat.[14] This opinion is based on the analogy to gold and silver, whose *zakatability* is confirmed by texts and *ijma'*. The Hanbali school does not make any distinction between metals treated with heat and metals that are not treated with heat. According to this school, all minerals that come from the earth are *zakatable*, whether solid like iron ore, lead, and copper, or fluid like petroleum. This opinion is shared by Zaid bin 'Ali, al Baqir, al Siddiq, and all Shi'ite jurists except al Mu'ayad, who excludes salt, petroleum, and asphalt.[15]

Abu Ja'far al Baqir was asked about salt mines. His answer was, "This mineral is subject to the one-fifth due." When asked about sulphur and petroleum, he replied, "These and their likes are charged one-fifth."[16]

It seems that the Hanbali view is supported by the linguistic meaning of the word "minerals" and by reasoning, since as far as *zakatability* is concerned, there is no difference between solid and liquid minerals or between those treated by heat or not so treated. All of them are kinds of wealth that must be dealt with similarly. If the great scholars from previous centuries had seen the importance of petroleum, which is even called black gold, in the economic life of the world today, they would not have hesitated about its *zakatability*. Ibn Qudamah gives the following points in support of this view.

A. The generality of the verse "and out of what We have produced for you from the earth . . . . ."

B. The general implication of the word "minerals" as a form of wealth extracted from the earth, which must be *zakatable*, like gold and silver.

C. Minerals are a form of wealth. If they are taken as war booty, they would be subject to a one-fifth due. The same wealth, taken from the earth, should be subject to *zakah*.[17]

SECTION THREE

THE RATE IMPOSED ON MINERALS

Abu Hanifah, his disciples, Abu 'Ubaid, Zaid bin 'Ali, al Baqir, al Sadiq, and all Zaidi and Imami jurists believe that the rate is one-fifth. Ahmad, Ishaq, Malik, and al Shafi'i argue that the rate must be like that of gold and silver, i.e. two-and-one-half percent.[18] Malikites distinguish between minerals that take cost and effort to extract, in which case two-and- one-half percent is obligated, and mineral that do not need cost and effort to extract, in which case twenty percent applies.[19]

There is yet another opinion known among Malikites, that all minerals and ores, liquid or not, are owned by the national treasury of the Islamic state, on the ground that they in fact belong to the whole society together and their exploitation must not be left to a few individuals. Their output must also be spent for the public interest of the Islamic society.[20] This opinion may derive support from a report by Abu 'Ubaid that Abyad Hammal al Mazini asked the Messenger of God (p) to grant him the salt in Ma'rib and the Messenger agreed to do so. Abyad adds, "When I left, the Messenger was told, 'Do you know what you have just granted him? You gave him wealth like running water.' The Prophet took it back from me."[21] Abu 'Ubaid says this granting and retrieving the grant indicates that the Prophet gave Abyad the land on the assumption that he was going to use it for reclamation and agriculture. When the Prophet realized that it was a huge amount of wealth in salt, he took it back from him. The Messenger's traditional practice with regard to pasture land, firewood and water, is that they belong to all people together as partners; he hated to give such property to one person alone. Consequently, such things as petroleum, iron ore, etc., must belong to all people together under the holdings of the Islamic state.[22]

The evidence of those who believe the rate is 2.5%

Malik reports in *al Muwatta* from Rabi'ah bin Abi 'Abd al Rahman, from more than one narrator, that the Messenger of God (p) granted Hilal bin al Harith the minerals of al Qibliyah (a coastal area five days walking distance from Madinah) in the direction of al Qar'a (a place between Madinah and Nakhlah). Those minerals are charged only *zakah* (meaning 2.5%) until today.[23] Al Shafi'i in *al Umm* says after reporting this saying, "This is not confirmed as authentic by critics of hadith. Even if it were accepted, all it indicates is that the grant was given by the Prophet. The application of the rate of *zakah* on minerals instead of the one-fifth rate is not narrated from the Prophet (p) in this saying."[24] Abu 'Ubaid says, "This saying from Rabi'ah on al Qibliyah has no acceptable chain.

Additionally, it does not mention that the Prophet ordered the rate; all it says is that *zakah* is collected from the minerals until today. If the choice of the rate was authentically reported from the Prophet, it would have been irrefutable evidence."[25]

The argument of those who believe the rate is one-fifth

A. Abu Hanifah and his disciples present the saying of the Messenger of God (p) "One-fifth is obligated on *rikaz*."[26] They add that two things can be extracted from earth: the first is treasures buried by human beings and the second is minerals created by God. The word *rikaz* includes both; its literal meaning is minerals and its allegorical meaning is treasures.[27]

On the other hand, Malik, al Shafi'i, and most Hijazi jurists argue that minerals are not *rikaz* and that *rikaz* only means treasures buried by people in the earth. They cite the saying, reported by the group, from Abu Hurairah that the Prophet (p) said, "Harm inflicted by animals is unclaimable, and harm inflicted while (working inside) a well is unclaimable, and harm inflicted while (extracting) minerals is unclaimable, and one-fifth is obligated on *rikaz*." They argue that since the Prophet makes a distinction between minerals and *rikaz*, using the article "and" between them, they must be two different things.

The opposing Hanafites then argue that minerals must be included in the Prophet's word *rikaz*, because when he mentioned minerals he was talking about the harm inflicted in their extraction. If he had then said, "and one-fifth is obligated on *them*," buried treasures may have remained uncharged. Because of that possibility of ambiguity, the Prophet used a more general word, *rikaz*, which includes both minerals and buried treasures.[28] No language specialist could put an end to this dispute, because both the Iraqi and the Hijazi jurists include people who are well versed in Arabic, such as Muhammad bin al Hasan and al Shafi'i.

It seems that the word *rikaz* has in fact two meanings. Al Qamus and other Arabic dictionaries define *rikaz* as minerals God put in the ground and what the ancients buried of metalic pieces of gold and silver.[29] Ibn al Athir in *al Nihayah* says that according to the Hijazis, *rikaz* means ancient treasures buried in the ground, and according to the 'Iraqis, *rikaz* means minerals. Linguistically, both meanings are possible because each of them is something put in the ground and made steady in it.[30]

Abu Hanifah presents another saying from Amr bin Shu'aib, from his father from his grandfather, that "A man asked the Messenger of God (p) about things found in old buildings that are being demolished. The Prophet said, One-fifth is obligated on this and on *rikaz*."[31] Abu Hanifah adds that the use of the additive article "and" must mean that the two things are different, so *rikaz* cannot mean buried treasures, and consequently must mean minerals. Some of Abu Hanifah's disciples add that even if minerals are not initially called *rikaz*, the common use of the word by people was in that meaning. Muhammad bin al Hasan, a reknowned scholar of the Arabic language, says, "Arabs say *rakaza* for mineral ore when it has a high ratio of gold and silver in it."[32] The author of al Bada'i writes "*Rikaz* is derived from the verb *rakaza*, which means to make stand still."[33]

B. The second argument given by Hanafites is the analogy between minerals and war booty. They say the minerals were inside the earth when it was in the hands of unbelievers, and when Muslims took over they did not a dig underground to reach these minerals, leaving them untouched. Their extraction later must be subject to the same principle applied to the unbelievers property above the ground, i.e. one-fifth must be charged.[33]

The argument is difficult to accept, because it is founded on assuming that underground wealth remains in the ownership of unbelievers until it is extracted. How could one make such an assumption about the lands of Islam and Muslims? And who is to tell us that these minerals were installed inside the land before or after Islam?

C. Imami jurists make the analogy between minerals and war booty on the basis of the meaning of the word *ghanimah* (war booty) mentioned in the verse, "And know that out of all the booty that ye may acquire, (in war), a fifth share is assigned to God, and to the Apostle, and to near relatives, orphans, the needy, and the wayfarer."[34] According to Imamis, not only war booty but also things extracted from land or sea.[35] The author of *al Rawd al Nadir* (in Zaidi Jurisprudence) says that such generalization of the word *ghanimah* is questionable, because first, the word mentioned in the verse applies only to war booty on the basis of its context, and second, the word *ghanimah* as used in the Qur'an and the sayings, like "*Ghanimahs* are made lawful for me," is a religious concept and not only an Arabic word. This argument is based on the principle known among the scholars of *usul* that a general word may be used for a specific meaning by additional indications in *Shari'ah*. When a word is used like this, it becomes restricted to that meaning alone. The judge 'Abd al Wahhab al Maliki wrote a chapter on restricting general words to specific intended meanings, in such a way that meaning of the word in *Shari'ah* becomes only that specific one, and the word may not be taken to mean its original linguistic meaning except by additional evidence, even though the absolute use of the word may imply that general meaning. Some disciples of al Shafi'i agree with that, including Abu Bakr, al Qaffal, and others. Ibn Daqiq al 'Id refers in his commentary on *al 'Umdah* to the principle that the context sometimes indicates the specific meaning of a general word or gives more weight to one or more of the meanings included.[36]

Summing up, it appears that the only strong argument for the rate of twenty percent on minerals is that minerals are *rikaz* and *rikaz* is charged one-fifth. This is the view selected by the great scholar Abu 'Ubaid, who also reports from 'Ali bin Abi Talib a statement in its support.[37]

A distinction made on the basis of the cost of extraction

Some jurists argue that if the cost of extraction is high, relative to the amount of mineral taken, the rate must be 2.5%. On the other hand, when the cost involved is small or negligible, relative to the amount of mineral extracted, the rate must be one-fifth. This is also a narration from Malik and al Shafi'i,.[38] This trend is induced by the attempt to reconcile the sayings which indicate that gold and silver, which are minerals, are charged 2.5%, and the sayings which indicate that the charge on minerals is one-fifth. Another inducement for this approach is the fact that the rate of *zakah* on agriculture differs according to irrigation costs.

Al Rafi'i, a Shafi'ite, says "In reconciling all texts together, minerals obtained without cost or sweat must be charged one-fifth, while these obtained by effort and cost must be charged 2.5%, just as irrigation costs change the rate on agriculture."[38] Obviously, "The difference between 20% and 2.5% is substantial. It may be reasonable to impose a rate of 10% or 5% according to the value of extracted minerals relative to cost involved. This is not an invention of new rates in *Shari'ah*, but application of clear analogy, because *Shari'ah* makes a similar distinction in rates according to the value of the item and the cost of its production.

SECTION FOUR

NISAB OF MINERALS

Is there a *nisab* on minerals?

Abu Hanifah, his disciples, and the scholars of Ahl al Bait believe that dues on minerals apply to any quantity regardless of *nisab*, on the grounds that the sayings do not refer to *nisab* or to the passage of one year on *rikaz*. Malik, al Shafi'i, his disciples, Ahmad, Ishaq argue that there must be *nisab*, and that it is equal to the *nisab* of money, since general sayings determine *nisab* for gold and silver, as in "No *zakah* is obligated on anything less that five *uqiyyah* (of silver) and nothing is obligated on a hundred and ninety (*dirhams*),"[39] and since *ijma* sets the *nisab* of gold at twenty *dinars*.

The correct view seems to be that we must consider *nisab*, but the passage of one year is not required, since, as al Rafi'i states, *nisab* is needed for the wealth to be substantial enough to relieve the recipient, while the passage of one year is given for wealth to be invested and to grow. Minerals extracted from the ground are themselves the increase, like plants and fruits. So, like on grains and fruits, there must be *nisab*, but there is no need for the passage of one year.[40]

The time span for the accumulation of *nisab*

Nisab need not be produced at one time. Things extracted are added together, and if they add up to the amount of *nisab* in a period of one year, then *zakah* applies, even though the output may be sold as time goes. This period is similar to the season in the case of crops. Small interruptions in production do not affect this accumulation, but after a long interruption a new period of accumulation starts.[41]

I believe such a matter should be left to specialists, in accordance with the advice in the Qur'an, "Before thee, also, the apostles We sent were but men to whom We granted inspiration. If ye realize this not, ask of those who possess the Message."[42]

SECTION FIVE

THE PASSAGE OF ONE YEAR

The majority of jurists argue that dues on minerals are payable at the time of extraction, after initial preparation and refinement. Malik notes, "Minerals are like crops." Dues on them are collected on similar dates, i.e. the day of extraction, without any need for the passage of one year."[43] According to al Nawawi, this is the view of the masses of scholars, from the precedent-setters and the later generations. It is confirmed in most Shafi'i writings,[44] and is the approved opinion in the school of Ahmad.[45]

Ishaq and Ibn al Mundhir disagree. They require the passage of one year because of the saying "No *zakah* is obligated on wealth until one year elapses."[45] This saying is, however, weak, and it is unanimously agreed that it does not apply on all cases, since agriculture is excluded. Minerals should likewise be excluded, by analogy. The author of *al Mughni* writes, "since minerals are wealth earned from the earth, then like agriculture and buried treasures, there is no need for the condition of the passage of one year. Moreover, this condition is put in order to allow wealth to grow. Minerals are, like fruits, the result of the process or growth itself, so there is no such condition."[45] The author of *al Muhadhdhab* says "Dues on minerals are payable when minerals are obtained, without any consideration of the period of one year, because the lapse of such a period is meant to give time for the asset to grow, but minerals are the fruits and growth of land, like agriculture."[46]

SECTION SIX

DISBURSEMENT OF DUES ON MINERALS

Jurists differ in categorizing dues on minerals. Abu Hanifah and a group of jurists classify these dues with fai' and argue that they must be disbursed the same way fai' is. Malik and Ahmad consider it *zakah*. We have two reports from the Shafi'ites. Some Shafi'ite jurists say it is like *zakah*, and others say it depends on the applied rate---if 20% is applied it must be treated like fai', but if 2.5% is applied it must be treated like *zakah*.

Those who do not classify this due as *zakah* apply the charge one-fifth to non-Muslims too, while those who classify it as *zakah* do not, because *zakah*, as a form of worship, is not applicable to non-Muslims.[47]

SECTION SEVEN

EXTRACTIONS FROM THE SEA

Materials extracted from the sea like pearls, marble, etc.

According to Abu Hanifah, his disciples, al Hasan bin Salih, and Zaidi jurists, nothing is due on such materials. This is also the opinion of Ibn 'Abbas, as reported by Ibn Abi Shaibah and others. Ibn 'Abbas writes, "Amber is not *rikaz*. It is something thrown out by the sea, and nothing is imposed on it."[48] Apparently, this means that no charge is obligated on it. Additionally, Jabir bin 'Abd Allah is reported to have said "Amber is not *ghanimah*. All of it goes to the person who acquires it,"[49] meaning that the one-fifth due on *ghanimah* is not obligated on amber. Abu 'Ubaid comments, "Here we find two Companions of the Prophet (p) believing it is not charged anything."[49]

On the other hand it is authentically reported that Ibn 'Abbas said about amber, "If anything is charged on it, it must be one-fifth." It seems that Ibn 'Abbas changed his opinion after a specific incident. 'Abd al Razzaq reports via a correct chain Ibrahim bin Sa'd, who was governor of Eden, asked Ibn 'Abbas about amber. Ibn 'Abbas reply was "If anything is charged, it must be one-fifth."[50] Eden was an area where amber was produced. Thus Ibn 'Abbas gave a different opinion in consideration of interests recognized in *Shari'ah*. It is reported via al Hasan bin al 'Amarah from Ibn 'Abbas from 'Umar bin al Khattab that one-fifth must be charged on amber and every jewel extracted from the sea.[51] Additionally, Ibn 'Abbas is reported to have said that Ya'la bin Mainah wrote to 'Umar about a piece of amber found at the coast. 'Umar asked the Companions who were present, and they suggested one-fifth be collected from it. 'Umar wrote, "One-fifth is obligated on it and on every jewel that comes out of the sea."[52] There is also another report from 'Umar that runs in opposition to this one, which says he wrote "Collect one-tenth from jewels of the sea and from amber." All these reports from 'Umar do not reach the level of authenticity and even if they were authentic they would simply indicate that the issue of rate is subject to *ijtihad.*

Obligating one-fifth on amber and pearls is reported from some Followers too. Abu 'Ubaid reports it from al Hasan al Basri and Ibn Shihab al Zuhri.[53] 'Abd al Razzaq and Ibn Abi Shaibah report it from 'Umar bin Abd al Aziz.[54] This is the view of Abu Yusuf.[55] Ahmad is reported to have said that amber and pearls are *zakated* like minerals.[56] Abu 'Ubaid selects the view that no charge is put on things extracted from the sea, arguing that people at the time of the Prophet and his successors used to extract materials from the sea and no charge on that is reported in Sunnah. This indicates these material are exempt, the same way horses and slaves are exempt. Those who obligate one-fifth on extracts from the sea and do so only by analogy to minerals extracted from land. Those who do not do so believe extracts from the sea and minerals are not alike, since the Prophet distinguishes between them by stating that one-fifth is obligated on *rikaz* and remains silent on extracts from the sea.[57] But one may argue, what is analogy but applying the ruling mentioned in the texts to something similar about which the texts are silent?

If extracts from the sea are not a form of *ghanimah,* they are then similar to minerals extracted, from the land and must be treated likewise. For these reasons, I choose to obligate a charge on such extracts, whether this charge is called *zakah* or not. The rate of this charge must be determined by people of wisdom and knowledge, as indicated by 'Umar when he consulted the Companions. Different rates are applied in *Shari'ah* on agricultural products, depending on the cost and effort involved in irrigation. Here, also, the rate must be chosen in consideration of expenses involved, as well as the value of materials extracted. Whenever costs minimum and value is high, the rate should be the higher one. There are reports from al Shafi'i and Malik to this effect concerning minerals. When I discussed the rate on minerals, I supported the view that through *ijtihad,* a rate of one-tenth or one-half of a tenth be selected according to interests considered. Abu 'Ubaid reports that 'Umar imposed one-tenth, and comments, "I know of no reason why one-tenth is selected, because sea extracts are now treated like *rikaz* (where 20% applies) or like minerals (where 2.5% applies) according to the view of jurists of Madinah. 'Umar imposed one-tenth, which seems to be taken by analogy to agriculture, and I know of no one else who expresses such a view."[58] This means that there is nothing to prevent new opinions on this matter, as long as they are founded on valid evidence and reasoning.

The obligation on fish

The fishing industry is important in today's economic life, producing millions of dollars worth of fish. What is its treatment in *Shari'ah* from the point of view of *zakatability*?

Abu 'Ubaid reports from Yunus bin 'Ubaid, "'Umar bin 'Abd al 'Aziz wrote to his governor of 'Oman, 'Do not take anything from fish until it reaches two hundred *dirhams* in value similar to *nisab* of money. Once it becomes two hundred *dirhams*, take *zakah* from it."[59] A similar view is reported from Ahmad.[59] Imamis believe the rate must be one-fifth, like on *ghanimah*. Here also I present the same opinion that I expressed regarding the extracts from the sea.

Footnotes

1. *Al Nihayah* by Ibn al Athir, Vol. 3, p. 82.

2. *Fath al Qadir*, Vol. 1, p. 537.

3. *Al Mughni*, Vol. 3. p. 23.

4. Mentioned in *al Muntaqa*. See *Nail al Awtar*, Vol. 4, p. 147.

5. *Sunan al Nasa'i*, Vol. 5, p. 114.

6. *Nail al Awtar*, Vol. 4, p. 140.

7. *Al Mughni*, Vol. 3, pp. 22-23.

8. *Nail al Awtar, Ibid*, and *Fath al Bari*, Vol. 3, p. 235.

9. *Al Mughni*, Vol. 3, pp. 20-22. Al Shawkani attributes the requirement of *nisab* to Malik, Ahmad, and Ishaq. This contradicts what is quoted in *al Mughni*, especially from Ahmad.

10. *Nail al Awtar* and *Fath al Bari*, op. cit.

11. *Nail al Awtar*, Vol. 4, p. 148.

12. *Al Mughni*, Vol. 3, p. 222.

13. *Sura al Baqarah*, 2:267.

14. *Al Mirqat*, Vol. 4, p. 149.

15. *Al Bahr al Zakhkha*, Vol. 2, p. 210.

16. *Jawahir al Kalam*, Vol. 2, p. 119-120.

17. *Al Mughni*, Vol. 3, p. 24.

18. *Al Majmu'*, Vol. 6, p. 83.

19. *Al Muntaqa*, Sharh *al Muwatta'*, p. 102.

20. *Halaqat al Dirasat al ijtima'iyah*, 3rd session, p. 250.

21. *Al Amwal*, pp. 275-276.

22. *Ibid*, p. 281.

23. *Al Muntaqa*, Vol. 2, p. 101.

24. *Al Umm*, p. 45.

25. *Al Amwal,* p. 342.

26. Reported by the group.

27. *Bada'i al Sana'i,* Vol. 2, p. 65.

28. *Sharh al Tirmidhi,* Vol. 3, p. 139.

29. *Al Qamus al Muhit,* Vol.1, the root rakaza.

30. *Al Nihayah,* Vol. 2, p. 107.

31. Reported by Abu 'Ubaid in *al Amwal,* al Hakim in *al Mustadrak* and Abu Daud. Al Mundhiri says it is reported by al Tirmidhi. al Nasa'i and Ibn Majah. Al Tirmidhi calls it good. See *Mukhtasar Sunan* Abu Daud, Vol. 2, p. 272.

32. *Al Rawd al Nadir,* Vol. 2, p. 420.

33. *Al Bada'i,* Vol. 2, p. 67.

34. *Sura al Anfal,* 8:41.

35. *Al Bahr al Zakhkhar,* Vol. 2, pp. 209-214.

36. *Al Rawd,* Vol. 2, p. 419.

37. *Al Amwal,* pp. 240-241.

38. *Al Sharh al Kabir and al Wajiz,* printed on the sides of *al Majmu',* Vol. 6, pp. 88-89.

39. Refer to these two sayings in chapter three of this part.

40. *Al Sharh al Kabir, op. cit,* p. 92.

41. *Al Wajiz,* by al Ghazali, *op. cit.* pp. 93-96.

42. Sura al Anbiya', 21:7.

43. *Al Muntaqa,* printed with *al Muwatta',* Vol. 2, p. 104.

44. *Al Majmu'*, Vol. 6, p. 81.

45. *Al Mughni*, Vol. 3, p. 26.

46. *Al Muhadhdhab* and its commentary, *al Majmu'*, Vol. 6, p. 80.

47. *Al Majmu'*, Vol. 6, p. 76.

48. *Al Musannaf*, Vol. 4, p. 21, and *al Amwal*, p. 346.

49. *Al Amwal*, p. 346.

50. *Al Muhalla*, Vol. 6, p. 117, *Musannaf Ibn Abi Shaibah*, Vol. 4, p. 21, also mentioned in *Nasb al Rayah*, Vol. 2, and in *al Talkhis*, p. 184.

51. *Al Muhalla, op. cit.*, al Hasan bin al 'Amarah is disregarded.

52. *Al Rawd al Nadir*, Vol. 2, p. 419.

53. *Al Amwal*, p. 346.

54. *Al Talkhis*, p. 184.

55. *Al Kharaj* by Abu Yusuf, p. 70.

56 *Al Mughni*, Vol. 3, p. 27.

57. *Al Amwal*, p. 347.

58. *Ibid*, p. 348.

59. *Al Mughni*, Vol. 3, p. 128.

CHAPTER EIGHT

ZAKAH ON EXPLOITED ASSETS

Section 1: *Zakatability* of exploited assets

Section 2: Computation of this *zakah*

Section 3: The consideration of *nisab*

SECTION ONE

ZAKATABILITY OF EXPLOITED ASSETS

Exploited assets are defined as forms of wealth used to produce exchangeable services or goods that are sold for profit without exhausting the exploited assets themselves. They include assets rented for profit, such as residential buildings, means of transportation, jewelry, and other material used for rental purposes. Also in this category are livestock raised for milk, wool, or meat, and factories, plants, or equipment used for producing goods. In chapter six, I discussed livestock products and concluded that they must be treated like honey, whereby one-tenth is charged on the net output, but the producing animals are exempted. Therefore, I will not include a discussion of livestock in this chapter.

The difference between assets used for exploitation and those used for trading is that the former remain as permanent capital, while the latter change hands. Exploited assets used in the industrial, transportation, and service sectors represent a large portion of the contemporary economy.

Those who restrict *zakatability*

Two extreme opinions exist among jurists. There are those who expand the concept of *zakah* to include all or most assets, and those who limit *zakah* to only a few kinds of wealth. Those who tend to limit the *zakatability* argue that:

1. The Messenger of God (p) defined the *zakatable* assets, and did not mention among them these exploited ones such as buildings, rented animals, and productive machinery. The principle is that people must not be obligated to pay any charge without a clear text. There is no such text.

2. Jurists throughout the history of Islam and in all its various countries did not obligate *zakah* on those assets.

3. We have on hand scholarly opinions that negate the *zakatability* of exploited assets. Jurists have stated that residential homes, craftsman's tools, transportation animals, home furnishings, etc., are all exempt from *zakah*. This means factories, buildings, cars, planes, and ships are not *zakatable*, regardless of their size, value, or income.

When the earnings of these assets are received, retained for one year, and exceed *nisab*, they are then *zakatable*, like money.

Restricting the kinds of assets that are *zakatable* is a well-established stance in jurisprudence. It is defended by Ibn Hazm and later by al Shawkani and Siddiq Hasan Khan, to the extent that some jurists exclude trading assets and fruits and vegetable from zakat. The author of *al Rawdah al Nadiyah* argues for this opinion, "Imposing *zakah* on assets that are agreed on as non-*zakatable*, such as residential buildings, real estate, and animals, simply because they are rented for profit without being exchanged in trade, was unheard of in the first generations of Islam, not to mention their lack of support from Qur'an or Sunnah."[1]

Those who expand the concept of *zakatability*

On the other side there are jurists who expend the category of *zakatable* assets and establish the *zakatability* of exploited assets like factories and buildings. This is the position of some Malikites, Hanbalites, and the followers or al Hadi among Zaidis. It is also the view of some contemporary scholars, including Abu Zahra, 'Abd al Wahhab Khallaf, and 'Abd al Rahman Hasan, as we shall see in this section. In my opinion, this approach is more valid, for the following reasons:

1. God obligates a defined due on each asset: "and in their wealth there is a defined due," "Out of their assets take a *sadaqah*." The Prophet (p) also exhorts us to "Pay the *zakah* on your assets." These texts do not distinguish between the different kinds of assets.

Ibn al 'Arabi disproves the opinion of the Zahiris, who negate the *zakatability* of trade assets for lack of a correct text. "The verse 'Out of their wealth take a *sadaqah*' is general," he says. "It includes all kinds of wealth, regardless of classification, name, and purpose. Whoever wishes to impose any restriction on this generality is asked to bring proof."[2]

2. The reason for which *zakah* is imposed with respect to assets is growth, as noted by jurists who look for the reasons behind *Shari'ah* rulings in order to use them in analogy. (They include practically all jurists of the Islamic nation except a few Zahiris, Mu'tazilies and Shi'ites.) Consequently, *zakah* is not obligated on houses inhabited by owners, clothes, jewelry, craftsmen's tools, or horses used for fighting, by unanimous agreement. This is also why *zakah* is waived from camels and cows used as personal transportation, and from every asset that does not grow on its own or by human action. Since the reason for the *zakatability* of an asset is its growth, then if growth exists, an item must be *zakatable*.

3. The objectives of the legislation of *zakah* imply that *zakah* must be imposed, because owners of exploited assets need to be sanctified and purified, the poor and needy need relief, and Islam and its state have many uses for the proceeds of this form of *zakah*. Al Kasani explains the reasoning behind the obligation of the one-tenth charge on the produce of the earth, "The payment of the tenth to the poor is an expression of gratitude for Grace, a relief for the incapable and poor so they can perform their religious and social role. It is also needed for the purification of the payer's soul from

miserliness and sin, and the sanctification of his or her spirit and wealth." Is it reasonable to claim that farmers need this sanctification, purification, and expression of gratitude, while owners of factories, buildings, ships, and planes do not, although the latter usually has higher income that the former?

Disproving the evidence of the restricters

1. The fact that the Prophet (p) does not mention a certain asset as *zakatable* is not in indication of non-*zakatability*, because the Prophets only mentions growing assets common in Arab society at his time, such as camels, cows, lambs, wheat, barley, dates, raisin, and silver money. Muslims throughout generations obligated *zakah* on many assets by analogy to these mentioned by the Prophet, because of the general terms used in the texts, and in consideration of the objectives of *zakah*. Some examples are:

A. Al Shafi'i says in *al Risalah* about the *zakatability* of gold, "The Messenger of God (p) imposed *zakah* on silver. Afterward, Muslims collected *zakah* on gold, either by virtue of a text from the Prophet that did not reach us, or by analogy, since gold is used by people as a determinant of value for their exchange, before and after Islam."[3] The possibility that there is a saying that did not reach al Shafi'i is very remote. The only reason, then, is analogy, as stated by Abu Bakr bin al 'Arabi in *Sharh al Tirmidhi*: "The Arabs' trade at the time of the Prophet used silver currency, so the Prophet mentions it to mean all money used. His mentioning of silver was understood as inclusive of all kinds of money, but when people in later generations started asking for a specific text on everything, God shut in their faces the door of guidance and they deviated from the track of their predecessors."[4]

B. There is no clear text about the *zakatability* of trade assets. In spite of that, Ibn al Mundhir reports that they are *zakatable* by *ijma'*. Only the Zahiris disagree.

C. 'Umar ordered *zakah* on horses because he realized that they had become valuable wealth. Abu Hanifah agrees with 'Umar on this issue as long as the horses are retained for growth and pastured naturally.

D. Ahmad obligates *zakah* on Money on the basis of the report from the Companions and by analogy to grains and fruits. He further obligates *zakah* on all minerals by analogy to gold and silver, and by virtue of the general verse, "And out of that which We have produced for you from the earth. . ."

E. Al Zuhri, al Hasan, and Abu Yusuf obligate a one-fifth charge on pearls. amber, and other extracts from the sea, by analogy to *rikaz* and minerals.

F. All known schools of thought utilize analogy in the rules of *zakah*. The Shafi'ites, for example, use analogy in the *zakatability* of food items although the sayings mention only a few of these items by name.

2. The claim that no Muslim jurists impose *zakah* on exploited assets is refuted on the basis that the concept of retaining the asset and exploiting it for production or rental is a modern innovation that did not exist at the time of the great Muslim jurists. Yet we find their statements indicate that such assets would be *zakatable*.

3. The fact that jurists exempt residential houses and craftsmens tools from *zakah* cannot be extended to include buildings exploited for rent and factories or plants established by industrial growth. Riding animals of the past are by no means similar to modern cars, planes, and gigantic ships, while personal home furnishings of the past differ substantially from today's furniture rental businesses. Our predecessors did not err when they decided that furniture and tools are not *zakatable*; they applied strictly and rationally the rules for *zakatability* to the circumstances of the age in which they lived. The author of *al Hidayah* rationalizes the exemptions of such items "because they are utilized for essential needs and also do not grow."[5] The author of *al 'Inayah* comments, "Each of these two traits is alone an obstacle to *zakatability*. Residential quarters are indispensable for people as is clothing. As for growth, it may either be a characteristic of the item itself, as in the case of gold and silver, or it may be merely by designation, as in the case of business inventory."[6]

Jurists unanimously agree that a house taken as a residence by its owner is not *zakatable*. This exemption is a expression of Islamic justice, especially when compared with most contemporary real estate taxes, which usually do not give such consideration.

It is essential to point out that the rationalization or the exemption of housing, clothing, tools etc., from *zakah* on the basis that they are non-growing and utilized for essential needs, is itself an indication that any of these items becomes subject to *zakah* if it is used for growth and for non-essential needs.

SECTION TWO

THE CALCULATION OF *ZAKAH* ON BUILDINGS, FACTORIES, AND SIMILAR ITEMS

Zakatable growing assets discussed in previous chapters are of two kinds:

First are assets whose *zakah* is calculated on the principal and its increments together one every year, such as *zakah* on livestock and trade assets. In this case, the asset and its increment are integrated very closely, and the rate of *zakah* is two-and-a-half percent.

Second are assets whose *zakah* is calculated only on the growth or increase once the harvest is obtained. The asset may be materially fixed, such as land, or non-fixed, such as bees. The rate of *zakah* on this kind of asset is ten percent or five percent as we have seen earlier in this book.

If buildings and factories are *zakatable*, on what basis must *zakah* be calculated and how are these assets to be treated with regard to *zakah*?

Two established trends

Many people may think that preceding jurists did not discuss the *zakatability* of rented houses because the practice was not common in the past. This justification is generally valid, but one may find a few jurists who expressed the view that such houses are *zakatable*, although they have different ways of calculating *zakah*. Some suggest that rented houses be treated like trade inventory, appraised every year and *zakated* on the appraisal value at a rate of two-and-a-half percent, while others calculate *zakah* on the income these assets bring in, to see if it reaches *nisab* and fulfills other conditions for *zakatability*.

The first trend: treatment similar to that of trade assets

This view requires an appraisal of the asset used for income such as rented buildings, airplanes, ships, etc., every year. *Zakah* is then charged on the basis of this appraisal plus whatever net earnings remain at the end of the year, at a rate of two-and-a-half percent. This view is shared by jurists from Sunni and Shi'i schools of thought.

Ibn 'Aqil, a great, sharp-minded Hanbali jurist, exposses this view, as quoted approvingly by Ibn al Qayim in his book *Bada'i al Fawa'id*: "Ibn 'Aqil, in application of Ahmad's belief in the *zakatability* of jewelry used for rent, says that *zakah* must also be applied to buildings designated fro rent and every assets or commodity that is used for rental purposes." Ibn al Qayim continues, "Ibn 'Aqil points out that this view is the logical extension of our treatment of jewelry. Jewelry, according to our school, is not subject to *zakah*, but if jewelry is used as a rental item, *zakah* becomes obligated. If the designation for rent obligates *zakah* on an item that was originally not *zakatable*, this must apply to all non-*zakatable* items, i.e., the *zakatability* of an item depends on its state. Gold and silver are *zakatable*, but when they are made into women's ornaments designated for personal use, *zakah* is abolished on them. If again that same piece of jewelry changes its state into a rental item, *zakah* is imposed on it again. This necessarily indicates that buildings, animals used for riding, utensils, and furniture become *zakatable* when they are rented out."[7]

In my opinion, this view of Imam Ahmad is very strong. It is based on the important principle that *zakah* is not obligated on non-growing assets or on assets used to fulfill essential needs, and is obligated on growing assets, An asset that generates rental income is undoubtedly a growing one. Lawful jewelry used as ornamentation does not grow, and also fulfills a need for the woman who wears it, but if it is used for rental purposes it becomes a growing asset subject to *zakah*. This opinion is also shared by Malik, according to Ibn Rushd.[8]

If we apply this principle to buildings, furniture, cars, ships, planes, machinery, and industrial equipment, we can find the answer to their *zakatability*. If any of these is assigned for personal use, *zakah* is not obligated, but when they are used for rental or for generating income, they become *zakatable*. *Zakah* on them is similar to that on trade assets as far as *nisab* and rates are concerned. "This means that owner of such assets must appraise their buildings, cars, etc., add to the appraisal value other cash capital and loans to others, and pay 2.5% on the total. The claim of exemption from *zakah* on the basis that these are fixed assets like the exempted store fixtures of merchants is disproved by the fact that the productive capital itself is these fixed rental assets. They are the ones that generate gains and profit. Exemption from *zakah* covers assets that are not themselves used for growth but help other assets to produce, such as buildings where industrial equipment is placed. The industrial equipment is the productive asset. On the other hand, land and structure in rented buildings, hotels, and cimas are themselves the productive assets.

The school of Hadawi

The author of *al Bahr al Zakhkhar* writes that the Hadawis, who are Zaidi Shi'ites, obligate *zakah* on all items used for making profit, on the basis that the verse "Out of their wealth take *sadaqah*" is general and applies to these assets. These assets are intended for income generation, and must be treated similarly to trade assets and *zakated* if they reach *nisab*.[9] The author of *Matn al Azhar* and its commentators, also Zaidi, adopt the same opinion regarding all assets whose benefits renew without exhausting the asset itself. Thus *zakah*, according to them is not obligated on horses, mules, donkeys, houses, etc., except when they are used for trade or productive exploitation.

Al Hadi is reported to have said that if a person purchases a horse for the purpose of selling its reproduction, the horse and its offspring are all *zakatable*. Al Mu'ayyad Abu al 'Abbas and Abu Talib say this is "because all become like trade assets." Al Mu'ayyad continues, "The same applies to the silkworm." Al Huqaini says the same also applies to the person who has purchased a tree in order to sell its fruits. It is also said to be applied to cows and sheep bred for their reproduction, milk, and dairy products and wool.[10]

The author of *al Bahr al Zakhkhar* states as evidence supporting this view:

1. The generality or the texts regarding the obligation of *zakah*.

2. The similarity between assets used for production and exploitation and trade assets; both are forms of wealth intended for profitable growth.[10]

Objections of the opponents

Scholars who tend to restrict the obligation of *zakah*, such as al Shawkani and Siddiq Hasan Khan, object to this opinion. This is no surprise, because they also object to the *zakatability* of trade assets and vegetables. Their argument concentrates on two points:

A. The text of the saying "No *zakah* is obligated on a Muslim's slaves and mares" is general in its exemption of horses from *zakah*. This exemption includes cases in which horses are used for renting or for trade.

B. The obligation of *zakah* on assets known to be exempted such as houses, buildings, and riding animals, simply because they are being rented, was unheard of among the Companions and the generations that followed them, not to mention its lack of support from Qur'an and Sunnah. In spite of the fact that they used to hire and rent their houses, orchards and animals, it never occurred to any of these people to pay, at the end of the year, a 2,5% tax on their real estate or animals, They passed away with their peace of mind unbroken by such harsh obligations, until the end of the third century of Hijrah when this form of *zakah* was claimed on the basis of mere analogy to trade assets, which itself is dubious. Moreover, this analogy is itself incorrect because in renting one exchanges the benefit of the asset, while in trade one exchanges the asset itself.[11]

In brief, this view says that people are not obligated to say anything in principle, except when there is clear evidence that requires then to do so. In the case on hand, such evidence does not exist. Nothing is reported from the precedent-setting scholars, no verse or saying talks about it. As for the analogy to trade assets, it is erroneous because of the difference between them.

Weighing and discussion

One can argue that the saying "No *zakah* is obligated on a Muslim's slaves and mares" founds the exemption on the basis that these items are for personal use that satisfies essential needs for services and transportation. The great majority of scholars, as early as the third generation, obligate *zakah* on them if they are designated for trade. Ibn al Mundhir even mentions that there is *ijma'* on this. The wording of the saying never prevented such understanding, The lack of reports from the Companions concerning the *zakatability* of rented and productive assets may be attributed to the rarity of such incidents at their time. The use of fixed assets for productive purposes or rent was not so common as to make it important enough for people to give their opinions about it. The author of *al Bahr al Zakhkhar* notes that the claim that Hadawis contradict *ijma'* on this issues is baseless, because there are no reports from our predecessces on this issues either way.[12] The author of *Sharh al Azhar* comments, "I believe that the view of al Hadi does not contradict *ijma'*, because the Companions and the Followers either discussed this issue and differed on it or agreed on an opinion [nothing is reported] or did not discuss this issue at all. No harm is done by discussing it a new and expressing opinions on it."[13]

The analogy between productive rented assets and trade assets makes some sense because each is a growing capital that produces income, and the owners of each are businessmen who intend to invest their capital in income generating activities for the purpose of profit. The difference between exchanging the utility of the item or exchanging the item itself is not substantial enough to warrant different treatment. One may even argue that a person who exchanges only the utility and preserves the principal has more guarantee of profitability than the person who exchanges the item itself. However, if we think deeply we may find a few differences between these two forms of assets.

First of all, the best definition of trade assets is anything obtained for the purpose of resale for profit, as stated in the saying from Samurah in which the Prophet (p) used to command them to pay *zakah* on that which they prepare for sale. It is obvious that buildings and factories are not prepared for sale by their owners but rather for rent and productive use. Contractors and building merchants buy buildings or build them for the purpose of resale.

Secondly, if we consider each owner of an assets that is productive and profitable a merchant, even though his or her assets are not themselves intended for sale, owners of agricultural land and or lands must be included implying that they are required to appraise the value of their land and trees each year and pay *zakah* at the rate 2.5%. This is not acceptable and contradicts the ample evidence that we have.

Thirdly, the productive use of these assets may be halted sometimes for any reason, such as a lack of raw material or market. In those cases, how can the owner pay his or her *zakah*? Owners of trade assets can sell some of them or pay *zakah* in kind. Are owner of real estate required to sell in order to be able to pay *zakah*? This is an obvious hardship which is not required in *Shari'ah*.

Fourthly, from the practical point of view, the required yearly appraisal is subject to many non-objective elements in addition to price and changes and depreciation because of wear and tear. It is a cumbersome practice that requires hiring specialized experienced people and involves the payment of substantial expenses that may end up being paid from the *zakah* itself.

For these reasons, I select the view that *zakah* on buildings and factories must be taken on the basis of their income, which coincides with the other two opinions, which differ only in whether the percentage of *zakah* is two-and-a-half, ten, or five percent.

The second trend: *Zakah* taken on an assets' income

Ahmad is reported to have said that *zakah* is obligated on the rent of rented houses whenever the rent is received. This is quoted by Ibn Qudamah.[14] In the writings of the Malikites, Zarruq states in *Sharh al Risalah* that "There are two opinions on the *zakatability* of assets used for income, such as rental housing. One, *zakah* is due on their value received when sold, and two, *zakah* is due on their income when it is acquired."[15] This second opinion is important and has its roots in older views from some Companions and Followers.

The view of a group of Companions and Followers

All those who say that earned funds are *zakatable* when acquired (without the passage of one year) apply the same rule with regard to *zakah* on income earned from the output of factories and rental income of cars, buildings, planes, equipment, furniture, and the like. We shall see in the text chapter that this is the opinion of Ibn 'Abbas, Ibn

Mas'ud, Mu'awiyah, al Nasir, al Baqir, and Daud. It is also attributed to 'Umar bin.'Abd al 'Aziz, al Hasan al Basri, al Zuhri, Makhul, and al Awza'i.[16]

The evidence for this opinion is the generality of the saying "One-quarter of one-tenth is obligated on minted silver." Some jurists add the same argument given by al Hadi, the analogy of assets designated for renting or production and assets designated for sale, on the grounds that selling the benefit of the item is like selling a commodity. But this analogy implies that rented assets' *nisab* should be the same *nisab* of money, two hundred *dirhams*, and the rate should be 2.5%, as stated by the author of *al Hasir Fi Madhhab al Nasir*.[17] Notably, according to this view, the condition of the passage of one year does not apply.

A contemporary view: Earned income is *zakatable* like crops and fruits

This opinion agrees with the second trend among the precedent-setting jurists in that *zakah* is due on earned income from exploited, rented, and productive assets, but it suggests that the applicable rate is that of agriculture, one-tenth or one-twentieths by analogy to agricultural land. There is similarity between owner of land who collects its fruits and produce, and the owner of a building or factory who collects its rent or output.

This is the opinion of the late scholars Abu Zahrah, 'Abd al Wahhab Khallaf and 'Abd al Rahman Hasan, which they expressed in a lecture on *zakah* in Damascus, 1952.[18] They classify assets into three categories:

1. Assets acquired for the satisfaction of personal and family needs, such as houses inhabited by the owner, foodstuffs stored at home for daily use, etc. These ar not *zakatable*.

2. Assets acquired for the purpose of making profit with them or with their help. These assets are usually stored in vaults or storage places. They are unanimously *zakatable*. They include the items mentioned by the Prophet (p) as *zakatable*. Other items are added to this category on the basis of similarity.

3. Assets that are sometimes used for growth or profit and sometimes for personal needs, such as jewelry and domestic animals. Jurists differ on the *zakatability* of these items.

The application of this classification to the kinds of assets we have in our time must necessarily lead us to include in *zakatability* items that are used today for growth and profit but were not at the time of our great predecessors. The three scholars mention two kinds of these assets.

First, industrial equipment, plants, and machinery that represent productive capital, because they are the assets that produce income. These machinery and plants are not like tools of the blacksmith or carpenter who works with his hands. These three scholars reach the conclusion that plant and equipment are *zakah* table because they are productive and growing. Jurists in the past did not obligate *zakah* on the tools of craftsmen because these tools were very primive, not much more than basic hand tools; production was in fact dependent upon the ability and skill of the craftsman himself.

On the other hand, today's plants and factories are the productive growing capital. Consequently, we conclude that craftsmen's tools which the owner uses personally are exempted from *zakah* because they are essential for his or her personal needs, but plants and machinery are *zakatable*. No one can claim that by stating this we stand against the opinion of preceeding jurists, since they never expressed an opinion on factories they never saw. If they had seen them, they would have given the same ruling. We are merely applying their standards and criteria to modern times.

Second, buildings designated for rental and not personal residence of the owner are growing assets and not assets that satisfy essential personal needs of their owners. Accordingly, we divide residential houses into two categories, houses that are residences of their owners, which are *zakah*-free as stated by the jurists, and houses designated for renting. Those are *zakatable*. In this manner we do not contradict the opinions of preceding jurists, who did not obligate *zakah* on houses, because they meant only houses occupied by owners. Rental housing was rare; it was an exception and not the rule. Today rental housing is a well-known and profitable form of investment, which must be *zakated* as a growing asset, especially since *zakah* is imposed on similar assets, like agricultural land. Justice requires that these two similar kinds of assets be treated similarly.

It is fair to mention that Ahmad used to pay *zakah* on the income of a few stores he rented, although that was his only source of income. (See *Manaqib al Imam Ahmad* by Ibn Abi Za'la, p. 224.) "We have seen that the Prophet (p) imposes *zakah* on mobile capital at the rate of a quarter of one-tenth, and we also find him imposing *zakah* on the income and not the principal of productive capital, because the principal is indivisible so one must collect from its output. Then the rate of *zakah* on the output becomes one-tenth or one-half of a tenth, in accordance with rates decreed by the Prophet (p) which distinguish between fixed and mobile assets. We conclude that productive assets of our time must also be *zakatable*, with the same distinctions between fixed and mobiles assets. On the mobile items, the rate of *zakah* must be one-quarter of one-tenth, while on the fixed it should be one-tenth or one-half of one-tenth, taken out of its income."

"This means that *zakah* on rented buildings and fixed industrial assets is taken out of their income and not out of the principal at the rate of one-tenth or one-twentieth. When it is possible to know the net income after deducting costs, as is the case in business corporations, *zakah* is calculated on the net income at the rate of ten percent. The Prophet took ten percent from crops watered by rain or natural springs, as if he were taking it from the net. When it is difficult to determine the net income, *zakah* is calculated at the rate of one-twentieth of the growth."[19]

This is the opinion of these three great scholars, who spent their whole lives studying and teaching Islamic jurisprudence. Their opinion can only be described as the opinion of one most experienced, and I believe it is correct *ijtihad*, based on sound analogy.

Discussion and consideration

The view of these three respected scholars is consistent with the second trend established by our predecessors in charging *zakah* on the income of buildings and factories. The only difference is in the rate applied. This opinion is most persuasive, since it is based on the sound analogy between the income of fixed assets and that of agricultural land. This is my selected view with the following remarks:

This opinion includes factories and buildings among *zakatable* assets, without providing general criteria that can be applied to all similar productive capital. This era of ours witnesses other forms of profitable investment, such as cattle and poultry farms and transportation rental firms. All these forms of invested capital are similar to factories and buildings and should be treated like them, without distinction between the different forms invested capital may take. we have noted that the Prophet (p) collected *zakah* from honey, which is the output of bees, a mobile asset, unlike buildings.

Also, the similarity between rented houses and agricultural land is not free of dispute. The claim that there is no difference between an owner who gets income from his agricultural land and an owner who collects income from buildings is rejected on the grounds that *zakah* on agriculture is not based on ownership of the land, but on ownership of the crops themselves, which can occur even though the land is rented. The sound analogy must be between the owner of rented land who gets only its rent, and the owner of a rented building who also obtains rent. Such an analogy must certainly be preceded by a discussion of the *zakatability* of rent on agricultural land, which was done in the preceding chapters, and the conclusion reached that is must be *zakated.*

Lastly, the analogy between buildings and agricultural land is not accepted, because agricultural land is a perpetual source of income that is not exhausted as years go by, while buildings have a certain number of years at the end of which they will be dehabitated and possibly demolished. This difficulty in analogy can be overcome by accepting the exemption of capital depreciation used in today's taxation systems, whereby a certain amount is deducted every year from the income of fixed assets, with the purpose of accumulating sufficient amount to acquire a new asset at the end of the old one's productive lifespan.[20] With this consideration of depreciation or amortization, the buildings and machinery that have a finite lifespan can become similar to agricultural land, whose lifespan is not finite.

SECTION THREE

NISAB OF BUILDINGS AND SIMILAR ASSETS

The three renowned professors do not discuss the issue of *nisab* on the income of buildings and factories. How much should this *nisab* be? Is it like that of crop and fruits, i.e. five *wasq*, or is it like the *nisab* of money? It seems that *nisab* should be set as similar to that of money, as long as owners of buildings and factories receive their income from rent in monetary form.

The period in which the *nisab* conditions is fulfilled

Since the flow of income is always time related, the question of the time for the accumulation of income arises. Should we apply *nisab* on the monthly, weekly, or yearly income? It seems that the yearly interval is the most suitable period of time for the consideration of *nisab*, especially since incomes of individuals and states, as well as rental proceeds, are usually estimated and considered on a yearly basis. It is mentioned that some of the scholars who believe that earned income is *zakatable* when acquired believe also that if the yearly rent reaches *nisab*, it must be *zakated* when rent is obtained.

Consequently, monthly earned rent and income will be treated like fruits that are collected periodically and then all the collections are added together, which is the opinion of the school of Ahmad. The author of *al Mughni* says, "Fruits collected on several pickings are added together as long as they are of the same year's harvest, whether they all ripen together or not, and when the first harvest comes, the second growing of the same plants during the year must be added to the first, like in the case of palm trees that carry fruit twice a year. Both harvests are added together."[21]

Deduction of expenses and debts from income

My opinion is that *zakah* must be calculated on the basis of net income, after deducting expenses and costs such as wages, maintenance, taxes, etc. Additionally, debts that are due to others and personal and family expenses are deductible, according to the opinion of 'Ata and others. 'Ata says to "Deduct your expenses and pay *zakah* on the rest." This is also supported by Ibn al 'Arabi in his *Sharh al Tirmidhi*.

Deduction of a minimum cost of living

Undoubtedly, there exist people whose only source of income is the rent from a house, the earnings from a small craftshop, or something similar. Such incomes may belong to an old retired person, a widow, or orphaned children. Are these and similar owners whose only source of income is rent of output derived from fixed assets allowed a certain amount as a deduction for their cost of living. Or must *zakah* be calculated on the gross income?

It is obvious that an exemption of a minimum cost of living is consistent with the justice of Islam, so long as such a minimum is determined by experts who are righteous. *Zakah* must be calculated on the residual only if it equals *nisab*. This opinion is substantiated by two points:

1. Jurists consider assets which are needed by owners to satisfy basic needs as exhausted and, with respect to *zakah*, non-existing. They give the example of water for thirsty person. A thirsty person can make ablution with soil [tayammum] in spite of the presence of water, because as long as the water is exhausted by the thirst of the person, it cannot be counted.

2. Sayings mentioned earlier ordain estimators of dates and grapes to make it easy on the owners. The Prophet told them to "discount one-third, and if you do not discount one-third, then discount one-fourth," This discount from the total *zakatable* quantity is a consideration for what they eat to fulfill their needs. It might even be easier and simpler in calculation to discount one-third or one-fourth, in compliance with the spirit of these saying.

Footnotes

1. *Al Rawdah al Nadiyah*, Vol. 1, p. 194.

2. *Sharh al Tirmidhi*, Vol. 3, p. 104.

3. *Al Risalah*, ed. Ahmad Shakir, pp. 193-194.

4. *Sharh al Tirmidhi*, Vol. 3, p. 104.

5. *Al Hidayah* with *Fath al Qadir*, Vol. 1, p. 487.

6. *Al 'Inayah*, p. 487.

7. *Badai' al Fawa'id*, Vol. 3, p. 143.

8. *Bidayat al Mujtahid*, Vol. 1, p. 237.

9. *Al Bahr al Zakhkhar*, Vol. 2, p. 147.

10. *Sharh al Azhar*, by Ibn Miftah and its commentaries, pp. 450-451, and 475.

11. *Al Rawdah, op. cit.*

12. *Al Bahr al Zakhkhar*, Vol. 2, p. 148.

13. *Sharh al Azhar*, Vol. 1, p. 450.

14. *Al Mughni*, pp. 29 and 47.

15. *Sharh al Risalah*, Vol. 1, p. 329.

16. See "*Zakatability* of Earned Income" in the next chapter.

17. *Hawashi Sharh al Azhar,* Vol. 1, pp. 450-451.

18. *Halqat al Dirasat al Ijtima 'iyah lil Jami'ah al 'Arabiyah,* third session, pp. 241-242.

19. *Ibid*, pp. 249-250.

20. *'Ilm al Maliyah* by Rashid al Daqr, p. 368.

21. *Al Mughni*, Vol. 2, p. 755.

CHAPTER NINE

ZAKAH ON EARNINGS OF LABORERS AND PROFESSIONALS

Labor is one of the most important source of income in our day. Earnings take the form of an independent professional's income or a laborer's wages. This chapter deals with the *zakatability* of these two forms of income, neither of which was common at the time of the great scholars who preceded us. This chapter has three sections:

Section one deals with jurists' opinions about the *zakatability* of this source of income.

Section two deals with the determination of *nisab*.

Section three discusses the rate of *zakah* on these incomes.

SECTION ONE

JURISTS' CONSIDERATION OF THE INCOME FROM LABOR AND PROFESSIONS

A contemporary opinion

The three late professors, 'Abd al Rahman Hasan, Muhammad 'Abu Zahra, and 'Abd al Wahhab Khallaf mention this matter in their lecture in Damascus in 1952, and conclude the following: "Income from labor and professions is subject to *zakah* if it reaches *nisab* and one year passes. We note that Abu Hanifah, Abu Yusuf, and Muhammad believe that *nisab* conditions must be satisfied at least in the beginning and the end of the year. On the basis of this opinion, *zakah* can be imposed on income from labor on a yearly basis. Earnings from labor are *zakatable* because of the same reason other earning are subject to *zakah*. The considerations of *nisab* is also a must, because *zakah* is imposed on the rich and *nisab* determines richness. The Hanafites approach to the fulfillment of this condition at the two ends of the year is easy to satisfy." Discussing the rate of *zakah* on different items, the three professors continue, "We know of no case similar to that of *zakatability* of income from labor and professions in existing jurisprudence. Perhaps the only exception is an opinion from Ahmad that rent, if it is acquired and reaches *nisab*, is subject to *zakah* at the time of acquisition, regardless of the condition of the passage of a year. This, in fact, is similar to income from labor, and consequently the latter is *zakatable* if it reaches *nisab*. This is in addition to what we remarked earlier upon, that professionals and workers are most likely to have *nisab* at least at the beginning and end of the fiscal year."[1]

Wages and salaries are earned income

The conclusion of their analysis is that *zakah* on salaries applies only to the last month of the year, because they require the fulfillment of the condition of *nisab* at the beginning of the year and at its end, i.e. they do not imposed *zakah* on the flow of income itself during the year, but only consider its two ends.

It is rather astonishing that they claim there is no similarity to the case of *zakah* on salaries in the writings of jurists except for rent, because the most similar case to earnings from labor is the well-known case of earned income, and I believe this similarity is the foundation for the *zakatability* or labor income. A group of Companions believed in the *zakatability* of earned income. This includes Ibn 'Abbas, Ibn Mas'ud, and Mu'awiyah. They are followed by a few jurists, such as al Sadiq, al Baqir, al Nasir, and Daud. This opinion is also reported from 'Umar bin 'Abd al 'Aziz, al Hasan, al Zuhri, and al Awza'i. *zakah* on earned income is discussed in several well-circulated books, including *al Muhalla* (vol. 6, p. 8), *al Mughni* (vol. 2, p. 6), *Nail al Awtar* (vol. 4, p. 148), *al Rawd al Nadir* (vol. 2, p. 412), and *Subul al Salam* (vol. 2, p. 129).

Analysis of the different views concerning earned income

It is extremely important to reach a strong ruling on this matter, because earned income is a major category of wealth in our era, including wages and salaries, professional income, gains from invested capital, etc. Earned income may be merely an increase in a *zakatable* asset, such as a profit from trade assets or increase in the number of cattle or sheep. These increments are added to the principal and become subject to zakah at the end of the fiscal year of the principal. On the other hand, earned income may be the acquired value of an already *zakated* asset, such as crops sold after *zakah* is paid on them. This earned income is not subject to *zakah* until one year elapses, in order to avoid duplication.

Our discussion is restricted to earned income not covered by the two previous cases, such as salaries of laborers, capital gains and its dividends, gifts, etc., whether the earned income is of the same kind as its source or not.

For such forms of earned income, is the passage of one year necessary, or must earned income be added to similar already-owned assets, applying the year of that asset on newly earned in cements? Or should earned income be *zakated* at the time of acquisition, provided that the necessary conditions such as *nisab*, non-existence of debts, and being in excess of essential needs, are met? In fact, each of these three propositions is taken up by a few jurists, although it is commonly known among scholars that the passage of one year is a required condition on all *zakatable* funds, whether they are owned assess or earned income. This is based on the general terms of the sayings on this matter, as understood by many jurists. Consequently, an analysis of these sayings and their indications is indispensable.

Sayings on the passage of one year are weak

The condition of the passage of one year is reported from four Companions, namely, 'Ali, Ibn 'Umar, Anas and 'A'ishah (m), but all these sayings are in fact weak and cannot substantiate the point on hand.

The saying from 'Ali is reported by Abu Daud under the title "*Zakah* on pastured livestock." Abu Daud says "Sulaiman bin Daud al Muhri informed me that Ibn Wahb told him that Jabir bin Hazim told him (and he named another) from Abi Ishaq, from 'Asim bin Damurah and al Harith al A'war from Ali that the Prophet (p) said, "And if you have two hundred *dirhams* and one year elapses on them, there is five *dirhams* [as obligated *zakah*], and nothing is obligated on you [concerning gold] until you have twenty *dinars*. When you have twenty *dinars*, and a year elapses, there is half a *dinar* [as obligated *zakah*]. What is above that is by proportion." The narrator adds, "I do not know whether 'Ali said 'by proportion' or attributed it to the Prophet (p)." "And there is no obligated *zakah* on a fund until one year elapses." Jarir says that Ibn Wahb adds in the saying the words "And there is no . . . elapses."

Critics of hadith have the following to say:

A. Ibn Hazm, followed by 'Abd al Haq in his Ahkam comments "Abu Ishaq mentions 'Asim and al Harith together in his narration, and al Harith is a liar. It may pass unnoted by that al Harith is the one who extends his narration to the Prophet, while 'Asim does not. Associating them together is incorrect. Su'bah, Sufian, and Mu'ammar narrate the same saying from 'Asim from 'Ali stopping there. This is also the way it is narrated by any trustworthy narrator. If it had been the narration of Jarir that extends the chain through 'Asim to the Prophet, the saying would have been accepted."[2]

B. In *al Talkhis*, al Hafiz says al Tirmidhi reports this saying from Abu 'Uwanah from Abu Ishaq from 'Asim from 'Ali, stated from the Prophet.[3] I argue that the word of the saying from Abu 'Uwanah does not include the passage of a year. No truth is more evident. Al Tirmidhi reports the following words:

"On each forty *dirhams*, pay one *dirham* [as obligated *zakah*]; nothing is due on a hundred and ninety *dirhams*, but if it reaches two hundred *dirhams*, pay its due *zakah*, five *dirhams*."[4]

C. 'Asim himself is not free of criticism. Al Mundhiri, in his *Mukhtasar*, says[5] "Al Harith and 'Asim are not accepted." Al Dhahabi says "The four report his narration, Ibn Ma'in and Ibn al Madini grade him trustworthy. Ahmad grades him higher than al Harith, and to me he is accepted." Al Nasa'i says he is all rights. On the other hand, Ibn 'Adi says he is singled in several sayings from 'Ali; the problem comes from him. Ibn Habban says that "He had a bad memory and made very bad errors. He often attributes the statements of 'Ali to the Prophet, and he deserves to be abandoned . . . . Anyhow he is better than al Harith."[6] This supports the opinion of al Mundhiri.

D. The saying has a defect in its chain, referred to by al Hafiz in *al Talkhis*.[7] He warns, "The saying just mentioned from Abu Daud has a defect discovered by Ibn al Mawaq: Jarir did not hear from Abu Ishaq. Trustworthy disciples of Ibn Wahb, namely Suhnun, Harmalah, Yunus, and Pahr narrate it from Jarir from al Hasan bin 'Amarah from Abu Ishaq. It seems that Sulaiman made the mistake of omitting the name of al Hasan bin 'Amarah, who is agreeably abandoned"[8] Al Hafiz does not criticize the opinion of Ibn Mawaq, which indicates that he probably changed his opinion, mentioned earlier in *al Talkhis* itself, that "the saying from 'Ali is all right as far as its chain is concerned; it is supported by other narrations, to the extent that makes it an acceptable evidence."[9]

In conclusion, this saying is unacceptable as evidence. It is apparent that this saying has so many problems that I speculate those who grade it good would have changed their opinions had they known these defects, especially the one mentioned by Ibn al Mawaq, that is so substantiated by correct evidence as to be overwhelming in its effect on the acceptability of the saying.

The saying from Ibn 'Umar is, according to al Hafiz, reported by al Daraqutni and al Baihaqi. In this chain there is Isma'il bin 'Ayash, and his narration is weak when it comes from other than narrators in Syria. Ibn Numair and Mu'tamer report it via 'Ubaid Allah bin 'Umar, from Nafi' as stopping at Ibn 'Umar. Al Daraqutni grades the narration that ends at Ibn 'Umar as correct.[9]

The saying from Anas Is reported by al Daraqutni. It has Hasan bin Siyah in its chain. He is weak. He narrates alone from Thabit, as in *al Talkhis*, p. 175. Ibn Habban says in his *al Du'afa'* that "his narrations are very absurd. Whenever he is narrating alone, he cannot stand as acceptable.[10]

The saying from 'A'ishah is reported by Ibn Majah, al Daraqutni, al Baihaqi, and al 'Aqili in *Al Duafa*. Ibn al Rijal, who is weak, is in its chain.[11] Ibn al Qayim says, "This saying is reported from 'A'ishah via a correct chain. Muhammad bin 'Ubaid Allah bin al Munada says that Abu Zaid Shuja' bin al Walid informed him . . . that 'A'ishah said: I heard the Messenger of God (p) saying 'No *zakah* [is obligated] on any fund until one year elapses. Abu al Husain bin Bishran narrates it from 'Uthman bin al Sammak from bin al Munada."[12]

I wonder how Ibn al Qayim could grade this saying as having a correct chain, since Shuja' bin al Walid is graded poor, not strong, and not acceptable by Abu Hatim. Even more importantly, he narrates from Harithah, who is graded weak by al Daraqutni and al Aqili. According to al Dhahbi, "Ahmad and Ibn Ma'in grade him weak, al Nasa'i says he is abandoned, al Bukhari says his narrations are absurd, and no one accepts him as narrator. Ibn al Madani says, 'Our colleagues still grade him weak,' and Ibn 'Adi says 'The bulk of what he narrates is absurd.'"[13] This means grading him weak and abandoning his narrations are agreed upon. How then could a narration he alone gives be graded correct? Confusion caused by not mentioning the full name of his father may have caused this is in the mind of Ibn al Qayim.

Saying about earned income

Al Tirmidhi reports from Abd al Rahman bin Zaid bin Aslam from his father from Ibn 'Umar that the Messenger of God (p) said, "He who earns income is not subject to *zakah* until a year elapses, as prescribed by his Lord." Al Tirmidhi also reports from Ayub from Nafi' that Ibn 'Umar said, "He who earns income . . . . " etc., without ascending it to the Prophet. Al Tirmidhi says that the last saying is more correct than the saying from 'Abd al Rahman. Ayub and 'Ubaid Allah bin Umar and others narrate from Nafi' from Ibn 'Umar the same saying as being said by Ibn 'Umar. 'Abd al Rahman is graded weak by Ahmad, Ibn al Madini, and others. He makes frequent mistakes.[14] The narration of 'Abd al Rahman is reported by al Daraqutni and al Baihaqi; al Baihaqi, Ibn al Jawzi, and others conclude that as ending at Ibn 'Umar, the saying is correct. [meaning it is not attributed to the Prophet]. Al Daraqutni mentions among the peculiarities of Malik, the same, and comments that "the saying is weak." However, Malik has a correct narration that stops at Ibn 'Umar. Al Baihaqi reports statements of

Abu Bakr, 'Ali, and 'A'ishah similar to that of Ibn 'Umar, and says we can count on those of Abu Bakr, 'Uthman, Ibn 'Umar, and others.[15]

This makes it clear that there is no authentic saying supporting the condition of the passage of a year regarding earned income, as confined by al Baihaqi. Even if there were a correct saying about the year, it would be applied to assets other than earned income, in order to compromise the different texts together. However, it is agreed upon that any *zakatable* item must not be charged another *zakah* until one year elapses. In this sense, *zakah* is yearly. Saying that imply *zakah* is not imposed until one year elapses may be interpreted in this manner, as was explained in detail in chapter one of this part. Lastly, the fact that the Companions are not agreed on this condition with regard to earned income implies that there was no correct text.

Difference among Companion and Followers on earned income

It is reported correctly from al Qasim bin Muhammad that Abu Bakr did not take *zakah* from any fund until the year had elapsed. Amrah bint 'Abd al Rahman narrates from 'A'ishah that "No *zakah* is due until a year elapses" regarding earned income. 'Ali is reported to have said, "He who earns income is not obliged to pay *zakah* on it until one year passes." A similar statement is reported from Ibn 'Umar.[16] On the other hand, Ibn Hazm quotes Ibn Abi Shaibah and Malik in al Muwatta as saying "It is correctly reported from Ibn 'Abbas that *zakah* is obligated on any income when acquired by any Muslim."[17] Ibn Mas'ud and Mu'awiyah, both Companions, and 'Umar bin 'Abd al 'Aziz, al Hasan, and al Zuhri, Followers, are also reported to obligate *zakah* on earned income when acquired.[18]

It is known that when the Companions differ on an issue, the matter is rendered to other texts and to the general principles of Islam. No one can claim any ijma' on such a disputed matter.

Reports from Companions and Followers on this issue

A. Ibn 'Abbas

Abu 'Ubaid reports from Ibn 'Abbas about a man who earns income, "He must pay its *zakah* the day he earns it.[19] Similar statements are reported by Ibn Abi Shaibah.[20] The report is correct from Ibn 'Abbas, as confirmed by Ibn Hazm. It obviously does not require the passage of one year for *zakah* to be obligated, as understood by most people from Ibn 'Abbas. Abu 'Ubaid disagrees, sayings that "People understand that Ibn 'Abbas meant gold and silver, but not believe that. In my opinion, Ibn 'Abbas knows better than that, because such a view would put him in opposition to the majority of people, I guess he only meant crops of agriculture, because people of Madinah call lands '*mal*' [the word used in the saying of Ibn 'Abbas] and there seems to be no other interpretation to his statement"![21]

Abu 'Ubaid is undoubtedly a leading expert in financial affairs and has a good insight into *zakah*, but I believe that his interpretation of Ibn 'Abbas view is weak. It contradicts what immediately comes to mind and the understanding of most scholars. If it were simply related to agricultural crops, nothing would be new about this statement and it would not be worth being pointed out by many people as distinguishing Ibn 'Abbas. In principle, words must be taken to mean their apparent meaning, except when that becomes impossible. Is there anything in this statement that prevents us from taking the apparent meaning of *mal*? The reason cited by Abu 'Ubaid is not acceptable for the following points:

Firstly, Ibn 'Abbas is not alone in this opinion. Both Ibn Mas'ud and Mu'awiyah agree with him, in addition to some Followers.

Secondly, a Companion who exerts efforts to find a Shari'ah ruling is not required to wait for agreement or approval of other scholars to express his or her own conviction.

Thirdly, a Companion may even be alone in expressing certain opinions, and this is not unusual in the history of jurisprudence. The fact that Ibn 'Abbas was alone in expressing this opinion must not be an excuse to twist the apparent meaning of his words to make them consistent with the opinions of other Companions.

At last, we must note that Abu 'Ubaid does not as certain his interpretation, because he uses the words "I guess."

B. Ibn Mas'ud

Abu 'Ubaid also reports from Hubarrah his saying that "'Abd Allah bin Mas'ud used to give us salaries in s*mal*l bags and to collect *zakah* from them."[22] Abu 'Ubaid also interprets this collection as related *zakah* that was due on assets other than these salaries.

This interpretation seems to be very far-fetched. It contradicts the apparent meaning of the statement. Moreover, it is also in contradiction with correct reports from Ibn Mas'ud which provide the obvious explanation. Hubairah says "Ibn Mas'ud used to collect *zakah* on salaries at the rate of twenty-five from each one thousand," as reported by Ibn Abi Shaibah,[23] and al Tabarani.[24] This explanation of the practice of Ibn Mas'ud is reported by Hubairah himself, but one may assume that Abu 'Ubaid did not hear of this second report.[25]

C. Mu'awiyah

In *al Muwatta'*, *Mal*ik reports from Ibn Shihab that "the first one who collected *zakah* from salaries was Mu'awiyah bin Abi Sufyan."[26] He probably means the first head of state, since Ibn Mas'ud collected it before him, or perhaps Ibn Shihab did not hear the report about Ibn Mas'ud. Mu'awiyah, as head of the Islamic state, used to collect *zakah* from salaries in the state administration. Many Companions lived during the era of

Mu'awiyah, and none of them objected to his action, although Mu'awiyah is the target of much criticism.

D. 'Umar bin 'Abd 'Aziz

Around the end of the first century after Hijrah, 'Umar resumed the practice of collection of *zakah* from salaries and grants. Abu 'Ubaid reports that when 'Umar bin 'Abd al 'Aziz paid anyone a salary, he collected *zakah* out of it. He also collected *zakah* or grants before they were delivered.[27] . . . . Abi Shaibah too reports that 'Umar bin 'Abd al 'Aziz used to collect *zakah* on salaries and prizes.[28]

Scholars from the Followers and otherwise

E.   The subjection of earned income to *zakah* is reported from al Zuhri, al Hasan, and Makhul, also mentioned is Ibn Hazm. Some of these reports will be mentioned in the next section. The same is also reported from al Awza'i. Even Ahmad is reported to have said similar things concerning rent on land. The author of al Mughni says "Ahmad and several others say that rent should be *zakated* when earned."[23]

F. Al Baqir, al Sadiq, al Nasir, and Daud

The view of the first three scholars from the descendants of the Prophet, and that of Daud, is that whoever earns the equivalent of *nisab* must pay its *zakah* immediately.[30] They argue that this is based on general texts which obligate *zakah* on money, such as the saying "[There is obligatory *zakah*] on currency, one-quarter of one-tenth." Agreed upon.

This removes the condition of the passage of one year, according to these scholars. *nisab* need only be fulfilled at the end of the year, as is apparent from the practices of the Prophet and his *zakah* collectors in taking *zakah* at the end of the year, without keeping records of the beginning of the year.[31]

Disagreement of the four schools about *zakah* on earned income

Ibn Hazm mentions that Abu Hanifah believes that earned income is not *zakatable* until a year passes, except when the owner has assets of the same kind as the earned income, in the amount of *nisab* from the beginning of the year. In this case, earned income is added to the assets in the calculation of *zakah*. *Ma*lik has a similar view on the requirement of the passage of a year regarding the presence of assets of the same kind, except when it comes to livestock. If the owner of livestock has assets of the same kind of ani*mal* from the beginning of the year in the amount of *nisab*, the total becomes *zakatable* at the end of the year. Al Shafi'i says earned income needs the condition of the passage of a year for *zakatability*, except in the case of baby cattle, provided that their mothers reach *nisab*.[32]

Ibn Hazm objects to all these opinions, describing them all as erroneous, and says "Their differences are themselves evidence that they are not based on solid proofs. They are all empty claim not supported by Qur'an, Sunnah, *ijma'*, *qiyas*, or rationality that can stand on its feet." Ibn Hazm himself considers the condition of the year obligatory with regard to all items, whether assets or earned income, thus contradicting his colleague Daud, who does not require this condition regarding earned income.

Zakatability of earned income when acquired outweighs other opinions

In view of the texts on *zakah* in general, its objectives, and the general interests of Islam and Muslims, I believe earned income, whether salaries, wages, professional income, or return on capital invested in other than trade, such as shipping, planes, and hotels, is *zakatable* when received, without the requirement of the passage of one year. This opinion is substantiated by the following points:

1.   The requirement of the passage of one year with respect to all funds, including earned income, is not based on any correct or good saying, which is necessary in order to derive a ruling in *Shari'ah*, or to restrict one of its general texts. All that exists are opinions of some Companions.

2.   Companions and Followers did not agree on requiring the passage of one year on earned income. Some obligate *zakah* when earned income is acquired. When Companions and Followers differ, no one can claim that the view of some must be taken, and the issue must then be settled by other texts in accordance with the general principles of Islam. God says, "If ye differ in anything among yourselves, refer it to God and His Apostle."[33]

3.   The lack of a text or *ijma'* allows for schools of jurisprudence to disagree on the issue of earned income to such a degree that Ibn Hazm accused them all of being mere claims, unfounded on correct texts from Qur'an Sunnah, *ijma'* analogy, or sound rationalization. I myself have examined these differences as well as differences on the same issue inside each school of thought, and noted many unnecessary details and complications, so many that I do not believe it is at all likely that our easy-flowing *Shari'ah*, which is addressed to all people, can accommodate such minute, complicated details, especially with regard to one of its essential and more predominant pillars.

4.   The view that the passage of one year is not required with regard to earned income is in fact closer to the generality of the texts. Texts of Qur'an and Sunnah that obligate *zakah* are general and absolute, and do not mention a condition of the passage of a year, such as the sayings, "Bring in one-fourth of one-tenth of your *amwal*" and "On money, one-fortieth is required." This is also supported by the general implication of the verse, "O ye who believe, give out of the good things which ye have earned.[34] Earning in the verse is general, and applies to trade, professional, or employment. Jurists use this verse to support the *zakatability* of trade; why can we not use it to support the *zakatability* of earned income. When jurists require the passage of one year with regard

to *zakah* on trade assets, it is only to allow for the principal to produce its earnings. The case of salaries is different. They are earned when they are received.

5. Sound analogy also supports our view. Earned income is most similar to crops and fruits when harvested; if farmers, even those who have rented the land, are charged on-tenth or one-twentieth, why not charge employees and physicians one-fortieth of their earnings, especially since God associates earning with the produce of land in the above-quoted verse that continues, "and of the fruits of the earth which we have produced for you." Why should we treat differently things that God associates together, while both of them are of the same grace of God. It is true that the grace of God is more dovioce in the produce of the earth, and consequently gratitude for that is more stressed, but this is not a sufficient grounds for exempting the other earnings from the obligation of *zakah*. The difference in applicable rates is sufficient reflection of the difference in the emphasis of thankfulness.

6. The requirement of the passage of one year regarding earned income implies the exemption of many highly paid employees and professionals from the obligation of *zakah*. These may either expend all their earnings during the year, thus escaping totally any *zakah*, or save and invest part or all of their earnings, thus becoming *zakatable* after one year. This approach results in putting all the burden of *zakah* on moderate or thrifty income earners and exempting extravagant spenders. It is improbable that our wise and just *Shari'ah* would make it difficult for the moderate spenders while making the burden of the extravagant spenders null.

7. The requirement of the passage of one year on earned income ends up creating imbalance in the distribution of the burden of *zakah*, which is undoubtedly contrary to the justice of Islam. Take the example of a farmer who rents his land. He is required to pay ten percent or five percent if his total output reaches 653 kilos of grain, while the owner of the land is not required to pay any *zakah* on the incoming rent money. Such contradiction cannot be reconciled except by applying *zakah* on earned income regardless of the passage of one year.

8. The obligation of *zakah* on earned income is more beneficial to the poor and other deserving categories. This form of *zakah* produces huge proceeds, especially since the cost of collection is mini*mal*, as *zakah* can be deducted at the source, as done by Ibn Mas'ud, Mu'awiyah, and 'Umar bin 'Abd al 'Aziz. Ibn Abi Shaibah reports from Hubairah, "Ibn Mas'ud used to deduct from salaries twenty-five out of each thousand." This is also reported by al Tabarani.[35] 'Awn bin Muhammad says "I saw the governors deducting *zakah* when they gave salaries."[36] "Umar bin 'Abd al 'Aziz is reported to have been deducting *zakah* from salaries and grants.[36] Moreover, *Mal*ik in al Muwatta reports from Ibn Shihab that "the first to take *zakah* from salaries was Mu'awiyah bin Abi Sufian."[37]

9. The obligation of *zakah* on earned income is consistent with the spirit of Islam in nourishing the values of brotherhood and caring. God describes believers as those who "spend out of what We have provided for them" and orders "O ye who believe, spend

out of what We have provided for you." The Prophet (p) obligated charities on Muslim out of their wealth and their earnings. Al Bukhari reports for Abu Musa al Ash'ari from the prophet (p) "A *sadaqah* is obligated on each Muslim." His listeners questioned, "O Prophet of God, what about the person who finds nothing to spend from?" He answered, He must work with his hands, so he can benefit himself and give charity." "And if he cannot find a job? they asked, "He replied, "He must help the person who is desperate for help." They asked, "What if he cannot?" The Prophet then answered, "He must do what is known as good and abstain from evil; this is a charity for him."[38]

The exemption of those renewable incomes from obligated *zakah* for the excuse of the passage of one year allows many people to earn, spend, and enjoy without sharing in the needs of others and without assigning part for the sake of God.

10. The elimination of the condition of the year's passing with respect to earned income provides administrative convenience and procedural easiness in the calculation and collection of *zakah* for the *zakah* administration, as well as *zakah* payers. The condition of a year implies that payers and the administration must keep records of every segment of income earned in order to monitor its changes for one full year, which means that the payment of *zakah* shall be as frequent throughout the year as the frequency of the segments of income acquired. This is very cumbersome and difficult to pursue, in addition to the cost involved in such an exercise.

A contemporary view

At the end of this section, and in fairness to contemporary Muslim writers, it is imperative to mention the opinion of Shaikh Muhammad al Ghazali, presented in his book, Islam and Economic Issues, more than twenty years ago. After stating that *zakah* is either on the stock of capital--such as *zakah* on money and business assets-- or on income--such as crops and fruits--continues.

The conclusion is that whoever has an income equal to that of *zakatable* formers must be subject to *zakah* on equal footing regardless of capital and related conditions. Consequently, physicians, lawyers, and other professionals and employees are subject to *zakah* on their income for the following two persons:

Firstly, the general texts: The verse "O ye who believe, give of the good things which ye have earned."[39] There is no doubt that the income of those categories is included in good earning referred to in the verse. It is by this obligatory spending that they become integrated among believers described in the verse, "Who believe in the unseen, are steadfast in prayers, and spend out of what We have provided for them."[40]

Secondly, it is beyond imagination to assume that Islam may impose *zakah* on a poor farmer and exempt the owner of buildings that produce manifold the income of the farmer, or a physician whose daily income may equal that of the farmer for one full year.

Accordingly, *zakah* must be obligated on all of them as long as they share the same reason for *zakatability*. This form of analogy does not accept hypocritic manipulation. A question may arise regarding the calculation on *zakah* and its rates. Its answer is found in the rules of *zakah* themselves. The rate of crops and fruits is one-tenth or one-twentieth, according to efforts involved in irrigation. *zakah* on income may likewise be related to efforts in earning. It is always possible to make details and refinements once the principle is agreed upon, although such an exercise must be done by a group of scholars.[41]

These are excellent words that reflect depth in understanding Islamic principles. The two substantiating arguments given by al Ghazali are undoubtedly strong, but the approach I selected in this chapter in providing evidence from the practice of some Companions and Followers is more consistent with jurists' methodology. Even though our results may not have precedents in the four known schools of jurisprudence, we are not obligated to follow any of these schools.[42]

SECTION TWO

THE *NISAB* OF EARNED INCOME

Zakah is only imposed on the rich, in order to realize the meaning of the excess or surplus, mentioned in the Qur'an as the subject of spending. "They ask thee how much they are to spend; say, 'what is beyond your need.'" The Prophet (p) also says, "No *sadaqah* is obligated except out of richness." All this requires the condition of *nisab* for *zakatability*. What should *nisab* be in regard to earned income? Al Ghazali, as quoted at the end of section one, determines this *nisab* as the equivalent of *nisab* of grains and fruits, but who can be sure whether or not this *nisab* was set for a special purpose related to agricultural products? Why not take the *nisab* of money, which is 200 *dirhams* of silver, 20 *dinars* of gold, or its equivalent, i.e., eighty-five grams of gold, especially since earned income is usually paid and calculated in money terms?

The time period for estimating *nisab*

Since we are talking about a flow of income, the question arises of whether there is any time span through which income accumulates with regards to the amount of *nisab*, especially since earned income is paid at intervals, sometimes equal like salaries, and other times not equal, like physician's fees. There are two opinion on this matter.

The first is that each amount of earned income is considered alone when it is received. Monthly salaries, if they reach *nisab* or more, are *zakatable*, payments received by professionals that equal, each one alone, *nisab*, are *zakatable*, while small income or segments of income received at short intervals are not *zakatable*, except for the payment that is equal to *nisab* or more. This opinion apparently exempts small salaries and wages from *zakah*. It is consistent with the apparent meaning of the report about the practice of the Companions and Followers. On the other hand, many highly paid professionals, such as physicians, receive their income in s*mal*l increments that add up to large amounts in one week and perhaps one day. Shall all these s*mal*l amounts be exempted from *zakah* while a salaried employee whose monthly income is just above *nisab* is *zakatable*? This explains the merits of the second opinion.

The second opinion is that increments of income and other earned funds must be added to each other as long as they are received at short intervals. We noticed earlier that when talking about minerals, jurists state that increments of an ore extracted at short intervals are added together in order to make *nisab*. The same thing also applies in the case of several crops of the harvest of the same year.[43] Consequently, the year must be considered as the time for the calculation of *nisab*, i.e. earned income received during the whole year is added together and *nisab* is considered on the basis of yearly income. In fact, a period of one year occurs in *zakah* studies on more than one occasion, like the condition of the passage of one year. It is useful at the end of this sub-section to mention some of the reports from our predecessors about how earned income is *zakated*.

Al Zuhri is reported to have stated, "If a person earns income and wants to spend it before the end of his fiscal year, he must pay its *zakah* then spend it. But if he plans to save it, then he must wait to pay *zakah* on the total at the end of his fiscal year."[44] Similarly, it is reported from al Awza'i that money received from the sale of non-*zakatable* items, like a residential house or a slave, must be *zakated* when received, except when the payer has already established a fiscal year with respect to *zakah*, in which case the *zakah* of the acquired money can be postponed till the end of the year.[45]

Makhul is reported to have said that if a person has an established fiscal year, earned income that is spent before the end of this fiscal year is not *zakatable*, but funds received in the months when *zakah* becomes due must be included in the calculation of *zakah*. When the person does not have an established *zakah* year, earned income must be *zakated* when acquired.[46]

It is clear that Makhul's opinion favors the payer who has an established fiscal year, which is awkward, because this privilege is given to the riche, who already owns some wealth, while those who have no previous wealth are disadvantaged.

This is why I select the opinion of al Zuhri and al Awza'i with regard to earned income that reaches *nisab*, and the opinion of Makhul for income--although no *nisab*--received in the same month when *zakah* is due on other wealth owned by the income receiver, observing, however, that income needed for personal and family expense is exempt from *zakah*. And for the case when received income is less than *nisab*, and the earner does not have previous assets that are *zakatable*, earned income must accumulate until it reaches *nisab* and then *zakah* becomes due.

Zakah applies on net earned income

Zakah on earned income applies on its net amount. Debts and a minimum standard of living for the income earner and his family are deductible, because they are among essential needs, and *zakah* is only obligated on a *nisab* that is above essential needs. Business expenses, for professional and other income earners are also deductible, in accordance with the view I select with respect to farming and palm trees that *zakah* is due on the residual after payment of expenses.[47] This is the opinion: of 'Ata and others.

After the above-mentioned deductions have been made if the residual of salaries or other earned income reaches during the year an amount equal to the *nisab* of money, then this residual is *zakatable*. That exempts small earnings and wages.

It should be noted that if earned income is *zakated* when received, the next *zakah* is not required untill one new year elapses, since two *zakah*s cannot be imposed in one year. When a person has an established fiscal year with respect to his or her *zakah*. He or she may delay the payment of *zakah* on earned income untill the end of that fiscal year. To give an example, a person earns income in the second month of his fiscal year, and pays its *zakah* as he earns it. *zakah* on the part saved from this earned income is not due at the end of the twelfth month of the fiscal year during which it is earned, but becomes due the next year on all assets then owned.

SECTION THREE

ZAKAH RATE ON EARNED INCOME

Al Ghazali calls for collective research on the part of Muslim scholars to determine the applicable rate on earned income. My personal opinion is to distinguish between earned income resulting from capital investment alone, earned income resulting from capital and labor together, and earned income resulting from labor alone.

Income that is earned as a return on capital or on capital and labor together is charged one-tenth of the net income, after the deduction of all expense, debts, and allowance for essential needs. This is in analogy to agricultural crops produced without irrigation costs. It applies to returns from factories, buildings, printings facilities, hotels, renting cars, transportation business, and the like. I mentioned earlier the opinion of Abu Zahra and his two colleagues that the rate of *zakah* on buildings and factories should be ten percent of the net income, if expenses and costs are determined and deducted, or five percent of gross income if expenses cannot be determined. This distinction is--in my opinions acceptable. It is noted, however, that capital in this regard does not include trade assets discussed earlier in chapter four.

Income that results from labor alone, such as employment compensation and professional income has a rate of one-fourth of one-tenth only, in application of general texts that obligate a rate of 2.5% on money, whether it takes the form of assets or earned income. It is also in accordance with the Islamic principle of reducing the applicable rate in proportion to effort spent, and with the practices of Ibn Mas'ud, Mu'awiyah, and 'Umar bin 'Abd al 'Aziz. Analogy of salaries and professional income with salaries paid by those leaders is much more sound than a claimed analogy with income from farming. On the other hand, income from farming may be closer to income from buildings and factories.

Lastly, the distinction means that income from labor is treated with consideration of effort spent , which reduces the rate as compared to income from capital. This is a principle also followed by contemporary taxation systems, in which it is considered just to charge higher rates on the return of capital than on employment income.[48]

Footnotes

1.   *Halaqat al Dirasat al Ijtima'iyah*, p. 248.

2.   *Al Muhalla*, Vol. 6, p. 3, *and Nasb al Rayah*, Vol. 2, pp. 328-329.

3.   *Al Takhils*, p. 182.

4.   *Sunan al Tirmidhi, part on zakah, chapter "Zakah* on gold and silver."

5.   *Mukhtasar al Sunan*, Vol. 2, p. 191.

6.   *Mizan al I'tidal*, Vol. 2, pp. 352-353, biography no. 4052.

7.   *Al Takhlis*, p. 182.

8.   See his biography in *Mizan*, Vol. 1, pp. 513-515, no. 1918.

9.   *Al Takhlis*, p. 175.

10.   *Nasb al Rayah*, Vol.2, p. 530.

11.   *Al Takhlis*, p. 175.

12.   *Tahdhis Sunan Abu Daud*, Vol. 2, p. 189.

13.   *Mizan*, Vol. 1, pp. 445-446, biography no. 1659.

14.   *Al Tirmidhi*, with commentary of Ibn al 'Arabi, Vol. 3, pp. 125-126.

15.   *Al Sunan al Kubra*, Vol. 4, p. 95, and *al Talkhis*, p. 175.

16.   Ibn Hazm reports these statements, *al Muhalla*, Vol. 5, p. 276.

17.   *Al Muhalla*, Vol. 6, p. 83. Abu 'Ubaid reports the same in al *Amwal*, pp. 413-414, and interprets it in a different, farfetched way.

18.   *Al Muhalla*, Vol. 6, pp. 84-85. The narration from 'Umar and al Hasan is slightly different.

19.   Al *Amwal*, p. 413, reported via two chains.

20.   Al Musannaf, Vol. 3, p. 160.

21.   *Al Amwal*, p. 414.

22.   Ibid, p. 412.

23.   Al Musannaf, Vol. 3, p. 114.

24.   The author of *Majma' al Zawa'id*, Vol. 3, p. 63, says its narrators are those of the correct books, except Hubairah , but he is trustworthy.

25.   Perhaps what helped Abu 'Ubaid in his interpretation is another saying. Abu 'Ubaid says it is attributed to Sufyan from Khasif from Abu 'Ubaidah that 'Abd Allah said "A person who earns income is not *zakated* until one year passes." But this saying is weak for two reasons. Firstly, Abu 'Ubaid does not determine the connection between him and Sufyan; he only says it is attributed to Sufyan. And secondly, Khasif is accused of having a bad memory and many illusions, to the extent that his narrations are disturbed, and do not stand as evidence. The best that is said about him may be the statement of Ibn Habban that "He was righteous, knowledgeable, and a good worshiper, but he makes many mistakes in what he narrates, and is singled out alone in narrations from famous men, while no one agrees with his narration. He is honest, due in fairness to him, he must only be accepted when his narrations coincide with those of the trustworthy and to be abandoned when they do not." See Tahdhib al Tahdhib, Vol. 3, pp. 143-144. In the case on hand, we notice that correct narrations from Ibn Mas'ud contradict that which is narrated by Khasif.

26.   *Al Muwatta'* with al Muntaqa, Vol. 3, p. 95.

27.   Al *Amwal*, p. 432.

28.   Al Musannaf, Vol. 3, p. 85.

29. *Al Mughni*, Vol. 2, p. 626 and Vol. 3, p. 29 and 47.

30. *Al Rawd al Nadir*, Vol. 2, p. 411, and *Nail al Awtar*, Vol. 4, p. 148.

31. *Al Rawd*, Ibid.

32. *Al Muhalla*, Vol. 6, p. 84.

33. *Sura al Nisa*, 4:59.

34. *Sura al Baqarah*, 2:267.

35. See footnotes 24. above.

36. *Musannaf Ibn Abi Sahibah*, Vol. 4, pp. 42-44.

37. *Al Muntaqa*, with *al Muwatta'*, Vol. 2, p. 95.

38. The correct Collection of al Bukhari, part on *zakah*, title, "On each Muslim there is *sadaqah*."

39. *Sura al Baqarah*, 6:267.

40. *Sura al Baqarah*, 2:3.

41. *Al Islam wal al Awdal al Iqtisadiyah*, fifth printing, pp. 166-168.

42. See the introduction of this book.

43. *Sharh Ghayat al Muntaha*, Vol. 2, p. 59.

44. *Al Musannaf*, by Ibn Abi Shaibah, Vol. 4, p. 30.

45. *Al Mughni*, Vol. 2, p. 626.

46. *Al Musannaf*, op. cit.

47. See the condition of being above essential needs, in chapter one of this part, and in chapter three also.

48. *Mabadi' 'Ilm al Maliyah al 'Ammah*, by Dr. Muhammad Fu'ad Ibrahim, Vol. 1, p. 284.

CHAPTER TEN

ZAKAH ON SHARES AND BONDS

Introduction

Stocks, shares, and bonds are forms of financial assets that were not known in the past. Many taxation specialists call for imposing certain taxes on these assets or at least on their returns.[1]

Shares or common stocks represent ownership of a certain part of the capital of a corporation. Bonds are certificates of loans borrowed by a corporation, government, or municipality. A Bond is usually paid back at a certain future point of time, and the loan it represents carries interest. The basic difference between a share and a bond is that the first represents a contribution to the capital and carries profits or losses, while the second is only a borrowing instrument that carries predefined terms of interest and series of repayments. Usually, bond holders do not have authority of controlling of administration on the corporation. When issued, both shares and bonds may have a market value that is different from the face value. They are traded in the exchange markets, like other commodities in their respective markets. Their prices go up and down according to different factors that affect their supply and demand, including the success of the corporation that issues them and the local and international economic and political situation.[2]

The issuance, holding and circulation of shares--in their common form--is permissible in *Shari'ah*, except when the very activity of the issuing corporation is prohibited in Islam, such as alcoholic beverage breweries or interest-based financial corporations. On the other hand, bonds are interest-bearing instruments, and interest is prohibited in Islam. But regardless of the matter of lawfulness of holding bonds, they represent capital owned by people and their *zakatability* must be discussed. Two broad opinions are formulated among contemporary scholars on this issue.

The first opinion

One view distinguishes between shares and bonds and deals with shares in accordance with the nature of the economic activity of the corporation whose capital they represent.

Shaikh 'Abd al Rahman 'Isa, in his book al Mu'a*mal*at al Hadithah wa Ahkamuha [Modern Transactions and Their *Shari'ah* Rulings] represents this opinion:

Some people who own corporation shares may not know the *Shari'ah* ruling on their *zakatability*, or think that *zakah* is obligated on all corporations' shares, and this too is wrong. It is imperative to distinguish between shares in accordance with the nature of economic activity of the corporation itself. The shares of purely industrial corporations that do not practice any trade activities, such as a corporation dealing with refrigeration, hotels, advertising, public transportation, shipping, and airline industries, are not *zakatable*, since the capital of these corporations and the shares which represent it is invested in machinery, offices, and buildings, that are not *zakatable*. But dividends distributed on these shares are added to the other assets of the shareholders and are *zakatable* at the end of the year, according to the rule of *zakah*.

Trading corporations that deal only with the purchase and sale of commodities, such as import/export dealers and retail trading, along with corporations that have a mixture of trading and industry, such as corporations that transform raw materials, extracted by the same corporation or purchased elsewhere, and sell their final products, are *zakatable* as far as their shares are concerned. Thus, the criteria for the *zakatability* of shares is whether the corporation is *zakatable* and that depends on the use of its assets. Shares are evaluated at their present value. A deduction is made for the percentage of capital used in buildings, machinery, and tools owned by these corporations. After deducting this percentage from the present value of the share, the residual is *zakated*.[3]

This opinion of Shaikh 'Isa is based on the well known view that factories, machinery, and buildings are not *zakatable*, neither on capital and profit together as with trade assets, nor on profit alone, as with agricultural land. Because of that, he differentiates between industrial and trading corporations. This means that people who own different shares, even of the same value, may be *zakated* differently according to whether these shares happen to be of a trading or industrial corporation.

In chapter eight of this part, the *zakatability* of buildings and factories was analyzed, and it was concluded that there are three opinions in addition to the traditional one of non-*zakatability*:

1. Treating them like trade assets and estimating *zakah* at the rate of 2.5% on their total net value at the end of each year.

2. Subjecting the return of factories and buildings to *zakah* like money, on the basis of being earned income.

3. Drawing an analogy with agricultural land and imposing *zakah* at ten or five percent, on their gross or net profit.

In chapter three, I selected this last view as being the most appropriate. Here I must add that the distinction between trade and industry has no foundation, or evidence from Qur'an, Sunnah, *ijma*, or sound analogy. There seems to be no sense in imposing *zakah* on the shares of trading corporations, while at the same time leaving exempt the shares of industrial corporations. Both kinds of shares are growing capital that earns annual renewable returns, which may in fact be higher in industries than in trade.

If such a distinction is to be made, I suggest that we treat corporations like individuals, whereby *zakah* is imposed at the rate of ten percent of the dividends of industrial shares, while it is imposed at the rate of 2.5 percent on the market value of trading shares, certainly after deducting the percentage invested in fixed assets, i.e. treating trading shares like we treat trade inventory.

Zakah on bonds

Regarding bonds, Shaikh 'Isa continues, "Since bonds represent a loan made by companies or the government of definite amounts at definite interest rates, the holder of a bond is like the creditor of a deferred debt. At the due date, when it is paid, it must be *zakatable* for only one year if it remains in the holding of its owner for one year or more, according to *Malik* and Abu Yusuf. Until the bond is redeemed, or if it is not in possession for one year,, it is not *zakatable*."[4]

It was sown earlier[5] that the most acceptable opinion about hopeful debts is that they are *zakatable* every year. This is the view of the majority, and the choice of Abu 'Ubaid and others, because hopeful debts are like assets on hand. Accordingly, bonds, being specific forms of debts that have legal assurances in addition to the interest they earn, must be *zakatable* every year. The fact that interest is prohibited is no reason for exempting these bonds from *zakah*, because a person who commits what is prohibited must not be given any privilege. It is known, for example, that jurists unanimously agree on subjecting prohibited jewelry to *zakah*, although they disagree on the *zakatability* of lawful jewelry.

The second opinion

This opinion treats all shares and bonds alike, regardless of the economic activity of the issuing corporation. Professors Abu Zahrah, 'Abd al Rahman Hasan, and Khallaf believe that shares and bonds are used in circulation, like commodities, purchased and sold, usually at a market value that is different from its face value. They are thus like commodities that are purchased for resale at a profit. Like any other business inventory, they must be *zakated*.[6]

This means that *zakah* is calculated on shares and bonds on the basis of their current market value plus all their dividends and interest, provided the totals equals at least *nisab*, or if added to other funds owned by the same holder, they make up at least *nisab*. The rate is 2.5 percent, and deductions for essential needs or minimum cost of living is applied in the case where shares are the only source of income. It seems to me that this opinion is more suitable to *zakah* payers, because it is simply and easy to know the market value and add earnings to it on all kinds of shares. This is as long as individuals are asked to make their own calculations, but if an Islamic state adopts the laws of *zakah*, it may be advisable to collect *zakah* directly from corporations, on the basis of the first opinion, that of Shaikh 'Isa.

Zakatability of corporations in addition to shareholders

If shares are treated like trade inventory and subjected to *zakah*, is it lawful to impose *zakah* on the earning of the corporations themselves, in additions to the *zakah* on the shareholders?

Professors Abu Zahrah and his two colleagues consider that since shares are treated like commodities owned by shareholders, corporations are *zakatable* on their own activities, because their assets are growing assets invested in business and industry, while shares for those who trade shares and hold them are merely trade inventory.[7] According to this opinion, the corporations should pay *zakah* on their earnings before distribution, and shareholders must also pay another *zakah* on their shares, including earned dividends. This means that the shareholders are *zakated* once on the earnings of the company and once on their own assets and distributed profits. This kind of duplication in *zakah* is prevented in *Shari'ah*. I believe that only one of these two *zakah*s must be applied in order to avoid such duplication.

It may be useful to give some examples from jurists' writings that can shed some light on this matter. We studied in chapter two that *zakah* is obligated on pastured livestock unanimously, and when livestock is obtained as business inventory by livestock merchants, it is only *zakated* either at the rate of livestock or at the rate of business inventory, but definitely not twice as business inventory and pastured livestock at the same time.

Ibn Qudamah discusses the difference in their treatment as following:

*Mal*ik and the new opinion of al Shafi'i say this livestock must be *zakated* at the rate applied to livestock on the grounds that *zakah* on livestock is stronger, being unanimously agreed upon and mentioned by name in the sayings. On the other hand, Abu Hanifah, al Thawri, and Ahmad say it must be *zakated* as trade assets because this *zakah* gives more benefits to the *zakah* recipients in addition to being proportional. If the number of livestock held by the merchant reaches, in value, *nisab* of business, but does not reach in number the *nisab* of livestock, *zakah* on trade assets applies indisputably.[8] . . but it is impossible to obligate the two kinds of *zakah* together, because this leads to duplication, which must be avoided in accordance with the saying of the Prophet (p), "No duplication in *sadaqah*."[9]

If *nisab* of livestock (40 sheep) is fulfilled, while the *nisab* of business assets (200 *dirhams*) is not, *zakah* becomes obligated at the rate applied on livestock, as if they were not being held for trading.

The author of al Mughni gives another example, the case of palm trees or land purchased for resale, but while held as inventory, the land was farmed, or the trees harvested. If the *zakah* year of business ends at the time of harvest, and the value of the land and/or trees equal *nisab*, then *zakah* on crops and fruits must be paid at the rate of ten percent or five percent, and *zakah* on the lot and trees must also be paid at the rate of 2.5%. This is according to Abu Hanifah and Abu Thawr. Al Qadi and his Hanbalite colleagues say that land and crops must totally be *zakated* at the rate of business assets, because all are considered business inventory. Ibn Qudamah argues that the first opinion gives more proceeds and is thus better for the poor and claims that this case is different from the case of livestock as inventory, since the rate of livestock is anyway below that on trade inventory.[19] One can reply that increasing the proceeds of *zakah* is not reason enough since *zakah* aims at providing a just and bearable burden on payers as well. The justice of Islam is featured in applying the high rate of one-tenth only on the return, while when *zakah* applies on the principal, the rate is 2.5 percent, as in business assets. It is not known that two rates can be applied together on the same principal and on its return. It is imperative to select one of the two forms of *zakah* in order to avoid duplication or payment of more than one *zakah* in the same year.

The argument that in the above-mentioned examples there are two reasons for *zakah*, namely, trade and agriculture, is not valid, because only one of them was originally intended. The other came incidentally, but only one form of *zakah* must apply. This is taken up by the author of Sharh al Ghayah, a Hanbalite, who says "A person who owns *nisab* of pastured livestock for the purpose of trading only is subject to *zakah* on trade assets alone, even if the year of *nisab* of livestock ends before *nisab* of business is reached, since the intention of holding inventory removes the description as holding livestock." By the same token, he argues that land held as inventory for trade is *zakatable* along with its crops or fruits at the form of *zakah* applied to trade assets, because crops and fruits at the form of *zakah* are clearly an increase in the inventory the owner had. But if the total does not reach 200 *dirhams*, while the fruit alone reaches their own *nisab*, or the livestock reaches its *nisab*, they must be subject to *zakah* applied on their own cases, so that *zakah* may not be waived at all.[11]

Ibn Hazm quotes al Hasan bin Hay, "What is farmed for business is subject to *zakah* on business, and nothing else."[12] Al Kasani says that "Our colleagues, the Hanafites, say 'ushri or kharaji land purchased for trade is only subject to 'ushr or kharaj, and *zakah* on trade may not be obligated at the same time as kharaj or 'ushr. This is their well-known opinion. Muhammad is said to have obligated 'ushr or kharaj along with *zakah* on trade, i.e. *zakah* of trade on the value of the land, and 'ushr on the crops, assuming these are two different properties. The rationale behind this is that trade's *zakah* is obligated on the land while agriculture's *zakah* is obligated on the crops; thus no two *zakah*s are charged to the same asset.[13]

I believe only one of the two forms of *zakah* must be applied, and that it is not correct to allow duplication in *zakah*, as is the common view of the Hanafites and others. As for which of the two forms of *zakah* should be selected. I think this should be left to the *zakah* administration or the *zakah* payer, each of these two alternatives has its reasons. We must recall that the bulk of Muslims jurists, perhaps all of them, do not approve of any duplication of *zakah* on the same asset, although in certain instances, we find some 'who disagree, such as the above-mentioned case of Muhammad.

Footnotes

1. *Mawarid al Dawlah* by Sa'd Mahir Hamzah, p. 180.

2. *Al Mu'amalatal Hadithah wa Ahkamuha*, pp. 68-69.

3. *Ibid*, pp. 73-74.

4. *Ibid.*

5. See chapter one of this part.

6. Halaqat al Dirasat al Ijtima'iyah, Third Session, p. 242, it is noted that the three professors treat stocks and bonds similarly, without the distinction made by Shaikh 'Isa. This unified treatment is, in my opinion, correct. One may object on the grounds that bonds represent debts and may change hands from one creditor to another, which makes them forbidden, according to many jurists. Their reply to this objection is to emphasize that bonds have become commodities which, if exempted from *zakah*, would encourage investors to hold more bonds. Exempting them from *zakah* is not a means to reduce undesired holdings and transactions. Moreover, it is not prohibited to spend unlawful earnings on charity when the original lawful source of that earning is not determined.

7. *Ibid.*

8. *Al Mughni*, Vol. 3, pp. 34-35.

9. Reported by Abu 'Ubaid in al *Amwal*, p. 275, and Ibn Abi Shaibah in al Musannaf, Vol. 3, p. 218.

10. *Al Mughni*, Vol. 3, pp. 35-36.

11. *Matalib Uli al Nuha*, Vol. 2, pp. 100-101.

12. *Al Muhalla*, Vol. 5, p. 249.

13. *Al Bad'i*, Vol. 2, p. 57.

www.ingramcontent.com/pod-product-compliance
Lightning Source LLC
LaVergne TN
LVHW080844240726
843527LV00047B/544